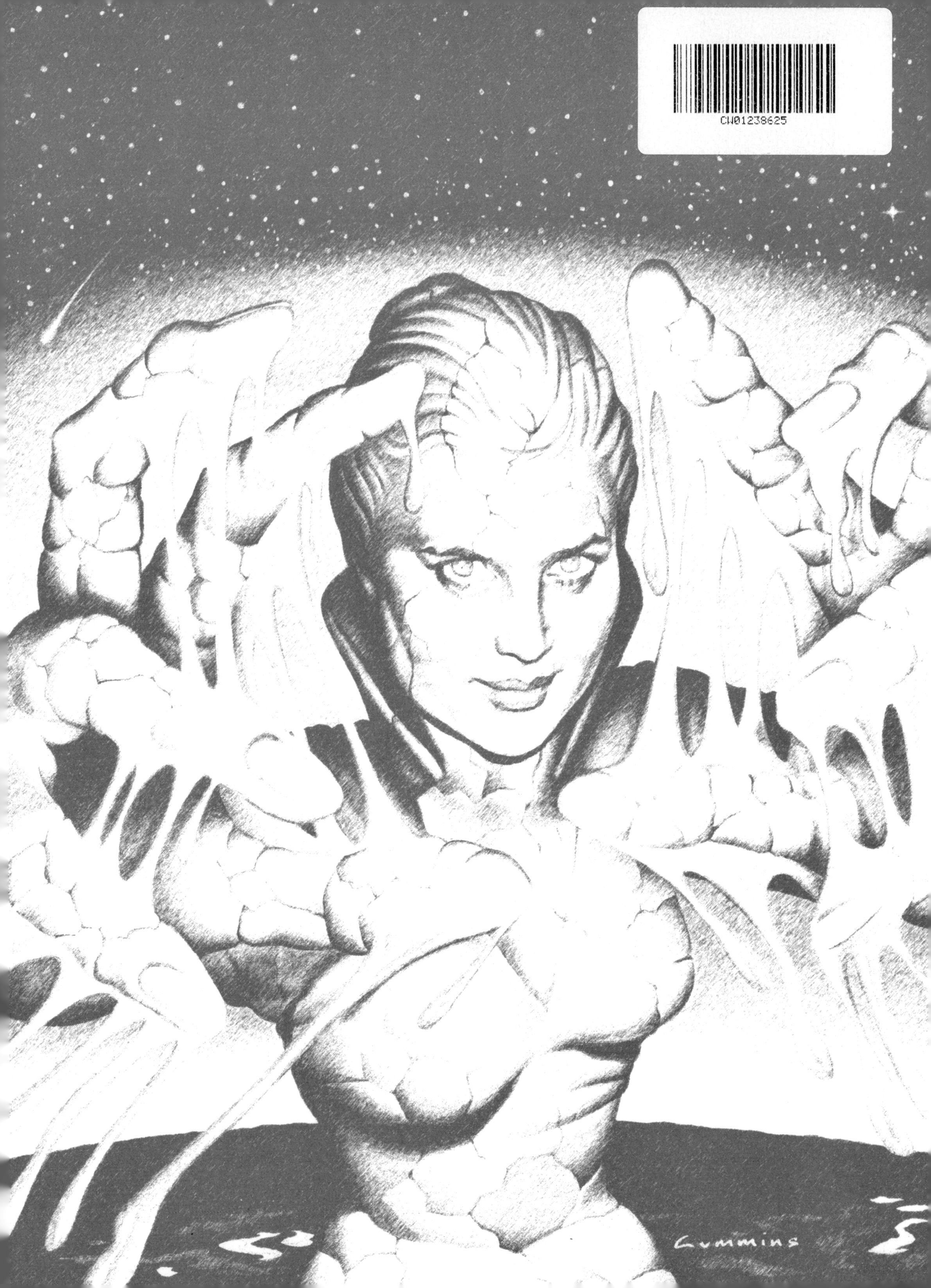
Cummins

THE WHO ADVENTURES

THE ART AND HISTORY OF VIRGIN PUBLISHING'S DOCTOR WHO FICTION

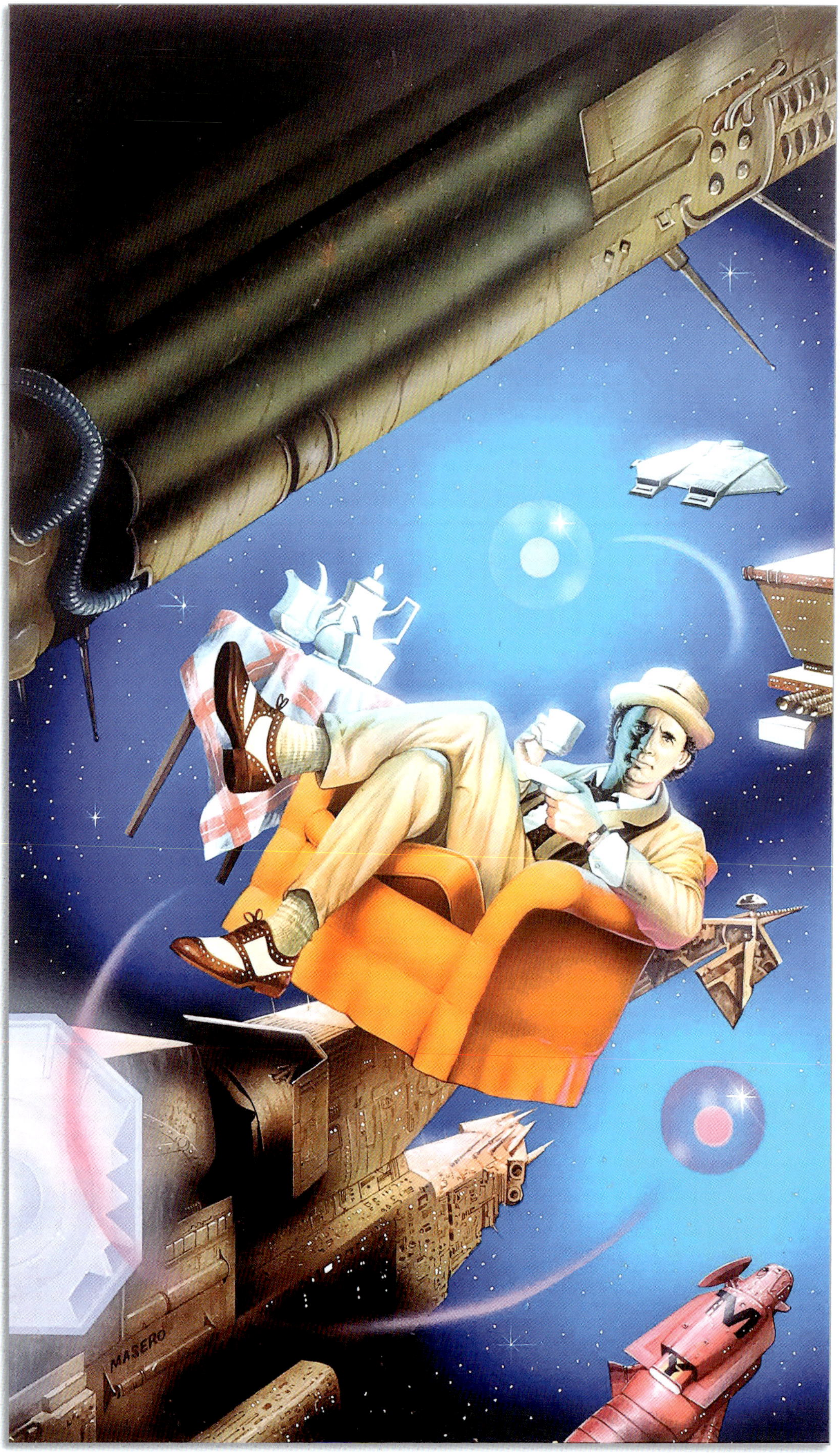
MASERO

THE WHO ADVENTURES

THE ART AND HISTORY OF VIRGIN PUBLISHING'S DOCTOR WHO FICTION

*To Will
Best Wishes
David J[?]*

DAVID J HOWE

First published in England by:
Telos Publishing Ltd, 139 Whitstable Road, Canterbury, Kent CT2 8EQ
www.telos.co.uk

Telos Publishing Ltd values feedback. Please e-mail any comments you
might have about this book to: feedback@telos.co.uk.

ISBN: 978-1-84583-185-1

The Who Adventures: The Art and History of Virgin Publishing's Doctor Who *Fiction*
© 2021 David J Howe

All original artwork reproduced in this book remains the copyright
of the artists, as credited, and is used with permission.

'Survival' location photographs on pages 14, 16 and 18 © Stephen James Walker
Photographs on pages 16 (top), 23, 39, 51, 61, 95 and 121 © David J Howe
Sophie Aldred photograph on page 146 © Robin Pritchard
Photographs on pages 171 (top) and 213 with thanks to Gallifrey One
Photographs on pages 13 and 235 © Peter Darvill-Evans
All other photographs accompanying biographies are either public
domain or © their respective subjects, unless otherwise noted.

The moral right of the author has been asserted.

Design, typesetting and layout by Stephen James Walker.

Printed in India by Imprint Press.

British Library Cataloguing in Publication Data.
A catalogue record for this book is available from the British Library.

This book is sold subject to the condition that it shall not, by way of trade or otherwise, be
lent, resold, hired out or otherwise circulated without the publisher's prior written consent
in any form of binding or cover other than that in which it is published and without a similar
condition including this condition being imposed on the subsequent purchaser.

DEDICATION

This book is dedicated to the ones we have lost. In particular remembering:

Terrance Dicks, Craig Hinton, Barry Letts, Peter Elson and Phil Bevan.

Also to Samantha Lee Howe for being my rock.

THANKS AND ACKNOWLEDGEMENTS

For the writing of the original *Doctor Who Magazine* articles that form the backbone of the written content for this book, I'm grateful first to Alan Barnes for commissioning them. Also to the following people for help with the writing of those pieces: Rebecca Levene, Chris Weller, Kate Orman and Jon Blum, Justin Richards, Martin Day, Daniel O'Mahony, Steve Lyons, Gary Russell, Stephen James Walker and Alister Pearson. Especial thanks to Peter Darvill-Evans, who was there at the start, there at the end, and for sharing his thoughts and memories with me.

In the preparation of this book, I'd like to thank the following for their support and enthusiasm and for permission to use their original materials: David Banks, Allan Bednar, David Bishop, Jon Blum, Daniel Blythe, Andy Bodle, Lee Brimmicombe-Wood, Simon Bucher-Jones, Christopher Bulis, Andrew Cartmel, Jeff Cummins, Peter Darvill-Evans, Martin Day, Bill Donohoe, Pam Elson, Brian Fennelly, Fred Gambino, Mick Hall, Colin Howard, Andrew Hunt, Kevin Jenkins, Mark Jones, Barry Jones, Matthew Jones, Daryl Joyce, Tim Keable, Andy Lambert, Andy Lane, Roger Langridge, Rebecca Levene, Steve Lyons, Shaun Lyon and Gallifrey One (www.gallifreyone.com), Stephen Marley, Tony Masero, Peter McKinstry, David A McIntee, Simon Messingham, Lawrence Miles, Mike Nicholson, Daniel O'Mahony, Kate Orman, Lance Parkin, Alister Pearson, John Peel, Neil Penswick, Marc Platt, Rod Ramos, Martin Rawle, Luis Rey, Nigel Robinson, Gary Russell, Mark Salwowski, Kerri Sharp, Andrew Skilleter, Nik Spender, Jon Sullivan, Lee Sullivan, Jason Towers, Mike Tucker, Richard Unwin, Stephen James Walker, Pete Wallbank and Mark Wilkinson.

Especial thanks to Kit Bevan for permission to use Phil Bevan's artwork.

With additional thanks to the following who have helped in smaller or greater degrees with the creation of this book: Paul Scoones, Jeremy Bentham, Gareth Kavanagh, Paul Rhodes, Robert Simpson, John Freeman, Siobhan Gallichan and Colin Brockhurst.

For the 'Behind the Book' box-outs, based on entries originally written by Paul Scoones for the fanzine *TSV*, sources: *Celestial Toyroom*, *TV Zone*, David Banks, *Doctor Who Magazine*.

ABOUT THE COVER

The cover of this book uses Tony Masero's original painting for the novel *The Also People*. 'I'm particularly pleased with *The Also People*,' says the artist, 'with its sweep of spaceships in the background and the Doctor sipping tea in his armchair whilst floating in space. It seems to encapsulate the mixture of madly bizarre and homespun avuncularity that was the foundation of the whole *Doctor Who* concept.'

CONTENTS

Chapter 1: Endings and Beginnings 9
Chapter 2: Agreement is Reached 15
Chapter 3: The Timewyrm is Born 19
Chapter 4: Cat's Cradle 37
Chapter 5: Future History 49
Chapter 6: A New Companion 77
Chapter 7: Arrivals and Departures 95
Chapter 8: The Stand-Alone Adventures 121
Chapter 9: The End of Ace 155
Chapter 10: Vile Problems 183
Chapter 11: Celebrating Fifty Books 207
Chapter 12: All Change 221
Appendix A: The Missing Adventures 237
Appendix B: Afterlife 271
Appendix C: Checklist: The New Adventures 311
Appendix D: Checklist: The Missing Adventures 315
Appendix E: Checklist: The Big Finish Audios 317
Appendix F: Covers Gallery 319
Afterword: The Legacy 333

Artist Richard Jennings' original painting for the cover of *The Dalek Book* (Souvenir Press, September 1964).

1: ENDINGS AND BEGINNINGS

'From the dark unexplored regions of outer space, a new planet moved into orbit around the Sun – what strange form of life had developed on this mystery planet? Earthmen wondered as they turned their telescopes towards this new world. The answer came swiftly and terribly – it was the planet of the Daleks, the machine creatures with superhuman brains. Their mission was to conquer the whole solar system and enslave the Earth.'

So begins *The Dalek Book*, which was issued in September 1964 and featured the first ever professionally-published *Doctor Who*-related fiction outside of the television show itself. It is telling that one of the first items of commercially-available *Doctor Who* merchandise should also have presented the first examples of tie-in fiction.

There is one range of original fiction that really broke the mould and established a storytelling platform on which a great many talented and creative writers got their start, eventually going on to make their mark elsewhere as well as continuing to develop adventures for the Doctor. This was a range of original novels published by Virgin Publishing during the early 1990s and collectively called the New Adventures.

Doctor Who tie-in fiction was well established long before this, however. Dalek adventures appeared not only in *The Dalek Book* but also in *The Dalek World* and *The Dalek Outer Space Book*, issued in 1965 and 1966 respectively, while comic strip escapades for the Doctor started in late 1964 in *TV Comic* (and have continued to this day, now residing in Panini's *Doctor Who Magazine* and Titan's *Doctor Who Comic*). There were also text stories in World Distributors' *Doctor Who* annuals; and Target Books, better known for their novelisations of the Doctor's televised adventures, ventured into the field of original fiction in 1986 when they published *Turlough and the Earthlink Dilemma* and *Harry Sullivan's War* as the first titles in their short-lived 'The Companions of *Doctor Who*' series.

Despite all this activity, with the television show bringing new adventures every year, the tie-in stories were sidelined.

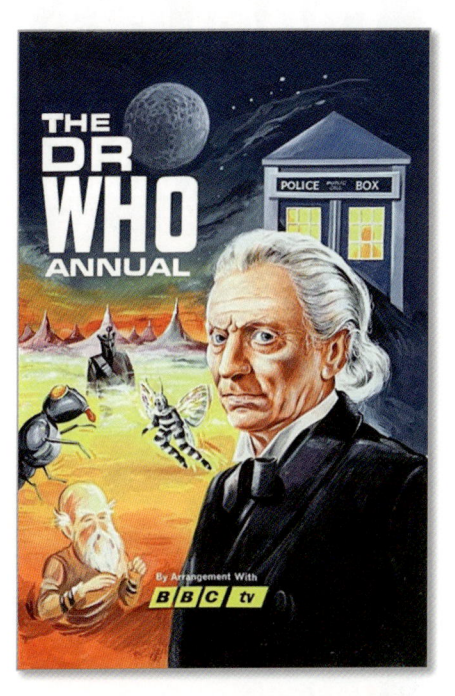

The original cover art, believed to be by either Walter Howarth or Stanley Freeman, for the first edition of *The Dr Who Annual* (World Distributors, September 1965); and a *Doctor Who and the Daleks* strip page on the cover of *TV Comic* (TV Publications, January 1967), with art by John Canning.

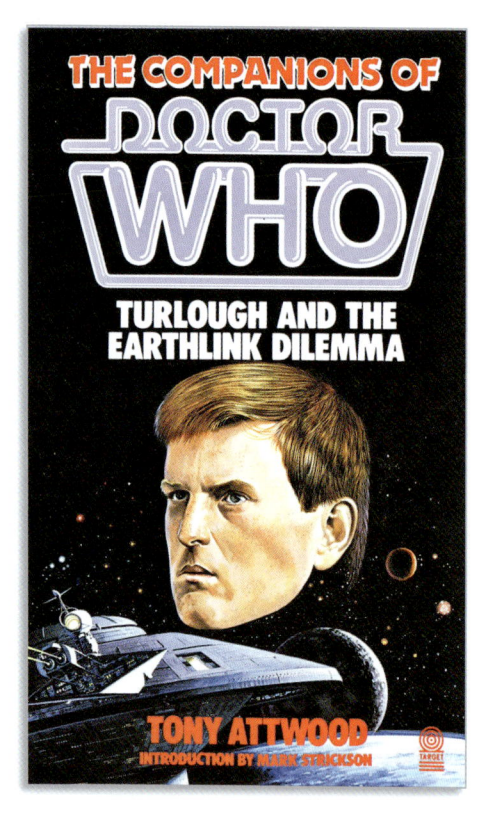

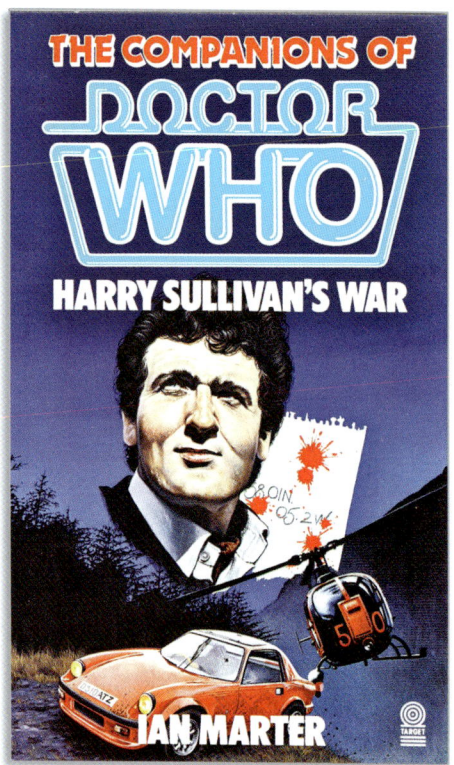

The two original books in 'The Companions of *Doctor Who*' series, both with cover art by David McAllister.

They were never regarded in the same way, or even with the same respect, as their television counterparts, and few fans would have argued, even half-heartedly, that they had any degree of validity. (Detailed debates about 'canon' were some years off.) In the mid-1980s, however, W H Allen, publishers of the Target novelisations, ran into a problem. On television, the number of episodes made each year had been slashed from 26 to 14; the number of stories from six to four. With a publishing schedule that demanded 12 new titles a year, this meant it was just a matter of time before all the stories that could be novelised, would have been, and at that point the future prospects for the range seemed dependent on whatever the BBC decided to do with *Doctor Who* – anything from reducing the number of stories made still further to, heaven forbid, cancelling the show altogether. Any holder of an existing and successful product licence will want to do their best to exploit it, and also to try to future-proof it, to break away from restrictions imposed from elsewhere and continue to profit from the franchise indefinitely. The answer? In this case, it was to publish original fiction.

But it wasn't that simple. First, permission had to be gained from the BBC: specifically from Wendy Sanders of BBC Books and John Nathan-Turner, producer of *Doctor Who*. Target editor Nigel Robinson was apparently the first to ask about doing original fiction, in the mid-1980s, and was turned down – save for gaining permission to publish the aforementioned 'The Companions of *Doctor Who*' range, a limited number of original novels featuring the Doctor's television companions. The latter venture, however, was cancelled in-house, as the sales of the two published titles, although quite respectable, were not as good as those of the *Doctor Who* novelisations.

The next approach came from Robinson's successor, Jo Thurm, just as she was departing from the editor's post in February 1989. This was followed up by her successor, Peter Darvill-Evans, in March of the same year. No response from Sanders is recorded, but it is likely that the matter was simply referred to Nathan-Turner, who took an active interest in all *Doctor Who* merchandise. At that time, as far as anyone knew, the television show was still ongoing;

however, by the middle of the year, rumours were rife that it would not return to production for a twenty-seventh season, and by October this was a certainty.

'When I arrived at W H Allen at the end of February 1989,' recalls Peter Darvill-Evans, 'I was aware that there had been some original tie-in fiction published by the company, things like the Harry Sullivan book, and also a *Blake's 7* book. I was also aware that these titles had done less well than the novelisations, and that wasn't a terribly good precedent.' This was an issue for Darvill-Evans, as he was determined to get a range of original fiction off the ground. 'I was able to finesse that problem,' he explains, 'and persuade everyone in the company by explaining that the poor sales were because those tie-ins didn't have the Doctor in. You can't have *Doctor Who* without the Doctor. (Luckily there was no-one around to remember my forceful arguments some five years later when we took the Doctor *out* of the New Adventures when the BBC took back the license …) I was also encouraged that "The Missing Stories" series published by Target – novelisations of television scripts commissioned by the BBC for the twenty-third season but then cancelled when the show changed direction – seemed to sell as well as the standard novelisations. That just strengthened my view that if the Doctor was present, then the books would do fine. I knew that the BBC's earlier argument for not allowing original fiction to be published revolved around their desire to see all the television stories novelised first; well, we'd now done that, and furthermore by October of that year, there were no immediate plans to do any more television stories, so all that just strengthened my argument that now was the time to do some original fiction.'

These thoughts culminated in Darvill-Evans meeting with Nathan-Turner in October of 1989 and the outgoing producer finally agreeing that original fiction could be published, but with the proviso that he would be involved in the setting up of the range. The novels were initially envisaged as continuing the Doctor's adventures directly on from the end of the final televised story, Rona Munro's 'Survival', and Darvill-Evans suggested starting the first original novel with the last lines of Munro's novelisation of

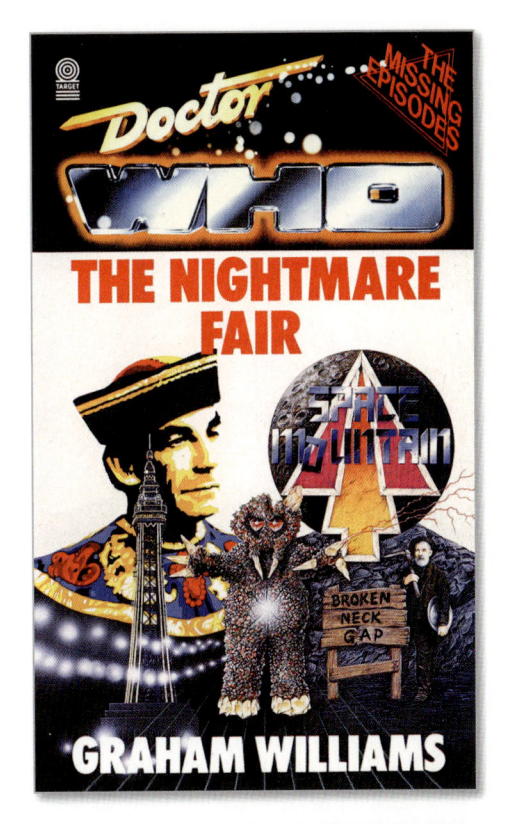

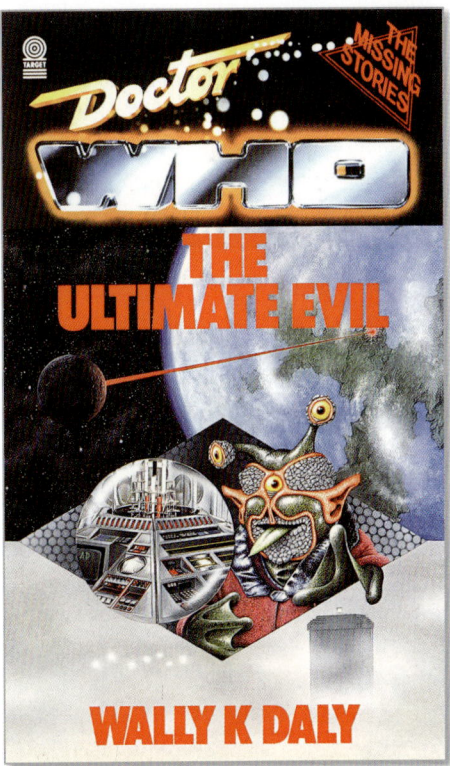

Two of 'The Missing Stories' books, both with cover art by Alister Pearson with Graeme Way.

THE WHO ADVENTURES

ANDREW CARTMEL

Andrew Cartmel was born in London and grew up in Canada. Ever since he first learned to read (Ray Bradbury, Robert Heinlein, the Oz books), Andrew never wanted to be anything except a writer. On returning to London to study at university, he began writing scripts for television while getting established as a novelist. This led to a distinguished sojourn as script editor of *Doctor Who* for three years (during which period he developed the so-called 'Cartmel master plan'). At the same time, very much under the influence of Alan Moore, he began writing for comics, first the *Doctor Who* strip and then *Judge Dredd* and, most recently, collaborating on the 'Rivers of London' series of graphic novels with its creator Ben Aaronovitch. Cartmel is also a passionate playwright, with several runs of his work already produced on the London fringe. He also had a brief career as a stand-up comedian. Cartmel is the author of the 'Vinyl Detective' series of crime novels. The fifth of these, *Low Action*, was published by Titan Books in 2020 and, at the time of writing, number six is already taking shape. Cartmel lives in London with too many books, too many records and just enough cats.

that story. Nathan-Turner wanted Darvill-Evans to involve Andrew Cartmel, the show's departing script editor, and the initial candidate for the author of the first book was Ian Briggs, both Darvill-Evans and Nathan-Turner having been impressed by his work on the novelisation of his story 'The Curse of Fenric'. By November, Darvill-Evans had authors 'foaming at the mouth' to write original fiction; however, negotiations with the BBC were proceeding very slowly, with letters to the rights and contracts department failing to gain any positive response – or indeed any response at all. Undaunted, Darvill-Evans pressed on with his plans.

Survival by Rona Munro, with cover art by Alister Pearson.

PETER DARVILL-EVANS

Peter Darvill-Evans was born in 1954 in Buckinghamshire and graduated in 1975 from University College London with a degree in History. In 1976 he joined the staff of Games Centre, a specialist games shop in London, becoming a Branch Manager and then Manager of Wholesale Sales. In 1979 he moved to work for Games Workshop, first as Trade Sales Manager and then as General Manager, also looking after their magazine *White Dwarf*. However, when the company relocated to Nottingham, he left.

Between 1986 to 1988 he was Marketing Director of the magazine distributor Argus Press Ltd, and also wrote two Fighting Fantasy gamebooks for Puffin: *Fighting Fantasy Gamebook 25: Beneath Nightmare Castle* (1987) and *Fighting Fantasy Gamebook 37: Portal of Evil* (1989).

In 1989 he joined publishers W H Allen Ltd as a junior editor, initially overseeing their Target imprint and their Nexus adult fiction range. Already part-owned by the Virgin group, W H Allen was then taken over in its entirety and drastically downsized; the *Doctor Who* and Nexus imprints survived in the new, much smaller business now named Virgin Publishing.

In 1991 Darvill-Evans launched the New Adventures range of original *Doctor Who* fiction for Virgin, followed in 1994 by the Missing Adventures range. Other lines he oversaw were Black Lace, a mainstream erotic fiction imprint targeted at women; the Crime and Passion imprint; Idol, a homoerotic fiction imprint for men; and Sapphire, a lesbian erotica line. He also found time to pen a third Fighting Fantasy novel, *Fighting Fantasy Gamebook 45: Spectral Stalkers* (1991). In addition, he expanded Virgin's output into non-fiction titles focused on various television franchises, including *Red Dwarf*, *Doctor Who*, *The Simpsons* and *The Avengers*. In 1998, among other projects, he managed the editing and production of Virgin's *Guide to British Universities* and personally supervised the copy-editing and proofreading of Richard Branson's autobiography *Losing My Virginity*.

Virgin closed its fiction department in 1999, and Darvill-Evans left the company. Subsequently he wrote several *Doctor Who* novels for BBC Books and took on a variety of other editing and writing work.

In 2001 he started working for the Inland Revenue and qualified as an Inspector of Taxes, a job he still enjoys today. He has continued to be involved in the worlds of *Doctor Who*, contributing to various DVD extras, and has appeared as a guest panellist at Fighting Fantasy conventions.

Sylvester McCoy as the seventh Doctor, on location for the final 'classic-era' *Doctor Who* television story, 'Survival'.

2: AGREEMENT IS REACHED

There were a number of things that helped to cement Darvill-Evans' ideas about the form the new original fiction range should take. First was his desire to match the high quality of the novelisations of recent television stories such as 'Remembrance of the Daleks' and 'The Curse of Fenric'. Second was his discovery that script editor Andrew Cartmel had formulated plans for *Doctor Who*'s future development on television, had the show not been cancelled. Cartmel had set out his ideas in a 'master plan' document, and Darvill-Evans was allowed sight of this 'on the strict instruction that I wasn't to tell anyone'. A third consideration was Darvill-Evans' perception of the relationship between the seventh Doctor, as played by Sylvester McCoy, and his final television companion, Ace, portrayed by Sophie Aldred. 'They were a very good team on screen,' he says, 'and I felt that this would translate well to the page. The obvious thing was to move forward. I didn't want to go back to the past. There has always been in *Doctor Who* fandom a terrible lust for nostalgia, and this was no good to me as a publisher, because we'd done that through the novelisations. The only way was to go forward. For this reason, I was initially very resistant to the idea of doing the Missing Adventures [the range of original novels featuring the Doctor's earlier incarnations, which Virgin eventually launched in 1994]. I was very worried about this backward-looking limitation. To create a brand that has value, you need to avoid relying on things you don't control – we had no control over the old stories, but we did control the new things we were doing.'

Over Christmas 1989, Darvill-Evans formulated an initial ten-page proposal for how he saw the range developing. The final version, dated 24 January 1990, laid out the basic premise and plot outline for an interlinked series of six original novels.

The document posited that, following the conclusion of 'Survival', the Doctor and Ace would return to the TARDIS only to find the Doctor's old enemy the Master at the controls. The Master damages the console, having already set destination coordinates, and flees into the TARDIS's corridors. The TARDIS arrives on the planet Fland, where civil war is raging:

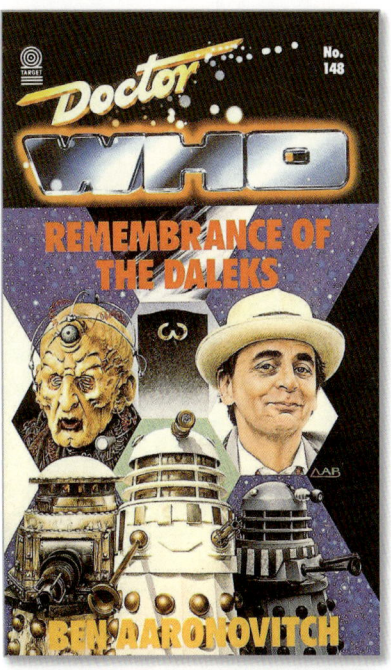

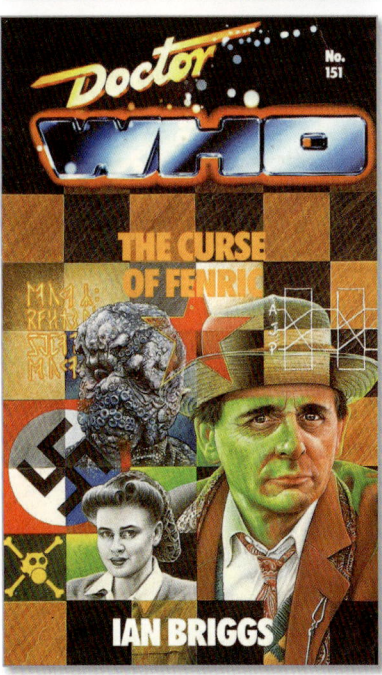

Two very influential Target novelisations, Ben Aaronovitch's *Remembrance of the Daleks* and Ian Briggs' *The Curse of Fenric*, both with cover art by Alister Pearson.

THE WHO ADVENTURES

Doctor Who books editor Peter Darvill-Evans, pictured at the time of the New Adventures' launch.

The Doctor's companion Ace, as portrayed on screen by Sophie Aldred – photographed here on location for 'Survival'.

Bitavian forces versus the Hokof Union. When the Doctor tries to escape in the TARDIS, Ace is caught in a boobytrap set by the Master in her room. The Master has linked together a genetic material condenser, a time loop generator and a trans-mat, and he uses these to condense Ace into a genetic pattern, of which he then fires randomly-selected segments out into space-time. The device has fired five times before the Doctor realises what is happening and puts a stop to it. This results in there being five slightly different versions of Ace scattered through the universe. The Doctor has to recover all of them to have any chance of restoring the real Ace.

Thus the scene was set for a six-book series, in which most of the first book and all of the following four would be self-contained adventures involving the Doctor hunting for the missing Aces, while the sixth would wrap up the overarching plot. This was reminiscent of the Doctor's search for the missing segments of the Key to Time in *Doctor Who*'s sixteenth television season. Darvill-Evans provided an outline of how the plot would finally be resolved, and also a draft of the opening section of the first book.

Unfortunately, Nathan-Turner's response to this initial proposal was less than enthusiastic: '"McGuffin" stories inevitably are very limiting,' he wrote, 'and personally I feel we should do something more subtle and less constraining.

'Also, the concept of five Aces roaming the galaxy as segments of a geometric pattern, may seem to some to be rather complex for the younger readers. Off the top of my head … may I suggest a much more vague linking theme? For example: the Doctor decides that Ace's history education is lacking and therefore he takes her on six adventures set in various historical times. Obviously this needs some sort of pay off. At its most coy and most basic, it could be as simple as Ace saying: "History is so full of mistakes, rape, pillage, violence etc, shall we move on to geography?"'

Nathan-Turner concluded by commenting, 'There is nothing wrong with your plot, but I think you should consider it a self-contained one, rather than a six-part linking structure for the series. Although you go to great lengths to explain that the writers of stories two to five should not be too constrained, I feel from experience from [the 14-part television story] "The Trial of a Time Lord", that a fully-fledged umbrella theme is too strapping.'

'I have absolutely no recollection of this outline,' says Darvill-Evans today. 'Clearly I wrote it, as it's got my name on, but I have no memory of it at all. It's nothing like anything we did in the end. It might have been written more to demonstrate what we could do – to prove that the books could continue on from the television show. Thinking about it, I very much doubt that Virgin would have gone for a six book series – to commit to that many before you even know how the first one has done is a massive leap of faith. It also seems very prescriptive …'

Darvill-Evans understands why he might have wanted to do this, though: 'In a very *Babylon 5* kind of way (to take a later show that impressively succeeded in creating an ongoing story arc), I wanted to tie people in for the long term. I wanted to encourage readers not to buy just one book, but to get into the habit of buying all of them. The only way I could think of to do that was to have elements of the story that carried on from book to book, so that you had to buy the next one to find out how things developed or were resolved – or not. That was the reason for the Timewyrm arc that eventually ran through the first few books. After those initial releases, we found we didn't really need to do that, although we did subsequently have some more story arcs running: there was the Cat's Cradle trilogy, a small arc of Future History stories and then, near the end, the Psi-Powers arc. We just liked the idea of linking and grouping the stories together: I remembered watching the Key to Time season on television, and that made you want to keep watching to see what happened. The problem with story arcs is that you need to deliver at some point, and come to a conclusion … or, in fact, you *don't* need to, as by that time you've achieved what you intended: to get people reading the books out of habit.'

Darvill-Evans took on board Nathan-Turner's feedback, as well as comments he received internally from within Virgin Publishing, and by mid-February 1990 he was considering that the initial run of books should number four rather than six. He was also happy to ditch any and all previous ideas in favour of something new. However, as he explained in a lengthy letter to Nathan-Turner, he still wanted to have some ongoing thread running through the first novels, feeling this to be paramount in

AUTHORS' GUIDES

Peter Darvill-Evans prepared a number of guides for prospective authors of the New Adventures. The first was undated and comprised 18 sheets of information under a covering letter. The contents consisted of: 'The Objectives' (taken from Virgin's initial pitch to BBC Worldwide regarding the range); 'Guidelines for Writers' (basic guidance on layout and grammar); 'Writing *Doctor Who* Novels' (notes regarding things that were and were not required, restrictions, copyright, settings, characters etc, and also how to submit); pointers from the text of the *The Curse of Fenric* novelisation (mainly about the character of Ace); and a 'Universal Background for *Doctor Who* Stories' (a general history of the key elements of the show's mythos).

A second guide was issued after April 1990, with *The Curse of Fenric* element and the 'Universal Background for *Doctor Who* Stories' section removed and a number of new inclusions: 'Background'; 'The Timewyrm Concept'; 'Example of a Four Book Series'; 'Advantages of Using Timewyrm'; and 'Thematic Unity'.

This was supplemented on 3 October 1990 by the first of two additional 'Time Travel in *Doctor Who*' documents, discussing that subject with reference to the show's mythos, the Time Lords and so on. The second document, issued on 29 October 1990, added into the mix sections on 'Pocket Universes', 'Travelling into the Past', and 'Creating New Stories'.

engendering readers' loyalty – hooking them to come back and buy the next book in the series each time.

There was another reason for this. 'I always thought that what I was trying to create was a series of books that could eventually exist without *Doctor Who*,' says Darvill-Evans. 'And the reason I wanted to do that was that I had at the back of my mind the thought that if the BBC never made another *Doctor Who* story on television, how long realistically could we continue to rely on *Doctor Who*? We might not be able to count on the good will of *Doctor Who* fans to keep the range going. I might need to reach a new readership and branch out. So, all along, I wanted to do something that could stand alone. It wasn't that I thought the BBC might withdraw the license, it was simply that I thought *Doctor Who* might cease to be popular. People might forget it. It was very much uncharted territory, a completely new situation, and I had little confidence that it would last forever.'

Above: an early promotional sheet for the New Adventures. Below: pictured on location for 'Survival', Sylvester McCoy and Sophie Aldred as the seventh Doctor and Ace – the Doctor-and-companion team with which the new range would be launched.

3: THE TIMEWYRM IS BORN

With ideas in hand for a linked four-book series, the next and most important step was to find some authors to work on the novels. 'I simply wrote lots of letters to those authors who I felt had written particularly good novelisations,' says Darvill-Evans. 'I contacted the ones whose style I liked – Ben Aaronovitch, Ian Briggs, Marc Platt among them – but also I very deliberately let it be known to the fan magazines that we were doing this. That was partly because I simply wanted the *Doctor Who* fans to be aware of what we were doing, but it naturally had the side effect of prompting people to write in and ask if we would look at their stories. I don't think we put out an appeal as such for fan writing, mainly because when we launched the books I wanted to be able to use the names of the authors as a selling point. That's why I badly wanted Terrance Dicks to do one, because he had a name way beyond *Doctor Who*, and was very well known in the book trade as an author who sold lots of copies of books. It meant a lot to me that he agreed to contribute to the range so readily.'

By June 1990, Darvill-Evans was finalising his ideas. 'I was looking for an overarching storyline that could link the books together,' he explains. 'It had to be something that could link through both time and space, so inevitably the Doctor had to have some sort of opponent who could also travel through time; and it was surprising how few ideas there were that hadn't already been done. The Timewyrm was what I eventually came up with, and this allowed the authors to develop their stories around that concept.'

That same month, Darvill-Evans wrote to former *Doctor Who* script editor and novelisation author Eric Saward to see if he might be willing to contribute to the range. This was something that Saward was interested in, subject to financial agreements. Darvill-Evans also approached former *Doctor Who* scriptwriter, director and novelisation author Peter Grimwade; and while Grimwade was interested, he urged Darvill-Evans to look at his novel *Robot*, which had been written for and published by W H Allen previously.

Also in June, Darvill-Evans sent fan authors Paul Cornell and John Peel some notes relating to Ian Briggs' Target

JOHN PEEL

John Peel was born in Nottingham, England, in 1954. He moved to New York, USA, in 1981 to marry his penpal, and they live there still with their rescue mixed breed dog, Dickens, and (currently) a flock of 13 lovebirds. Alongside his *Doctor Who* novels, Peel has penned books based on various *Star Trek* series, *The Outer Limits*, *The Avengers* and *Quantum Leap*. His original series for young adult readers include the *Diadem* and *Dragonhome* books. He's written more than 100 novels and is currently penning the *Doctor Omega* series (with *Doctor Who* artist Andrew Skilleter), novels in the *Lethbridge-Stewart* series and a new take on *Dracula*.

Andrew Skilleter's original artwork for the first New Adventures novel, *Timewyrm: Genesys*.

THE TIMEWYRM IS BORN

novelisation of 'The Curse of Fenric', as this was seen as being very influential to the development of the New Adventures range. In a letter of 22 June to Peel, Darvill-Evans wrote: 'I'm looking for someone who can quickly come up with the first book of the first series; in order to describe the Timewyrm and set the parameters for the series.'

Peel remembers this approach well. 'I was a full-time writer by then (this would actually be my ninth book), but I was a fan, and wanted very badly to be the first original novelist. I faxed Peter an outline the next day, based on his idea that if the universe could be described by using mathematics, then the Timewyrm was like the universe having a computer virus. The outline had the Doctor and Ace landing on a world where everyone is part of a central processing unit – human parts of a gigantic computer that the Timewyrm has constructed; she uses their minds like floppy discs, wiping them when she desires. The Doctor and Ace fall into some unformatted people's hands, and the usual *Doctor Who* revolt against tyranny ensues. Peter responded that he wanted something with Mesopotamians in it ...'

Peel duly submitted a revised outline and an opening chapter. 'Luckily for me,' he says, 'I was just as fascinated by mythology as Peter, and could readily work up a plot that brought the Doctor and Ace into contact with the legendary god-king Gilgamesh, and also the ungodly Ishtar – the front, as it were, for the Timewyrm. Originally, I had described the Timewyrm as a sort of mechanical spider, but I decided that was rather silly, since it was called a "wyrm", and switched it to a snake instead. The idea had intrigued me, and I started wondering how such a creature might come into being. That gave me the title of the book: *Genesys*. After that start, I was pretty much left to my own devices as to what I did with the plot.'

The novel was formally commissioned on 12 July 1990. Being familiar with the period in which the story was set, Peel pointed out to Darvill-Evans that the base material, *The Epic of Gilgamesh*, contained a lot of sex, as one of Gilgamesh's problems was an overactive libido. Darvill-Evans replied: 'I have no objection to Ishtar's temple being a sort of brothel, as long as it's believable; I suppose if Ace were in danger of being processed to serve temple duty it would add a certain frisson of

Top: Andrew Skilleter's original rough for the cover of *Timewyrm: Genesys*.

Bottom: as part of their promotional effort for the new range, Virgin produced a short give-away sampler of *Timewyrm: Genesys*; pictured here is the front cover.

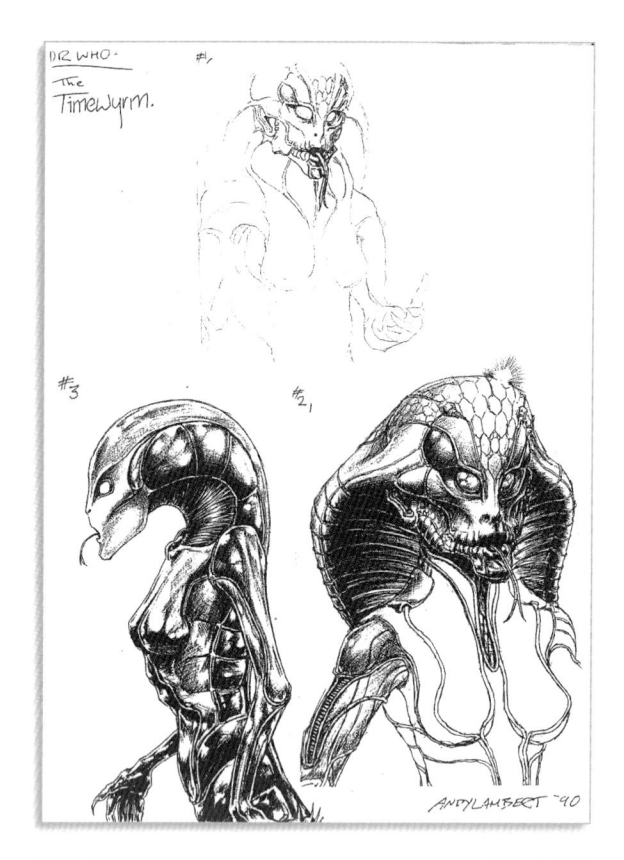

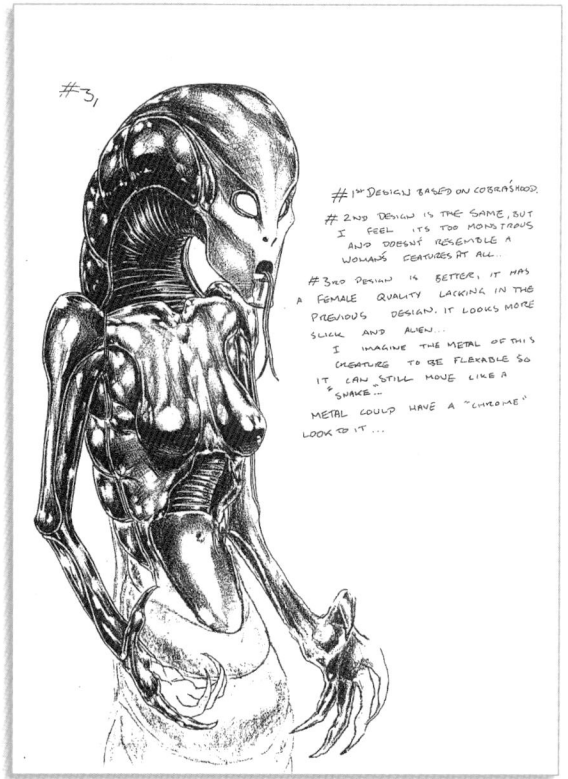

THE WHO ADVENTURES

fate worse than death that is absent from most *Doctor Who* stories. On the other hand, I don't see any reason to indulge in gratuitously detailed descriptions of sexual practices; unless they're artistically necessary, of course …'

The sexual content of the book ultimately proved controversial with some readers. Peel, however, says: 'To be perfectly honest, I thought the sex in *Genesys* was very subdued! Mostly it's just talk, and there's no real sex at all, except for Gilgamesh's clumsy passes at every girl in sight – which was meant more to show his obnoxious character than to titillate.

'The other thing about *Genesys* for me was that I had never liked the seventh Doctor on television. (Hence the continuity errors that some reviewers picked up in the novel!) I particularly disliked the Machiavellian aspect of his character, and decided from the start that my interpretation of him would include him making some grave errors. He had to be seen as fallible, rather than some omniscient game-player – otherwise, where was the suspense? So I knew he would have to be the inadvertent creator of the Timewyrm.

'To set this up, and because Peter asked me to open the novel in such a way that people who didn't really watch the show could pick up on the storyline, I decided the best way to begin was to start with Ace having amnesia, and then clue the readers in via her discoveries. So much better than simply writing a "what's-gone-before" block! And that gave me the chance to show the Doctor screwing up to start with, to presage what would happen at the end of the novel.

'Though I dislike the seventh Doctor on television, Sylvester and Sophie are two of my favourite people. I felt that with better stories, they would have run a lot longer. As a result, I was the one who approached Sophie about writing the introduction to the first novel. She's a big SF fan anyway, and she was very happy to agree.'

The first draft of *Genesys* was completed on

Above: artist Andy Lambert's design concept sketches for the Timewyrm.

TERRANCE DICKS

Terrance Dicks is by far the most prolific of the *Doctor Who* authors, both within and beyond the range, with over 220 books to his name. Born in East Ham, London, in 1935, he was educated at the local grammar school and went on to read English at Downing College, Cambridge. After national service, he got a job as an advertising copywriter. This lasted for five years, during which time he started writing radio scripts as a sideline. Eventually he switched to full-time freelance writing, first on radio plays and comedy series, then on television shows including *The Avengers* and *Crossroads*.

He began working on *Doctor Who* in the late 1960s. He was script editor on the show for part of the sixth season (1969) and for the whole of the Jon Pertwee era (1970-1974), and contributed several scripts to the show thereafter.

Aside from *Doctor Who*, Dicks also served as script editor on *Moonbase 3* (1973) and the BBC's classic serials, all alongside producer Barry Letts. He took over as producer on the latter serials before they were cancelled by the BBC in 1988. He also contributed a script to ITV's *Space: 1999* ('The Lambda Factor', 1976).

He was approached by Target editor Richard Henwood in 1973 to novelise some of the *Doctor Who* serials he was then overseeing. This led to a 17-year stream of *Doctor Who* titles for Target and started Dicks on the road as an author.

When Virgin Publishing started their range of original *Doctor Who* novels, Dicks contributed *Timewyrm: Exodus* (1991), *Blood Harvest* (1994) and *Shakedown* (1995), and he continued writing original *Doctor Who* fiction for BBC Books with *The Eight Doctors* (1996), *Catastrophea* (1998), *Players* (1999), *Endgame* (2000), *Warmonger* (2002), *Deadly Reunion* (with Barry Letts, 2003), *World Game* (2005) and the novella *Made of Steel* (2007).

Dicks' original fiction for children began with two series of books for Target. First in 1986 was *The Mounties* trilogy – *The Great March West*, *Massacre in the Hills* and *War Drums of the Black Foot* – and then came the *Star Quest* trilogy – *Spacejack*, *Roboworld* and *Terrorsaur!*.

In 1978, Dicks began a series of ten adventure books featuring *The Baker Street Irregulars*. This ran from *The Missing Masterpiece* (1978) to *The Criminal Computer* (1987). All were published in hardback by Blackie & Son Ltd. The same publisher also issued Dicks' series of six inter-connected contemporary children's horror novels, starting with *Cry Vampire!* (1981). Other titles recounted the adventures of *T R Bear* (a walking, talking teddy bear), *Sally Ann* (a determined ragdoll), *Goliath* (a golden retriever), *Harvey* (a St Bernard) and *Magnificent Max* (a talking black-and-white cat).

Dicks also wrote for a teenage audience: the *Changing Universe* series (three titles, 1998-2000) and the *Second Sight* series (four titles, 2000-02). In addition, he penned the 12 book *The Unexplained* series, investigating paranormal goings-on.

Alongside these series and one-off works of fiction for pre-school to teenage readers, Dicks wrote several non-fiction titles, including *Europe United* (1991), *A Riot of Writers* (1992), *Uproar in the House* (1993) and *A Right Royal History* (1994).

Dicks died on 29 August 2019.

THE WHO ADVENTURES

Above: one of two early cover concept roughs produced by the Slatter-Anderson design agency and dated 4 December 1990.

11 December 1990, and with some minor revisions and additions, the book was finished by 8 January 1991.

Terrance Dicks was, like Peel, specifically approached for the range, and was interested in writing the second book. He suggested setting it in 1930s Europe. 'I had to know about the Timewyrm,' Dicks later recalled, 'and where it had been, but otherwise the story was up to me. I also had to introduce the Timewyrm into the story at some point, and then get her on her way at the end. I've always been very keen on the Nazis as characters, so choosing a period in which to set the book was fairly easy. When I came to write *Endgame* for the BBC range more recently, I realised that the book was set in the same period as *Exodus*, so I couldn't resist writing in a sequence where the eighth Doctor sees the seventh Doctor and Ace at the 1951 Festival of Britain, which was where *Exodus* started.'

Dicks had something approaching 70 novelisations of *Doctor Who* television adventures under his belt; but, as he recalled, it never got any easier: 'I always grumble like mad about doing a novel – they're longer and harder than the novelisations and are also pitched at a different level. I found

Below: the original design sketch and a drawing of Ace produced by artist Andrew Skilleter for the cover of *Timewyrm: Exodus*.

24

Andrew Skilleter's original artwork for the cover of *Timewyrm: Exodus*.

NIGEL ROBINSON

Nigel Robinson's first book was *The Tolkien Quiz Book* (1981), a collaborative effort with his schoolfriend Linda Wilson. He began his association with *Doctor Who* with three *Doctor Who Quiz Books* (1981-85) and *The Doctor Who Crossword Book* (1982), all for Target. He went on to take over editorship of the Target range from 1984 until April 1987. He wrote four novelisations based on serials from the 1960s and also completed *The Rescue* after the original author Ian Marter died with the book unfinished. After the Target range came to its end, he wrote two of Virgin Publishing's New Adventures, *Timewyrm: Apocalypse* (1991), and *Birthright* (1993).

Robinson has also written novelisations based on the TV shows *Baywatch* (four books, 1993), *The Young Indiana Jones Chronicles* (four books, 1993), *The Tomorrow People* (four books, 1995) and *Dragon Flyz* (four books, 1996-97), and tie-ins for the *Free Willy* films. His original fiction for young readers include the science fiction trilogy *First Contact* (1994), *Second Nature* (1996) and *Third Degree* (1997), a horror novels series (seven books, 1994-95) and the *Luke Cannon Showjumping Mysteries* (four books, 1996). He has also penned five romance novels for teenage girls for Scholastic (writing as Robyn Turner) and has ghost-written for kids' early '90s telly stars Phillip Schofield, Andy Crane and Yvette Fielding.

His *Doctor Who* work on audio includes adapting for Big Finish the scripts for the unmade stories *Farewell, Great Macedon* and *The Masters of Luxor*, and for AudioGo (re)novelising the first televised adventure as *An Unearthly Child*, which was recorded for the show's fiftieth anniversary but is currently in copyright hell.

Robinson currently works as a freelance journalist, mainly in the LGBT+ press, and is the editor of *Pride Life*, the UK's largest distributed LGBT+ title.

Photo: Peter Clark.

---

writing *Exodus* very hard work – it was the longest thing I'd ever written at that time.'

Dicks' initial synopsis, titled *Exodus of Evil*, was dated 21 August 1990, and the first draft manuscript was delivered to Virgin around the start of February 1991. 'Peter said it was too straightforward,' recounted Dicks. 'He has this theory that when writing for older fans, the novels should be more complex and convoluted. I also had to break it up more – Peter has a mania for seeing events from different characters' points of view, whereas I prefer to follow just one character at a time.' After much discussion, Dicks agreed to perform a rewrite, generally increasing the novel's sophistication and making it more challenging for the reader, in line with Darvill-Evans' aspirations and intent for the range. 'It was a lot of hard work,' repeated Dicks, 'but I was very pleased with the end result. After all those novelisations of other people's stories, it was nice to see one of my own turning out so well.

'I remember Peter didn't like the title *Exodus*. He kept saying that we'd change it, but we never did, and the books all ended up with Biblical titles.

There was one further requirement that came later. Paul Cornell, who was writing the fourth book, got in touch with me as he needed a traitorous character to use in his novel, and so I created Hemmings for him to pick up at the end – that happened while I was writing the book.'

The third book in the series was written by Nigel Robinson, someone very familiar with the *Doctor Who* range, as he himself had been editor of the Target novelisations from 1985 to 1987. 'I suspect I may have heard rumours about the new novels on the fan circuit,' recalls Robinson, 'but my first definite recollection comes from having attended the farewell party for Mike Bailey, ex-Editorial Director, at the W H Allen/Virgin offices in St John Street, where I was first introduced to Peter Darvill-Evans and the idea was mooted to me. That was around June of 1990, and I thought it was about bloody time that original novels were finally going to happen – it was something I had always wanted to do when I was in charge of the *Doctor Who* range.

'Peter asked me to submit a proposal, and I came up with one called *The God-Machine*. After a revised submission, that became *Timewyrm: Apocalypse* – although I really wanted to call it *Apotheosis*. I was contracted in September 1990 and the manuscript was delivered (two weeks late) in the first week of January 1991.

'I was given the concept of the Timewyrm as well as John's synopsis for *Genesys* and the *Guide for Writers* stuff that Peter had produced. Peter told me that the Timewyrm had to top and tail the novel, but it was up to me how much of a role it played in the book. In *Apocalypse*, my character the Grand Matriarch is ultimately revealed to be the Timewyrm. Little was changed from my submitted manuscript to the published book, although I do recall Peter inserting a two-paragraph resumé of the events of the previous two books, as well as a throwaway comment from Ace about whether or not there are any cats in the TARDIS, as a teaser for the forthcoming *Cat's Cradle* series. I also recall that the quote at the beginning from *Logopolis* [Christopher H Bidmead's novelisation of his script for the final fourth Doctor story] was included at Peter's insistence and not mine. I think it made for an overly portentous intro to what was essentially just an old-fashioned romp.

'I found it very strange writing original material for the Doctor, without the benefit of scripts or videos to fall back on, but

---

QUOTE, UNQUOTE

The Doctor: 'I'm a wandering scientist and scholar and you're my niece. Be as enigmatic as possible and give the impression that I'm a strange and mysterious character with a number of mystic powers.'

Ace: 'Just stick to the truth, you mean?'

Timewyrm: Exodus

PAUL CORNELL

Paul Cornell is a writer of science fiction and fantasy in prose, comics and TV, one of only two people to be Hugo Award-nominated for all three media. He's written *Doctor Who* for the BBC, *Action Comics* for DC, and *Wolverine* for Marvel. He's won the BSFA Award for his short fiction, an Eagle Award for his comics, and shares in a Writer's Guild Award for his television. He lives in Gloucestershire with his wife and son.

THE WHO ADVENTURES

Andrew Skilleter's original artwork for the cover of *Timewyrm: Apocalypse*.

McCoy's incarnation was a joy to write for – as was his new companion Benny in my second New Adventure, *Birthright*, which I must say I enjoyed writing far more than *Apocalypse*. It was also great fun inserting some bits with the second Doctor, as played by Patrick Troughton, although I think we all overdid past-Doctor appearances in the first four New Adventures. I did try to keep continuity references down to a minimum, however.'

The final book in the Timewyrm series came from a writer new to professional publishing, Paul Cornell. 'It was just a darn good story,' says Darvill-Evans. 'I was very impressed with the writing style, and I thought, "Well, I've got a slot, let's just go with it." Also, I wanted to demonstrate that we weren't barring new authors. I did encounter a certain amount of opposition to this within the company, from people who wanted to know why we didn't have well-known authors for all four books, but I wanted to make a selling point of finding new talent, something that is very important to me.'

'I'd read the announcement that Peter Darvill-Evans put out in various fanzines and in *Doctor Who Magazine*,' explains Cornell. 'I already knew it was coming, from hearing about it on the grapevine, and I'd already had a short story published in *Doctor Who Magazine* by that time. I thought it was about time that original fiction was published; it was the obvious thing to do. And that it was going to change everything.

'The Timewyrm was in place in the material that Peter sent out to prospective writers. I think I got commissioned because I took that stuff and

Andrew Skilleter's initial proposal to Peter Darvill-Evans for the cover of *Timewyrm: Apocalypse*, and his subsequent colour rough of the artwork.

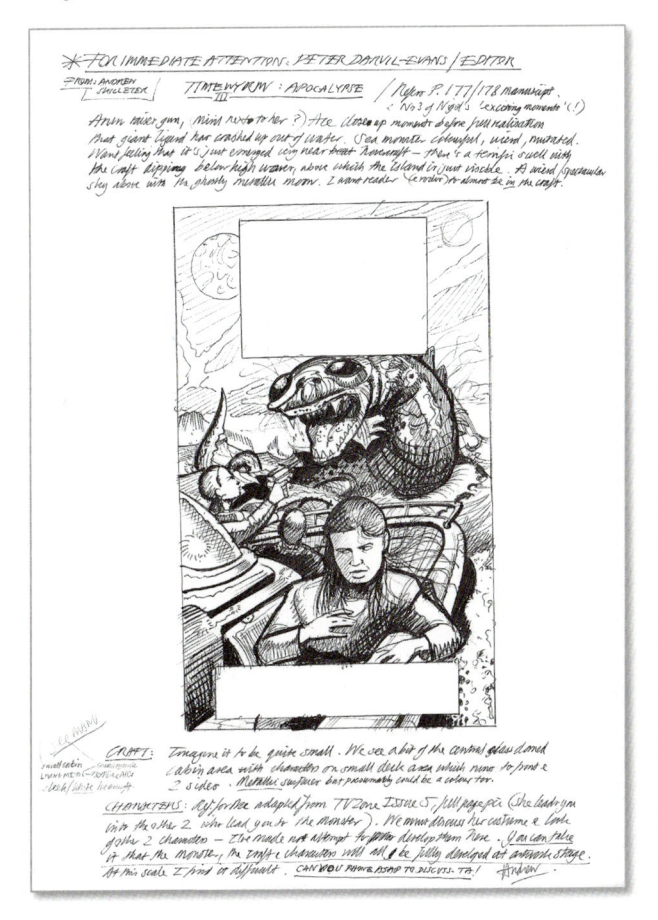

Issues 5 and 7 of *Queen Bat*, the 1980s fanzine in which was published Paul Cornell's multi-part story 'Total Eclipse', the starting point for *Timewyrm: Revelation*. Issue 5's cover art was by Phil Bevan, who would go on to illustrate *Doctor Who Magazine* Preludes to many of the New Adventures (see the next chapter) and provide internal illustrations for the Missing Adventure *The English Way of Death*.

The novel's concept of Saul the sentient church came from another of Cornell's earlier short stories, from the fanzine *Paradise Lost*.

developed it/ignored it/wasn't constrained by it. I took the view that if the Timewyrm had all the aspects that Peter had outlined for it, then it was going to be a big universal creature, and for those things all bets are off in terms of limits to their powers. And, of course, being inside the Doctor's mind changed it too. It became more an archetypal thing, more about the Doctor.

'For my initial submission, I rewrote a chunk of, and the plot of, "Total Eclipse", a story published in several issues of the fanzine *Queen Bat*. I turned the demon that's the villain of that story into the Timewyrm, and the original team of the fifth Doctor, Nyssa and Tegan into the seventh Doctor and Ace. The section I submitted was, I think, Ace in the garden maze in the Doctor's mind.'

This was sent in to Virgin in around July 1990, and Darvill-Evans was impressed. 'If you're not careful,' he wrote to Cornell at the time, 'you'll find yourself writing the fourth Timewyrm novel.'

'I was standing in my hallway in Manchester when I picked up the slim letter from Virgin, fully expecting another rejection,' recalls Cornell. 'I literally leapt up and down. And then I grew worried: how "careful" did I have to be? It happened at the same moment in my life that I got my first radio work out of the BBC and had my first play on TV. But the book was first by a week or two, and was the thing that gave me a career, changed my life, saved me, gave me a peer group. Peter has my eternal loyalty for that.'

Cornell duly submitted a revised outline called *Total Eclipse Rewrite or Book of Revelation or Synthesis*. This was met with enthusiasm, and on 21 September 1990 he was formally commissioned to write the novel, making him the first of many previously unpublished fiction writers from the *Doctor Who* fan community to contribute to Virgin's ranges.

In the course of writing the book, Cornell consulted some fan friends. One of them, Siobhan Gallichan, made suggestions that led him to rewrite Chapter 9; much of the original draft, which featured the group the Happy Mondays, a submarine of goblins and a talking parrot, was published by way of a teaser in Vol 5 Issue 3 of the fanzine *Skaro*, dated May 1991.

For the covers of the new books, Darvill-Evans initially asked regular novelisations artist Alister Pearson if he would like to try his hand. One idea for the design was to have an image of the Timewyrm around the lower title/author credit box, and Darvill-Evans' handwritten brief to Pearson suggested: 'Movie poster style; full bleed out to page edge; elements of swashbuckling; *Who*-ness, and sex appeal –

Gilgamesh fighting, the TARDIS and/or Doctor, Ishtar and/or Ace respectively. Also keep it quite simple – I guess that means a few big images, perhaps only one, but you could include a lot of detail small/in background.'

'I can't actually *design* anything to save my life,' claims Pearson, 'so faced with the apparent need for a Timewyrm figure, I enlisted the help of artist Andy Lambert, whom I'd met at a convention and whose inventiveness and design skills impressed me enormously. He provided me with some extraordinary drawings. [See page 22.] I found I couldn't seem to get all of Peter's requested elements to mesh, so I ended up sketching something involving Sylvester McCoy, Sophie Aldred and the Lambertesque Timewyrm – a typical Pearson heads-floating-about-in-mid-air piece, which was precisely what Peter didn't want. I started the picture on 8 December 1990 and abandoned the project just before Christmas, leaving Peter very little time to organise an alternative.'

The alternative came in the form of a piece from artist Andrew Skilleter, who had previously handled covers for the *Doctor Who* range, and who was at the time working on the jackets for BBC Video's *Doctor Who* releases.

The brief supplied to Skilleter was slightly more refined: 'I guess we want a narrative picture,' wrote Darvill-Evans, 'a picture that extends to all edges of the front cover; and I think the whole thing can be achieved with a film poster look, i.e. a background that bleeds to the cover edge, a middle ground that consists of close-ups of the stars, and a foreground that consists of an exciting narrative shot from the action … Some suggestions [for the] background: the TARDIS in close-up – blue panels, a glimpse of the words at the top; or the walls of Kish, covered with intricate copper circuitry; or the face of Ishtar, beautiful, malevolent, metallic.'

'Peter asked if I could do it,' wrote Skilleter in his book *Blacklight: The Art of Andrew Skilleter*, 'and in a matter of days. Having been given so little time, I put most of my efforts into creating and painting Ishtar, and as a consequence the rest of the painting is not ideally as I would have liked it to have been.' Skilleter went on to handle all four covers for the books comprising the Timewyrm sequence.

Throughout 1990 and 1991, Darvill-Evans was in regular contact with the BBC, trying to sort out the actual license agreement for the original fiction. In 1992, in desperation, and with the book range already up, running and available to buy, he

---

ANDY LAMBERT

Andy Lambert originally hailed from the North East of England, but relocated to Cambridge to study illustration. Although his work has graced various commercial items over the years, including Big Finish audio releases and issues of *Doctor Who Magazine*, he mainly treats art as a hobby.

Lambert now lives by the Sussex coast. He continues to illustrate – both traditionally and digitally – and produces the occasional cover for the *Doctor Who* Appreciation Society fanzine *Celestial Toyroom*.

LONG AGO …

As a narrative conceit, Paul Cornell chose to end his *Doctor Who* New Adventures with similar lines. *Timewyrm: Revelation* ends with 'long ago in an English winter', *Love and War* ends with 'long ago in an English autumn', *No Future* ends with 'long ago in an English summer', and *Human Nature* ends with 'long ago in an English spring'. *Happy Endings* closes with 'And a love for all seasons.' And a song and dance routine.

Andrew Skilleter's initial compositional sketch (left) and more detailed proposal (right) for the cover of *Timewyrm: Revelation*.

drew up his own version of the agreement and asked the BBC if they would sign it, which they did. 'That's how our contract came to be,' laughs Darvill-Evans. 'It was great, as I was able to incorporate into it all the things I needed there to be for Virgin to be able to continue with the books, such as the ability to use "*Doctor Who*" as our imprint logo. It was not an ideal situation, but we simply couldn't have waited any longer for the BBC to come back to us.'

The first in Virgin's range of original fiction, with a logo proclaiming the books to be 'The New *Doctor Who* Adventures', went on sale on 20 June 1991. John Peel's *Timewyrm: Genesys* was marketed with the cover blurb, 'Full-length science fiction novels: stories too broad and too deep for the small screen'; and to add an element of continuity to the proceedings, it featured the aforementioned introduction by Ace actress Sophie Aldred.

The novel met with a rather mixed reaction. 'A good story,' wrote Gary Russell in *Doctor Who Magazine*, 'but perhaps I expected too much and found myself a little disappointed with the end product.' The *Doctor Who* Appreciation Society's newsletter, *Celestial Toyroom*, presented several members' views. 'A trifle unoriginal,' claimed Doug Potter, 'but all very enjoyable … a good start.' In the same issue, Stephen Parsons commented, 'Overall I did find the book enjoyable and readable. I just wish I knew who they were writing for. The whole idea of writing the books to appeal to a different audience seems suspect … The books should be in the same style as the series,

THE TIMEWYRM IS BORN

Andrew Skilleter's original artwork for the cover of *Timewyrm: Revelation*.

at least that would keep the present audience ... I enjoyed the book but I wouldn't have bought it. I doubt I'll buy the sequel.' John A Collins was more enthusiastic: 'I enjoyed this book tremendously and could not put it down. It is true that it has many flaws, though.'

There were, of course, detractors, most notably the often-controversial fanzine *DWB*, which managed to obtain a first draft of the opening chapters and a very early draft synopsis of Peel's novel and proceeded, in a review published in its Issue 88, to trash the entire book on the basis of this material. When the novel was eventually published, the fanzine backtracked somewhat, as assistant editor David Gibbs gave his verdict in Issue 91: 'If you like historical adventures, or you dig weird and wonderful computer concepts, or if you just want to find out what the Doctor and Ace did next, then take a look. Ignore the bad sex, the occasional clumsy phrasing and the ghastly continuity references and underneath you'll find good, solid, honest *Doctor Who*. A promising start to a new series.'

Publicity for the range was boosted, albeit in a strange way, when the *News of the World*, a weekend tabloid newspaper with a penchant for sensationalism, picked up on the fact that one of Peel's characters was a harem girl, and that his novel featured prostitutes as a presence in Gilgamesh's court – something that Peel himself had been concerned about. As *DWB* had noted, the narrative also contained a number of less-

Below: *Timewyrm: Genesys* provokes controversy in the 11 August 1991 edition of the Sunday newspaper the *News of the World*.

ANDREW SKILLETER

Born on the Isle of Wight, Andrew Skilleter studied Graphic Design at Bournemouth and Poole College of Art, then pursued a career as a freelance illustrator, gaining commissions for magazines, books, advertising and merchandise.

He has been a significant presence in the world of *Doctor Who* art for over 40 years. From 1979 to 1995, he was professionally involved with the franchise, his work including the iconic *Radio Times* cover for 'The Five Doctors'; book covers, including for over 40 of the legendary Target and related range; BBC VHS covers; books; calendars; and prints, establishing him as the most prolific professional *Doctor Who* artist of that period.

In the 1980s he created Who Dares Publishing, issuing licensed printed *Doctor Who* art merchandise and a number of books, including *Cybermen* by David Banks.

Blacklight: The Doctor Who Art of Andrew Skilleter, was published by Virgin Books in 1995.

Outside of *Doctor Who*, Skilleter maintained a busy career from the 1970s as a versatile illustrator producing hundreds of covers for adult, teenage and children's books across numerous genres. His work has also appeared on magazines, CDs, computer games, TV and video.

Late in 2016, Skilleter, along with Matthew Doe, revived the Who Dares Publishing imprint and launched the *Andrew Skilleter Target Art Calendar* and other innovative art collections.

Skilleter lives in Dorset with his artist and writer wife. He continues to produce artwork using traditional materials, and is always busy with private commissions while dreaming up new projects to self-publish. As time allows, he is also currently writing and illustrating an epic retro-style space mystery graphic novel, featuring Miss Midnite and fellow travellers.

You can see a range of his work on his website at www.andrewskilleter.com and follow him on Instagram and on his Facebook page at: http://www.facebook.com/artofandrewskilleter.

Who Dares is at: www.who-dares.co.uk.

---

than-subtle passages of a sexual nature. On 11 August 1991, the newspaper ran a half-page story with the headline 'Sexterminate Him! Dr Who's Too Blue' and the subheading 'Fans zap porno timelord' (sic). The basis of this story was offence apparently taken at the book by two fans, Matthew Smith and David Houlgate, as expressed in letters published in Issue 92 of the fanzine *DWB* (although actually Houlgate's letter had praised aspects of the book). Subsequently, on 21 August, Virgin complained to the Press Complaints Commission of unfair and inaccurate reporting. The *News of the World* strongly denied the allegations, arguing that the book did contain 'adult' material and that their coverage wholly reflected the way that *Doctor Who* and Sylvester McCoy had been generally portrayed in the press. Despite a spirited defence by Darvill-Evans on Virgin's behalf, on 11 September, the complaint was not upheld. This exchange did nothing to diminish the book's reception; on the contrary, it generated additional awareness, and sales were good enough for the range to be proclaimed a success. The New Adventures had arrived!

THE WHO ADVENTURES

Artist Pete Wallbank's proposed cover for *Cat's Cradle: Time's Crucible*, which ultimately went unused.

4: CAT'S CRADLE

With the publication of the first of the New Adventures in June 1991, Virgin Publishing realised that they had something very special on their hands. Editor Peter Darvill-Evans had always argued that there was a market for original *Doctor Who* fiction, but had now demonstrated this to his superiors. The first title, *Timewyrm: Genesys*, had gained some good reviews – and some controversy courtesy of the *News of the World* – and excellent sales: the first printing of 20,000 copies had sold out before publication, and a reprint of 5,000 copies had nearly sold out by 11 July 1991. Comments about the other three titles in the *Timewyrm* arc proved equally positive.

'On finishing *Genesys*, I felt that there would be problems maintaining such high quality,' wrote Richard Houldsworth in his *TV Zone* magazine review of Terrance Dicks' contribution, *Timewyrm: Exodus*. '*Exodus* extinguishes such fears; instead it improves upon the first book, and expands our knowledge of the two leading characters … *Exodus* is really one of *Doctor Who*'s finest adventures.' Keith Topping, writing in *DWB*, agreed, and added, 'Happily Terrance is familiar enough with how to tell a rattlingly good old-fashioned action story.'

Nigel Robinson's *Timewyrm: Apocalypse* was likewise praised by Houldsworth: 'A good, traditional *Who* tale, featuring a subjugated population, monsters, mutants and the end of the universe … What really sets *Apocalypse* apart is the outstanding dialogue, much of it given to the Doctor. … A pleasing read. It doesn't quite reach the excellence of *Exodus*, and hardly matches Virgin's hype of being "too broad and too deep for the small screen". It is good, standard *Doctor Who*, and there's nothing much wrong with that.'

Above: Pete Wallbank's rough for his proposed version of the cover art for *Cat's Cradle: Time's Crucible*.

Strangely, Paul Cornell's *Timewyrm: Revelation*, which has since won acclaim as a pivotal point in *Doctor Who* publishing and is now widely regarded as one of the best in the range, was not well reviewed at the time. Richard Houldsworth felt it to be '… a bizarre tale from Paul Cornell, a *Who* fan turned writer, who has taken the plunge and written the novel for the adult audience the publisher intended … *Revelation* is another "Warriors' Gate" [a narratively challenging *Doctor Who* television story from 1981], with elements of Clive Barker and Stephen King thrown in for good measure.' Peter Linford, writing in *DWB*, took a different stance:

THE WHO ADVENTURES

Peter Elson's original artwork for the cover of *Cat's Cradle: Time's Crucible*.

'*Revelation* is a difficult book. I don't know what the average readership age for the *Doctor Who* range is, but assuming it to be around 16 or 17 then I have reservations about their making any sense of this book at all. If most of its deeper concerns and themes are lost on them then there will be not much left. But perhaps I do them a disservice. We shall see.' This comment is especially ironic, given that where the earlier novelisations were concerned, fans had generally been calling for less literal 'script-to-book' type works that would treat the source material in a more sophisticated way. Perhaps the key lies in Houldsworth's comment that Cornell was 'a *Who* fan turned writer' – a fact that may have made it difficult for certain other, non-published fans to accept and embrace his novel. Regardless of its reception, Virgin felt that *Timewyrm: Revelation* was a strong enough book to enter it for the prestigious Arthur C Clarke Award. It did not, however, make the shortlist selected by the judging panel.

Publishing has a long lead time, and Darvill-Evans was already thinking about the next run of books before the first New Adventure had even hit the bookshops. Therefore he continued on the basis that the books needed to feature a running theme: 'As with the *Timewyrm* series, and as we hadn't actually sold any copies at that point, I was still thinking along the lines of needing to draw readers along, to get them to buy the next one in the series. There was a comment at the time that we should have numbered the books, but if you number them, the implication is that you need to start reading from number one. I wanted to allow people to start reading at any point, but then to get them to read the next book as well.'

On 11 December 1990, Darvill-Evans wrote to three authors who had submitted ideas and formally told them that they were to be commissioned to write New Adventures novels. These were Marc Platt, Andrew Hunt and Andrew Cartmel. At that stage, only one of the three proposals had a working title, and that was Marc Platt's *Cat's Cradle*. Darvill-Evans decided that the publication order of the books should be first Platt's, then Cartmel's, then Hunt's. Furthermore, he encouraged the authors to work as a team, and suggested they swap addresses and telephone numbers and meet up to discuss the three-book series. Having decided to use *Cat's*

MARC PLATT

Marc Platt wrote the 1989 *Doctor Who* television story 'Ghost Light', which he also novelised along with the preceding story 'Battlefield'. He wrote the direct-to-video drama *Downtime* (Reeltime Pictures), which he also novelised as a Virgin Missing Adventure. He wrote the Virgin New Adventures *Cat's Cradle: Time's Crucible* and *Lungbarrow*.

He has written many audio dramas for Big Finish Productions, including numerous *Doctor Who* stories: *Loups-Garoux, Spare Parts, The Cradle of the Snake, The Silver Turk, The Behemoth, The Skin of the Sleek, Purgatory 12, An Earthly Child, Relative Dimensions* and *The Tyrants of Logic*. In addition, he has contributed a number of the *Doctor Who Companion Chronicles* range, including: *Frostfire, Mother Russia, Quinnis, The Flames of Cadiz, The Beginning*. Philip Hinchcliffe Presents: *The Ghosts of Gralstead, The Devil's Armada, The Genesis Chamber, The Helm of Awe* and *The God of Phantoms*. For the *Doctor Who Lost Stories* range: *Point of Entry, The Children of Seth* and *Thin Ice*.

Other work for Big Finish includes: *Blake's 7 – Traitor, Flag and Flame, The Sea of Iron* and *Drones*; *Timeslip – The War That Never Was*; and classic book adaptations of: *The Wonderful Wizard of Oz* and *The Time Machine*.

Cradle as an overall title for this arc, Darvill-Evans apologised to Platt, saying, 'You've come up with a title that's just too good to ignore. It's mysterious, memorable, conveniently brief, and rolls off the tongue – perfect.' Darvill-Evans went on to outline the basic premise for the series: that the Doctor would be on a quest to locate TARDIS components, with the TARDIS itself being the one doing the searching, so that he would not know where he would arrive each time. A mysterious cat, included in Platt's proposal, would also feature as a recurring element. However, Darvill-Evans admitted that, at that stage, he had no idea how the arc would resolve itself … 'It's going to have to have something to do with the cat, isn't it?' he wrote. 'Maybe it disappears at last, having served its purpose (keeping the Doctor on the right track for TARDIS spare parts), and when Ace seems peeved, the Doctor says mysteriously that the cat's gone to a good home.'

By 28 February 1991, Platt's book had the working title *Old Haunts*, Cartmel's was called *Escape*, and the ideas behind the series were coming together, based on Platt's initial ideas and concepts. At their most basic, these concerned the TARDIS having suffered damage. Thus Platt's book focused on the TARDIS's internal structure and resonances from Gallifrey's ancient past. Peter wanted the other two books to take on board: the damage to the TARDIS, the plot mechanism that would spring the series from story to story; the concept of the TARDIS as a cat's cradle of dimensions, an infinite space within which anything can happen and which is also a semi-sentient artificial intelligence of awesome power and alien nature; and, finally, a silver cat. Peter concluded with a request that all the authors think visually, as he needed inspiration for cover images!

The three titles were eventually published in February, April and June 1992, forming the second tranche of novels from Virgin.

Darvill-Evans was clear as to the sort of covers he wanted to use for the books: 'I knew I wanted to use narrative images, as that is the sort of image you generally find on science fiction paperbacks. I wanted to draw a distinction between these original novels and

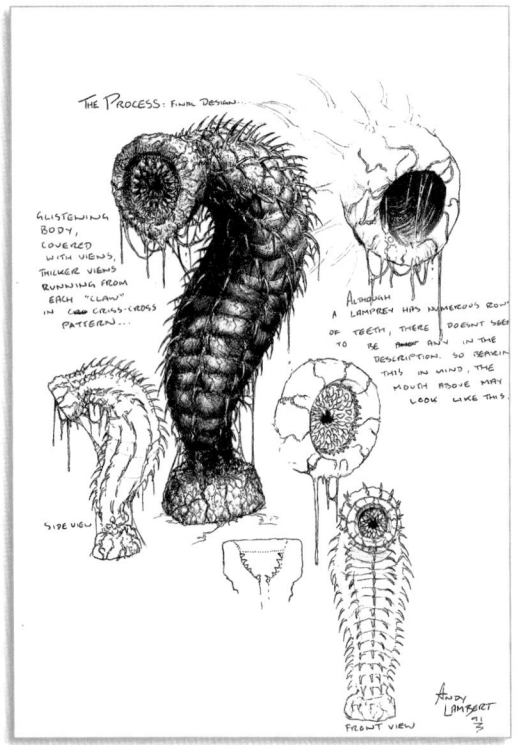

Top: author Marc Platt sketched this design idea for the cover of *Cat's Cradle: Time's Crucible*.

Bottom: Andy Lambert's concept sketch for the appearance of the Process creature featured in the story.

the Target paperbacks, which featured collages of images, and I wanted them to look like ordinary science fiction novels. This unfortunately counted out Alister Pearson who, while expert at designing collages and geometric images for the novelisation covers, could not manage the narrative approach I wanted. He was far more suited to the Missing Adventures range; and, indeed, we used his work extensively on that.

'I used Andrew Skilleter for the first four books as I wanted to develop a series look and therefore didn't want to use different artists. Thereafter I wanted to have variation, so I got a number of artists all from the same agency. I looked around at various agencies, but the Sarah Brown Agency seemed to have the range of talent I was after.'

The Sarah Brown Agency had been set up in 1977 by artist Peter Elson and his friend Carol Butfoy. 'The name was a combination of Sarah (a name Peter liked) and Brown (which I thought sounded reliable),' explains Butfoy on Elson's website. The Agency specialised from the outset in science fiction and fantasy artwork, an area that interested Elson.

Working for the Agency was Brian Fennelly, a long-time friend of Elson and Butfoy.

'Carol started it back in the day, with Peter Elson,' Fennelly explains. 'I joined in 1992, probably around the time when the New Adventures got going. By then, Carol had other things on her plate, so it was a good idea for her to ease out and do other things and for me to ease in and carry on with the Agency, which is what I did.

'I'd spent a little time at art college, but only on a part-time basis. I always maintained an interest in the Agency and in SF and fantasy too, so it was a natural fit for me in some ways. It was certainly more interesting than insurance, the business I was in before!

'We worked with publishers, games companies, magazine companies ... you name it ... and it was mostly me at the time. Specialising in science fiction and fantasy artwork, it wasn't like we were dealing with advertising companies, who have a lot of money to spend. The kind of work we were doing was very painstaking and time-consuming.

Three preparatory roughs produced by Peter Elson for his cover for *Cat's Cradle: Time's Crucible*.

THE WHO ADVENTURES

HUNGARIAN EDITION

Only one of the New Adventures was translated into another language back in the 1990s: Marc Platt's *Cat's Cradle: Time's Crucible*. This edition (see top right), titled *Új Doctor Who Kalandok: Az Idö Fogságában* (which means, in English, *New Doctor Who Adventures: In the Captivity of Time*), was published in January 1993 by a firm called Android, based in Budapest, Hungary, with ISBN 963-7755-81-0. The translator was Bihari György.

The cover art (the original of which is reproduced below) was by British artist Tim White, and was not specially-commissioned: it had previously appeared on a 1978 New English Library edition of Frank Herbert's 1968 novel *The Santaroga Barrier* (see bottom right). The Hungarian book, however, credits Gál László for the cover.

Despite the number '1' appearing with the *Doctor Who* logo on the spine, no further Hungarian editions were published.

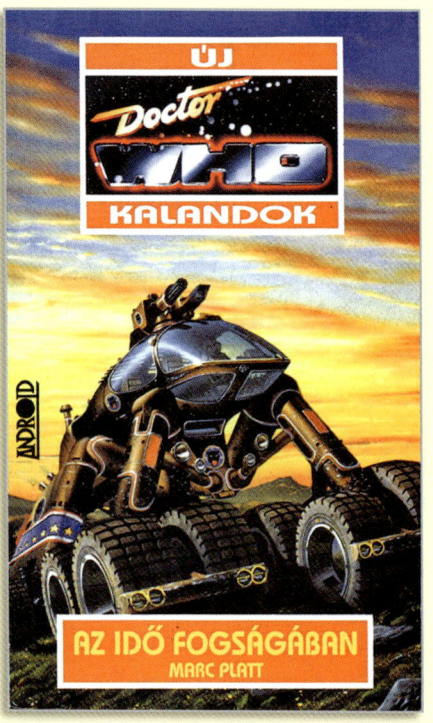

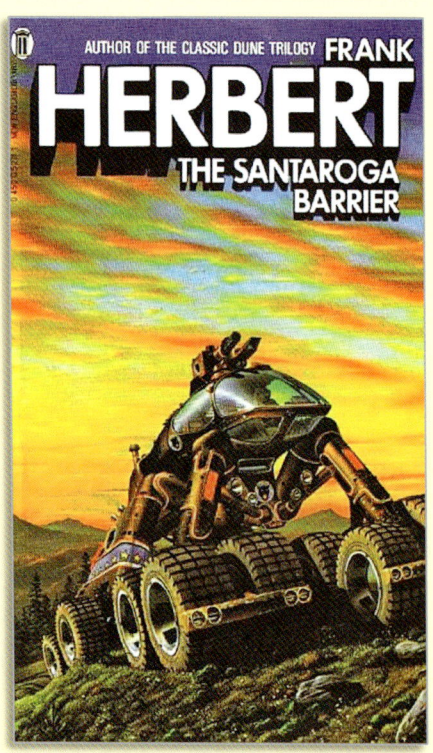

PETER ELSON

Peter George Elson was born in 1947, and did a year in Fashion Design at the Ealing School of Art before changing to Graphics. On leaving Ealing, he specialised in painting space hardware, winning a *Science Fiction Monthly* competition in 1975.

Elson was based in Colchester and needed someone in London who could look after his clients and find new ones, so he and his friend Carol Butfoy set up the Sarah Brown Agency. The Agency went on to represent many artists, and was the main one used by Virgin Publishing to source the cover art for their *Doctor Who* ranges.

Elson's career mirrored the chronology of the Golden Age: he was prolific through the '70s and '80s, still important in the '90s, but slid out of fashion with the advent of the initial wave of do-it-yourself 3D computer-generated images.

Elson's work graced a great many book covers and art collections over the years. Authors whose books featured iconic Elson covers included John Wyndham, A E van Vogt, Harry Harrison, Theodore Sturgeon, Poul Anderson and Isaac Asimov. Among his last work was the sleeve to a 1998 CD of music inspired by the works of Allan Cole, called *When the Gods Slept*. A book of his paintings, entitled *Parallel Lines*, was published in 1981.

Elson died aged 52 in March 1998 in Skegness, while he and some colleagues were relaxing in the hotel bar after a day spent working on a mural at Butlins. His work can be seen at https://peterelson.co.uk/.

'This was all before digital, and it used to take the artists quite a while to paint and create the images – particularly Peter Elson. The amount of detail they'd put in with a brush was extraordinary. So the paintings took some time to do, and it was difficult for the artists to make it cost-effective. They used to produce beautiful work, and it all took time, but the clients would never pay quite enough to cover the amount of effort they had to put in. But they loved doing it. And we loved doing it as well.

'I remember Peter Darvill-Evans or [his assistant] Rebecca Levene would ring up and say that they'd got some covers they wanted to commission, so would I come down and visit them.

'I'd go to their offices and they would give me an idea of what the story was, and discuss what kinds of visuals they had in mind, who might would be good for it, and so on. They'd look at some artwork samples – because I'd bring the folders with me with the various artists' work in.

'I remember that they in most cases wanted artwork that was fairly character-driven. In other words, they usually wanted a picture of some person on the front: the Doctor, Ace, [new companion] Bernice Summerfield or whoever. Therefore, they'd want an artist who could do figures. Oddly, Peter Elson wasn't actually that good at people, but he was so good at everything else that he managed to get selected a great many times. Virgin would give me the brief for the cover, and I'd go away and commission it with the artists.'

The Sarah Brown Agency eventually closed down. 'Basically, agencies like ours didn't have

Peter Elson's initial roughs for the cover of *Cat's Cradle: Warhead*.

much of a purpose when the internet really got going, because the publishers could find the artists through their own websites without needing to check with us,' explains Fennelly. 'We started to find more and more that the artists were being approached direct. Also, many of the publishers started to find that they could create their artwork in-house, so they started knocking out covers themselves using a few stock photos and other manipulated imagery. It was much cheaper for them than actually hiring and paying an artist to create a cover. If you ask me, those early digital covers didn't look nearly as good as the sort of paintings we used to produce for them, but there was nothing we could do!'

Of Elson, who sadly died in 1998, Fennelly recalls: 'Peter was a very sensitive sort of guy, and very artistic – although it might sound a bit funny saying "very artistic" about somebody whose life was painting pictures. Some artists were fairly phlegmatic, and would just get on with the job and do it on time, with no nonsense, while others were, for want of a better word, more flaky, and we'd have problems getting things done to deadline. Peter wasn't at all flaky, but he was a perfectionist. He got so into the image of the work that he had inside his head that he wanted to make sure that, when it got on the page, it really was what he had intended. That's a painstaking process that can take some time to achieve.

'Peter was an amazing artist, and always worked in physical media: canvas, boards, paints and brushes. He never got into digital art and was still painting right up until he died.

'One fascinating story about Peter: he could paint machinery as if he was an engineer. But it was intuitive for him. You need only look at his art featuring spaceships and other machinery and vehicles! I remember, there was a commission we had from – I think it might have been Transworld – and the art director rang me up, concerned that a painting of Peter's was overdue – it might have been a day or so late or something. And what I had to do at that time was to write a letter to Peter and ask him to call me. Peter would then, when he got the letter the next day, go down the road to his local phone box and ring me up, so that I could find out the status of the work and get back to

CAT'S CRADLE

Peter Elson's original artwork for the cover of *Cat's Cradle: Warhead*.

ANDREW HUNT

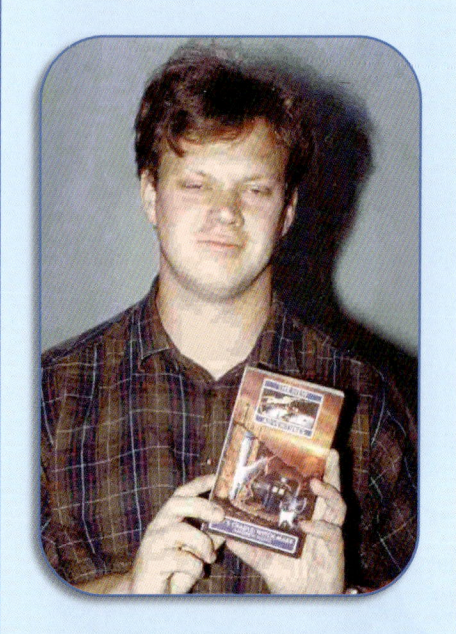

Andy Hunt was a member of the Lancaster and Morecambe *Doctor Who* Local Group when he was a teenager in the 1980s. He was studying for a veterinary degree and wrote *Witch Mark* before he turned 20. He worked for a veterinary charity, the PDSA, for 20 years, and was one of their senior vets, in charge of one of their hospitals. His work involved moving around the country, from Liverpool to Kent, until he settled in the Midlands. He now specialises as a part-time GP caring for pets owned by people on low incomes. 'It isn't just about the pets,' he says, 'it's also about helping people who sometimes have only their pets to give them love and to give them a reason to get up in the morning. I'm a strong believer that pets are good for our self-esteem and mental health. And although pets are a luxury, a lot of the people we help either took on pets before losing their jobs/income or need them to keep on going from day to day.'

Hunt is still in love with *Doctor Who*, though not involved in fandom. When asked, he will write stories. Has two cats and five chickens.

the art editor! I found it just so extraordinary that here was a guy who seemed to know the ins and outs of machinery, and science fiction hardware, and spaceships ... and yet he didn't have a phone!'

Darvill-Evans considered Peter Elson's work to be the best available: 'I asked them to do some sample work, and clearly Peter Elson was the one we thought had the right combination of being able to do superb science fiction illustration but also acceptable likenesses of people's faces: specifically Sylvester McCoy's and Sophie Aldred's. Furthermore, we wanted artists who could do likenesses without directly copying photographs – a difficult thing to ask of anyone. Peter's likenesses weren't perhaps the best, but his obvious talents at science fiction illustration swung it in his favour.'

Reviewers continued to be kind to the books. *TV Zone*'s Richard Houldsworth suggested that *Cat's Cradle: Time's Crucible*, as Platt's book was eventually titled, was 'a good read; perhaps not quite as good as the pre-publicity suggested,' and that Cartmel's *Cat's Cradle: Warhead*, retitled from *Escape* at Cartmel's request on 8 August 1991, was 'certainly beyond the range of normal *Doctor Who* in terms of its exotic locations, the three-dimensional characters, and the adult, very depressing themes it encompasses,' while Hunt's *Cat's Cradle: Witch Mark* received the poorest review of the three: 'The book combines the *Doctor Who* we know with the style of Tolkien and C S Lewis. *Witch Mark* is Andrew Hunt's first professional work, and sadly it shows. Characterisation is thin on the ground ... and there is also a painful amount of continuity, seemingly dredged from every era of the programme. It demonstrates Hunt's wide knowledge, but he should have more faith in his own material ... Not the best in the series, then, but still readable and entertaining.'

Anthony Brown, writing in *DWB*, was impressed with Platt's work: '*Time's Crucible* will probably be remembered as the book that explained how the Doctor could be a contemporary of Rassilon – or at least as the book that provided enough clues for the answer to become obvious, although it's made clear that, even in the Old Time, *the Other* wasn't exactly one of the Gallifreyan people ... Those

Peter Elson's original artwork for the cover of *Cat's Cradle: Witch Mark*.

Promotional items produced by Virgin around the time of the New Adventures' launch: a wall card bearing the range name; and a cardboard 'dump bin' offered to bookshops for use in displaying the books – this particular example stocked with multiple copies of the debut title, *Timewyrm: Genesys*.

who've enjoyed the uncertainty of the last few years shouldn't be worried, though, as *Time's Crucible* leaves a lot of questions still to be answered ... Hold on – the McCoy era explained? A subplot that describes the rise of Rassilon? A main plot in the tradition of "Warriors' Gate"? ... *Time's Crucible* is superb! Just get your thinking caps on before starting it ...'

Brown, too, enjoyed *Warhead*, though not as a *Doctor Who* story: 'Andrew Cartmel has got a bright future as an author of science fiction thrillers ahead of him, but it also demonstrates, once and for all, that he doesn't understand *Doctor Who*.' He also found much to like about *Witch Mark*: 'Under its fantasy trimmings, *Witch Mark* is a very traditional *Doctor Who* story, done with some style, in a way that fully exploits the freedoms the New Adventures have brought. It's rather reminiscent of *Apocalypse* in some ways, though undoubtedly superior; and, despite a few loose ends, I imagine that it'll be the most widely popular of the *Cat's Cradle* books.'

The *Cat's Cradle* series marked the end of Darvill-Evans' desire to market the books with arc titles. This was mainly because the first few books in the range had already been published by the time he started thinking about post-*Cat's Cradle* entries, and their sales figures, combined with feedback both from Virgin's sales teams and from fans, indicated that having an overarching title like '*Timewyrm*' or '*Cat's Cradle*' made little difference to the books' appeal. 'The crucial element was that there was no difference in sales terms between the first four titles,' explains Darvill-Evans. 'We didn't need to entice people to read the books; they were buying them as they came out. In addition, some of the authors were commenting that it was too constricting to theme the titles, and the fans were saying that they didn't care about the theming ... It was also difficult editorially. So we dropped the idea after *Cat's Cradle*.'

5: FUTURE HISTORY

Peter Darvill-Evans as usual put together a fairly detailed document describing what he was aiming to do with the range post-*Cat's Cradle*. Although there would be no further arc titles as such, he referred to the next half-dozen or so books as the 'Future History Cycle', indicating that they would be linked by their taking the Doctor to various points in Earth's future. He also developed a rough background for the authors to work to. This involved the TARDIS having been infiltrated by a speck of alien intelligence at some point during the events of *Cat's Cradle: Witch Mark*. The intelligence has been absorbed into the fabric of the TARDIS and starts to cause random and unpredictable changes in the Doctor's ship. Ace is convinced that the Doctor knows something he's keeping from her, or is pretending he cannot see the phenomena. What is really happening is that the Doctor himself has been infected along with the TARDIS and is keeping Ace in the dark until he can work out how to expel the intelligence. He needs Ace safely out of trouble, and out of the TARDIS, so that he can reconfigure the ship's interior and shut off areas of his mind. He therefore contrives to ensure that she stops travelling with him for a time – although she will rejoin him later on, when she will have matured and grown, away from his presence.

In another undated note, Darvill-Evans went on to outline elements of 'Future History' that he envisaged the novels could explore: warp drive; advanced communications; corporate power; colony planets; the 2160 Dalek War; the First Cyber War in 2200; the second Dalek War at the start of the 25th Century; and so on.

In October 1991, Darvill-Evans issued a further note to authors, this time with a brief update as to how things were going: the *Cat's*

LEE SULLIVAN

Lee Sullivan has been a comic book artist since 1987, working on *Transformers*; *Doctor Who Magazine* (semi-regularly, becoming well-known for his drawings of the Daleks); *RoboCop* and *William Shatner's TekWorld* for Marvel US; *Judge Dredd* and *Mercy Heights* in 2000AD; *Radio Times'* short-lived *Doctor Who* comic strip; the *Amulet of Samarkand* graphic novel; five years on *Thunderbirds Magazine*; five years on Fabbri's *Doctor Who: Battles in Time* comic strips; three years of *Doctor Who DVD Files* illustrations; various *Doctor Who* comic book covers for Titan; a comic strip for the Royal Mail's *Doctor Who Prestige Stamp Book*; and IDW's *Doctor Who: Prisoners of Time*, celebrating the show's fiftieth anniversary. His work has also appeared on the show itself in the Series 8 episode 'Time Heist'. He completed the *TV Century 21* 'Dalek Chronicles' strip story for *Vworp Vworp* magazine, and has also supplied box artwork for Big Chief Studios' Gerry Anderson 1/6 scale figures.

Between 2015 to 2018 he provided the art for six graphic novels in Titan's *Rivers of London* series – continuing on from Ben Aaronovitch's successful novels featuring Peter Grant – scripted by Aaronovitch and Andrew Cartmel.

Since 2018 Sullivan has worked as a concept artist for the TV industry, drawn graphic novels for the Penguin Readers series and produced two album covers for his sax-playing hero, Roxy Music's Andy Mackay.

Cradle books were in production, and there were promotional plans including 'dump bins' with Dalek header cards, posters and banners, and even a full-size Dalek! Darvill-Evans also noted that he had started commissioning the next batch of books, 'looking for a fairly mixed bag of novels, with varied settings and quite probably with different companions.' He went on: 'The main requirements are, as always: an exciting, original, large-scale, complex, satisfying *Doctor Who* story, with plenty of *Who*-ishness, action and drama. It needs to be well written, and to stand out from the herd it needs Wow! Factor – something that makes the reader think Wow!'

With Ace temporarily absent, Darvill-Evans was keen to see other companion characters introduced. By the time of his October 1991 note, he had decided that the first of these should be Professor Bernice Summerfield, a 26th Century archaeologist introduced in Paul Cornell's second novel, *Love and War*. Other books would be seeded with characters who, although they would not join the TARDIS team straightaway, might reappear later on, the main one of these being Kadiatu Lethbridge-Stewart, introduced in Ben

KADIATU LETHBRIDGE-STEWART

Ben Aaronovitch's initial submission for *Transit* – originally entitled *Stunnel* – included some notes on the new potential companion character Kadiatu Lethbridge-Stewart. These indicated that she was 6 foot 1 inch tall, with an athletic build, strong African features, very dark skin and black eyes. Aaronovitch went on to explain that she was the daughter of Yembe Lethbridge-Stewart and Mariama Kumara, two genetically-modified supersoldier veterans of a Thousand Day War against the Ice Warriors on Mars. Yembe, a distant descendant of the Doctor's old friend Brigadier Lethbridge-Stewart, named Kadiatu after the Brigadier's granddaughter, the original Kadiatu – a character included by Aaronovitch in his novelisation of the TV story 'Remembrance of the Daleks' as the daughter of the Brigadier's illegitimate son Stephen, conceived as the result of an affair with a local woman while he was serving in Sierra Leone in the 1950s.

Aaronovitch noted of the new character: 'Kadiatu herself was conceived in a laboratory (using genetic material from her parents) as part of the proposed second generation of supersoldiers. Vigorous lobbying and finally direct action by the Veterans Association closed down the project but by that time Kadiatu had already been born (alright – decanted). Yembe and Mariama took her home and raised her and the whole supersoldier project was buried under a mound of official secrets.' Although she grew up believing herself to be a normal human, Kadiatu's origins meant that she had enhanced capabilities – 'faster reflexes, greater tolerance to heat and cold, better stamina, super-acute vision' and greater strength.

Above: feminist American playwright and poet Ntozake Shange, a photo of whom from an issue of *Ms.* magazine was used by author Kate Orman as the basis of the physical descriptions of Kadiatu in her New Adventures novel *Set Piece*.

Aaronovitch's *Transit* as a descendant of the television show's popular Brigadier character.

'It became clear that, while the Doctor needed to be present in (almost) every story,' explains Darvill-Evans, 'to limit yourself to one companion – Ace – was too restrictive. I was loath to use older *Doctor Who* companions, because I wanted to look forward and not back; and also, even at that early stage, I wanted to build new characters who could sustain the series should the *Doctor Who* element be removed. I also wanted to do something serious and noteworthy in the range, and the obvious thing was to lose Ace; but to do that I needed substitutes. Losing Ace was the only big, dramatic, gesture I could make.

'It is worth pointing out that there was a lot of input from the authors, as well as from within Virgin, as to which direction to go in. The authors were very influential in choosing the path the books took. There was a contingent that wanted me to get rid of Ace altogether, but I didn't want to do that. I did, however, feel that we could rest Ace and bring her back as an older and wiser version – which I eventually did in my own contribution to the series, *Deceit*.'

The 'Future History Cycle' ultimately contained the following titles: Mark Gatiss's *Nightshade*; Paul Cornell's *Love and War*; Ben Aaronovitch's *Transit*; Gareth Roberts' *The Highest Science*; Neil Penswick's *The Pit*, which was developed from a proposal titled *O Lucifer, Son of the Morning*; Peter Darvill-Evans' *Deceit*; and *Lucifer Rising* by Andy Lane and Jim Mortimore. For the covers of these latest books, Darvill-Evans decided on another change of approach. On 12 December 1991 he distributed a note to a

BEN AARONOVITCH

Ben Aaronovitch is the son of economist Dr Sam Aaronovitch and the younger brother of actor Owen Aaronovitch and British journalist David Aaronovitch. He contributed the scripts for two of the *Doctor Who* television stories, 'Remembrance of the Daleks' (1988) and 'Battlefield' (1989). The former was novelised for Target to much acclaim by Aaronovitch himself, while the latter was novelised by Marc Platt.

'Remembrance of the Daleks' was Aaronovitch's first television work. He had been put in touch with *Doctor Who* script editor Andrew Cartmel by a BBC producer, Caroline Oulton. Since *Doctor Who*, he has written for *Casualty* ('Results', 1990), *Jupiter Moon* (1990) and *Dark Knight* (2001).

For Virgin Publishing's New Adventures range Aaronovitch wrote *Transit* (1992) and *The Also People* (1995) and contributed the outline and some textual material to *So Vile a Sin* (1997), which was completed by Kate Orman.

In 2006, *Genius Loci*, Aaronovitch's first book in ten years, was published as the latest in Big Finish's range of adventures featuring one of the Doctor's companions from the original novels, Bernice Summerfield.

2011 saw the publication of Aaronovitch's *Rivers of London* (retitled *Midnight Riot* in the USA), the first in a series of well-received urban fantasy novels about Peter Grant, Detective Constable and trainee wizard. In 2020, the eighth novel in the series, *False Value*, entered the *Sunday Times* bestseller list at #1.

THE WHO ADVENTURES

wide range of fan and professional artists, inviting them to submit pencil, ink or watercolour roughs for *Nightshade*. He succinctly described the scene he wanted to appear on the cover. Amongst those who contributed ideas were Pete Wallbank and Colin Howard; but Alister Pearson, who also received the note, elected not to do so. Ultimately Peter Elson was offered the commission. Now taking on the role of principal artist on the range, Elson also completed the covers for *Transit*, *The Highest Science* and *The Pit*. Comics artist Lee Sullivan, who had worked extensively for *Doctor Who Magazine* in the late '80s, provided the cover for *Love and War*. Luis Rey, a Spanish-Mexican artist, was chosen by Darvill-Evans to paint the cover for his own *Deceit*. Jim Mortimore provided the cover for his and Andy Lane's *Lucifer Rising* – making this the first *Doctor Who* novel to have featured a cover by one of its authors.

Reproduced on this page, ultimately unselected sketches pitched for the cover of *Nightshade* by Pete Wallbank (left), Colin Howard (below left) and a third, currently unidentified artist (below right).

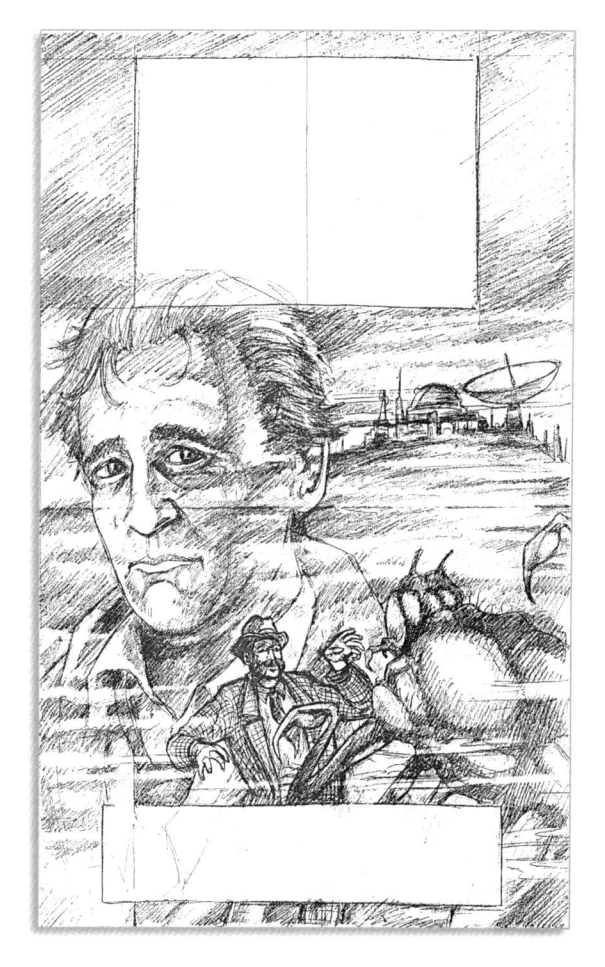

FUTURE HISTORY

MARK GATISS

Mark Gatiss was born on 17 October 1966 in Sedgefield and graduated from Bretton Hall Drama College with a BA (Hons) in Theatre Arts. He is an actor, comedian, screenwriter, director, producer and novelist. His work includes writing for and acting in the TV shows *Doctor Who*, *Sherlock* and *Dracula*, and acting in the fantasy series *Game of Thrones*. Together with Reece Shearsmith, Steve Pemberton and Jeremy Dyson, he is a member of the comedy team the League of Gentlemen, who found success on television in 1999 and ran until 2017.

His New Adventures novel *Nightshade* was his first published fiction. It was followed in 1994 by *St Anthony's Fire*. The same year, he started working with independent video producers BBV, contributing scripts for four of their heavily *Doctor Who*-influenced dramas: *P.R.O.B.E.: The Zero Imperative* (1994), *P.R.O.B.E.: The Devil of Winterborne* (1995), *P.R.O.B.E.: Unnatural Selection* (1996) and *P.R.O.B.E.: Ghosts of Winterborne* (1996). He also appeared in all but the 1996 offering.

In 2004 he released his first mainstream novel, *The Vesuvius Club*, which was followed by *The Devil in Amber* (2006) and *Black Butterfly* (2008).

Below: Peter Elson's rough sketch submissions for the cover of Mark Gatiss's novel *Nightshade*, on the basis of which he was commissioned to provide the final artwork.

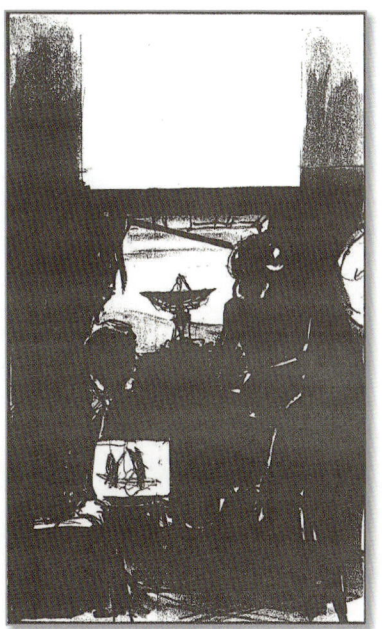

THE WHO ADVENTURES

Peter Elson's original artwork for the cover of *Nightshade*.

FUTURE HISTORY

PHIL BEVAN

Phil Bevan was born in Edgware Hospital in 1953. He was a prolific self-taught artist from an early age, with interests encompassing Marvel comics, the band Pink Floyd, Gerry Anderson, Dinky toys, and everything *Doctor Who*. He was constantly drawing and honing his skills; everything from funny cartoons to serious self-expression and experimentation. He was wary of using colour at first, preferring to illustrate in black-and-white, but by using coloured pencils and inks he created his own comic strips and pieces of art. He dropped out of school and eventually settled into a job at the Borehamwood Fire Research Station, where he set up a drawing-board in his office and forged his own little empire. Bevan felt he struggled with likenesses, and so evolved a technique of photographing images off the television in order to get likenesses that were not from the usually-known images of actors. 'If I want to see a recognisable photograph, I'll go and buy one!' he is quoted as saying. If he needed to draw a spaceship he would build it as a model first, photograph it and then draw from the reference. Bevan also involved family and friends in his projects: he dressed them up as vampires, robots and characters from *Doctor Who*, then photographed them and committed them to paper in his own special style.

Although he contributed no covers to the New Adventures, he provided artwork for a series of *Doctor Who Magazine* 'Prelude' pieces (see page 56), the first of which was for *Nightshade*, plus internal illustrations for the Missing Adventure *The English Way of Death*.

Alongside an increasing demand for his *Doctor Who* artwork, Bevan continued to express himself by drawing from his own imagination; either single pieces or short-form comics. In his last years he was dogged by ill health and depression and he died in April 1998, aged only 44.

Below: a 1989 self-portrait by Phil Bevan, titled 'The Gray Man'.

THE WHO ADVENTURES

PRELUDES

Issue 175 of *Doctor Who Magazine*, dated 10 July 1991, previewed the New Adventures by way of an introductory piece supplied by author John Peel and an abridged opening to his novel *Timewyrm: Genesys*, with five black-and-white illustrations by artist Paul Vyse. In Issue 186 of the magazine, dated 13 May 1992, this was followed up by a Brief Encounters piece entitled 'Cathedral Heart', written by Paul Cornell and featuring the setting and characters from his *Timewyrm: Revelation*. Then, starting from Issue 190, dated 2 September 1992, the magazine began running a series of Preludes to the forthcoming novels. Each took the form of a prequel or tie-in short story contributed by the author, generally presented over a double-page spread with two or three black-and-white illustrations and an inset picture of the book's front cover.

There were, in all, 31 of these Preludes: the first was for Mark Gatiss's *Nightshade*; the last, in Issue 226, dated 7 June 1995, was for Cornell's *Human Nature*. Shown here, as examples, are the respective spreads for *Nightshade* and *Human Nature*. All of the Prelude illustrations are also reproduced across this and subsequent chapters.

Below: Phil Bevan's illustrations for the *Doctor Who Magazine* Prelude of *Nightshade*.

COVER STORY: *LOVE AND WAR*

Lee Sullivan was the artist chosen to create the cover for *Love and War*. He explains its development: 'In late 1991, I was asked by the New Adventures editor, Peter Darvill-Evans, to provide designs for the character of Bernice Summerfield – Benny for short – created by writer Paul Cornell. I suppose Virgin already knew that they would feature the character strongly in the rest of the novels series; and *Doctor Who Magazine* editor John Freeman wanted to achieve a tie-in between the New Adventures, the show and the magazine's comic strip. Benny was described to me by Paul as rather like actress Emma Thompson, who at that time was just coming to prominence in movies like *The Tall Guy* and *Dead Again*. I think the resemblance is fairly clear, though I believe I didn't actually reference Thompson, just used my memory of what she looked like and the impression she gave.

Below: the original compositional brief given to Lee Sullivan for his *Love and War* cover artwork, with Peter Darvill-Evans' handwritten notes in the margin.

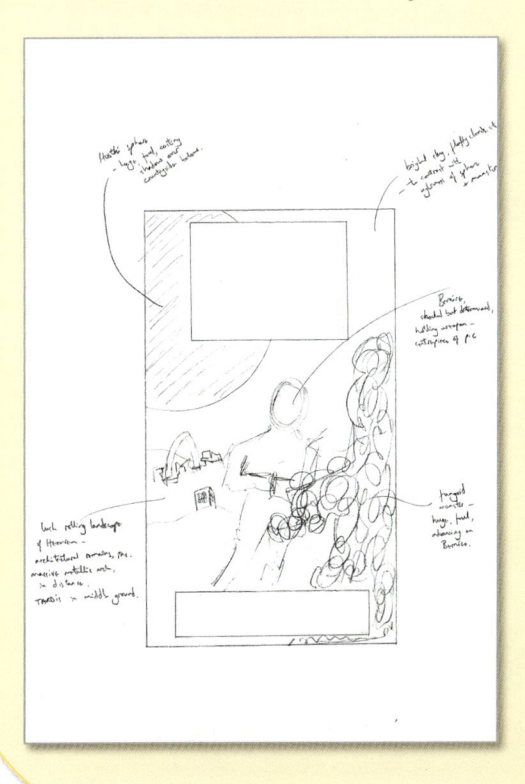

Above: one of Lee Sullivan's pencil sketches for the cover of *Love and War*, with a detail showing Bernice's expression.

'I produced some sketches [see page 78], and these would be used as the visual template both for Benny's comic-strip appearances and for her book cover appearances for the next few years. I read somewhere that this was the point at which it was decided to give me the commission to paint the cover for *Love and War*.

'Peter, Paul and I met at the Virgin offices, and there was a fair amount of discussion about getting the look of the cover right. There was a very loose rough presented to me to show what was required, along with a description that was very precise: that the monster, the planet, the arch, the pyramid, the TARDIS and Benny were pretty much to be shown as they eventually were. I knew that Benny wore jeans and a very bright jumper. All of the colours were to be as bright as possible, bar those for the sphere and the monster; I think this was to contrast with the more sombre look of the previous covers. There was certainly a colour rough produced.

'I was thrilled to be asked to do what was my first book cover, and everyone was terribly pleased with the art when it was delivered. It was the most technically accomplished piece of art I had ever created, and I hoped it would lead to other New Adventures covers, at least. Then the book was reviewed somewhere, and I still have (I think) a sharp memory of the opening line: "If you can get past the awful cover by comics artist Lee Sullivan, this is a fine book." I was never offered any further work for Virgin, and I think they probably decided they'd made a mistake with both the cover and, by extension, me. So my first book-jacket illustration became my last, for some time at least.'

Lee Sullivan's original artwork for the cover of *Love and War*.

FUTURE HISTORY

Above: Lee Sullivan's ink sketch for the cover of *Love and War*, developed from the pencil one reproduced on page 57. Sullivan submitted this to editor Peter Darvill-Evans for his approval before going on to produce his colour rough.

Below: Phil Bevan's *Doctor Who Magazine* Prelude illustrations for *Love and War*.

THE WHO ADVENTURES

Peter Elson's original artwork for the cover of *Transit*.

On publication, Ben Aaronovitch's *Transit* became notorious for its inclusion of strong expletives, and received some harsh criticism in the letters pages of *Doctor Who Magazine*. Nick Walters felt that the book was 'a cheapening and lessening of all that makes *Doctor Who* unique'; Ian Scales wrote, 'If the insertion of swear words, violence and sex is some attempt to make the stories more "adult" then I suggest the words "childish" and "puerile" spring to mind'; and 12-year-old Louise Ward asked, 'Do they need swearing in them to make the stories better? The stories on television were good without swearing, weren't they?' A reader named Graham Cox sent letters of complaint to Virgin, the BBC and the BBC's Director General, in a one-man campaign against the book.

In response to this deluge of criticism, Darvill-Evans took the unprecedented step of writing an open letter to readers in Issue 200 of *Doctor Who Magazine*. 'I don't believe *Transit* needs to be defended,' he said. 'Some – perhaps many – people may not like it, but I, and some other people who don't review books for *Doctor Who* fanzines, think it's terrific. Because Ben Aaronovitch was heart-stoppingly late delivering

GARETH ROBERTS

Gareth Roberts was born on 5 June 1968 and studied drama at King Alfred's College, Winchester and at Liverpool Polytechnic. He also worked as a clerk at the Court of Appeal.

During the 1990s, alongside his *Doctor Who* fiction, Roberts also penned for Virgin some novelisations of the police series *Cracker* and, under the pseudonym Christopher Summerisle, an erotic novel, *The Velvet Web*. In the 2000s, Roberts wrote for *Doctor Who Magazine* and co-wrote audio plays and short stories for Big Finish. His other *Doctor Who* novels, for BBC Books, include *Only Human* (2005), *I am a Dalek* (2006) and *Shada* (2012).

Christmas Day 2005 saw the broadcast of a special 'interactive' *Doctor Who* mini-episode written by Roberts, entitled 'Attack of the Graske'. Roberts also scripted a series of 'Tardisodes', short videos available online and via mobile phones, promoting the 2006 *Doctor Who* series.

Roberts has written four full episodes of *Doctor Who*: 'The Shakespeare Code' (2007), 'The Unicorn and the Wasp' (2008), 'The Lodger' (2010) and 'Closing Time' (2011). He co-wrote 'Planet of the Dead' (2009) with Russell T Davies and 'The Caretaker' (2014) with Steven Moffat.

Roberts also co-wrote with Russell T Davies 'Invasion of the Bane', the pilot episode of the *Doctor Who* spin-off *The Sarah Jane Adventures*. He then contributed two two-part stories to that show's 2007 series, and a further two two-part stories to its 2008 series.

Away from *Doctor Who*, Roberts worked with comedian Charlie Higson on the sitcom *Swiss Toni*, and in 2001 collaborated with him on scripts for the second series of the revived *Randall and Hopkirk (Deceased)*. In 2015 he reteamed with Higson for the superhero-style series *Jekyll & Hyde*. Amongst his many other credits, in 2005 Roberts contributed sketches to the Channel 5 sketch show *Swinging*, and in 2017 he scripted an episode for the fantasy series *The Librarians*.

THE WHO ADVENTURES

his manuscript, I didn't read the whole book in the right order until it was printed and bound. Once I'd started it, I couldn't put it down … However much some people may like it and others loathe it, it is no more typical of the New Adventures than *Time's Crucible* or *Nightshade* or *Love and War* or *Exodus* – each of which is the favourite of one group or another. And I'm very glad that there is no such thing as a typical New Adventure.'

As before, reviewers were, with one or two

Below: Phil Bevan's *Doctor Who Magazine* Prelude illustrations for *The Highest Science*, one of them featuring the turtle-like Chelonians, who would go on to appear in numerous other *Doctor Who* novels and audio dramas and be mentioned in the 2010 TV episode 'The Pandorica Opens'.

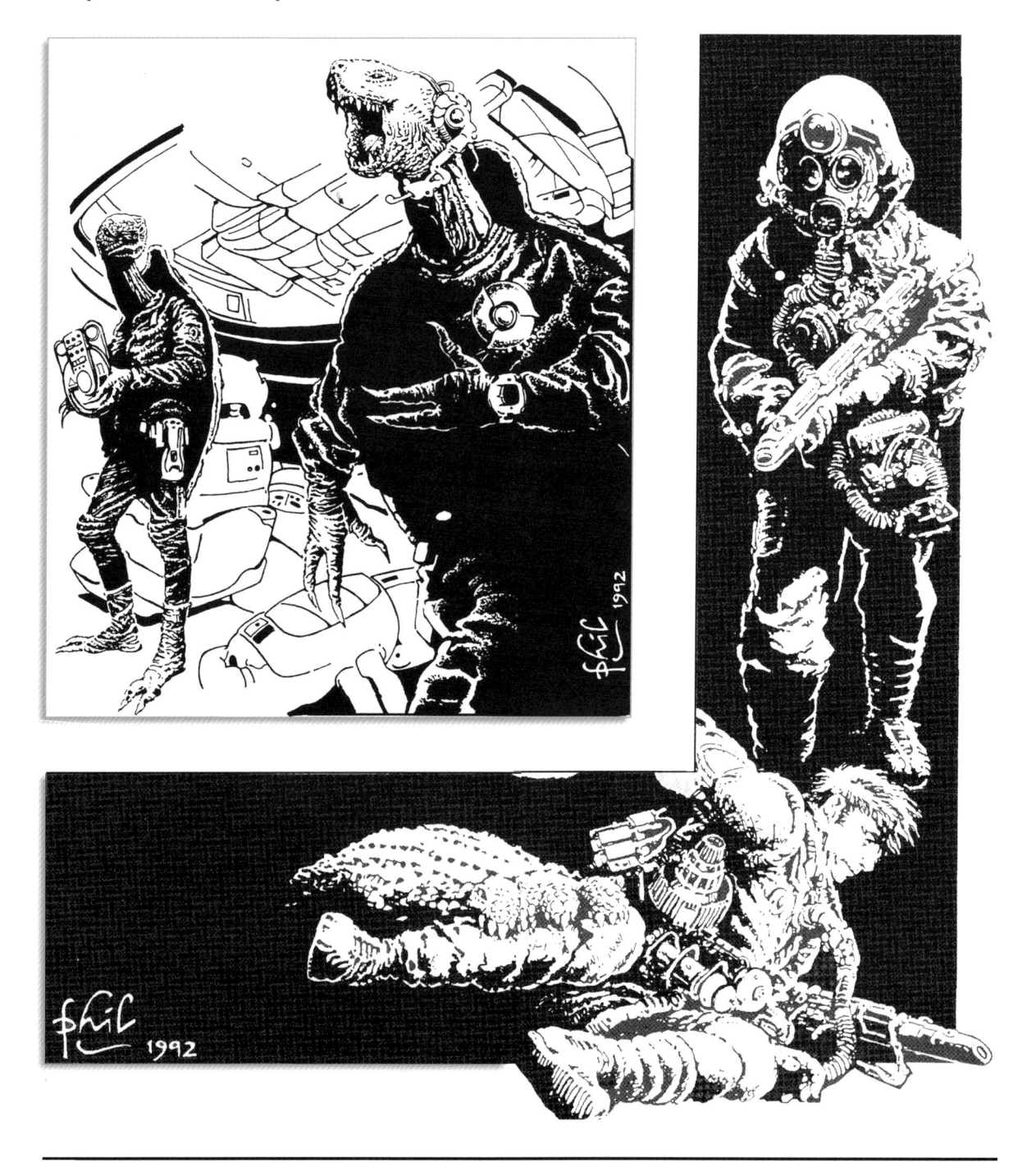

Peter Elson's original artwork for the cover of *The Highest Science*.

Peter Elson's original artwork for the cover of *The Pit*.

NEIL PENSWICK

In the 1980s Neil Penswick was a writer and director in the theatre in the North of England. He won a BBC film screenplay competition with a murder mystery set in the Sikh community. *Doctor Who* script editor Andrew Cartmel met him to discuss writing for *Doctor Who* and later for *Casualty*. Penswick later adapted his proposed three-part *Doctor Who* script, 'Hostage', into the New Adventures novel *The Pit*.

For over 30 years, Penswick has pursued a career nationally and internationally in social work, in particular aiming to improve services for vulnerable children and young people. He has a number of professional and academic qualifications in this field and also spent time studying and working in the Netherlands.

While he no longer writes as much as he once did, he remains a member of the Writer's Guild of Great Britain. He agrees with Ray Bradbury, who said: 'I am an emotional person and I must write regularly. To express my emotions.' He enjoys writing contemporary thrillers and dark fantasy, and this has recently included published short stories, a radio series about strange phenomena, a children's television series about an alien invasion and a horror movie script set in Edwardian London for a major UK company. He is currently writing a children's novel and adapting a script. In 2020 he returned to the *Doctor Who* world when he was commissioned to write a novel for the *Lethbridge-Stewart* tie-in range; this is due to be published in 2021.

exceptions, broadly positive about the titles in the 'Future History Cycle'. Gary Russell, reviewing regularly in *Doctor Who Magazine*, tended to speak for the majority: *Nightshade*: '… an incredible atmosphere that just reeks with that essential *Who*-ishness'; *Love and War*: '… probably the most mature and intelligent of the run so far. Miss it at your peril!'; *Transit*: '… the most puerile, non-*Doctor Who* book it has ever been my misfortune to read'; *The Highest Science*: '… nothing short of marvellous … full of drama, humour, intelligent and concise writing and a total understanding of what makes *Doctor Who* both unique and highly successful'; *The Pit*: '… a good example of an attempt to stretch the format as Andrew Cartmel's *Warhead* did … Nice words, shame about the tale they tell'; *Deceit*: '… coherent, entertaining, pleasantly easy to follow and, above all, it has a darned good story to tell with a beginning, a middle and an end'; and *Lucifer Rising*: 'Those exasperated by some New Adventures novels will be overjoyed to know that in this book the Doctor is the lead character – indeed the whole

Below: Peter Elson's rough for the cover of *The Pit*.

THE WHO ADVENTURES

Phil Bevan's *Doctor Who Magazine* Prelude illustrations for *The Pit* (left-hand column) and *Deceit* (above).

During the period when *Doctor Who Magazine* was running the Prelude feature, Ben Aaronovitch's piece for *Transit* was the only one to have no illustrations accompanying it. The feature was eventually dropped when Gary Gillatt took over from Gary Russell as the magazine's editor.

FUTURE HISTORY

book revolves around him as he moves in Holmesian manner around the base where a murder has occurred … an evocative science fiction novel.'

Other commentators singled out different aspects of the books. Craig Hinton, writing in *TV Zone*, liked *The Highest Science*: 'Gareth Roberts' version of the Doctor is perfect, a mix of humour and unspoken menace that seems to have eluded previous authors (perhaps with the exception of Paul Cornell), and his Bernice … well she was underused in *Love and War* and controlled by a sentient subway in *Transit* so this is our first real opportunity to get to know her – and it's a pleasure … it's what a New Adventures book should be like.' *The Pit* was disliked by Jan Vincent-Rudzki, also in *TV Zone*: 'This nearly lives up to its name. It doesn't quite reach "The Pits", it's only good enough for one. It is a hotchpotch of ideas, badly written and relatively unimaginative.' David Owen, reviewing for *DWB*, liked *Deceit*: 'I felt very reassured, after reading *Deceit*, that the New

Above: Luis Rey's original rough for the cover of *Deceit*.

LUIS REY

Luis Rey is a Spanish-Mexican artist residing in London. He trained at the San Carlos Academy (UNAM) in Mexico and obtained a Visual Arts MA. He has been a Symbolist and Surrealist painter, sculptor and amateur paleontologist for most of his life. A professional illustrator for more than 30 years, he devotes most of his time today to nature illustration and paleontological reconstructions.

Rey is fascinated by the study of dinosaurs and has worked on dinosaur-related books published by Usborne, Kingfisher, Wayland, Marvel Comics (*Dinosaurs: A Celebration*) and many others, while at the same time carrying out independent research and continuing with dinosaur restorations of his own. This has been appreciated by private collectors in the US, who regularly commission him to do paintings for their own exhibitions and collections.

Rey's work technique is mixed media using acrylics and inks with airbrush, colour pencils and markers over cardboard. He also does clay modelling and has recently moved into digital media.

THE WHO ADVENTURES

Luis Rey's original artwork for the cover of *Deceit*.

Adventures are in good hands and that Peter Darvill-Evans actually cares a great deal about this series of books. And for the first time since the New Adventures saw print, I am looking forward to the next book.' Craig Hinton, again in *TV Zone*, raved about *Lucifer Rising*: 'Probably the best New Adventure book I have read, and shows exactly what can be achieved with the format. It even has a gratuitous appearance by [the Doctor's old enemy] the Master!'

In retrospect, the most important book of this period was probably Paul Cornell's *Love and War*, notable for its introduction of new companion Bernice Summerfield – a development that will be discussed in greater detail in the next chapter.

The older, more mature version of Ace from the post-*Deceit* New Adventures, as depicted by artist Colin Andrew in Marvel's ongoing *Doctor Who Magazine* comic strip.

DWM TIE-INS

From Issue 192 in October 1992 to Issue 210 in February 1994, the *Doctor Who Magazine* comic strip was explicitly tied in with the New Adventures continuity. The first of these stories, 'Cat Litter', written by Marc Platt and drawn by John Ridgway, saw Ace discover a new TARDIS bedroom, destined to be occupied by Bernice Summerfield; Bernice then made her comic strip debut in the following issue, a month after her New Adventures debut in *Love and War*.

A final seventh Doctor, Ace and Bernice comic strip story, 'The Last Word', written by Gareth Roberts and drawn by Lee Sullivan, appeared in Issue 305 in June 2001, to mark the New Adventures' tenth anniversary.

JIM MORTIMORE

Jim Mortimore is the author of more than 20 novels and audios relating to a number of television and literary properties, including *Doctor Who*, *Babylon 5*, *Cracker*, *The Tomorrow People* and *Bernice Summerfield*. Original works include *Skaldenland* (a fantasy novel), *Keys* (*Doctor Who* as it might perhaps have been if created by John Carpenter), *Erimem: A Pharaoh of Mars* (one of the range of novels featuring Erimen, a companion character created for Big Finish's *Doctor Who* audios) and *The Sun in the Bone House* (a short story collection). His books have been published by Virgin, Big Finish, Macmillan, Bantam, Doubleday, Dell, Thebes and BBC Books. His short story 'The Sun in the Bone House' was suggested for a Nebula Award. His unofficial, self-published *Doctor Who* novel *Campaign*, described by him as a loopy literary wake-up call, is now in its second decade in continuous print. His first *Cracker* novel was translated into Japanese, French, Finnish, American and two different audiobooks – one for each ear, he points out, if you come from this planet.

Apropos of ears, Mortimore has also written music since he was very young, having abandoned piano lessons for a Casio VL Tone and two reel-to-reel tape recorders in a fevered (but not yet entirely cured) attempt to emulate Mike Oldfield. He's inspired by early radiophonica, such as may be found fulgariously conglobing 1960s *Doctor Who*. As well as writing Big Finish *Doctor Who* audio plays, he's also done sound editing and written music for them, and for live local performances. Delia Derbyshire, Karlheinz Stockhausen, Tangerine Dream and Jerry Goldsmith are amongst his muses.

His mountain of unofficial-o-bilia can be obtained from the deviantart and bandcamp websites, and by e-mailing him direct at: jimbo-original-who@hotmail.com.

BEHIND THE BOOK: *LUCIFER RISING*

Lucifer Rising had its origins in a *Doctor Who* fan audio play script, written by Jim Mortimore, in which the Cybermen were the villains. The script was abandoned in favour of a New Adventures novel also featuring the Cybermen; however, after much revision, Andy Lane and Mortimore finally decided to take out the Cybermen.

The novel's plot was inspired by the science fiction work of Arthur C Clarke; the title, *Lucifer Rising*, was taken from that of the last section of his novel *2010: Odyssey Two*.

The authors wrote the book on IBM-compatible systems and swapped disks through the post. Mortimore wrote all the odd-numbered chapters, Lane did the evens; they revised each other's work, then rewrote the revisions. Lane wanted to put in more humour, Mortimore wanted more 'gut-wrenching' emotion.

The book took about ten months to complete. Most of it was written in Bristol and London – the authors' respective home cities – but parts were done in America and the Falkland Islands.

Mortimore persuaded Virgin to let him paint the cover, and the authors also managed to get approval for internal illustrations to be used. These were drawn by Lee Brimmicombe-Wood, a friend of the authors.

The cover layout was altered slightly between the advance publicity version and the final printing, including a reduction to the size of the title box and changes to some of the back cover text.

(From *TSV* Issue 35 – courtesy Paul Scoones.)

Below: the original proof front cover of *Lucifer Rising* (left) and the slightly revised as-published version (right).

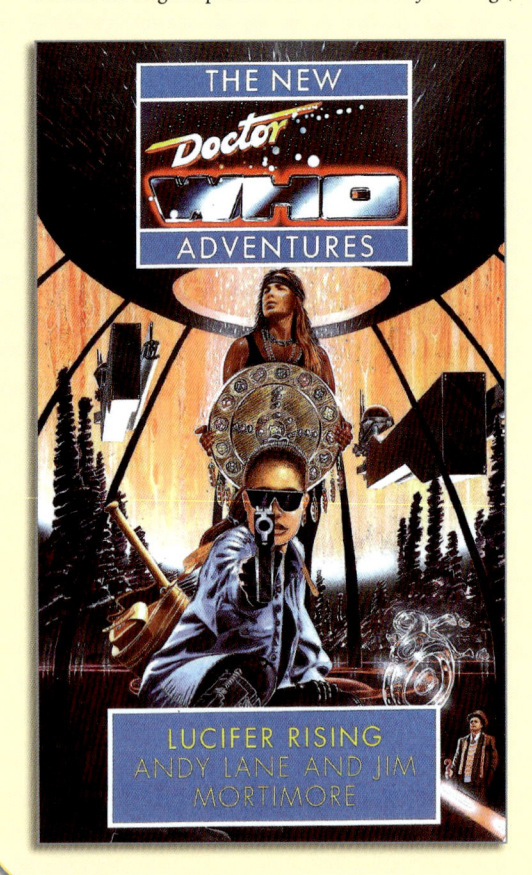

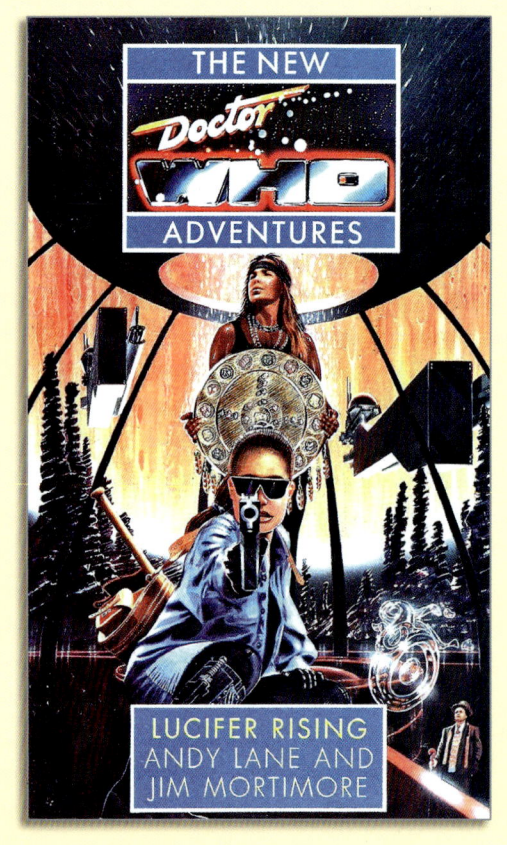

Above: the first two of Lee Brimmicombe-Wood's eight internal illustrations for *Lucifer Rising*.

LUCIFER RISING CONTINUITY REFERENCES

Lucifer Rising is a *Doctor Who* reference-spotter's delight. The following guide to some of the TV story continuity references within its pages is by no means a definitive one:

The Adjudicators and IMC are from 'Colony in Space'. The titles Krau (Ms) and Trau (Mr) originate in 'The Caves of Androzani'. The Knights of the Grand Order of Oberon (pg.51) were mentioned in 'Revelation of the Daleks'. The Ice Warrior invasion of 2090 (pg.171) is a reference to the events of 'The Seeds of Death', while the Dalek invasion of 2158 (pg.337) is 'The Dalek Invasion of Earth'.

Other, more obscure reference origins are as follows: Rutan (pg.33): 'Horror of Fang Rock'; Hydrax (pg.59) and the vampire swarms (pg.332): 'State of Decay'; Drashig (pg.65): 'Carnival of Monsters'; Zyton 7 (pg.71): 'Vengeance on Varos'; Hymetusite (pg.71): 'The Horns of Nimon'; Parranium (pg.71): 'Death to the Daleks'; Panorama Chemicals (pg.84): the Target novelisation of 'The Green Death'; Venusian lullaby (pg.95 and pg.165): 'The Daemons' and 'The Curse of Peladon'; Arcturans and Alpha Centaurians (pg.320): 'The Curse of Peladon'; Delphons (pg.101): 'Spearhead from Space'; Rills (pg.102): 'Galaxy 4'; Trisilicate (pg.117): 'The Monster of Peladon'; Azure (pg.132) and Vraxoin raids (pg.189): 'Nightmare of Eden'; Kroagnon (pg.189): 'Paradise Towers'; Macra (pg.189): 'The Macra Terror'; Ange (pg.262): 'Survival'; Draconians (pg.334): 'Frontier in Space'.

(From *TSV* Issue 35 – courtesy Paul Scoones)

THE WHO ADVENTURES

LEE BRIMMICOMBE-WOOD

Lee Brimmicombe-Wood is a London-born illustrator and games designer, and author of the *Aliens: Colonial Marines Technical Manual*. He works in both boardgames and computer software games. His boardgame titles include *Downtown*, *The Burning Blue* and *Wing Leader*. Softography includes *Far Cry 3*, *Killzone: Mercenary* and the *Dark Pictures* series. Currently he resides in Cambridgeshire with his family.

Below: the other six internal illustrations by Lee Brimmicombe-Wood for *Lucifer Rising*.

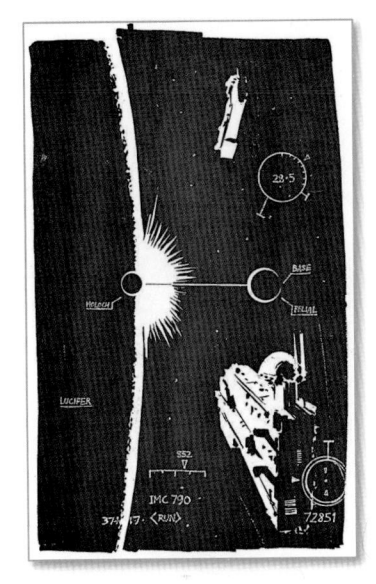

This page: Lee Brimmicombe-Wood's original roughs for seven of his eight internal illustrations for *Lucifer Rising*. These are in most cases very close in composition to the finished pieces, as reproduced over the previous two pages. The most significant differences come in the fourth and seventh, and particularly in the way Benny is depicted in the fifth – her clothes and hairstyle were both changed for the final version, to reflect the character's established image.

No rough is available for the eighth illustration, which was presented right at the back of the published book. This piece was unusual in that it included, albeit only in cloud form, a representation of a Dalek. The Daleks – *Doctor Who*'s most famous monster race – featured in neither the New Adventures nor the Missing Adventures, save for a handful of oblique and passing mentions. This was because the rights to the creatures were controlled by Roger Hancock Ltd, the agents of their creator Terry Nation, and were not covered by Virgin Publishing's licence agreement with BBC Worldwide. (This is also why some of the 1960s Dalek stories were amongst the last to be novelised in the Target range; permission was eventually obtained only because author John Peel was a friend of Nation's.)

THE WHO ADVENTURES

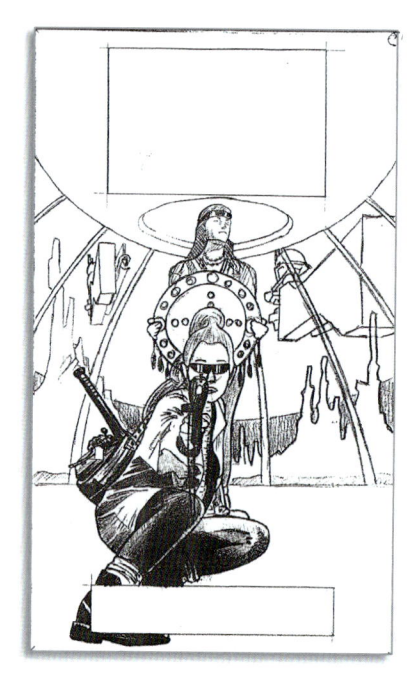

Above: three roughs produced by Jim Mortimore for his cover for *Lucifer Rising*. Below: Phil Bevan's two *Doctor Who Magazine* Prelude illustrations for this novel.

ANDY LANE

Since the publication of his three New Adventures, Andy Lane has written or co-written 26 other novels (including three ghosted crime novels) and nine non-fiction books. He has also strayed back into *Doctor Who*-space with ten audio dramas for Big Finish and one for the BBC. Outside *Doctor Who* circles, he is best known for the eight books in his young adult *Young Sherlock Holmes* series. His most recent books – the *Secret Protector* trilogy – were published only in Germany, while his *Crusoe* trilogy was published only in the USA.

Jim Mortimore's original artwork for the cover of *Lucifer Rising*.

THE WHO ADVENTURES

Lee Sullivan's original colour rough for the cover of *Love and War*, introducing new companion character Bernice, aka Benny.

6: A NEW COMPANION

'It all came down to Bernice in the end,' explains Darvill-Evans. 'We used to refer to her character as "Indiana Jones in Space". This was before the *Tomb Raider* games and Lara Croft, and the idea was for her to be an academic, someone who's getting on for the Doctor's intellectual equal, an adult character, somewhat spiky, but who could also supply a certain amount of sex appeal as well as being able to handle a heavy weapon. That kind of character was always in the back of my mind. Paul Cornell came up with the rounded character, however, and we had lots of meetings and telephone conversations where we discussed what she should be like. In the end, it all came down to Paul's writing ability to realise a fully-rounded human character in print – not an easy thing to do, but something Paul excelled at.'

Love and War was initially titled *Heaven*, however Cornell's 19-page plot outline had the published title up-front, with *Nightmare of the Hoothi* and *The Storming of Heaven* as suggested alternatives. Cornell also supplied a character outline for the new companion – see page 79 – and, in addition, a character breakdown along the lines of those presented in Ian Marsh's and Peter Darvill-Evans' 1991 *Doctor Who* role-playing book *Time Lord* – shown here to the right.

Cornell later explained in the book *Doctor Who: Companions* that he 'wanted to create a companion who was more mature than usual, and also one who was, as much as possible, a bit more like a real woman. I mean that, rather than being Rambo with ovaries, this is someone who thinks that the whole macho thing is a bit silly and that the most powerful group of people in the world are four women with a jug of sangria between them.' When asked about any other influences on the character, Cornell would joke: 'She's me in a frock!'

While the 'Future History' titles were in preparation, Darvill-Evans was already turning his mind to what would come next. His plans were thrown into turmoil, however,

---

CHARACTER BREAKDOWN

Character: Bernice Surprise Summerfield
Apparent Age: Early thirties
Species: Human, colonist

Equipment: Revolver (wounds 5, range 4)
　　　　　　Various minor practical items
　　　　　　Archaeology kit

Strength: 3
Cheat Death: 1

Size: 4

Weight: 3

Control: 4
Bench-Thumping: 1
Brawling: 1
Dancing: 2
Edged Weapons: 2
Marksmanship: 2

Move: 3
Driving: 1
Riding: 1
Running: 1

Knowledge: 5
Computing: 1
Detective Powers: 1
First Aid: 1
History: 2
Linguistics: 2
Science: 1

Determination: 5
Command: 1
Independent Spirit: 1
Strong Passion (Missing Father): 1

Awareness: 4
Bargaining: 1
Bureaucracy: 2
Intuition: 1
Precision: 2
Striking Appearance: 2

Lee Sullivan's original character sketches for Bernice, used as a template for her visual depiction both in the New Adventures novels and in the ongoing *Doctor Who Magazine* comic strip, into which she was introduced to create a tie-in between the two. Originally in black-and-white, the sketches were later coloured by Sullivan for use in the book *Doctor Who: Companions*.

when, with sales looking increasingly healthy, Virgin decided that the books could be published monthly, rather than every other month as had been the case so far. He explained the implications of this change in a May 1992 note to all past and potential contributors to the range: 'From February 1993 we will double the publication rate: from one every two months to a month. This is undeniably good news, but it does have one drawback: I had thought that the next book I had to commission would be for publication in October 1993, but now I need to find more books and much more quickly. There isn't much time to organise the books for the summer of 1993.'

His workload having already grown due to his decision to contribute his own novel, *Deceit*, Darvill-Evans admitted that after the loose 'Future History Cycle' he would no longer be able to invest editorial time into developing detailed overarching plots: 'Increasingly each New Adventure stands alone,' he told the authors. 'I had thought that the next few novels would be strung together with a theme: the idea that some external agency was pulling the TARDIS to locations where the Doctor could meet and collect a band of recent companions (Ace is already on board, and he could pick up Kadiatu in one story, the couple from Warhead in the next) because – as is revealed in yet another story – all their separate and joint skills are needed to avert a terrible catastrophe. Something like that. However, I don't think there's going to be time. I need to commission the first few books very soon, and I'll have to pick those that can be delivered earliest rather than the ones that best fit a complicated theme. On the other hand, I will definitely continue to create continuity from story to story, and I will be on the lookout for stories that suggest a larger thematic possibility.'

Darvill-Evans also confirmed that Ace was being temporarily 'rested', that Bernice was being introduced, and that Kadiatu Lethbridge-Stewart was another potential new companion. He went on to encourage prospective authors to think big and think wide; to move away from Earth history and not to use 'changing the timeline' type plots, sub- or mini-universes or stories that moved tens of thousands of years back or forward in Earth's timeline. Finally, he recommended buying a basic book on cosmology, as the universe is really, really big!

After the loosely-themed 'Future History

Below: a flier produced by Virgin in 1993 for distribution to bookshops, promoting the New Adventures range along with John Peel's novelisation of the 1966 TV story 'The Power of the Daleks' – one of the last of the Target range.

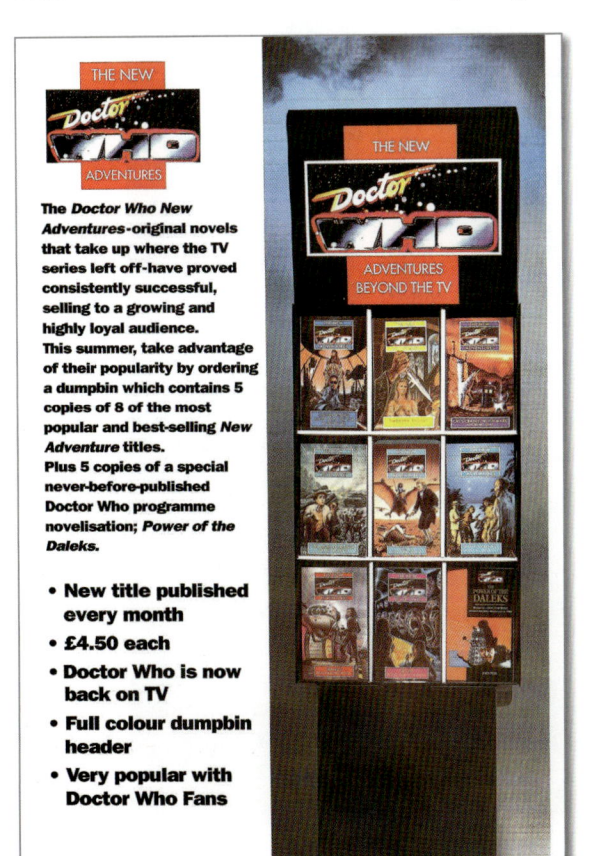

CHARACTER OUTLINE

The following is the original character outline for Bernice Summerfield, as submitted by author Paul Cornell to editor Peter Darvill-Evans. Note that the character's surname was spelt differently at this stage:

'Benny' Sommerfield is a Professor of Archaeology, from the future Earth of the Federation. She's 30, and frustrated with the establishment. A kind of female 'Indiana Jones' in attitude, she likes a challenge or a mystery. She's very intelligent, with a vast practicality, and she sometimes gets annoyed by those a bit slower. This manifests itself in a biting, sarcastic wit. This is never directed at the Doctor, who she sees as a fellow scholar, and rather like her father. Her wit is her way of defying the enemy.

Benny's parents died when she was young, leaving her an orphan. She had a seriously disastrous love affair at college, and since then has put her career before any romance.

She is skilled in self-defence and the use of weapons, and a good leader, having headed a team of excavators for the past two years. Benny isn't as kind as the Doctor, and on occasion can appear somewhat bitter, especially to those she sees as stupid. She's always just one step behind the timelord [sic], and occasionally overtakes him. They play chess regularly, discussing moves during adventures. Benny's curiosity is the equal of the Doctor's own, and she'd only admit to one weakness, an urge to stop and help the helpless or those alone. Thus, she often takes care of individual suffering when the Doctor is concerned with the big picture.

A visual reference to Benny would be the actress Emma Thompson, who plays a similar character in the movie *The Tall Guy*.

The idea behind Benny is to give the Doctor a 'Mrs Peel' figure, somebody who complements him, but isn't dominated by him. She has all of Ace's inquisitiveness, and a large dose of cheekiness that so offsets the seventh Doctor's cosmic concerns. However, the only 'teaching' element is that of an intelligent human being learning from a vastly-wise old timelord [sic]. As with the latest Sherlock Holmes, the Doctor's brilliance will shine greater as a result.

Peter Elson's original artwork for the cover of *White Darkness*.

A NEW COMPANION

Cycle', during the publication of which the books moved to their new monthly schedule, came four unconnected titles: David A McIntee's *White Darkness*, Christopher Bulis's *Shadowmind*, Nigel Robinson's *Birthright* and David Banks' *Iceberg*, the latter featuring the Doctor's old adversaries the Cybermen. Peter Elson painted the covers for *White Darkness* and *Birthright*, Christopher Bulis supplied that for his own book, and Andrew Skilleter, who had previously collaborated with Banks on the large-format book *Cybermen*, was commissioned for *Iceberg*.

White Darkness was David A McIntee's first novel. Prior to it being accepted, he had sent in outlines entitled *Moebius Trip*, *Symbiote* and *Haitian Story*. Reviewers enjoyed his blend of *Doctor Who* and the works of popular American horror author H P Lovecraft: 'Mixing an effectively atmospheric background drawn from historical events with a Lovecraftian storyline, it proves to be my kind of book,' wrote Anthony Brown in *DWB*. 'It rather restored my faith in the New Adventures. There's nothing wrong with the hard-SF books we've been getting almost consistently since late last year – provided they form part of a balanced diet. But there's more to *Doctor Who* than

> **BEHIND THE BOOK: *WHITE DARKNESS***
>
> Author David A McIntee's first submission to Virgin was a story called *Moebius Trip*; editor Peter Darvill-Evans liked this and made it an emergency back-up, to be used in the event of any of the other planned novels falling through at the last minute – although, as things turned out, this didn't happen.
>
> The initial inspiration for *White Darkness* came from McIntee watching the Wes Craven zombie horror movie *The Serpent and the Rainbow*, which he describes as 'notoriously atrocious'. Many long hours were spent researching the historical and geographical background detail for the story – all carried out at the Stirling Library in Scotland, which McIntee acknowledges in the book.
>
> *White Darkness* was first planned as a purely historical story, but Peter Darvill-Evans encouraged the introduction of fantasy horror elements.
>
> (From *TSV* Issue 35 – courtesy Paul Scoones.)

Peter Elson's initial roughs for the cover of *White Darkness*.

81

THE WHO ADVENTURES

Above: sketches submitted to Peter Darvill-Evans by author David A McIntee, showing the costume he envisaged Ace wearing in his novel *White Darkness*. Below: Phil Bevan's two *Doctor Who Magazine* Prelude illustrations for *White Darkness*; this Prelude was unusual in that it featured appearances by the third Doctor and his friend and associate Brigadier Lethbridge-Stewart.

just science fiction …' In *Doctor Who Magazine*, Craig Hinton agreed: '*White Darkness* is an enjoyable adventure story – a good pseudo-historical interlude amongst all the space operas of late – with strong similarities to [the 1976 television story] "The Masque of Mandragora" (stellar alignments, human hosts) and links with Lovecraft's Cthuhlu mythos (Great Ones, cyclopean chambers, impossible angles).'

Christopher Bulis's *Shadowmind* was also a first novel, but reviewers were less enthusiastic about this one: 'I'm not sure it's a *Doctor Who* novel … it's all a little too *Star Trek*-y for my taste,' opined P Mantora in *TV Zone*, while Peter Linford in *DWB* commented: 'I suppose it's not bad, exactly, but it's deeply derivative and unoriginal, and doesn't manage to freshen things up with a new style.'

Birthright, which Nigel Robinson had first pitched in November 1991, introduced a mysterious character called Muldwych, whose origins and motivations were hotly debated by fans. 'Who is Muldwych?' asked Craig Hinton in *Doctor Who Magazine*. In his original outline for the book, Robinson gave Darvill-Evans a footnote on the subject: 'The whole idea of Muldwych is that the Time Lords (and indeed the Doctor), self-appointed guardians of the universe, spend half their time correcting their own mistakes. I intend to leave this thing very, very open, but there will be a suggestion (and only a suggestion!) that Muldwych is, in fact, a future incarnation of the Doctor – a Doctor gone wrong, not in the tradition of the Valeyard, but more in that of the Meddling Monk …'

Birthright received one of the warmest receptions from reviewers, with David Richardson in *TV Zone* commenting: '[It is] magnificent *Doctor Who* … a mixture of [acclaimed TV stories] "The Talons of Weng-Chiang" and "The Ark in Space"; but that implies plagiarism, and it's too ingenious for that. An essential purchase.' Amanda Murray in *DWB* enthused: '[This is] one of the best books there's been for ages, with one of the best covers too.'

Robinson's original outline for *Birthright* had

DAVID A McINTEE

David A McIntee wrote three New Adventures and three Missing Adventures, plus six BBC *Doctor Who* novels. He has written various other tie-in novels for franchises such as *Star Trek* and *Final Destination*, as well as audio dramas for Big Finish and others, and comics including an authorised sequel to the classic Ray Harryhausen movie *Jason and the Argonauts* and an adaptation of William Shatner's *Quest For Tomorrow*. He has also written media non-fiction on various subjects, including *Star Wars*, *Star Trek*, and *Sapphire and Steel*, and for Telos Publishing he penned *Beautiful Monsters*, covering the *Alien* and *Predator* franchises.

In recent years has been writing and editing mostly non-fiction in the fields of mythology and military history for the likes of Osprey Publishing, but still dabbles in fiction too.

Away from writing, he's a martial artist, an historical fencing practitioner and instructor, and a con-runner. He is married with four cats.

QUOTE, UNQUOTE

The Doctor: 'Everything is history if you look at it from the right perspective.'

Lucifer Rising

featured the Doctor and Benny, but in the final novel, it was decided to have the Doctor absent – his part in the action was taken by Benny, while Benny's activities in the original outline were now performed by Ace. This allowed the story to mesh with David Banks' *Iceberg*, which had been developed as a companionless book and, in the event, explained what the Doctor was up to while Benny and Ace were involved in the events of *Birthright*. Banks had played the Cyber Leader in several 1980s *Doctor Who* stories on TV, and had also explored the Cybermen's history in the aforementioned large-format book *Cybermen*, published by Who Dares, as well as in a series of independently-released Cyber-History audio-books (which were also offered to Virgin to publish in book form, but rejected as being too specialised). Banks' initial outline for *Iceberg*, then entitled *Flipback*, had started life as a proposal for the TV show itself, back in 1986. It had then been reworked into a potential Make-Your-Own-Adventure book in the *Doctor Who* range

COVER STORY – *SHADOWMIND*

The cover for *Shadowmind* was painted by the author, Christopher Bulis. He explains the process: 'I produced four different colour roughs for the cover, each with variant ideas as to what it could include [see opposite]. The fourth was chosen, and there was an editorial request to modify the design to show Bernice without her helmet on, more brightly lit and turned more to the viewer, which I think lost some of the drama of the composition. In the end the final cover was adequate, but I know I could have done better.'

Below: Christopher Bulis's detailed black-and-white rough for the final selected cover design for *Shadowmind*.

A NEW COMPANION

Christopher Bulis's colour roughs suggesting four possible compositions for his *Shadowmind* cover artwork.

CHRISTOPHER BULIS

Shadowmind was Christopher Bulis's first published work. This was the only seventh Doctor novel he wrote; his next five books all featured earlier Doctors and appeared in the Missing Adventures range: *State of Change* (1994), *The Sorcerer's Apprentice* (1995), *The Eye of the Giant* (1996), *Twilight of the Gods* (1996), and *A Device of Death* (1997).

When Virgin lost their licence to publish *Doctor Who* fiction, Bulis repeated this pattern with BBC Books, writing one novel for the current incumbent Doctor as part of the Eighth Doctor Adventures range, and then several others as part of the Past Doctor Adventures range. His BBC Books novels were: *The Ultimate Treasure* (1997), *Vanderdeken's Children* (1998), *City at World's End* (1999), *Imperial Moon* (2000) and *Palace of the Red Sun* (2002).

Bulis also wrote the Bernice Summerfield novel *Tempest* in Virgin's post-*Doctor Who* continuation of the New Adventures range, and the short story 'Hot Ice' for Big Finish's *Short Trips* series. While doing other creative things, including 2D and 3D art and design work, he is also writing a major fantasy story for young teens and up, various versions of which he has been tinkering with for years, and which he now hopes finally to get finished!

---

published by Severn House, but this had been curtailed when the initial titles did not sell well enough. In keeping with the Make-Your-Own-Adventure style, Banks wanted to write the novel entirely in the first person from the point of view of Ruby, a character who would have been 'played' by the reader in the activity book. Unfortunately, Darvill-Evans did not share Banks' enthusiasm for this type of narrative. 'If the whole book is narrated by one character, you are restricted to the narrowest field of vision,' he told Banks in a note dated 17 October 1991. 'Adventure stories and thrillers are usually written in the third person, often from a god-like position with only occasional glimpses into the thoughts of various characters, for the very good reason that this style allows the author to use the full range of techniques for building dramatic tension.' Ultimately Banks was

Right: a *Shadowmind* illustration produced by author Christopher Bulis for publication on the cover of the *Doctor Who* Appreciation Society fanzine *Celestial Toyroom*.

Christopher Bulis's original artwork for the cover of his novel *Shadowmind*.

THE WHO ADVENTURES

convinced, and the completed novel was written mainly from a third person perspective, with only a few sections 'narrated' by Ruby remaining from the original concept.

Despite its rather rocky road to publication, *Iceberg* was generally liked. 'A decent novel, but I suspect that the targeted audience of *Who* fans may lose patience in the first half,' remarked David Richardson in *TV Zone*. 'The Doctor does not materialise until page 147, and the Cybermen remain pretty low profile for much of the time as well.' Anthony Brown in *DWB*, meanwhile, felt it was 'an enjoyable read which captures something of the style of the '60s monster nightmares … a little better than average.' Sounding a more sour note, Craig Hinton, writing in *Doctor Who Magazine*, considered the book 'a grave disappointment, lacking the ideas and excitement that characterise a good

Left: *Doctor Who Magazine*'s Prelude illustrations for *Shadowmind*. Uniquely, these were supplied not by Phil Bevan but by the novel's author, Christopher Bulis, and there were three of them rather than the standard two.

BEHIND THE BOOK: *SHADOWMIND*

Christopher Bulis wrote the first third of *Shadowmind* in 1991, and in the same year submitted a proposal for the novel to Virgin's Peter Darvill-Evans. Darvill-Evans liked it, but wasn't able to commission the book until July 1992, at which time Bulis was asked to complete the manuscript by the end of November. In four months, he had not only to write the remaining two-thirds of the book, but also to revise the first third to include Bernice, change Ace's character and move the adventure's setting from the 28th Century to the 27th. Bulis cites *Star Trek* as a major influence in his work, particularly in the creation of other worlds. He set himself the task of finding convincing scientific principles for futuristic technology, especially as regards spacecraft. One of his first ideas was to create a future in which the people and places encountered by the TARDIS crew were nice for a change.

Bulis describes himself as an artist first and a writer second. He received the commission to paint the cover and submitted four colour roughs with suggested compositions – see page 85.

(From *TSV* Issue 36 – courtesy Paul Scoones).

Andrew Skilleter's original artwork for the cover of *Iceberg*.

Phil Bevan's *Doctor Who Magazine* Prelude illustrations for *Iceberg*, depicting characters from the 1968 TV story 'The Invasion'.

DAVID BANKS

David Banks studied drama at Manchester University and at Bristol Old Vic Theatre School. Stage roles have included Dracula; Sherlock Holmes; Andrew Aguecheek; Falstaff; Mowgli; Aslan the Lion; Gandalf the Wizard; and Karl – and briefly, when star Jon Pertwee fell ill, the Doctor himself – in *Doctor Who: The Ultimate Adventure*.

As Cyber Leader in *Doctor Who* on TV throughout the 1980s he was destroyed by a succession of Doctors. As singing teacher Ray in Melvyn Bragg's *A Time to Dance* (BBC TV), he was described by critic Simon Hoggart as 'the ugliest man on television'. He was 'axe murderer' Dennis Smalley in *Going Under* (BBC TV); 'suspected murderer' Graeme Curtis in *Brookside* (Channel 4); and, as Max Armstrong in L!ve TV's ambitious soap *Canary Wharf*, he was annihilated by aliens.

Plays he has written and directed include *Severance*, an intimate story of Heloise and Abelard, and *Five Marys Waiting*, a tragicomedy of grief and belief. He has also directed Jimmie Chinn's *Talking to John*, Simon de Deney's *Between the Lines* and, most recently, T S Eliot's *Four Quartets*. He won Best Play award for his production of Alan McMurtrie's *The Prisoner's Pumpkin* at the Old Red Lion in 1992. His voice work embraces radio, commercials, video narration and many audiobooks (the latter including J RR Tolkien's *The Lord of the Rings*). Recently re-inhabiting the CyberLeader in the Big Finish audio plays *Hour of the Cybermen* and *Warzone/Conversion* he was again

Photo: Maureen Purkis, 1991

destroyed by the Doctor. Twice.

His published books include *Iceberg* (Virgin); *Cybermen* (Who Dares); and *Not Somehow* (Virtual Angels), the story of Mina Banks and her lifelong career in nursing.

His latest play is *A New Way to Play an Old Game* – though Banks claims it was written in 1674 by the spy Aphra Behn, the first Englishwoman to earn a living as a playwright.

THE WHO ADVENTURES

BEHIND THE BOOK: *BIRTHRIGHT*

The initial outline that author Nigel Robinson submitted to editor Peter Darvill-Evans followed basically the same plot as the finished novel, but had the Doctor trapped with Ace in the London of 1909. Robinson was at first shocked at Darvill-Evans' request to remove the Doctor (so that the story could be presented as being concurrent with the following, companionless one, *Iceberg*), but then saw what a good idea and a challenge it could be.

The Doctor does however have quite an influence over the book's events. Robinson sees him 'as an alien being of slightly dubious morals who isn't to be trusted,' and considers that if the Doctor is capable of plotting events in advance, then there is no need for him to be around when his plans come to fruition.

Several mentions of past companions of the Doctor, such as Victoria and Barbara, crop up in the narrative. Robinson thinks that such continuity references should not be ignored as long as they are important to the plot; when self-referencing becomes irrelevant or intrusive, however, he considers this a mistake – one he feels he made with his previous New Adventures novel, *Timewyrm: Apocalypse.*

The background of 1909 London – where most of the story is set – comes mostly from Robinson's knowledge of the society and politics of the time. He also received a wealth of useful information from Coutts Bank in the Strand. The Soho pub that Bernice frequents really existed, and in fact still operates today, but under a different name – Robinson drinks there himself on occasion!

(From *TSV* Issue 36 – courtesy Paul Scoones.)

New Adventures novel.'

By September 1993, 18 New Adventures had been published. Not only had one of the titles, *Revelation*, been nominated by the publishers for a prestigious literary award, but material from two of the others, *Lucifer Rising* and *White Darkness*, had been selected by the British National Corpus for inclusion in their major research resource. The books had been generally well-received by readers and reviewers alike, sales were healthy, and the range was going from strength to strength.

Below: Phil Bevan's two *Doctor Who Magazine* Prelude illustrations for *Birthright*, the second of them depicting the Doctor with Victoria Waterfield, companion to his second incarnation on TV in the 1960s.

A NEW COMPANION

Peter Elson's original artwork for the cover of *Birthright*.

A NEW COMPANION

Above: Andrew Skilleter's rough for his cover artwork for *Iceberg*, with detailed handwritten notes around the edges for editor Peter Darvill-Evans. The box-like structure on the right-hand side is the Jade Pagoda, an 'escape pod' offshoot of the Doctor's TARDIS, featured for the first time in *Iceberg* and then again in the later New Adventure *Sanctuary*.

Left: Skilleter's preparatory sketch of the novel's main character, Ruby Duvall.

BEHIND THE BOOK: *ICEBERG*

Iceberg began life in 1986 as a TV script submission to *Doctor Who* script editor Eric Saward. This was at first called 'Flipback' and later 'The Tallness of Terror'. Saward liked the plot, but when he left the show's production team soon after, the proposal went no further. Banks promptly sold the idea to Severn House, publishers of the *Doctor Who* Make-Your-Own-Adventure books, but they then decided not to continue with the range.

Banks next submitted his story to Virgin Publishing, before the New Adventures series was even under way. The long delay before the book finally reached publication was due in part to the lengthy discussions that took place before Banks was able to persuade editor Peter Darvill-Evans to let him write the book as a companionless one, without either Ace or Bernice. To accommodate Banks' wishes in this regard, Darvill-Evans asked Nigel Robinson to turn his *Birthright* into a Doctor-less book, to serve as a concurrent adventure.

Iceberg followed a Cyberman chronology that David Banks had first developed for his *Cybermen* reference book; this was derived primarily from the events of the TV stories 'The Tenth Planet' and 'The Invasion'.

Iceberg's central character, Ruby Duvall, was named after Banks' own young daughter Ruby, born around the same time he first developed the TV script proposal that eventually became the novel.

(From *TSV* Issue 37 – courtesy Paul Scoones)

THE WHO ADVENTURES

Jeff Cummins' original artwork for the cover of *Blood Heat*.

7: ARRIVALS AND DEPARTURES

His original assistant Riona MacNamara having left Virgin in mid-1992 – her final copy-editing contribution being on *Transit* – Darvill-Evans recruited toward the end of that year two new assistants: editorial secretary Kerri Sharp and, a month or so later, editorial assistant Rebecca Levene, known to friends as Bex. This was essential, as Virgin's fiction department was starting to expand rapidly. Alongside the New Adventures, now on a monthly publication schedule, they were preparing to launch the Black Lace erotica range, written by women for women, to complement their popular Nexus titles, and also in the initial planning stages were the past-Doctor novels that would eventually appear as the Missing Adventures. Sharp was quickly promoted to editor of the Black Lace titles, while Levene worked on the *Doctor Who* ones.

'I was working in the House of Commons as a personal assistant and researcher for Dr David Clark, who at the time was the shadow agriculture minister,' explains Levene. 'I worked for him up to the 1992 election, which Labour spectacularly lost. David Clark then wrote a history of his local Labour party, which I edited for him – which is how I got some editing experience – while hunting around trying to find another job. It took me ages, and I'd been to several failed interviews, before I saw the advert in the *Guardian* for the job at Virgin, which looked ideal – copy editor for *Doctor Who* and erotica. It was the *Doctor Who* that attracted me. I loved *Doctor Who* as a kid.

REBECCA LEVENE

Rebecca Levene was educated at Clare College, Cambridge. After graduating, she worked for a Labour MP. She then applied for a job at Virgin and began as an assistant to Peter Darvill-Evans, working on the New Adventures. She later took over as editor of all Virgin's *Doctor Who* lines and worked on other projects at the company, including their *Judge Dredd* series and their gay erotica line Idol.

For television, she worked as a storyliner for *Emmerdale* in 1998 and as story editor in 1999, and in 2002/3 as a writer on Sky One's *Is Harry on the Boat?*. In 2005 she wrote an episode of *Swinging* for Channel 5 and in 2006 was associate producer of the first series of *Wild at Heart* for ITV. In 2009 she co-wrote, with Paul Mackman, a video game called *Rogue Warrior* for Rebellion and also penned a spin off novel from the game.

Her first novel, the post-*Doctor Who* New Adventure *Where Angels Fear*, was co-written with Simon Winstone. She has written for publisher Black Flame, including a *Strontium Dog* novel, *Bad Timing*, and a *Final Destination* novel, *End of the Line*. She has also written for Big Finish, including *Doctor Who* short stories and a *Tomorrow People* audio drama.

Other books include a series called *The Infernal Game* (two titles: *Cold Warriors* and *Ghost Dance*), and a series called *Hollow Gods* (three titles: *Smiler's Fair*, *The Hunter's Kind* and *The Sun's Devices*).

KERRI SHARP

Kerri Sharp is a London-born film studies and psychoanalytic psychology graduate with a particular interest in 'freak/extreme' culture, horror and supernatural cinema, cult TV and disquieting fairy stories. She has worked in UK book publishing since 1992, heading up lists of erotica and true crime and latterly specialising in memoir and music biographies by the likes of John Lydon, Peter Hook and Tricky. She has been the editor/author of numerous texts including *Inappropriate Behaviour* (Serpent's Tail, 2002), and a contributor to *Horror: The Definitive Guide to the Cinema of Fear* (Andre Deutsch, 2006), as well as being a compère and interviewer at numerous independent film events and the Port Eliot literary festival in the UK.

QUOTE, UNQUOTE

The Doctor to William Blake: 'The future of mankind? Just remember these words – Auschwitz, Stalingrad, Hiroshima and Nagasaki. Just words. Gladys Aylward, Mother Theresa, Albert Schweitzer. Just names. Somewhere between the words and the names lies the future of mankind.'

The Pit

I collected all the Target books, but I drifted away from it at college – I stopped watching around the time of "The Trial of a Time Lord" – and didn't pick it up again until the end of the McCoy era when people at college were saying it had actually got quite good again, and indeed it had. I was never really a fan in that I did anything other than just watch it occasionally. I hadn't even heard about the Virgin novels until I got the interview for the job, at which point I went out and bought as many as I could find and very quickly read them before the interview. I was quite taken aback at how good they were. I hadn't imagined that there might be something like that out there. I was very keen to work on them once I'd read them.

'I liked the books a lot. I felt they were designed to appeal to me as an adult in the same way as the show had appealed to me as a child. I liked the fact that they weren't exactly like the show, but felt true to the spirit of the show. I found them exciting – *Timewyrm: Revelation* for example, the emotional depth and truth in that was something you never found in the show. Much as I loved it, it never made me cry as some of the books did. You don't really care about characters in a TV show, but books don't work that way, they can't just work on spectacle and breezy humour, because they last a lot longer and require a lot more commitment from the reader. I thought what Peter had done with the New Adventures really addressed the challenge of how you take a TV series and turn it into a range of books. I don't think any other TV tie-in range has done that so well.

'My first job was to collate the proofs of *Transit*, and *The Highest Science* was the first title I copy-edited – correcting grammar, spelling and sense. A copy editor doesn't usually ask for changes to the plot or structure, that's the desk editor's job. It was a gradual transition, really. Although the first book I desk-edited was *Tragedy Day*, it had been commissioned by Peter, and the first book that I commissioned myself was, I think, *Parasite*.'

1993 saw Virgin launch not only the Black Lace books, which proved to be a major hit for the company, but also a range of original novels based on the popular comic character Judge Dredd from *2000AD*; a series of books

ARRIVALS AND DEPARTURES

based on the Sega gaming hero Sonic the Hedgehog; and the first of their non-fiction episode guides for shows other than *Doctor Who*. The latter, a book on *Red Dwarf* by Chris Howarth and Steve Lyons, was wildly successful, was reprinted several times and reissued in revised and updated editions, and spawned a series of unofficial paperback guides to series as diverse as *Buffy the Vampire Slayer* and *The Simpsons*. With the Missing Adventures also on the horizon, the increasing workloads led to another person being recruited to join the team. This was Andy Bodle, who acted as editorial assistant to Levene and Sharp.

As 1993 drew to a close, so the New Adventures range started off on another story arc. This time it was the loosely-themed 'Alternate Universe Cycle', beginning with Jim Mortimore's *Blood Heat*, which included five internal illustrations by artist Tim Keable, and continuing through Daniel Blythe's *The Dimension Riders*, Kate Orman's *The Left-Handed Hummingbird* and Steve Lyons' *Conundrum* before reaching a conclusion in Paul Cornell's *No Future*, originally titled *Anarchy in the UK* (both titles being taken from tracks by the Sex Pistols), in which it is revealed that all the historical meddling witnessed in these novels has been the doing of none other than the Doctor's old sparring partner the Monk, here given the name Mortimus.

As with his previous novel, *Lucifer Rising*, Jim Mortimore sought permission to paint the cover for *Blood Heat* himself. On 9 January 1993 he sent through to Virgin three rough sketches of potential compositions. He suggested that it might take him a week to produce a finished sketch, by the end of March, and the final painting by the end of April at the latest. Rebecca Levene responded positively on 11 February, confirming that they would like 'Sketch Three' to be developed: 'with some ruins in the background, and with the Silurian moved a bit to the left, and Ace a bit to the right.'

Right: the first of Tim Keable's five internal illustrations for *Blood Heat*. These were commissioned by Virgin on 18 March 1993, on the basis of seven rough sketches that Keable had provided – see page 99.

TIM KEABLE

Tim Keable is an artist based on the south coast. Over the years he has contributed to many fan publications as well as *Doctor Who Magazine*, Virgin Publishing, Big Finish and Spiteful Puppet. He is also the artist on the independent comic book *West*, written by Andrew Cheverton. Most recently he has contributed art for Gerry Anderson Productions to commemorate the sixtieth anniversary of *Supercar*.

THE WHO ADVENTURES

The other four internal illustrations produced by Tim Keable for *Blood Heat*.

ARRIVALS AND DEPARTURES

This page: Tim Keable's original black-and-white roughs for his *Blood Heat* internal illustrations. Five of these were developed into the finished pieces shown over the previous two pages, some of them with adaptations, while two went unused. Elements from one of the latter, featuring a Silurian riding on a dinosaur's back with a large moon in the sky above, were added into the first of the finished pieces, and strongly recalled a 1991 painting by Colin Howard published in the *Doctor Who* fanzine *The Frame* – as shown to the right.

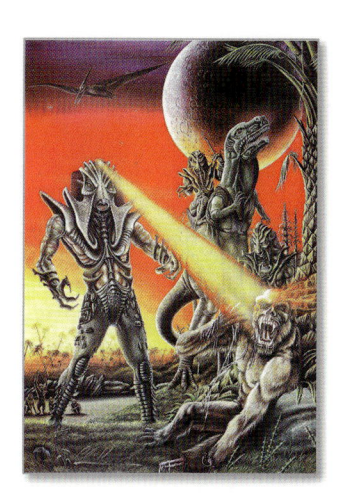

99

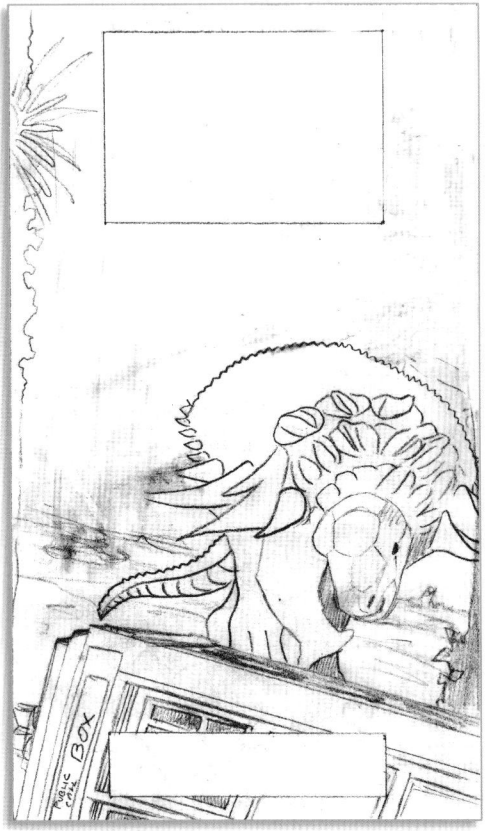

Mortimore produced several further sketches and a completed cover painting, taking on board Levene's editorial comments. In the end, though, Virgin were unhappy with how the piece had turned out. They therefore passed the project over to artist Jeff Cummins, who supplied, in record time, a substitute painting based on Mortimore's ideas.

Cummins had previously provided the covers for some of the 1970s Target *Doctor Who* novelisations (including those for *The Face of Evil, The Talons of Weng-Chiang* and *The Mutants*) and was the first of three of their artists to return to work on the New Adventures. This arose out of the fact that, in the early part of 1993, *Doctor Who*'s thirtieth anniversary year, author David J Howe had contacted many of the Target artists while researching *Timeframe*, a celebratory factual book that would be illustrated with original cover artwork. Several of the artists had expressed to Howe an interest in working on *Doctor Who* again, and sent sample cards of their work. These were passed on to Darvill-Evans, who liked what he saw and started approaching the artists. As well as Cummins, Bill Donohoe (whose novelisation covers had included those for *The Cybermen* and *The Enemy of the World*) and Tony Masero (responsible for *The Reign of Terror, The Macra Terror* and *The Romans*, amongst others) were subsequently contracted to work on the New Adventures.

When W H Allen, the precursor company to Virgin, had moved offices in 1990, Darvill-Evans had not long taken over as editor of the Target range. 'I rescued all the *Doctor Who* material I could find,' he says, 'including files, books and loads of artwork from the previous 20 years of *Doctor Who* publishing. I had no idea who the artists were, but when we did *Timeframe*, David was able to identify them and, in many cases, ensure that the art

Left: two of Jim Mortimore's initial compositional sketch suggestions for the cover of *Blood Heat*. Although neither of these two was selected for further development, one element from the second – the TARDIS lying askew on the ground at the bottom of the frame – was used in adapted form by Jeff Cummins when he produced the book's final, substitute cover painting – see page 94.

ARRIVALS AND DEPARTURES

Shown on this page are three stages in Jim Mortimore's development of his ideas for the *Blood Heat* cover artwork. Top left: the initial black-and-white sketch, one of three that Mortimore submitted to Virgin on 9 January 1993. Bottom left, a colour 'visualisation', taking on board Rebecca Levene's editorial comments of 11 February to include some ruined buildings in the background and move the Silurian a little to the left and Ace (on horseback) a little to the right. The depiction of Ace in this rough includes elements cropped from a photograph. Top right: Mortimore's completed colour painting for the cover. When Jeff Cummins was called in to provide a replacement piece, he retained the idea of having a Silurian riding on a dinosaur's back, which had also been used by Tim Keable in one of his roughs for the book's internal illustrations. Again this recalled the Colin Howard painting previously published in the fanzine *The Frame* – see page 99.

BEHIND THE BOOK: *BLOOD HEAT*

This novel began as a non-*Doctor Who* short story inspired by the real-life discovery of bones that turned out to belong to Seismosaurus and Ultrasaurus, the two largest dinosaurs. Mortimore's plot, which involved cloned dinosaurs, preceded the use of a similar idea in Michael Crichton's novel *Jurassic Park* (on which the successful movie franchise was based). As Mortimore's story developed, the *Doctor Who* Appreciation Society became interested in publishing it in their fan fiction journal *Cosmic Masque*, so he 'bunged the Doctor in'. The story however continued to evolve to the point where it was becoming novel-length.

Mortimore was then made redundant from his day job as a graphic designer and turned to writing novels as a way of earning a living. He submitted two proposals to Virgin; one with Andy Lane for *Lucifer Rising*, the other for his own dinosaur novel, which by this time involved the Silurians, originally created by scriptwriter Malcolm Hulke in 1970 for the third Doctor TV story 'Doctor Who and the Silurians'. The latter proposal consisted of three chapters of prose and a detailed plot synopsis of roughly 30,000 words.

Lucifer Rising was accepted, but Peter Darvill-Evans was at first reluctant to publish *Blood Heat* due to its alternate universe setting. Eventually he decided to make it the first in a linked series of alternate universe novels. Mortimore had six months in which to produce the final manuscript.

Bernice wasn't included in the original draft, so Mortimore developed a subplot to get around the need to perform extensive rewrites on what he had already written. The story forms a sequel of sorts to 'Doctor Who and the Silurians'; the characters Morka and Dr Meredith are both derived from that story, while Robin Ridgway and Tony Mitchell come from its TV sequel, Hulke's 'The Sea Devils'. Frank Hobson, uncle to the third Doctor's companion Jo Grant, who also features, is taken from Hulke's novelisation of his 1971 TV story 'Colony in Space'. However, despite some suggestions in the novel that another of the characters is the fourth Doctor's companion Harry Sullivan, Mortimore says this is not in fact the case.

Mortimore's finished manuscript overshot the maximum permitted word-count by about a quarter of the total length, so he had to remove 25,000 words. Approximately 20,000 words were cut through simply tightening up the prose, while the remaining 5,000 were lost by removing ten scenes. Many of the excised sections were set in 1973, at the time of the Silurians' emergence from their shelters and the release of their plague attack on humanity, as seen in 'Doctor Who and the Silurians'. The character Billy Wilson was introduced in one of these, and in another Jo Grant tries to convince her uncle to allow her to become a spy. There was also to have been a 1973-set prologue in which the crew of an ice-breaker try and fail to communicate with the Silurians at the North Pole.

Other 1993-set scenes lost from the finished work included part of one in which Bernice and the new character Julia hunt for Ace in the ruins of Bristol; one involving Bernice and Ace in the Complex sick bay the following day; one of Ace and her friend Manisha seeing a Triceratops and a Tyrannosaurus Rex fighting; one of the Doctor reintroducing flowers (which no-one has seen for 20 years); and one revealing that further time divergences have occurred on Earth prior to 1973, as there are buildings Ace doesn't recognise.

(From *TSV* Issue 37 – courtesy Paul Scoones.)

Jeff Cummins' rough for his final version of *Blood Heat*'s cover artwork.

ARRIVALS AND DEPARTURES

was reunited with the artists. Of course, this meant that I had a number of grateful artists talking to me, and as a result we used several of them on the New Adventures.'

Reviewers again seemed to be generally appreciative of this latest batch of novels. *TV Zone*'s Andrew Martin enjoyed *Blood Heat* – 'The pace never lets up,' he wrote, 'and there is always a feeling of wanting to know what happens next' – and considered *The Dimension Riders* to be 'one of the best-written novels to date'. On the other hand, he expressed some concern over Kate Orman's *The Left-Handed Hummingbird*, feeling that although the books were becoming more sophisticated, 'it could be argued that the resultant loss of innocence is taking things too far from the naïve charm of the television series'. He also had

Right and below: Phil Bevan's *Doctor Who Magazine* Prelude illustrations for *Blood Heat*.

103

THE WHO ADVENTURES

Jeff Cummins' original artwork for the cover of *The Dimension Riders*.

ARRIVALS AND DEPARTURES

some harsh criticisms to make about *No Future*: 'The storyline is complex, featuring the usual cod-psychology and wearisome New Age sub-PC bollocks. However, although the continuity references are well-integrated with the plot, it is this sort of emphasis which will keep the New Adventures within the bounds of fan fiction, rather than mainstream SF writing.'

Writing in *DWB*, David Owen was similarly

Three roughs produced by Jeff Cummins for his cover art for *The Dimension Riders*. This piece was commissioned from him before the *Blood Heat* replacement, and he initially drew the title box in the wrong format, based on that used on some reissue editions of the Target novelisations. He was asked to correct this for the final rough – see bottom right – which, unusually, he drew in purple.

> ### DANIEL BLYTHE
>
> Daniel Blythe is an acclaimed writer of novels for children and adults, and of non-fiction on subjects as diverse as politics, popular music, collecting gadgets and games, parenting and the history of robotics. He has written several of the officially-licensed *Doctor Who* novels.
>
> Blythe's first book with a teenage narrator was *The Cut*, which was followed by further novels *Losing Faith* and *This is the Day*. In 2012 his first supernatural fantasy novel for young readers, *Shadow Runners*, was published. *Emerald Greene and the Witch* Stones, for readers aged 9 to 12, came out in in 2015, and a sequel, *Emerald Greene: Instruments of Darkness*, in 2017. His first Badger Learning novel for reluctant and dyslexic readers, *New Dawn*, came out in autumn 2015, and was followed by *I Spy* (nominated for the Leicester Reading Rampage Award 2018), *Fascination*, *Kill Order*, *Hope and Truth* and *Kiss the Sky*. His most recent novel for older teenagers, a sci-fi mystery called *Exiles*, was published in autumn 2019.
>
> Blythe has worked as a visiting author in over 400 schools and has taught on the MA course in Creative Writing at Sheffield Hallam University. He mentors, advises and edits writers of all ages through Cornerstones UK and the Faber Academy. He is a regular judge on the Novel Slam for the Off the Shelf festival and leads classes through the Sheffield Writers' Hub. He lives in the Peak District with his wife and their two student children.

impressed with *Blood Heat*, citing a number of striking set pieces 'that remain etched on the memory long after putting the book down – the Silurian airships gliding in to attack, Ace and Manisha finding the Doctor's tomb, the sight of the TARDIS in the corner of UNIT HQ, unused for 20 years. Most of all, the image of a horde of pterosaur-borne Silurians flying through the night, their presence marked by the red glow of their third eye.' Anthony Brown was full of admiration for *The Left-Handed Hummingbird*, describing it as 'a book which continually strikes the breath from your throat, as yet another outrageous idea hits home. It's a book so packed with continuity as to be fanboyish – if any of it was obtrusive. It's a book in which the Doctor can take LSD, gush blood and be more vulnerable than he has been since about 1984 without anyone batting an eyelid … perhaps the best New Adventure I've ever read.' Keith Topping, meanwhile, praised *Conundrum*: 'It has more gumption and a hell of a lot more imagination than 90 percent of the New Adventures output … Buy this, because you might never find another quite like it.' Over in *Doctor Who Magazine*, Craig Hinton thought that *The Dimension Riders* was 'wonderful,' adding, 'Blythe has a confidence and flair of writing that makes every page a joy to read.' He also enjoyed *The Left-Handed Hummingbird*, describing it as 'the most adult New Adventure yet, and the most gripping. This is how they should be taking risks while telling a damn good story'. *Conundrum* was likewise praised, and Hinton listed some of the things he liked: 'Things to watch out for: Ace being attacked by flying New Adventures novels, John and Gillian from the *TV Comic* strip, the

ARRIVALS AND DEPARTURES

BEHIND THE BOOK: *THE DIMENSION RIDERS*

Daniel Blythe had had the basic idea for *The Dimension Riders* lying around for some time, so when the New Adventures were first launched, he revamped it and sent it off to Virgin.

The publishers liked the idea, but requested changes. The most notable of these was the inclusion of Bernice – which proved tricky, as Blythe had already put together a fair amount of the novel without her. He solved this problem by expanding on an existing subplot set around St Matthew's College, Oxford, to give her something to do. The fictional St Matthew's was based in part on the real St John's, where Blythe had studied French and German as an undergraduate.

Blythe enjoyed writing for Bernice and the Doctor, but found Ace difficult.

(From *TSV* Issue 37 – courtesy Paul Scoones.)

QUOTE, UNQUOTE

The Doctor: 'This isn't my job. I don't get paid for it. I don't get any kind of reward … I've never asked for any. Sometimes there are some. The smile of the baby child. The first sunset on a soft and new-born world. The taste of the purest spring water, untouched by any pollution of Man's making … But it's not enough.'

The Dimension Riders

Phil Bevan's *Doctor Who Magazine* Prelude illustrations for *The Dimension Riders*.

107

Dreadlox from Marvel's *Professor Gamble* strip, Benny and the Batcave ...' *No Future*, however, was found sorely lacking: 'Paul's once innovative style of writing – street-cred cyberpunk – now seems stale and dated, and, dare I say it, too clever by half ... a disappointment and a retrograde step. And it has the worst New Adventures cover ever.'

Despite the criticism in *TV Zone* that the New Adventures were glorified fan fiction, Darvill-Evans recognised that the fanbase, and ideas from that arena, were very important to the range. He wanted the authors, including newcomers like Daniel Blythe, Steve Lyons and Kate Orman, to discuss their work amongst themselves, and to add new layers to it, all fuelled by their enthusiasm and knowledge as fans of the show and of the books.

'We always encouraged the authors to talk to each other,' he recalls, 'and I know a lot of them met up – and indeed still do – at a monthly pub gathering in London, at the Fitzroy Tavern. There they would exchange ideas, and although I rarely went along, these meetings helped in the development of both our fiction and our non-fiction. Some authors started going along there after they had their first book published by us, while others were talking by telephone or via the internet.'

Kate Orman had been active in Australian *Doctor Who* fandom for some years before getting *The Left-Handed Hummingbird* accepted. She ended up being the only female and the only non-British writer to contribute to the New Adventures range. Her novel revolved around Aztec legends, and Orman explained the background to Craig Hinton in an interview printed in Issue 208 of *Doctor Who Magazine*: 'It began as a short story for a fanzine, which is intact in the book as Chapter 12. I liked [the 1964 TV *Doctor Who* adventure] "The Aztecs", and a friend of mine wanted me to use the *Titanic*, so they both went in. And I thought of the villain while standing about in a bookshop in Sydney.'

As part of her research work for the novel, in November 1992, Orman located a book, *Pre-Columban*

Pete Wallbank's original rough for his cover artwork for *The Left-Handed Hummingbird*, and the second draft he was asked to produce of one element: the figure of the Doctor.

ARRIVALS AND DEPARTURES

Pete Wallbank's original artwork for the cover of *The Left-Handed Hummingbird*. As reference for the figure of the Aztec warrior, Huitzilin, Wallbank used a Chris Achilleos illustration of actor Jackie Chan from the poster for the 1985 movie *The Protector*.

THE WHO ADVENTURES

KATE ORMAN

Kate Orman was born in Sydney, Australia, and grew up in Canberra, Melbourne, and McLean, Virginia, USA.

The Left-Handed Hummingbird was Orman's first novel. She was the first woman to write for the New Adventures range, and the first Australian. She went on to write or co-write numerous *Doctor Who* novels for Virgin and later for BBC Books, plus the Aurealis award-winning novella *Fallen Gods*, co-authored with her husband Jonathan Blum, for Telos Publishing. She has also written non-fiction about the *Doctor Who* stories 'The Talons of Weng-Chiang' (published in *Doctor Who and Race*, 2013) and 'Pyramids of Mars' (Obverse Books, 2017). She has written several *Doctor Who* short stories for Big Finish, co-written the *Blake's 7* novel *Mediasphere* with Blum, written stories for the short-lived *Torchwood* magazine, and edited *Liberating Earth*, an all-woman Faction Paradox anthology for Obverse.

Orman's original short fiction has been published in *Realms of Fantasy*, *Interzone* and *Cosmos*, and in Australian anthologies. Her ambition is to publish more original science fiction, and especially an original SF novel. In her spare time she battles Bipolar II Disorder and helps rescue street cats.

Phil Bevan's two *Doctor Who Magazine* Prelude illustrations for *The Left-Handed Hummingbird*.

Literatures of Mexico by Miguel León-Portilla (1969), which contained some ancient Aztec poetry. She contacted the publishers, asking for permission to quote from it, but when Virgin received the details, they commented to Orman: '$2.50 a line seems a bit exorbitant to us. How about making up some of your own in the similar style?' However, as Orman was responsible for clearing and paying for such things herself, she duly arranged for permission to use one poem, which appears on page 42 of the published book.

ARRIVALS AND DEPARTURES

STEVE LYONS

Steve Lyons wrote four novels for the New and Missing Adventures series. Prior to this, he was a writer on the *Red Dwarf Smegazine* and co-author of the *Red Dwarf Programme Guide*. He has continued to write *Doctor Who* in various media, including more novels (*The Stealers of Dreams*, *The Witch Hunters*), audio dramas for radio and CD (*Blood of the Daleks*, *The Architects of History*), talking books (*Destiny of the Doctor: Smoke and Mirrors*) and comic strips (for *Doctor Who Adventures* and *Doctor Who Magazine*). He has co-written two books about the series and is a regular contributor to *Doctor Who Magazine*. He has also written in other fictional universes, including those of *Warhammer*, *Blake's 7*, *Sapphire & Steel*, *Stargate*, *2,000AD* and both Marvel and DC Comics.

When Ace returned to the New Adventures in *Deceit*, after a period spent away, she had become a mercenary fighter. As *Doctor Who Magazine* wanted to establish continuity between their regular comic strip and the novels, an artist called Rod Ramos, who was working for a time at the offices of the magazine's publishers Marvel, was asked to come up with a new look for both Ace and the Doctor. Ramos's new costume design sketches (below), based on descriptions given to him by Peter Darvill-Evans, were intended for use as reference both for the comic strip and for the novels, and their influence can be seen in the covers for *Conundrum*, *First Frontier* and *Warlock*.

111

THE WHO ADVENTURES

1.
2.
3.

112

ARRIVALS AND DEPARTURES

This page and opposite: Jeff Cummins' evolving cover design for *Conundrum*.

1. Two initial composition ideas, one featuring Ace in the foreground and the Doctor Nemesis character in the background, the other featuring just the latter.

2. A more developed version of the Doctor Nemesis idea, in what Cummins called a 'comic strip style'.

3. A revised sketch of the alternative idea, which Virgin preferred. Cummins' handwritten note to editor Peter Darvill-Evans was, 'Will work on him [i.e. Doctor Nemesis] & background. But … you get the gist?!!!' The response, added at the top of the page, was, 'I phoned – said – better, but figures still too big. Sent, in post, more reference for Ace.'

4. A further refined sketch, Cummins commenting, 'Hi Peter. Post hasn't arrived yet! But I think this works with existing ref.' In reply to this, Cummins was phoned on 28 June 1993 and told that the piece needed more perspective, with hills, snow, a 'chocolate box' town, and Ace perhaps scaled down.

5. In response, Cummins produced this 'Additional, extremely rough sketch with revised "village" scene!'

6. The final, as-published cover of the book.

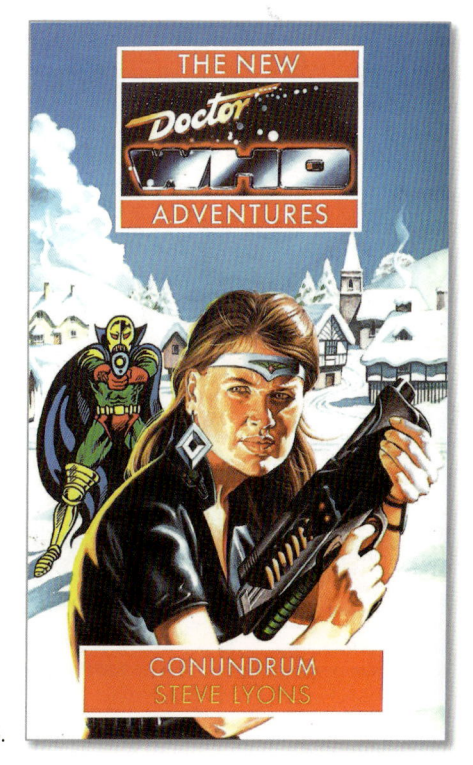

4.

5. 6.

113

THE WHO ADVENTURES

Phil Bevan's *Doctor Who Magazine* Prelude illustrations for *Conundrum*.

JEFF CUMMINS

Jeff Cummins discovered his talent for art at school in the '60s. He grew up in North Wales before joining a London-based marketing company as a graphics artist in 1974. He moved on in 1976 and got commissions from pop artists such as Paul McCartney and Wings, Elvis Costello, Ted Nugent, Whitesnake and, with the design group Hipgnosis, Pink Floyd, Led Zeppelin, the Moody Blues, Rainbow and Peter Gabriel.

In 1976 he painted the first of his covers for the Target *Doctor Who* range. Alongside his work on the novelisations, he also provided covers for three titles in the *Doctor Who Discovers ...* series (*Space Travel*, *Prehistoric Animals* and *Strange and Mysterious Creatures*) and for the first two books in Terrance Dicks' *Star Quest* trilogy, also published by Target.

His cover for 'The Time Meddler' in 1988 marked a return to the novelisations range after almost a ten year break. It was his last project for Target, but he then painted eight covers for Virgin's *Doctor Who* ranges through the first half of the '90s – although he himself was less than happy with his work on these.

Around the time that he was producing his earliest covers for Target, he was also providing illustrations for a short-lived British SF poster magazine called *TV Sci-Fi Monthly*, one of which was a portrayal of Tom Baker as the Doctor. These were amongst his earliest commissions.

Cummins has gone on to provide covers and illustrations for dozens of books and magazines, including *Radio Times*. He has worked as a freelance illustrator and designer and produced ideas for children's animation. He now works as a storyboard artist for an animation studio based in Chester and has moved back to North Wales.

ARRIVALS AND DEPARTURES

Jeff Cummins' original artwork for the cover of *Conundrum*.

THE WHO ADVENTURES

BEHIND THE BOOK: *CONUNDRUM*

Steve Lyons' original inspiration for *Conundrum* came from watching the 1968 *Doctor Who* TV story 'The Mind Robber' and wondering what a sequel would be like. He decided that things would be updated by having a new Master of the Land of Fiction, and that the fairy tales and children's classics of the original would be replaced by superheroes and the Famous Five. He originally had the Land of Fiction simply surviving after 'The Mind Robber', but in order to fit his idea into the 'Alternate Universe Cycle', he changed this so that the Monk had altered time to bring the Land of Fiction back into being. The Master of the Land was originally to have addressed his story to the Gods of Ragnarok, as seen in the 1988/89 TV story 'The Greatest Show in the Galaxy', but Lyons changed this to the Monk. 'Again, that was only a matter of altering a few lines,' he says. Lyons particularly enjoyed writing for the pairing of Bernice and his character Norman, the retired superhero, but found the new version of Ace difficult, as her reintroduction story, *Deceit* was published less than a month before his submission deadline. The changes made to the book by the editor were consequently almost all to do with Ace's character.

(From *TSV* Issue 43 – courtesy Paul Scoones.)

Above: Pete Wallbank's original rough for the cover of Paul Cornell's *No Future*.

PETE WALLBANK

Pete Wallbank was born on 23 October 1968 in Staffordshire. He has loved drawing ever since seeing the film *King Kong vs Godzilla* at a young age; it stirred a life-long fascination with all things film and TV and the desire to illustrate them. Early inspiration came from Andrew Skilleter, who at the time was working on novelisation covers for *Doctor Who*, one of Wallbank's favourite childhood TV shows.

Wallbank initially trained in Graphic Design at Matthew Boulton College in Birmingham but swapped this for more drawing-based illustration soon after. He was first employed as an illustrator for an advertising agency, but his desire to go it alone and become freelance soon took over. He considers himself fortunate in having been able to illustrate many books, magazines, DVDs, video covers and associated published materials.

He continues to work enthusiastically with many clients worldwide.

ARRIVALS AND DEPARTURES

Pete Wallbank's original artwork for the cover of *No Future*.

THE WHO ADVENTURES

Keri — This is what "Benny" will look like on No Future

Not too Liza Minelli-ish is she?

Speak to you soon

Above: a note by artist Pete Wallbank to Kerri Sharp at Virgin about his depiction of Bernice on *No Future*. This was approved on 17 June 1993.

Left: one of Phil Bevan's *Doctor Who Magazine* Prelude illustrations for *No Future*.

In February 1994, Darvill-Evans and Levene revamped the Writers' Guidelines document that had been created by Darvill-Evans as a means of communicating their requirements to any interested authors. The document included basic information for potential contributors, but also a 'Universal Background for *Doctor Who* Stories' section that sketched in some of the details of the 'New Adventures Universe', including ancient Gallifrey (female priest-rulers, similar to Hellenic Greece but with space travel), Rassilon (one of a political triumvirate including Omega and 'the Other', who, it is stated, is *not* the Doctor), the fall of the Time Lords (due to a genetic nano-technological bug) and lots more information about the Time Lords – this section is five pages long! The document also contained a further six pages on what to avoid and what to include in submissions. Overall, the document ran to a daunting 41 pages. Along the way, Darvill-Evans identified the key New Adventures titles so far: *Timewyrm: Exodus*: '[Terrance Dicks] knows more about *Doctor Who* storytelling than anyone else', *Cat's Cradle: Warhead*: 'an example of how the New Adventures can use non-traditional writing styles'; *Love and War*: 'the introduction of Bernice Summerfield'; *Transit*: 'an example of how far the novel medium can take *Doctor Who*'; and *Deceit*: '… written by me. Nuff said.'

Regarding the list's inclusion of his own novel in the list, Darvill-Evans says: 'When Bex started at Virgin, I asked her to use *Deceit* as a benchmark for submissions, as in my opinion, anything that was better than *Deceit* was probably worth considering. I considered it to be a minimum standard for a *Doctor Who* novel rather than one of the greatest entries in the range.'

ARRIVALS AND DEPARTURES

Phil Bevan's second *Doctor Who Magazine* Prelude illustration for *No Future*.

Jeff Cummins' original cover artwork for *Tragedy Day*.

8: STAND-ALONE ADVENTURES

With the conclusion of the 'Alternate Universe Cycle', the New Adventures proceeded during 1994 as a succession of stand-alone adventures – although character development continued as usual from book to book. The titles published were: Gareth Roberts' *Tragedy Day*; Gary Russell's *Legacy*; Justin Richards' *Theatre of War*; Andy Lane's *All-Consuming Fire*, which had internal illustrations by Mike Nicholson; Terrance Dicks' *Blood Harvest*; Simon Messingham's *Strange England*; David A McIntee's *First Frontier*; Mark Gatiss's *St Anthony's Fire*; Daniel O'Mahony's *Falls the Shadow*; and Jim Mortimore's *Parasite*, originally titled *Book of Shadows*. Peter Darvill-Evans' policy of encouraging new writers was clearly paying dividends; seeing their first novels in print here were Russell (then editor of *Doctor Who Magazine*), Richards, Messingham and O'Mahony, while Roberts, Lane, McIntee, Gatiss and Mortimore were all returning with new works. The range seemed to have found a core of talent that could keep it going almost indefinitely.

Below: an early 1990s gathering of Virgin Publishing authors with their editor. Kneeling at the front: Paul Cornell, Ben Aaronovitch, Gary Russell. Middle row: David J Howe, a Dalek, Paul Leonard, Peter Darvill-Evans, Stephen James Walker. Back row: Jim Mortimore (with eyes shaded), Gareth Roberts, Simon Messingham, Mark Gatiss, Mark Stammers, Andy Lane.

THE WHO ADVENTURES

Top left and right: Jeff Cummins' original roughs for his cover artwork for *Tragedy* Day, the second featuring in the margin a detail of the Doctor's face.

Above: a photograph that Cummins had taken of himself as reference for the Doctor's pose. Cummins added the speech bubble as a joke, suggesting a resemblance between himself and Francis Rossi of the band Status Quo.

Left: the more refined rough that Cummins faxed to editor Peter Darvill-Evans for his approval, with marginal notes 'I'll try to make the city look grotty!' and 'I'll improve the gun!' The coloured brush marks were added by Cummins later, when he was actually in the process of painting the final cover.

STAND-ALONE ADVENTURES

BEHIND THE BOOK: *TRAGEDY DAY*

Gareth Roberts feels in retrospect that his novel has 'far too many ideas' packed into it, and that he should have trimmed it so that the importance of the central concept was more apparent. 'I dolloped it on a bit too much. Totally my fault ... I should have made the plot simpler.' The central message Roberts wanted to get across was about the role that giving money to charity plays in our lives; that people give money 'simply to feel good, rather than to change things for the better.' Linked with this was the concept of a carnival. *Tragedy Day* also deals with the notion of social fatalism, 'where society just accepts its decay and decline.'

(From *TSV* Issue 43 – courtesy Paul Scoones.)

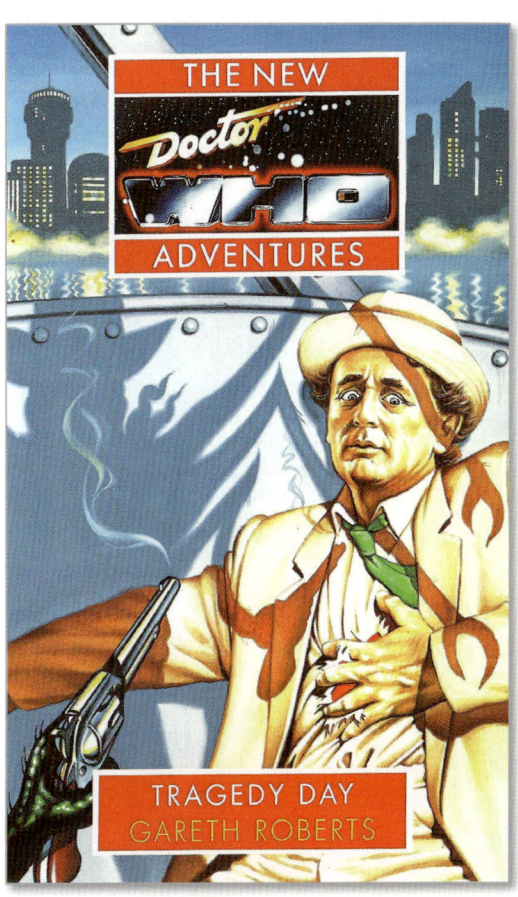

Top left and bottom right: Phil Bevan's *Doctor Who Magazine* Prelude illustrations for *Tragedy Day*. Bottom left: the book's as-published final cover.

THE WHO ADVENTURES

Peter Elson's original artwork for the cover of *Legacy*.

GARY RUSSELL

Gary Russell had a ten-year career as a young actor (which he plans to write a book about one day), then moved into other areas of the industry, working as a runner/assistant director/AFM, and spending a period of time in press and publicity and brand management for the BBC. As a freelance writer he has contributed to a number of national magazines and periodicals such as *Radio Times*, *Mojo* and *Time Out*. For Marvel UK he served as an editor and then group editor in both magazine and comic book departments, before moving on to work for gaming magazines and *TV Soap*.

He has written over thirty *Doctor Who*-related novels and factual books, including both the novelisation of the 1996 *Doctor Who* TV Movie and the behind-the-scenes 'making of' book about the same production. As well as *Doctor Who*, he has written non-fiction books on *The Simpsons* and *Frasier* and a number of *New York Times* best-selling hardbacks about the Peter Jackson-directed *The Lord of the Rings* movie trilogy.

In 1997 he helped establish Big Finish Productions, for whom he was the executive producer, overseeing all their audio drama and book publishing; script-editing, producing and directing over 200 hours of original audio drama. After eight years at Big Finish, he rejoined the BBC as a script editor at BBC Wales Drama, where he stayed for nearly six years, working on *Doctor Who*, *Torchwood*, *The Sarah Jane Adventures* and *Wizards vs Aliens*. While at BBC Wales he also produced and directed a number of *Doctor Who* animation and game projects, including 'The Infinite Quest', 'Dreamland' and the BAFTA-winning 'The Gunpowder Plot' adventure game.

Photo: Alex Mallinson.

In 2013 he temporarily relocated to New South Wales, Australia, to be executive producer on a 26-part ABC Me children's animated series, from Planet 55 Studios, called *Prisoner Zero*. He returned to the UK in 2016 and wrote the *Doctor Who Infinity* video game 'The Orphans of the Polyoptera'. Working with Big Finish Creative, he most recently oversaw the making of the animated version of the 1968 *Doctor Who* adventure 'Fury From the Deep' for BBC Studios.

Russell lives in Cardiff with his collections of 'friends', which everyone else refers to as books, comics, action figures, Converse hi-tops and a ridiculous number of CDs and DVDs. He is allergic to onion and terrified of cows and spiders.

BEHIND THE BOOK: *THEATRE OF WAR*

The starting points for Justin Richards' novel were the concepts of a dream machine and a play entitled *The Good Soldiers*. W H Auden's 1937 poem 'As I Walked Out One Evening' provided inspiration; according to Richards, 'It captures the essence of what I wanted the final performance to be about. Basically it talks about how time will get us all in the end.' *Theatre of War* was a complicated book to write, because Richards wanted to make it multi-layered, with a number of hidden and misleading clues to keep the reader guessing until the end. His intention was to write a book 'you could read several times and still get something out of, so even if you know what's going on and what the twist is, you can still read back through, see the clues, and reinterpret the evidence.'

(From *TSV* Issue 43 – courtesy Paul Scoones.)

THE WHO ADVENTURES

Above: Phil Bevan's two *Doctor Who Magazine* Prelude pieces for *Legacy*.

> **LYRICAL CHAPTERS**
>
> Many of *Legacy*'s chapter titles were taken from Gary Numan song titles: 'Unknown and Hostile'; 'In a Glasshouse'; 'Machine and Soul'; 'Strange Charm'; 'A Game Called Echo'; 'Are "Friends" Electric'; 'Soul Protection'; 'I Die, You Die'; and 'Dark Mountain'.

Two of the this year's new titles had literary influences: Justin Richards' *Theatre of War* was partly inspired by the works of Shakespeare, including *Hamlet*, and by W H Auden's poem 'As I Walked Out One Evening', while Andy Lane's *All-Consuming Fire* was presented as a story of Arthur Conan Doyle's fictional British detective Sherlock Holmes, written from the point of view of Homes' associate Dr Watson and featuring internal illustrations similar to those that originally accompanied Holmes' stories in *The Strand* magazine. In light of Peter Darvill-Evans' desire to introduce new companions into the range, Lane suggested that a character called Tir Ram from his novel might become an ongoing one; he produced a three-page character outline for him in August 1993. Ultimately, *All-Consuming Fire* saw Tir Ram make his only appearance. The character had not featured at all in Lane's original outline for the book, and in the published version, he is killed by Ace as he is being converted into one of the novel's rakshasa creatures.

Of his decision to use Conan Doyle's Dr Watson to tell his story, Lane says: 'It's such a wonderfully relaxing experience, sinking back into Watson's way of phrasing things as narrator. No problems with wondering what to write next – the words just flow from the quill pen! If you can find a voice to write a book with, then half the battle is won. Nicking a voice – the way I did with Watson – solves half your problems.'

'Andy Lane was always very prolific with ideas,' notes Peter Darvill-Evans. 'Unfortunately this meant that we had to turn him down an awful lot. That happens. We had to really squeeze some other authors to get anything out of them at all.'

STAND-ALONE ADVENTURES

Above: Phil Bevan's two *Doctor Who Magazine* Prelude illustrations for Justin Richards' *Theatre of War*.

JUSTIN RICHARDS

Justin Richards was born in Epping, Essex, on 14 September 1961. After attending Dean Close School in Cheltenham he obtained a BA (Hons) in English and Theatre at the University of Warwick.

Richards' first professionally published works were in Virgin's New Adventures, Missing Adventures and Decalog series. He continued to write *Doctor Who* novels after they were taken over by BBC Books. As well as producing numerous novels, audio books, activity books and reference books ,he acted as creative director for BBC Books' *Doctor Who* range until around 2017.

In 2003, Richards began writing *The Invisible Detective* series of children's crime novels, the parallel plots of which – split between the 1930s and the present day – show a fascination with time and temporal paradox that is also evident in his *Time Runners* series that came out in 2007-2008. More action-oriented books include the *Agent Alfie* stories for younger readers, and a series of action-adventure novels for young teens, co-written with Jack Higgins. Other books have had a more supernatural plot element, including the *Department of Unclassified Artefacts* novels and the *School of Night* books.

Richards' book *The Chaos Code* won the Hull Children's Book Award 2008. *Demon Storm*, from the *School of Night* series, was shortlisted for the Southampton's Favourite Book award 2011.

Richards has also written audio plays produced by Big Finish and original audiobooks, and scripts for television, including on Five's soap opera *Family Affairs*.

In 2011, Richards ventured into electronic publishing through his own company, Braxiatek. His novel *The Skeleton Clock* was made available later that year in electronic formats only (for the Amazon Kindle and for other ebook readers).

As well as his literary career, Richards has worked as a technical writer, editor, programmer, and user interface designer at IBM, and as an errand boy in a hotel.

Richards is married with two sons, and lives in Warwickshire.

127

THE WHO ADVENTURES

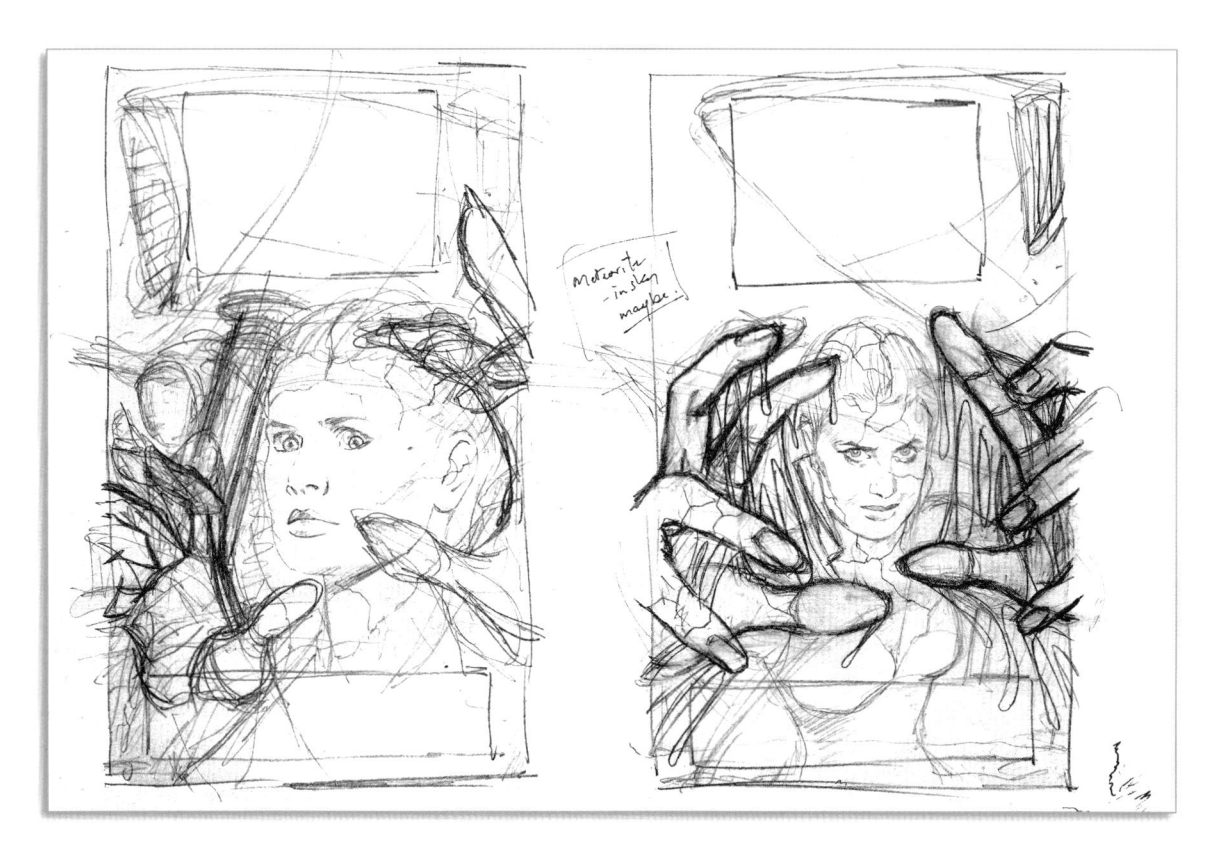

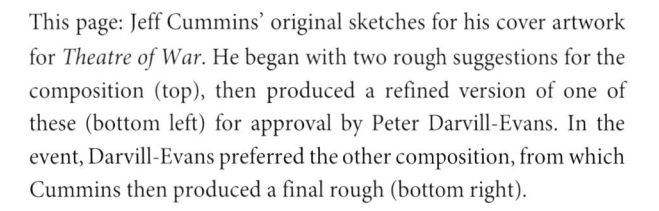

This page: Jeff Cummins' original sketches for his cover artwork for *Theatre of War*. He began with two rough suggestions for the composition (top), then produced a refined version of one of these (bottom left) for approval by Peter Darvill-Evans. In the event, Darvill-Evans preferred the other composition, from which Cummins then produced a final rough (bottom right).

128

STAND-ALONE ADVENTURES

Jeff Cummins' original artwork for the cover of *Theatre of War*.

THE WHO ADVENTURES

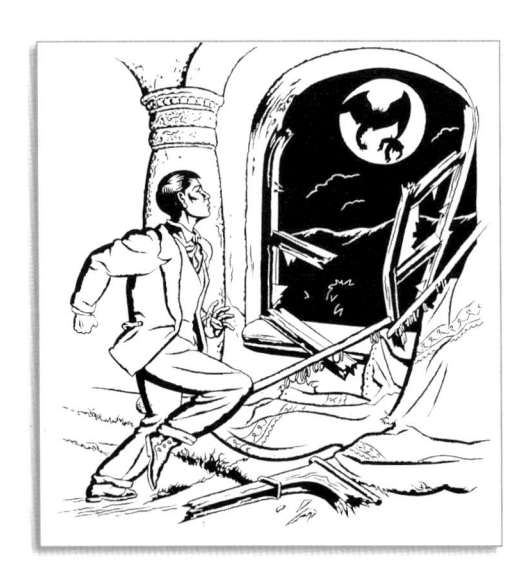

Mike Nicholson's six small internal illustrations for *All-Consuming Fire*.

STAND-ALONE ADVENTURES

MIKE NICHOLSON

Mike Nicholson is a London-based illustrator, storyboard artist and lecturer. He was born and brought up in Westmorland, but undertook his 1980s illustration training at St Martin's School of Art in London's Covent Garden. His illustration career then focused on editorial and publishing – including a book each for Virgin's New Adventures and Missing Adventures ranges.

Moving into a parallel career storyboarding for commercials, TV and film, he later worked with many luminaries of the British comedy scene since the mid-'90s, including Armando Iannucci, Paul Merton, Charlie Higson, Vic Reeves and Bob Mortimore, the League of Gentlemen, Sacha Baron Cohen and Matt Berry. Working on *Randall & Hopkirk (Deceased)* (2000 - 2001) meant that – although he missed David Tennant, who was a guest star in Episode 1, Series 1 – he enjoyed many a chat with Tom Baker between takes and at the lunch van. These were just as entertaining as he would have hoped.

When BBC Wales was powering up to bring *Doctor Who* back to TV in 2005, Nicholson sent in a comprehensive batch of storyboard samples to the new production office, but was told that they didn't plan at that point to use storyboards.

Nicholson says that even had he not been lucky enough to have worked on the Virgin titles written by his long-time pal Andy Lane, the books of that period would still hold a very special place in his heart: their strange, parallel continuation of the TV show expanded and deepened the character of the Doctor that first fascinated him when viewing Patrick Troughton in the role in the 1960s and continues to do so today, a quarter of a century after the last of the Virgin tales was told.

Left: Mike Nicholson's original roughs for three of his six small internal illustrations for *All-Consuming Fire*.

THE WHO ADVENTURES

Mike Nicholson's frontispiece and endpiece illustrations for *All-Consuming Fire*, reproduced alongside the equivalent roughs.

STAND-ALONE ADVENTURES

A colour version of his *All-Consuming Fire* frontispiece that Mike Nicholson submitted to Virgin on spec to see if they might be interested in commissioning a cover painting from him.

Jeff Cummins' original artwork for the cover of *All-Consuming Fire*.

STAND-ALONE ADVENTURES

Above: Phil Bevan's *Doctor Who Magazine* Prelude illustrations for *All-Consuming Fire*. Below left: Jeff Cummins' original rough for the book's cover artwork.

Terrance Dicks' *Blood Harvest* started life as a proposal for a single book containing two separate but linked stories. The Virgin team suggested splitting the stories into two different books. In the event, some of the content of the second story, which Dicks titled *Vampire Planet*, was included within *Blood Harvest*, while the idea of publishing two linked titles was progressed by having Paul Cornell's *Goth Opera*, the debut title in the Missing Adventures range, form a sequel to this.

'*Goth Opera* was the first Missing Adventure,' explains Darvill-Evans, 'and the inspiration for having it be a sequel to *Blood Harvest* was purely commercial. I wanted readers of the New Adventures to read the Missing Adventures as well, so a sequel seemed like the best way to achieve that; and I wanted the first Missing Adventure to be written by one of our star New Adventures authors, so Paul Cornell got the job. I believe Terrance and Paul discussed aspects of the stories together; and indeed they had done something similar before, when

THE WHO ADVENTURES

Terrance had created the character of Hemmings in his New Adventure *Timewyrm: Exodus* for Paul to use in *Timewyrm: Revelation*.'

Before *First Frontier*, David A McIntee had submitted several other ideas to Virgin, including one titled *Dying Time* and another called *Sidhral*, the latter of which he later reworked into *Autumn Mist* for the BBC's *Doctor Who* range. (Several other ideas rejected by Virgin eventually became BBC novels. These included John Peel's *War of the Daleks* and Steve Lyons' *The Witch Hunters*.) In another significant step for the New Adventures, *First Frontier* saw the return of the Doctor's old adversary the Master, now regenerated into a form described by McIntee as resembling actor Basil Rathbone (whose likeness had already been used for Sherlock Holmes – a character he often played on screen – on the cover of *All-Consuming Fire*).

Right: Phil Bevan's two *Doctor Who Magazine* Prelude pieces for *Blood Harvest*.

Below: Bill Donohoe's roughs for his *Blood Harvest* cover.

STAND-ALONE ADVENTURES

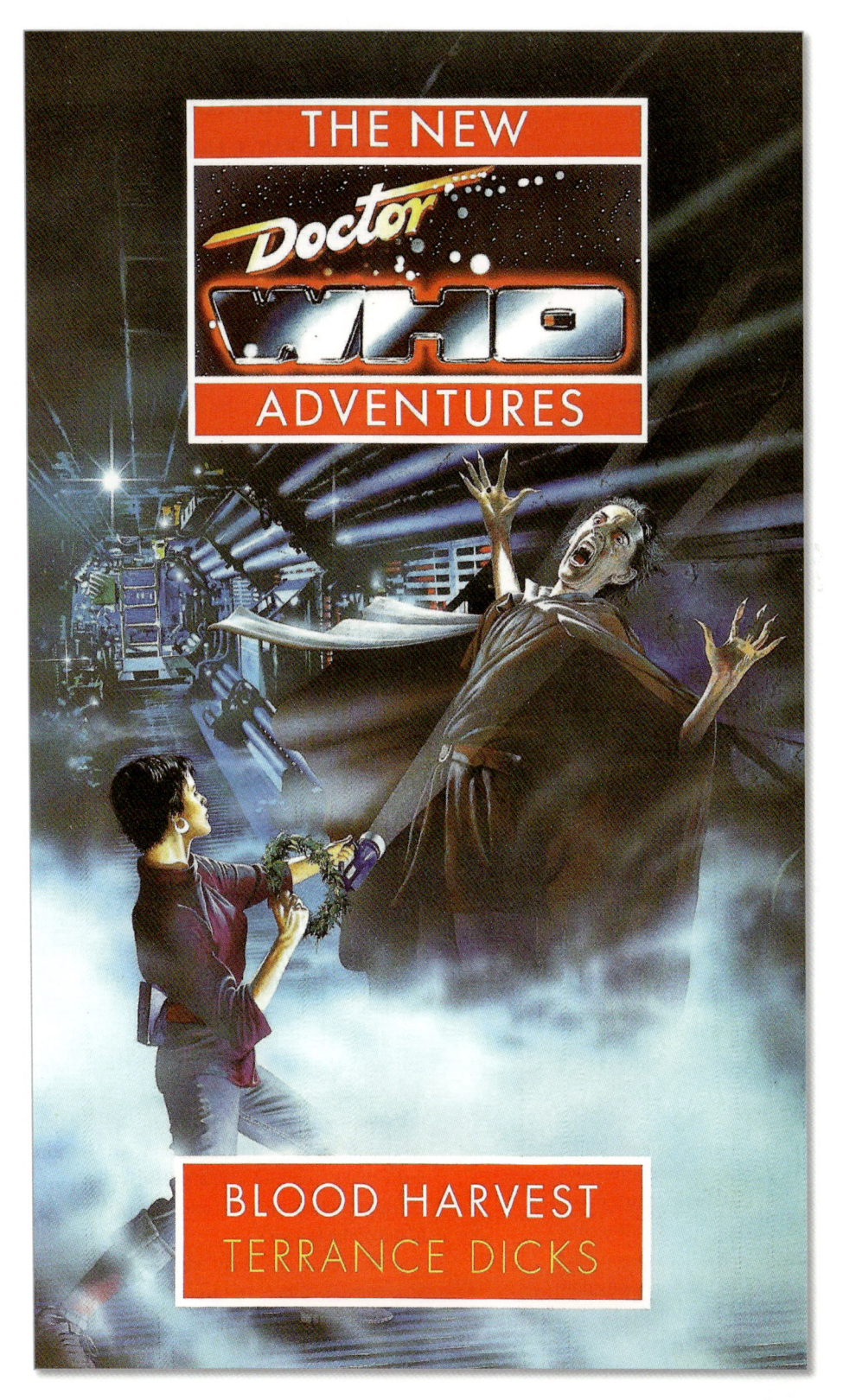

Blood Harvest by Terrance Dicks, with cover by Bill Donohoe, who based the spaceship interior on that of the *Nostromo* from the movie *Alien*. As in a number of other cases, sadly the whereabouts of the original artwork for this cover are currently unknown.

BILL DONOHOE

After leaving Brighton Art College in 1978, Bill Donohoe travelled for a while before settling into work as a full time freelance illustrator. With an agent in London, for many years he undertook a variety of work, the emphasis being primarily on book and video covers. He tackled everything from illustrated books and part-works to reference books, magazines and encyclopaedias. Consequently he was commissioned by most of the major publishers, along with many design groups, advertising agencies and web designers.

Since 1997, for his commercial work Donohoe has moved away from the traditional methods of painting to computer-based methods, using mainly Photoshop and Illustrator programs. He is still active as an illustrator, but away from professional work he is Chairman of Sussex County Arts Club, where he runs a weekly drawing session. He has a wide interest in all forms of art, music and sport, as well as being a struggling blues guitarist. He is married and lives with his wife Carrie. His two sons now both work in the creative digital arts sector in London.

Examples of his work can be seen at www.billdonohoe.com.

BEHIND THE BOOK: *STRANGE ENGLAND*

The plot of Simon Messingham's *Strange England* wasn't originally devised for a *Doctor Who* novel. It started life as a comic strip idea he'd formulated with his friend, the renowned *2000 AD* comic-strip artist Tim Bollard, 'about a Victorian cleric who went around England finding odd animals and plants.' Once Messingham had decided to develop his idea as a New Adventure, however, he aimed 'to do the ultimate *Doctor Who* novel'. He explains:' I wanted a story that would have the Doctor questioning why he does what he does. A story where the very act of his arriving somewhere and expecting an adventure would be the cause of the adventure itself!'

Inspiration came from the stories of noted author and conservationist Robert Aickman, so Messingham created the character Richard Aickland as a form of acknowledgement. In Messingham's view, the novel is about experience and gaining knowledge: 'If a person never experiences any bad things, are they any less a person than someone who has? I'm sure that Charlotte, Garvey and the other characters would have been just fine without the Doctor arriving. However, even they realise that they live in the real world, and have to deal with that. At the other extreme we have Rix, full of challenges and experiences. Too full, and it has turned his mind.'

Messingham makes no secret of his unhappiness with the way the final published book turned out. The problem, as he sees it, lies in the ending, which was not what he'd intended: 'I'd wanted the ultimate anticlimax. Everything is going wrong, people are dying, what can the Doctor do? He realises that he is responsible for the decay, and the only thing he can do is go away and never come back, hoping that things will get better. Great ending!' Virgin, however, refused to countenance this, and so Messingham was instructed to come up with a 'proper' ending, for which he devised the character of a Time Lady sculptor who is an old friend of the Doctor's.

'I would definitely change the ending,' insists Messingham. 'I hate it. Overall, I would like less of the sci-fi stuff and more of the slow-burning "strangeness".'

(From *TSV* Issue 43 – courtesy Paul Scoones.)

Above: Phil Bevan's two *Doctor Who Magazine* Prelude illustrations for Simon Messingham's *Strange England*.

SIMON MESSINGHAM

Simon Messingham, the author of the New Adventure *Strange England* and seven BBC Books *Doctor Who* novels, now lives on the south coast of England, producing films and theatre with his company Button Pressed Productions. His first original, non-tie-in novel, the black comedy *Sirens*, was published in Australia in 2017. At the time of writing, he is currently finishing his first young adult novel, *House Trafalgar*, based on the award-winning short film of the same title released in 2012 by Future Sun Films.

In the 1990s and 2000s, Messingham was one half of the comic duo Kirk & Messingham, who played the London comedy circuit and wrote and performed in the UK Play series *The Dave Saint Show*, starring John Thompson, and the BBC Choice series *Tales of Uplift and Moral Improvement*, starring Rik Mayall.

In the past, Messingham has won the British Fantasy Society Short Story Competition for his story 'Baby' and been a runner-up in the 1994 London Writer's Competition with 'Anderson's Ghost'. His short stories have been published worldwide. He has also written the plays *The Ealing Inheritance* – performed at the Brighton Fringe 2018 – and, in 2020, *The IVF Pistols*, a comedy about men and the humiliation of IVF.

Before being put on hiatus by the lockdown of 2020, Simon was halfway through filming *Disco*, a loose comic adaptation of the film *The Stud*. Meanwhile, to keep working, he wrote and produced a new Button Pressed comic web series, *Liz and Jessie's Undiscovered Country*, filmed in summer 2020 for release in early 2021.

THE WHO ADVENTURES

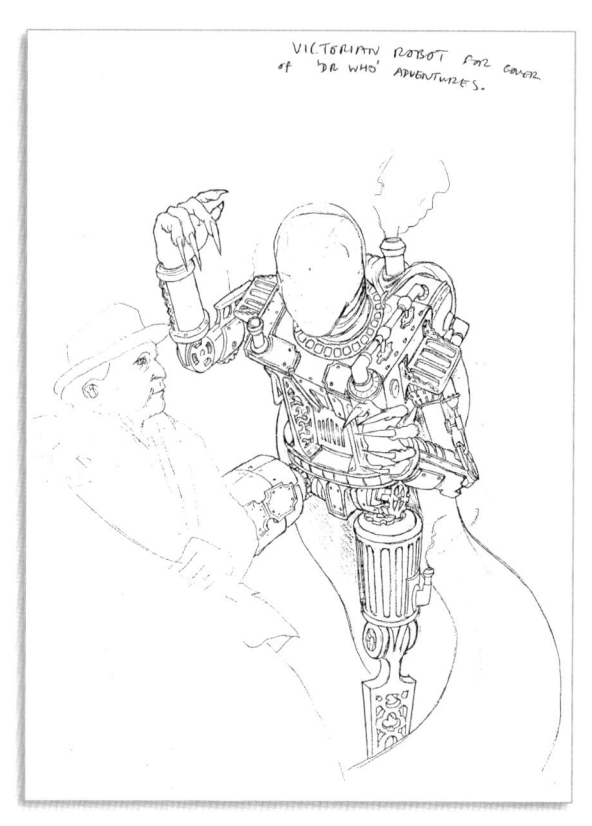

Paul Campbell's original sketches and roughs for the cover of *Strange England*.

STAND-ALONE ADVENTURES

Paul Campbell's original artwork for the cover of *Strange England*.

THE WHO ADVENTURES

Above: two sets of sketches of the Doctor's face submitted by Paul Campbell to Virgin; it was on the basis of these that he gained his New Adventures commissions. Below: further preparatory sketches by Campbell for the cover of *Strange England*.

STAND-ALONE ADVENTURES

BEHIND THE BOOK: *FIRST FRONTIER*

After his first New Adventure, *White Darkness*, David McIntee submitted three or four pure SF proposals for follow-ups, all of which were rejected. His next idea was to write a UFO novel in which the aliens turned out to be 'creatures from a parallel dimension that occasionally slipped into our own, feeding on fear and paranoia. Once, they had been thought of as elves and fairies, but by the '50s, they were seen as aliens in UFOs.' Virgin rejected the 'elves and fairies from another dimension' aspect, since this had already been a plot aspect of *Cat's Cradle: Witch Mark*, but they liked the UFO element.

The first half of the book remains much the same as McIntee originally intended. It was McIntee's idea to include the Master, but at first he'd wanted to make this the last story of the character's original incarnation, as portrayed on TV by actor Roger Delgado. When he was instructed instead to follow on from the 1989 TV story 'Survival', McIntee – with the aid of Gary Russell – managed to persuade Virgin to allow the Master to be regenerated.

The new Master's likeness was based on that of actor Basil Rathbone as he had appeared in the film *The Adventures of Robin Hood*. The personality was a mix of those of the character Karswell from the film *Night of the Demon*, Timothy Dalton's character from *The Rocketeer*, Julian Glover, Ricardo Montalbán and even a little of McIntee himself! The Master's alias, Major Kreer, was an in-joke, since Roger Delgado had played a malevolent hypnotist of that name in an episode of *The Avengers*. It was McIntee's idea to keep the Master's involvement a surprise; Virgin had wanted to put him on the book's cover. 'In a way,' says McIntee, 'the Master is the hero … the Tzun leave the Earth voluntarily, but vow to return. And then the Master destroys them in the same way that the Doctor destroys the Daleks in "Remembrance of the Daleks."'

(From *TSV* Issue 43 – courtesy Paul Scoones.)

One of Phil Bevan's *Doctor Who Magazine* Prelude pieces for *First Frontier*, depicting the second Doctor and companion Jamie.

THE WHO ADVENTURES

Left: author David A McIntee's sketched suggestion for the *First Frontier* cover. Right: Tony Masero's rough for the final version.

FROCKS AND GUNS

The sequence of novels that begins with *First Frontier* was singled out by writer Jonathan Blum as being when a significant change took place in the tone of the New Adventures novels. He described this in July 1996 in a newsgroup posting in response to comments by author John Peel.

'There was a massive change in the direction of the NAs, triggered in large part by two incidents: the rise of Rebecca Levene, who took over editorship ... around the time of *Tragedy Day*; and the declaration by a number of the authors, led by Gareth Roberts, that the NAs needed "less guns and more frocks".

'Gareth was drawing a distinction between the two kinds of writing in the NAs. "Gun" books are those that feature lots of militaristic mayhem, women in spandex combat suits, titillating naughty sex (straight or occasionally lesbian, but never gay male), cardboard superhero-esque angst, and a general sense of self-importance.

'On the other hand, "frock" books are ... well, even now people still haven't quite pinned it down, but generally it's the antithesis of "gun". Lots of emphasis on little personal events. Characters matter. Telling stories about people, not stock SF cardboard cut-outs. When people die, we stick around for the funeral. When people fall in love, we stick around for the wedding. A sense of community. There's a greater willingness to indulge in camp and self-parody. At times it can descend into the trivial and inconsequential, but it doesn't have to – you can deal with huge galaxy-shattering events, but you have to make them mean something to the people involved. Angst is okay, if used sparingly and effectively. The Doctor can agonise about weighty decisions, but he also takes time to go fishing, juggle, and watch the sunset. Remembering the simple joys of real life. A greater emphasis on the things that really matter to all of us ... like baking bread and making love.'

STAND-ALONE ADVENTURES

Tony Masero's original artwork for the cover of *First Frontier*.

THE WHO ADVENTURES

First Frontier was broadly enjoyed by the critics. *DWB*'s John Molyneux described it as 'a traditional action runaround as ... good *Who* frequently is, but with an extra maturity which raises it above the simply banal and superficial.' Andrew Martin in *TV Zone* found it 'captivating ... as someone remarks, it's all a bit like a Bond film, which is probably what makes *First Frontier* such an enjoyable romp.' The latter point was echoed by *Doctor Who Magazine*'s Craig Hinton, who described it as 'a full-blooded homage to those wonderfully kitsch films of the '50s.'

This year's other New Adventures also gained generally positive reviews, including from Martin and Hinton in their respective magazines. One exception was *Strange England*, which Hinton found 'increasingly difficult to sustain my attention ... not a bad book, just mediocre,' while Martin described it more bluntly as 'confusing and irritating'.

Two titles received a somewhat mixed reception. *St Anthony's Fire* was enjoyed by Hinton, who liked the characters and found it 'compellingly written,' although, curiously, he also considered it 'dull'. Martin, meanwhile, commented that it was 'worthwhile and diligent'. *Parasite* managed to divide opinion even more. Anthony Clark,

Top left: in a photo-shoot for her 1996 book *Ace!*, actress Sophie Aldred gets back into character as Ace, in a costume inspired by her New Adventures persona and a pose similar to that on the *First Frontier* cover.

Bottom left: the other of Phil Bevan's *Doctor Who Magazine* Prelude pieces for *First Frontier*.

TONY MASERO

Tony Masero was born in London. His late father, Gino Masero, was a renowned woodcarver, and therefore the young Masero's interest in art was heartily encouraged. He studied Graphic Design at Hornsey College of Art, where a request to transfer to Illustration was arbitrarily dismissed by the headmaster. After graduation in 1963, he found employment as a graphic designer working for a number of advertising agencies around London's vibrant Soho area.

Masero hawked his illustration portfolio around several publishing houses with little success until David Larkin, the art director at Pan Books, gave him some constructive advice that eventually led to Cecil Smith, the art director at the New English Library, commissioning him to provide the covers for a series of their horror novels. Other early work in the 1970s included covers for NEL's top-selling Western series *Edge* and *Adam Steele*.

Throughout the '70s, '80s and '90s, Masero juggled producing book covers with supplying illustrations for advertising. In the mid-1980s, W H Allen's art director Mike Brett commissioned him to produce ten covers for the Target range of *Doctor Who* novelisations. What should have been his final cover for the range, for 'Time and the Rani', went unused in favour of a photographic substitute. He also provided the covers for two of W H Allen's large-format *Doctor Who* hardback specials written by Peter Haining, *The Doctor Who File* (1986) and *The Time-Travellers' Guide* ((1987).

Other work for W H Allen included covers for some titles in their Target Classic range, including *The Adventures of Professor Challenger* (1985), *Allan Quatermain* (1986) and *Ayesha* (1986). Masero returned to *Doctor Who* when he was commissioned to supply the covers for six of Virgin's original novels in the mid-1990s.

These days, although he is retired, Masero still creates book cover artwork and also writes his own successful Western and thriller novels. He divides his time between living in the UK and Portugal and has had solo exhibitions of his art in both countries.

BEHIND THE BOOK: *ST ANTHONY'S FIRE*

After his first novel, *Nightshade*, Mark Gatiss submitted two further proposals to Virgin, both of which were rejected. One of them, *Maniac's Tear*, dealt with Jack the Ripper and was considered too similar to *Birthright*. *St Anthony's Fire* was his third attempt at a follow-up, and was deliberately set away from Earth, since *Nightshade* had been Earth-bound. Gatiss consciously made the alien Betrushians anthropomorphic, both because he sees this as is in keeping with the style of *Doctor Who* and because he felt that if he made the society too alien he might lose his readers. He wanted to capture the gritty crudeness of the First World War, hence the inclusion of machine guns in place of lasers. The 1969 TV story 'The War Games' provided inspiration in terms of pace, changing from initial 'grim-and-grittiness' to 'campness', as Gatiss puts it. 'So I went from the grim warfare on Betrushia to some of the campest performances ever seen in a *Doctor Who* book!' His inspiration for the religious leader was a Bond villain. The anti-religious tone of the novel came from Gatiss's dislike of organised religion: 'It's the source of most of the world's worries, and the hypocrisy of some faiths makes me very angry.' The book was originally to have concluded differently: Gatiss wanted a 'really downbeat ending. The Doctor realised that after the organism had originally spent itself, it became part of the planet – including the Betrushians. So, to prevent it from escaping, they had to sacrifice themselves.'

(From *TSV* Issue 43 – courtesy Paul Scoones.)

THE WHO ADVENTURES

Paul Campbell's original artwork for the cover of *St Anthony's Fire*.

writing in *Dreamwatch*, disliked it. 'I hated this book because it's badly written … If you're the sort of person who likes bland, two-dimensional characters served up in a truly ludicrous plot with pretensions of epic grandeur and with only a pinch of mystic gibberish for flavouring, then this is the book for you.' Martin, on the other hand, found it 'all very impressive, but there is a feeling that it is not how well it is done that is remarkable, but that it is done at all. There is a sense of doom about the book, a sense of the ultimate hopelessness of mortality, and the inconclusive ending serves to reinforce the notion that nothing in life is ever as over as you'd like to think it is…' Finally, Hinton described it, more succinctly, as 'a first rate science fiction novel.'

The covers for the 1994 books were provided by a number of different artists, some of them new to the range: Peter Elson (*Legacy*), Jeff Cummins (*Tragedy Day*, *Theatre of War*, *All-Consuming Fire*), Bill Donohoe (*Blood Harvest*), Tony Masero (*First Frontier*), Paul Campbell (*Strange England*, *St Anthony's Fire*, *Parasite*) and Kevin Jenkins (*Falls the Shadow*). Peter Elson and Kevin Jenkins were commissioned via the Sarah Brown Agency. Jenkins was one of the first artists to use computer imaging, and his other work included covers for Harry Turtledove's *World War* books and Tom Arden's *Orokon* series. Paul Campbell initially submitted several black-and-white images of Sylvester McCoy's face to Virgin

Below: Paul Campbell's original rough for the cover artwork for *St Anthony's Fire*, as faxed to Rebecca Levene at Virgin.

Right: Phil Bevan's two *Doctor Who Magazine* Prelude pieces for this novel.

THE WHO ADVENTURES

(see page 142); Peter Darvill-Evans was impressed by these, and asked him to tackle *Strange England*. Campbell then went on to contribute extensively to the range, and also provided covers for several of the Missing Adventures – the books featuring stories of the Doctor's earlier incarnations.

Aside from the ongoing schedule of New Adventures, 1994 also saw the first few Missing Adventures appear, and the launch of a series of annual *Doctor Who* short story collections with the umbrella title *Decalog*, devised and edited initially by Mark Stammers and Stephen James Walker, plus a range of novelisations, written variously by Jim Mortimore, Gareth Roberts and Liz Holliday, of the ITV crime drama series *Cracker*. These all meant further success for Virgin, but allowed no let-up in the workload of Darvill-Evans and his team.

Right: Phil Bevan's two *Doctor Who Magazine* Prelude illustrations for *Falls the Shadow*.

KEVIN JENKINS

Kevin Jenkins began his career working on book jackets and games art. He painted covers for Stephen Donaldson novels and Fabled Lands game-books, and created the first iconic *Worms* game art. He then progressed to visual effects work on the BBC's *Walking With Dinosaurs* series before continuing in film design. As art director and lead concept artist, Jenkins led a design unit onto over 50 visual development projects, covering a huge range of work including the zombie waves of *World War Z*, the intricate sets for *Zero Dark Thirty*, *Edge of Tomorrow* and the environments of Marvel Studios' *Thor 2*, *Guardians of the Galaxy* and *Avengers: Age of Ultron*.

Jenkins joined Lucasfilm to work on the *Star Wars* sequel trilogy, finishing the final film, *The Rise of Skywalker*, as production designer. His most recent project at the time of writing is *Jurassic World: Dominion*, again as production designer.

STAND-ALONE ADVENTURES

BEHIND THE BOOK: *FALLS THE SHADOW*

Daniel O'Mahony first had the idea for the plot of *Falls the Shadow* back in 1989, when through the fan network he heard some advance rumours about the TV story 'Ghost Light'. By piecing together all these rumours, he wrote a story that turned out, in the end, to be not at all like 'Ghost Light'. His original outline was called *Freakshow*, and it went through many changes, including at one point the removal of the Doctor, before O'Mahony finally submitted it to Virgin in July 1992. The novel's unusual title is a quote from T S Eliot's poem 'The Hollow Men': 'Between the idea and the reality, between the motion and the act, falls the shadow.' However, O'Mahony found this line in a book of quotations, and it wasn't until he was redrafting the book that he actually read the poem itself, and subsequently added more T S Eliot references. Virgin's standard requirement for author submissions was a synopsis and a sample chapter, but O'Mahony wrote the whole book and sent it in to them in an attempt to get them to accept it. Virgin did agree to publish it – provided he made some cuts, as it was a hundred pages over their maximum length, and also was considered too violent and gory. O'Mahony was instructed to rewrite Bernice's part, since he hadn't known much about her to begin with, and in addition to rewrite the ending. He feels the ending, in particular, was improved in the process: 'It ties up the loose ends, and the last two chapters are thematically better.' He does however regret that the loss of the hundred pages of material included an insight into the motivations of the character Sandra, who he feels consequently doesn't come comes very well.

The beings known as Tanith and Gabriel are, as the cover artwork suggests, based on the characters Sapphire and Steel from the classic ITV telefantasy series of the same title. O'Mahony says however that the pair changed as he wrote the book, becoming very unlike that original inspiration, and he is therefore disappointed that the cover is so suggestive of *Sapphire & Steel*.

(From *TSV* Issue 43 – courtesy Paul Scoones.)

DANIEL O'MAHONY

Daniel O'Mahony was born in Croydon, Surrey on 24 July 1973. The eldest of five children, he grew up in suburban London, the Republic of Ireland and the New Forest. He harboured ambitions to write from a very early age. His first professional publications were for Virgin's *Doctor Who* ranges: *Falls the Shadow* (1994) and *The Man in the Velvet Mask* (1996). For Telos he wrote the *Doctor Who* novella *The Cabinet of Light* (2003) and the original novel *Force Majeure* (2007). He also contributed *Newton's Sleep* (2008) to Random Static's Faction Paradox novels series. He lives in Hampshire, where he works for a wildlife charity while continuing to write.

MORE TITLE TATTLE

The chapter titles in *Falls the Shadow* all reference film, TV or song titles: including *Apocalypse Now*, *Edge of Darkness*, Led Zeppelin's 'Stairway to Heaven', *Virtual Murder*, *The Masque of the Red Death*, Philip K Dick's *The Man In The High Castle*, J G Ballard's *The Atrocity Exhibition* and 'Hark the Herald Angels Sing'.

Kevin Jenkins' original artwork for the cover of *Falls the Shadow*.

STAND-ALONE ADVENTURES

Left: Phil Bevan's striking illustration for the *Doctor Who Magazine* Prelude on *Parasite* – unusually, the only one he was asked to produce for this particular novel; the Prelude ran to just one page in this instance, rather than the standard double-page spread.

QUOTE, UNQUOTE

The Doctor: 'I have been to the Eye of Orion, have been caught in the clutches of the black hole of Tartarus, been hunted through the universe by the Daleks, and played backgammon with Kublai Khan. And you say I don't know what I'm talking about? Have you ever seen the skies above Metebelis Three, tried the experiential grid on Argolis, or watched the space yachts of the Eternals race against the stars? Of course you haven't.'

Theatre of War

BEHIND THE BOOK: *PARASITE*

Jim Mortimore first came up with the idea for *Parasite* before writing his debut New Adventure, *Blood Heat*. At that time, it was envisioned as a comic strip. The idea was salvaged for his next proposal, which was an historical adventure set in Alexandria. Mortimore then subdivided the concepts into two separate stories, one of which became the short story 'The Book of Shadows', published in the first *Decalog*, and the other of which became *Parasite*.

Originally the book did not have a villain, but Virgin asked Mortimore to include one. The plot underwent many changes in the process of getting accepted, and Mortimore was far from satisfied with the end result. He also disliked the cover, which he felt does not reflect what he'd envisioned.

The book's prologue had originally been meant to form the *Doctor Who Magazine* Prelude piece – consequently Mortimore had to come up with something different for the latter. In the course of writing the novel, he experimented with adopting the styles of various other authors, including those of Arthur C Clarke and *Cracker* scriptwriter Jimmy McGovern. He also had to take time out to novelise the first *Cracker* story for Virgin – a task he enjoyed far more than his work on *Parasite*.

Mortimore says that, given the chance, he'd 'remove the villain and rewrite the ending a little, setting up a tiny part of the Artifact's life-cycle so that the Doctor could resolve the problem with Ace in a way that was more internally consistent.'

(From *TSV* Issue 43 – courtesy Paul Scoones.)

Paul Campbell's original artwork for the cover of *Parasite*.

9: THE END OF ACE

The next year, 1995, saw the first significant change to the New Adventures since Ace had matured and Bernice joined. Ace was to leave.

'I think I wanted rid of Ace more than Peter did,' muses Rebecca Levene. 'We were both a bit tired of her. The intention had been for Ace to get rid of all her teenage angst by leaving for a period, and then Peter brought her back in *Deceit* as an older and wiser person. However, what ended up happening was that she had more angst than ever and became a very dull character. I never thought she worked when she came back. I was never happy with her. We did give notes to the writers not to emphasise the angst, but somehow it never sank in. She became even more one-dimensional, which was the opposite of what we wanted. Paul Cornell had created a brilliant, rounded character in Bernice, and the other writers had picked her up and run with her, and Ace suffered by comparison. I couldn't bring myself to care about her; I had cared about her in the original books and the series, and we had lost that. Also, the more characters you have, the more cluttered the story becomes and the less freedom you have, so that was another benefit of losing Ace. I think we might have had a meeting with the authors about getting rid of her, and Kate Orman, I think, suggested that she'd like to write her out. And as we'd loved *The Left-Handed Hummingbird*, which was a very character-led book, we thought that would be a good idea. Kate came up with a nice setting, and she just went for it.'

Ace's swansong thus came in Orman's *Set Piece*, published in February 1995. Orman had visited England in the latter half of 1993 and

> ### AMERICAN ADVENTURES
>
> On 6 January 1995, Virgin Publishing issued a press release about the *Doctor Who* novels' availability in North America:
>
> 'For several months *Doctor Who* fans in the USA have had difficulties obtaining *Doctor Who* books. *All-Consuming Fire*, published in Britain in June 1994, was the last New Adventure on sale in the USA; American fans were deprived of the launch of the Missing Adventures, and of new non-fiction titles such as *The Seventies* and *The Handbook: The First Doctor*.
>
> 'This interruption of normal service came about because Virgin Publishing was in the throes of changing its system of distribution in the USA. We apologise to everyone who has been disappointed or frustrated in trying to obtain *Doctor Who* books.
>
> 'Now for the good news.
>
> 'First, the next five New Adventures – *Blood Harvest*, *Strange England*, *First Frontier*, *St Anthony's Fire* and *Falls the Shadow* – were shipped to the USA last year and have now been distributed. This has been done under the old system, with Carol Publishing acting as distributor in the USA.
>
> 'Second, from 1 January 1995, *Doctor Who* books will be handled by London Bridge, a new company specialising in the distribution of selected British books in the USA. With a warehouse in New York State and teams of trade salespeople operating in every State, including Hawaii and Alaska, the availability of *Doctor Who* books should be better than ever before. Retailers in every corner of the United States can now order *Doctor Who* books easily and reliably.
>
> 'The first books distributed by London Bridge will be available in American shops in March …
>
> 'By June 1995 the Missing Adventures will have "caught up" with the New Adventures and from then on one of each series will be released each month, matching the UK publishing schedule but always a couple of months behind.'

THE WHO ADVENTURES

met up with Darvill-Evans and Levene, and this indirectly led to her being commissioned to write the character out. Her initial, eleven-page outline was entitled *Faust Forward*. Levene prepared two pages of notes on this, suggesting how it might be improved. On one thing Levene was determined: 'Ace needs to go out with a bang,' she wrote. After *Set Piece* was suggested as a title, the book was also known as *Butterfly Wings* for a time, before reverting to *Set Piece* around February 1994.

The books published in 1995 were: Andrew Cartmel's *Warlock*, originally titled *Warlord*; Kate Orman's *Set Piece*, which featured an afterword by Ace actress Sophie Aldred; Daniel Blythe's *Infinite Requiem*; David A McIntee's *Sanctuary*; Paul Cornell's *Human Nature*, developed from a plot by Cornell and Orman; Andy Lane's *Original Sin*, with internal illustrations by Tony Masero; Dave Stone's *Sky Pirates!*, originally titled *The Eyes of the Schirron*, with internal illustrations by Roger Langridge; Gareth Roberts' *Zamper*; Paul Leonard's *Toy Soldiers*, originally titled *Toy Solstice*; Steve Lyons' *Head Games*; Ben Aaronovitch's *The Also People*, originally titled *That Which Does Not Kill Us*; and Terrance Dicks' *Shakedown*. The latter, a story involving the Doctor's old enemies the Sontarans, was adapted from a screenplay written by Dicks for a fan video drama of the same title made in 1994 by the independent production company Dreamwatch Media, and the video's associate and executive producers, Jason Haigh-Ellery and Gary Leigh,

Below left: Phil Bevan's two *Doctor Who Magazine* Prelude illustrations for *Warlock*. Below right: Tony Masero's original rough for the cover of this novel, as faxed to Virgin.

THE END OF ACE

Tony Masero's original artwork for the cover of *Warlock*.

THE WHO ADVENTURES

Set Piece, with cover art by Tony Masero.

Above left: Tony Masero's original rough for the cover of *Set Piece*, as faxed to Virgin. Right: Phil Bevan's *Doctor Who Magazine* Prelude illustrations for this novel.

provided a foreword. The book also included in the middle an eight-page black-and-white section of photos from the production, and at the back an advertisement for the video. The main change made by Dicks in adapting and expanding the script into the novel was to incorporate the Doctor, who had not appeared at all in the original.

The majority of this year's books were written by authors who had contributed to the range before. Of the newcomers, Dave Stone had been writing *Judge Dredd* novels for Virgin and so was already known to the editorial team, while Paul Leonard was a writing friend of Andy Lane's. 'We'd found a core of good authors,' explains Levene, 'and in any fan group there's going to be only so many who can actually write novels – I think we'd pretty much found them all.' Despite this, in June 1995 Darvill-Evans, Levene and Bodle reissued their Writers' Guidelines, reducing it to 35 pages, simplifying the series background and including a new section on the Missing Adventures. The list of titles recommended as touchstones for anyone wanting to contribute to the range now read: *Timewyrm: Exodus*; *Transit*; *First Frontier* ('a fine demonstration of how to use an old enemy'); *Warlock* ('a good sci-fi story outside the traditional *Who* style'); *Set Piece* ('Kate's compelling writing style is a good example to everyone'); *Human Nature* (an

THE WHO ADVENTURES

excellent character-led story that manages to stretch the boundaries of the genre'); and *Original Sin* ('a good, solid sci-fi adventure').

'To be honest,' says Levene, 'once the Missing Adventures started, there were so many books we had to commission each month that it was a struggle sometimes to find anything that was suitable. We didn't have enough time. The plates were constantly spinning and we didn't have time to step back and think what design of plate we wanted; just any plate would do, as long as it would spin. This is why there were no predetermined story arcs in that

Above: one of Phil Bevan's *Doctor Who Magazine* Prelude illustrations for Daniel Blythe's *Infinite Requiem*.

Below: Barry Jones' original rough for the cover of Blythe's novel, as faxed to Rebecca Levene at Virgin with his handwritten notes around the margin.

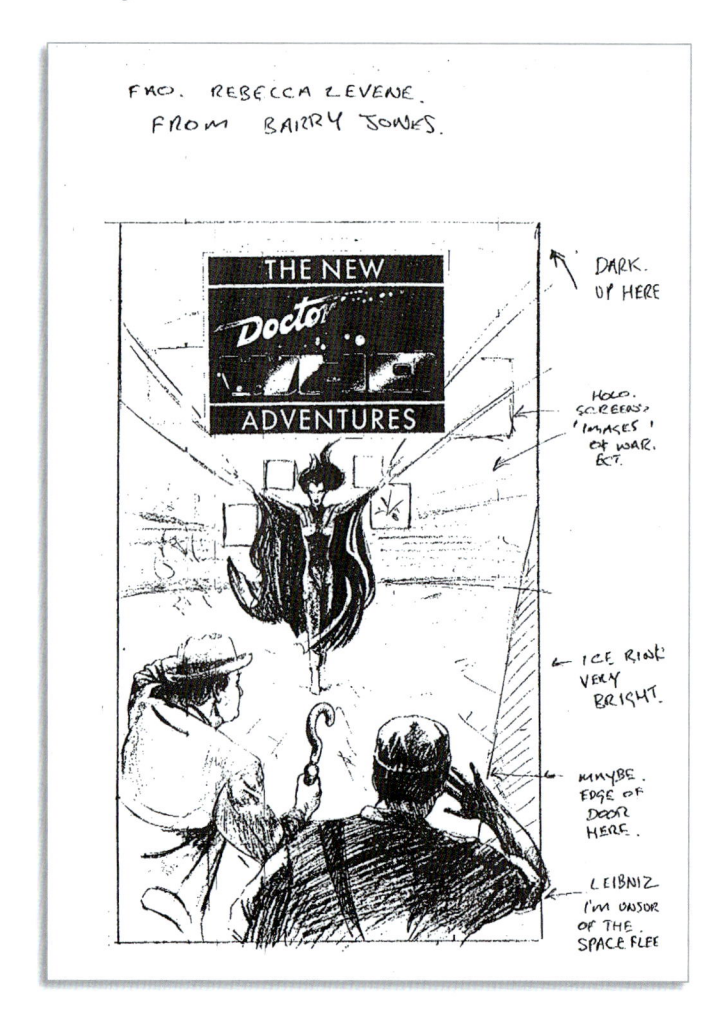

BARRY JONES

Barry Jones studied at the Reading College of Art and Design from 1977 to 1980. He worked on *Doctor Who* behind the scenes from 2006 to 2010, managing the fabrication of props. Then in 2010 he became a lead modeller on Tim Burton's *Frankenweenie* movie, before moving on to three seasons of the Starz television show *Da Vinci's Demons* (2012-2014). In 2018 he started working at Bad Wolf Productions, on projects including the Wes Anderson film *Isle of Dogs* (2018) and, for the BBC, *His Dark Materials* (2020).

Infinite Requiem, with cover art by Barry Jones.

THE WHO ADVENTURES

CYBERTECH

In February 1994, musicians Adrian Pack and Michael Fillis, who the previous year had composed the title music for the charity *Doctor Who* skit 'Dimensions in Time', released through Jump Cut Records a CD called *Cybertech* (see below left) featuring music inspired by *Doctor Who*. In July 1995 they followed this up with a second Cybertech album, *Pharos* (see below right), including tracks titled after and inspired by the New Adventures novels *Time's Crucible*, *First Frontier*, *Iceberg*, *Nightshade* and *Legacy*. The tracks also included various vocal contributions from *Doctor Who* stars Jon Pertwee, Sylvester McCoy, Caroline John and Sophie Aldred and author Mark Gatiss.

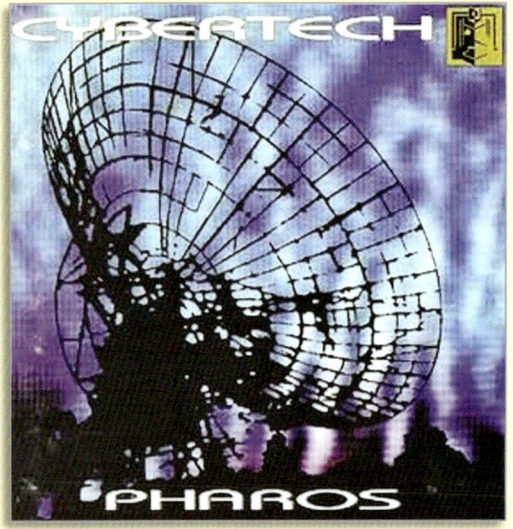

Below: the second of Phil Bevan's two *Doctor Who Magazine* Prelude illustrations for *Infinite Requiem*.

period. It was just too hard to make that work.

'When we did have arcs, it was difficult not to be too prescriptive with the authors. We didn't want to keep giving them ideas, otherwise we might as well have been writing the books ourselves. We wanted them to come to us with ideas, and then once they had the idea, we didn't want to have to twist it too much to make it fit a series. In fact, when the arcs did come along, it tended to be because we'd received a cluster of ideas that could be fitted

THE END OF ACE

neatly together; then we'd tweak them a bit to make them fit.'

Ace having been written out partly because it was felt that the TARDIS was a little too crowded, it was perhaps something of a surprise that Andy Lane's novel *Original Sin* introduced two new characters to travel with the Doctor and Bernice.

'It wasn't our initial intention to introduce two characters,' protests Rebecca Levene. 'In the first version of *Original Sin* there was an older tramp character who was going to be the new companion. Andy and I had talked about it and thought it would be a good idea to have a character who was actually fatherly toward the Doctor, who seemed older than him.'

This character was 'Old Tom', a tramp whose real name was Thomas Acheson. As with Tir Ram, Lane produced a character outline for this proposed new regular; this suggested that writers might like to seek out George Orwell's *Down and Out in Paris and London* for insight into the day-to-day realities of living on the streets, and Samuel Beckett's *Waiting for Godot* for the archetypal aspects of being a tramp. 'If you really want to imagine an actor playing the part,' wrote Lane, 'look for someone with a lined, lived-in face who isn't as old as they look. John Hurt, for instance, or Don Henderson. It's the weather-seasoned Navaho look we want to aim for.'

In the book *Doctor Who: Companions*, Lane recalled that the idea had first been mooted at a party thrown in 1993 for the various contributors

Below: one of Phil Bevan's *Doctor Who Magazine* Prelude illustrations for David A McIntee's *Sanctuary*.

THE WHO ADVENTURES

Peter Elson's original cover artwork for *Sanctuary*.

THE END OF ACE

to the *Doctor Who* books. 'I was pushing very hard for a change in the way the people in the TARDIS related to each other,' he explained. 'What I wanted was an elderly companion, someone who looked a lot older than the Doctor and who could treat the Doctor as a son, much to the Doctor's disgust. I proposed a 70-year-old tramp character called Old Tom, whose brain was half-fried from various experiences in his past and an awful lot of drink, but who had some deep, dark, terrible secret. In fact, the secret that I hadn't actually told Virgin was that he was Bernice's dad.'

Unfortunately, Old Tom was not to be. 'When I got the first draft of *Original Sin*,' explains Levene, 'Roz and Chris were infinitely more fun to be with than Tom, and I suggested we picked them up instead.'

'I never really wanted Old Tom,' admits Peter Darvill-Evans. 'I just didn't want an old man as a companion. You've already got a senior male in the TARDIS – the Doctor – and how would our readership empathise with an old tramp, especially one with a drink problem? He was a very unsympathetic character. When we saw Roz and Chris developing, I was all for using them instead. Anything but the tramp!'

Roslyn Forrester and Chris Cwej (properly pronounced 'Shvay', though he generally goes by 'Kwedge' to avoid having to keep correcting people) were devised as two Adjudicators from Earth's future – law-enforcers loosely related to the one impersonated by the Master in the 1971 TV story 'Colony in Space'. 'They had started as minor characters,' said Lane, 'but I had grown to like them more and more as I was writing the book ... I found them to be a strange mix between Han Solo and the Wookiee Chewbacca from the *Star Wars* films, and also characters from the television series *NYPD Blue*. This made it a lot easier to write distinctive dialogue for two very different characters.'

'A lot of what Roz turned into was due to *The Also People*, where Ben fleshed her out a lot,' comments Levene. 'He was very interested in her. Ben's wife is

Right: the second of Phil Bevan's two *Doctor Who Magazine* Prelude illustrations for *Sanctuary*.

ANDY BODLE

His editorial assistant job at Virgin was Andy Bodle's first full-time post after he completed his French degree at Oxford University. He went on to a career in journalism, working mostly as an editor at the *Guardian*, but with stints on a number of publications. As well as the *Guardian*, he has written numerous articles and features for *The Times*, the *Daily Mail* and several magazines and websites, as well as three episodes of the US animated series *Slacker Cats*. He still holds out hope of having his own hit sitcom made. His only contribution to the *Doctor Who* canon (to date) has been a story, 'The Tunnels To Heaven', in the *Bernice Summerfield: Missing Adventures* collection, edited by Rebecca Levene and published in November 2007 by Big Finish.

THE WHO ADVENTURES

African and he also does a lot of research. As I recall, Andy had almost arbitrarily given Roz a background of a particular country or tribe in Africa, and Ben then did a huge amount of research into it and got it all right. The TARDIS was a little overcrowded with the two of them, Bernice and the Doctor, but I felt they worked. They added some humour, which is always important, and also they had a relationship between themselves – a slightly soapy aspect of will-they-won't-they, which was fun.'

The stand-out books for the critics in 1995 included *Warlock*, about which *Doctor Who Magazine*'s Craig Hinton enthused: 'Against a powerful plot, Andrew has let loose a cast of characters that demand sympathy, loathing, hatred and pity; there isn't a single emotion that he doesn't wring out of the reader during the course of the book. *Warlock* is nasty. *Warlock* is unpleasant. *Warlock* is sick. And *Warlock* is a triumph for Andrew Cartmel'; *Set Piece* was hailed by Charles Packer in *Dreamwatch* as 'A cut above usual *Who* fare,' while Hinton proclaimed it to be 'a masterpiece'. In *TV Zone*, however, Andrew Martin took it to task for overambition: 'Kate Orman … gives us user-

Phil Bevan's *Doctor Who Magazine* Prelude illustrations for *Human Nature* – the last novel for which the magazine ran this feature. For the seated figure, Bevan used as reference the likeness of actor Simon Callow.

166

THE END OF ACE

Bill Donohoe's original artwork for the cover of *Human Nature*.

THE WHO ADVENTURES

Tony Masero's original cover artwork for *Original Sin*.

THE END OF ACE

Left: Tony Masero's rough for the cover of *Original Sin*. Note that, unlike in the final version, the Doctor is wearing his TV outfit here.

Above: a concept sketch produced by Masero for the visual depiction of new companions Chris Cwej and Roz Forrester.

friendly text, but has the usual problem that if a story is action-driven – as adventures must surely be – it can be hard to have characters with lives of their own who will consent to do what the plot requires, rather than cardboard ciphers, who just get on with it and don't quibble with the author.'

Human Nature received perhaps the highest praise. 'Very nearly unputdownable,' said Martin, while Hinton claimed it was 'definitely Paul Cornell's finest *Doctor Who* book, and if it's his last, it's a shame. I'd go so far as to say that it's the finest *Doctor Who* book to date.'

The Also People was described by Charles Packer in *Dreamwatch* as 'an enjoyable, adult stab at *Who*', a feeling echoed by Hinton, now writing in *TV Zone*: 'a stunning piece of fiction … offbeat but entertaining, and reads like the illegitimate offspring of Douglas Adams and Isaac Asimov – madcap space opera'. *Doctor Who Magazine*'s new reviewer David Owen, however, thought he had spotted a different influence: 'It is in all but name an Iain M Banks novel … a glowing eulogy to Banks' epic (and wonderful) Culture novels.'

LAST ORDERS

In a letter accompanying his second draft of the outline for *Human Nature*, author Paul Cornell requested that, if and when the book was put on the schedules, Virgin emphasise that this would be his last New Adventure. In the event, it wasn't: *Happy Endings* followed it a year later.

THE WHO ADVENTURES

Tony Masero's two internal illustrations for *Original Sin*, shown alongside the equivalent roughs as faxed to Virgin.

THE END OF ACE

DAVE STONE

Dave Stone was born on 12 June 1964. *Sky Pirates!* was his first original *Doctor Who* novel, but he went on to complete eight others – six for Virgin and two for BBC Books. He also wrote the *Doctor Who* novella *Citadel of Dreams* for Telos and three novels and two audio dramas for Big Finish's *Bernice Summerfield* ranges. In addition, he has authored a number of *Judge Dredd* tie-in novels and contributed extensively to *2000 AD* and the *Judge Dredd Megazine*; series he has written for these publications include *Soul Sisters*, a joint creation with fellow Virgin books author David Bishop and the artist Shaky Kane; *Armitage*, his take on *Inspector Morse*, but set in a future London; and the ongoing *Judge Hershey*.

ROGER LANGRIDGE

Roger Langridge – who drew four internal illustrations for Dave Stone's *Sky Pirates!* – was born in 1967 in New Zealand, where he grew up wanting to become a professional cartoonist. In a country without a comics industry, this aspiration proved difficult to achieve, so in 1990 he bought a ticket to London and, with the exception of a short gap in the 1990s, has lived and worked there ever since.

An incomplete list of his credits over a 30-year career includes work on *Doctor Who Magazine*, *Popeye*, *Mandrake the Magician*, *Betty Boop*, *John Carter of Mars*, *The Muppet Show Comic Book*, *Bill and Ted are Doomed*, *Thor the Mighty Avenger*, *The Goon*, *Batman: Legends of the Dark Knight*, *Horrible Histories Magazine*, *Rocky and Bullwinkle*, *The Rocketeer*, and various things for anthologies such as *Heavy Metal*, *Dark Horse Presents*, *Deadline Magazine*, *The Judge Dredd Megazine* and *2000 AD*. He has also worked on numerous projects of his own, most notably his critically-acclaimed comic book *Fred the Clown* and the Eisner Award-winning, Lewis Carroll-inspired adventure *Snarked!*. Other work has included *The Baker Street Peculiars*, *Abigail and the Snowman* and an adaptation of Jim Henson's unmade TV project from the 1960s, *The Musical Monsters of Turkey Hollow*, which won a Harvey Award.

Langridge currently lives in London with his wife Sylvie and their two children.

THE WHO ADVENTURES

Pictured on this page are three of the four black-and-white internal illustrations that artist Roger Langridge produced for Dave Stone's novel *Sky Pirates!*. These all reflect the novel's comedic tone. The one at top right takes the form of a mock front cover for a fictional comic book, titled *The 45 Second Piglet*, with a logo similar to that of the famous US company DC. The one to the left was used a total of six times in the published book, at breaks between the different parts of the text, characterised by Stone as 'Cantos'.

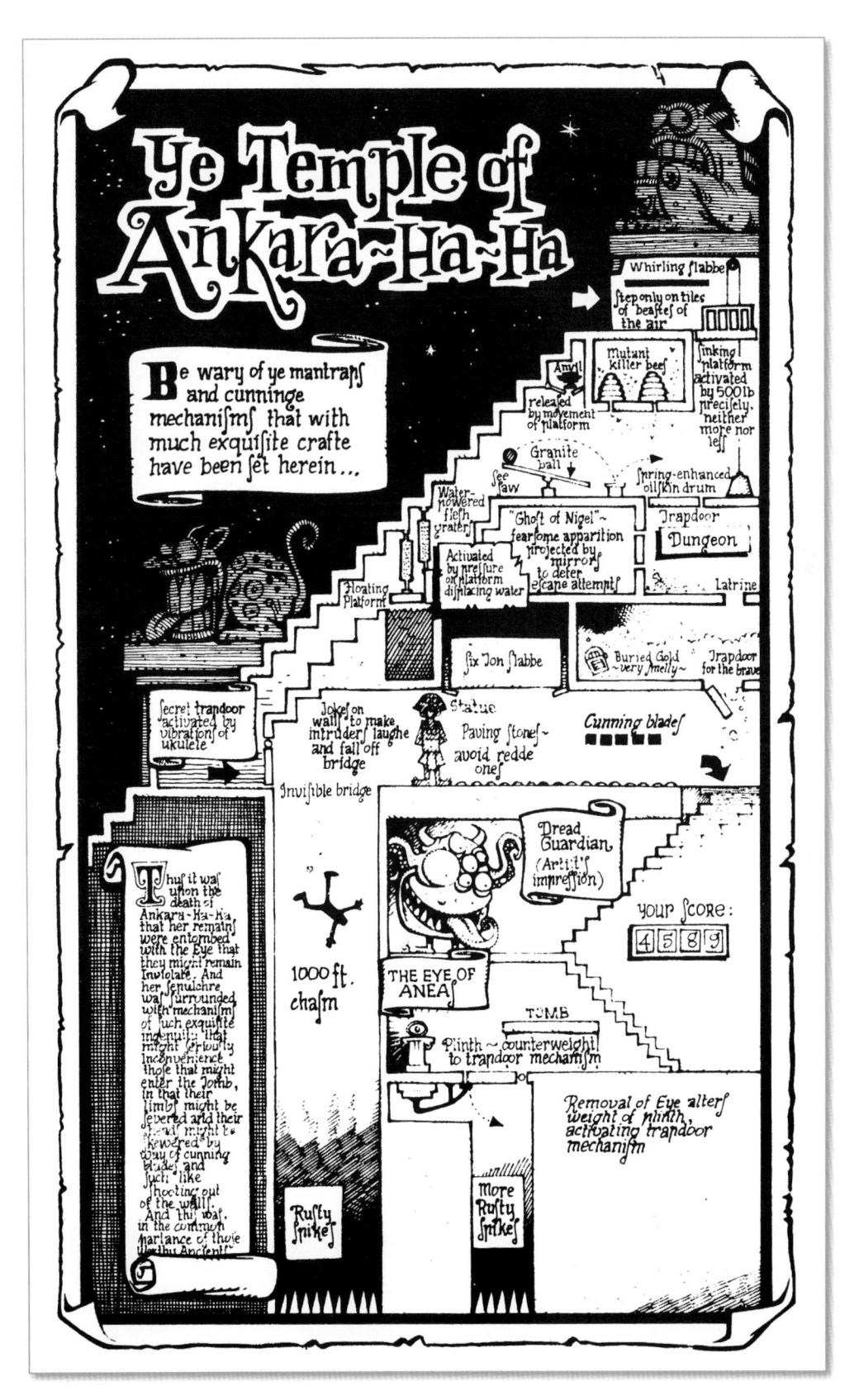

The fourth of Roger Langridge's internal illustrations for *Sky Pirates!*.

THE WHO ADVENTURES

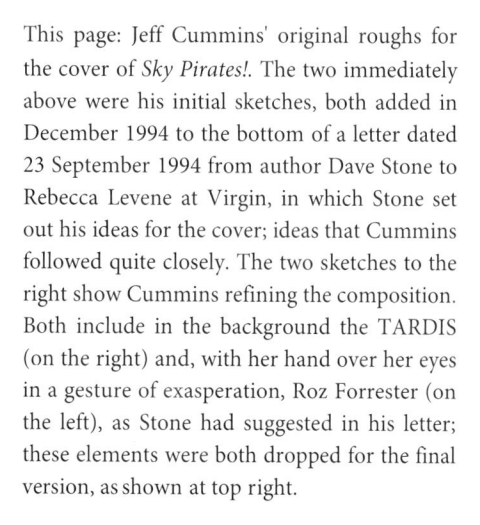

This page: Jeff Cummins' original roughs for the cover of *Sky Pirates!*. The two immediately above were his initial sketches, both added in December 1994 to the bottom of a letter dated 23 September 1994 from author Dave Stone to Rebecca Levene at Virgin, in which Stone set out his ideas for the cover; ideas that Cummins followed quite closely. The two sketches to the right show Cummins refining the composition. Both include in the background the TARDIS (on the right) and, with her hand over her eyes in a gesture of exasperation, Roz Forrester (on the left), as Stone had suggested in his letter; these elements were both dropped for the final version, as shown at top right.

THE END OF ACE

Jeff Cummins' original cover artwork for *Sky Pirates!*.

175

Tony Masero's original cover artwork for *Zamper*.

THE END OF ACE

Looking back at the New Adventures published in 1995, Rebecca Levene is quietly pleased with the output. 'If there was anything I tried to bring to the books, it was a more human thing. I've always liked fantasy more than science fiction, though generally I don't read that much of either. I think fantasy is more about people – I can't finish William Gibson's books because I can't relate to the people in them. If anything, that was what I was trying to do. I also think that the humour appealed to me more than it did to Peter. Something like *Sky Pirates!* really made me laugh like a drain, and so I wanted it in there.'

Peter Darvill-Evans is actually in complete agreement. 'I loved *Sky Pirates!* too,' he protests. 'Bex wasn't the only one in fits of laughter over it.'

In the space of one year, Ace had left, the TARDIS had gained a feline occupant in the shape of Wolsey, a cat introduced by Paul Cornell in *Human Nature*, two new companions had joined, two others had been mooted but hadn't quite made it, and Virgin's annual output of *Doctor Who* novels had doubled from 12 to 24 with the addition of the Missing Adventures.

'Those three years – 1993 to 1995 – were really the heyday of Virgin Publishing's fiction department,' smiles Darvill-Evans. 'There were no clouds on the horizon, there was lots of enthusiasm, the books were selling really well, and we had won some major industry awards, for our work on the Black Lace titles especially. There was a sense of fun and community within the department, as well as with the authors. We arranged several parties and gatherings for the authors, at which we talked about new ideas and directions for the range. Barely a week went by when we weren't lunching with authors and potential authors and getting them to talk to each other. We used some of the *Doctor Who* authors to launch other ranges like the *Cracker* novels and the non-fiction programme guide range … It was an incredibly happy and productive time for everyone involved.'

Andy Bodle moved on during 1995 and his place in the Virgin fiction department was taken by Simon Winstone – another editorial assistant recruited specifically to help with the *Doctor Who* ranges. Darvill-Evans recalls that other people were also hired to help with Sharp's increasing workload on the erotic novels side – the Black Lace titles were now being published two a month. In addition, author Gareth Roberts was recruited on a freelance basis to help with reading manuscripts from the ever-growing 'slush pile' of *Doctor Who* submissions, as well as to provide holiday cover and other assistance in the department.

Tony Masero's two original roughs for the cover of Gareth Roberts' *Zamper*, featuring the return of the Chelonians, the turtle-like monster race created by the same author in his earlier New Adventure *The Highest Science*.

Peter Elson's original artwork for the cover of *Toy Soldiers*.

Head Games, with cover artwork by Bill Donohoe.

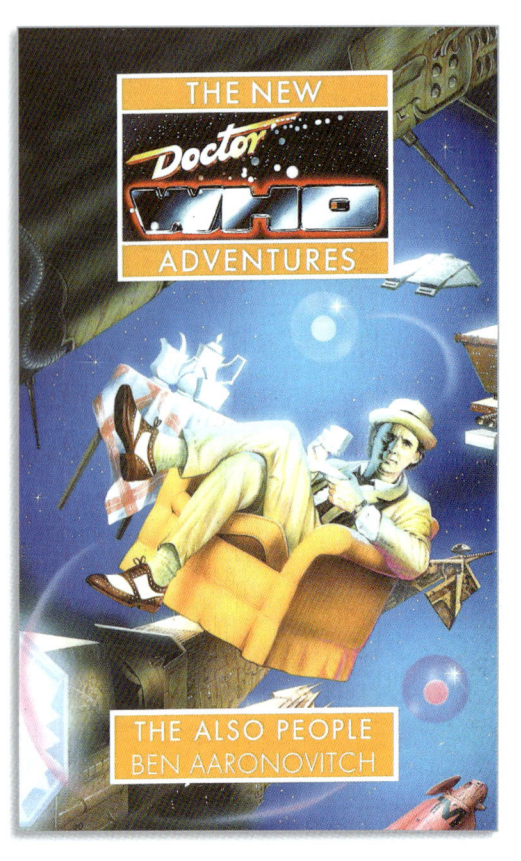

THE WHO ADVENTURES

Above: a polaroid photo that artist Tony Masero had taken of himself for use as reference for his cover artwork for *The Also People*.

Right: the final cover of *The Also People*. Masero's original artwork for this is reproduced at the front of this book.

Below right: Peter Elson's original rough for the cover of *Shakedown*.

PAUL LEONARD

Paul J Leonard Hinder, who writes under the pseudonym Paul Leonard and has also been published as P J L Hinder, is best known for his *Doctor Who* tie-in work. His first novel, *Venusian Lullaby* (1994), was one of the earliest of the Missing Adventures. It was followed by two others in that range, *Dancing the Code* (1995) and *Speed of Flight* (1996). For the New Adventures he authored *Toy Soldiers* (1995) and, with Nick Walters, *Dry Pilgrimage* (1998), the latter being one of the entries with Bernice Summerfield as the central character. Leonard was also a contributor to the fourth volume of Virgin's *Decalog* short story collections, after which he was asked to co-edit the fifth volume with Jim Mortimore. He went on to write five novels in BBC Books' Eighth Doctor Adventures range. In addition, he has written short stories for the *Short Trips* collections from the BBC and Big Finish.

THE END OF ACE

Peter Elson's original cover artwork for *Shakedown*.

Nik Spender's original cover artwork for *Just War*.

10: VILE PROBLEMS

Virgin kicked off 1996 with publication of another New Adventure from a first-time author, Lance Parkin. *Just War* was a purely historical tale, set during World War II and pitting the seventh Doctor against the Nazis.

'*Just War* was one of the best first books we ever got from a writer,' says Rebecca Levene. 'It's funny, looking through the slush pile of unsolicited submissions, there was a lot of stuff that was awful, but also a lot that was just average. We'd reply and get the authors to do more work on their submissions, but the work was still just average. I don't know what it is, but there's a skill that those people lacked, maybe the ability to make you really care about their characters, and it's not something that can be taught, you just have to be able to do it. It was a rare joy to come across something in the slush pile that was any good.'

Parkin was contracted to write *Just War* almost exactly a year before it was published, and part of his research was into the African Xhosa tribe of which the Doctor's then companion Roz Forrester was a member. On 27 January 1995 he sent Virgin some notes on her origins: a two-page

Below left: a rough by artist Mark Jones for his proposed *Just War* cover artwork, which ultimately was not selected for use.
Below right: Nik Spender's rough for the novel's final cover artwork.

LANCE PARKIN

Lance Parkin is a British author, biographer and essayist. He is probably best known for writing fiction and reference books related to TV shows, in particular *Doctor Who* and its tie-ins and spin-offs, including the New Adventures range and the Bernice Summerfield and Faction Paradox series.

Over a 20-year career, Parkin has written for publications including *TV Zone*, *Doctor Who Magazine*, *Star Trek Magazine* and the *New Statesman*, produced non-fiction guidebooks to the *Doctor Who* and *Star Trek* universes and worked on the series *Emmerdale* as a storyline writer.

Recent work includes biographies of the comics author Alan Moore (*Magic Words: The Extraordinary Life of Alan Moore*), and of Gene Roddenberry (*The Impossible Has Happened: The Life and Work of Gene Roddenberry, Creator of Star Trek*).

NIK SPENDER

Nick Spender, aka Nik Spender, studied at Epsom School of Art and Design for five years, and during that time was notably tutored by Frank Hampson, creator of *Dan Dare*. He is a life-long fan of *Doctor Who* and lucky enough in the early years to be commissioned by Target Books to provide the covers for the novelisations of the TV stories 'The Aztecs', 'The Highlanders', 'Inferno' and, a few years later, 'The Sensorites'. Then, after working steadily on other projects, he was commissioned to paint the cover for *Just War* for Virgin Publishing. Other early *Doctor Who* work included a series of portraits of all the Doctors up to and including Sylvester McCoy for a set of fridge magnets; and, during the same period, a 'Delta and the Bannermen' cover painting for the *InVision* fan reference publication. Some years later, BBC Audio commissioned him to paint a cover for the audio release of 'The Visitation'. Further covers for them were curtailed, however, when the company went into liquidation.

Spender has always painted in a combination of airbrush and gouache, as he finds this to be fast and easily corrected. Other clients include Ladybird books and Penguin, and he has done lots of graphic non-fiction books for David West, children's books and other sci-fi covers for most of the major publishers, magazine covers, *Star Trek* and *Star Wars* art for Hamilton plates, and poster art for the London Motor Show. He has also self-published two e-books on Amazon: *Dam Busters* and *Everest*.

Spender still watches *Doctor Who* to this day, and, if ever asked, his favourite Doctor was number two, Patrick Troughton. He clearly remembers hiding behind the sofa while watching the 1968 story 'The Web of Fear'!

document that summarised all that he could find about the tribe, their background and history. He noted: 'As Forrester is from a thousand years in the future, her people's beliefs might well have changed beyond all recognition from what we know today … There is certainly room to explore what Xhosa concepts she might believe in. If nothing else, the occasional use of a Xhosa word would serve to remind the reader that Forrester isn't a white middle-class Englishwoman.'

He went on to specify several Xhosa words that, he suggested, could be used from time to time in the novels. These included *usana* (meaning baby); *isithunzi* (strength of character); *ukurumreka* (being abandoned); and *ubuntu* (humanity).

Reaction to Parkin's book was extremely positive. 'Nothing short of a masterpiece … a gripping psychological thriller that I had to read in one sitting,' enthused Craig Hinton in *TV Zone*, while *Doctor Who Magazine*'s Dave Owen described it as 'a surprisingly mature first novel … almost impossible to put down.'

Following *Just War*, the majority of the novels planned for 1996 slotted into a story arc referred to as the 'Psi-Powers Series'. Those that comprised or contributed to this were: Andrew Cartmel's *Warchild*; Kate Orman's *SLEEPY*, with internal illustrations by Jason Towers; Lawrence Miles' *Christmas on a Rational Planet*; Kate Orman's *Return of the Living Dad*; Simon Bucher-Jones' *The Death of Art*; Russell T Davies' *Damaged Goods*; and Ben Aaronovitch's *So Vile A Sin*, which eventually gained a co-author in Kate Orman. By the time this arc started, Levene had realised that it was going to become rather more complex than she had imagined.

'When we planned the Psi-Powers Series we had meetings with the authors to chat about the ideas,' she explains, 'but I wasn't that aware of the authors themselves also working together on ideas, although apparently it did happen. To be honest I was glad of anything that reduced my workload. Some authors did talk together while others were out of the loop, so to speak, because of where they lived – this was the early days of the internet. These days it's a lot easier to communicate.

THE FORRESTER FACTOR

Research into Roz Forrester's lineage was carried out by a number of authors, particularly Ben Aaronovitch and Lance Parkin. By the time Aaronovitch came to work on *So Vile A Sin*, there was in existence at Virgin a document, writer unknown, summarising the established details of Roz's background:

Roz's sister's name – Leabie Forrester.
Roz's tribe (Xhosa subgroup): Tshangase.
Roz's clan name is Inyathi (buffalo).
Roz's title (as the sister of a Baroness): the Honourable Roslyn Forrester. Given the power of the Forrester family many commoners or sycophants would call her LADY FORRESTER but other aristocrats would probably make a point of using her correct title.

The FORRESTER family estate (where Roz grew up) is situated at KIBERO PATERA on IO. This is a large sulphur volcano in the southern hemisphere. The estate proper consists of the central caldera (cone) which has been domed over and terraformed to resemble the idealised patch of veldt. (Since Roz has been away her sister has added genetic reconstructions of southern African wildlife). The caldera is approx 80 km by 60 km. The Forrester family OWNS the entire moon.

Before she split with her father when she was 18, Roz was the favoured heir, rather than Leabie; she would have inherited but now Leabie has instead. Roz like the rest of the universe thinks that Leabie is a rich socialite who spends her days doing charitable works and her evenings hosting masques and balls.

Continuity Notes:

Roz wears an emerald engagement ring on her wedding finger. She was given this by LT GEORGE REED in 1941.

'Often things weren't planned and they came from the writers being retroactive. They would see something that had gone before and pick up on it and make it look like it had been planned all along, which of course it hadn't. What I liked about the books was an almost soap-like character development and the lack of a reset button. I liked the fact that Bernice gets married in one of the books, and then she has problems. Actions have an effect and you can't go back and pretend they never happened. Sometimes we made a rod for our own backs with that. For example, there's nothing some writers liked more than angst, and the endless "Ace agonising about how she had become a killing machine" nonsense that we had, used to drive me demented. I always preferred the New Adventures to the Missing Adventures as the Missing Adventures never went anywhere, and the point of a novel – a proper novel – is that it's about a character going on a journey and developing, leaving them different at the end than at the beginning. And we could do that in the New Adventures. We owed a lot to the BBC for letting us do this – we were lucky franchisees. Most other licensed ranges like *Star Trek* and *Buffy the Vampire Slayer* don't have that luxury. You know nothing's going to happen to the characters there. At least in the New Adventures you knew someone might die, and indeed they did.'

As the ideas for the Psi-Powers Series started to come together, Levene issued a document to all the writers involved, trying to give some background. 'This has turned into a horribly complex proposition,' she wrote. 'Basically we have a series featuring two opposing forces: the Doctor and the Brotherhood. The Brotherhood are a secret cabal of psi-powered humans, and their experiences move forward in linear time. Well, they would. The Doctor, on the other hand, is investigating the phenomenon of human psi-powers and gradually discovering the secret society behind them. As a time traveller, he's able to hop backward and

Left: on 19 June 1995, artist Jeff Cummins faxed these two roughs to Rebecca Levene at Virgin as suggested compositions for his cover for *Warchild*. The second was the one selected for use.

VILE PROBLEMS

Jeff Cummins' original cover artwork for *Warchild*.

Mark Wilkinson's original cover artwork for *SLEEPY*.

forward in time, as he follows clues and chases consequences.'

Levene went on to describe how the plot looked both from a linear time perspective – linking the development of psi-powers to the Pythia and the Time Lords' banishment of magic, and their seeding of the galaxy with N-forms to destroy any non-Time Lord psi-powers, leading to events in some of the recent and not-so-recent New Adventures – and from the Doctor's perspective – in essence a summary of the books that would form the Psi-Powers Series. Levene ended her note with a plea for ideas to resolve some of the hanging threads: 'What happens to the Grandmaster? Do the Brotherhood and the Family merge completely, remain different factions within the same organisation or remain bitter enemies? But this should give everyone something to think about/scream about/write me irate letters about/write me useful letters about telling me how we can tighten it up. And, obviously, those who've already written their books (yes, Kate and Andrew, I mean you) will have to add a few scenes hinting at this larger story. Sorry!'

Australian Kate Orman's two solo contributions to the arc were SLEEPY and *Return of the Living Dad*, the latter of which was originally titled *Big Trouble in Little Chalfont* on the outline she submitted to Virgin. 'SLEEPY was begun before the Psi-Powers arc was planned,' Orman confirms, 'so references to the Brotherhood were added during the writing. Bex also suggested that FLORANCE, the artificial intelligence who cameoed in Ben Aaronovitch's earlier book *Transit*, make a reappearance.

'*Return of the Living Dad* went through numerous drafts (and titles) – Department C19's involvement was added along the way, and it wasn't until I was actually writing the book that I decided their safe house was the same place the Doctor was held in during *The Left-Handed Hummingbird*. I think Woodworth, the C19

Right: Mark Wilkinson's two roughs for the cover of SLEEPY, as faxed to Rebecca Levene on 27 and 28 July 1995 respectively.

THE WHO ADVENTURES

JASON TOWERS

Jason Towers is an Australian writer and illustrator whose work has been published in magazines, newspapers and comics. He says he was once paid actual money to draw Jar-Jar Binks, and that he spent far too much of the 1990s contributing to *Doctor Who* fanzines; his collaborations with Kate Orman led to him being asked to supply two illustrations for *SLEEPY*. His website is at jasontowers.com.

Left: Jason Towers' original artwork for the frontispiece of *SLEEPY*.
Below: the frontispiece (left) and endpiece (right) as published.

190

agent, was also improvised during the actual writing. Bex suggested that Department C19 be revealed as the descendant of the Shadow Directory from *Christmas on a Rational Planet*, but that seems to have got lost somewhere along the way. Readers often have the impression that story arcs are carefully thought-out, but they're a mix of planning, last-minute revisions, authors pinching one another's ideas, and sheer coincidence.'

Of the other authors working on the Psi-Powers Series, three – Lawrence Miles, Simon Bucher-Jones and Russell T Davies – were all making their *Doctor Who* novel debuts. Miles' submission for *Christmas on a Rational Planet* stands out in Rebecca Levene's mind because it had been misfiled. 'It had been sitting in the slush pile for about a year and a half,' she says, 'and this pile of manuscripts, letters and ideas was constantly moved, sorted, looked through and re-sorted. Author Gareth Roberts was at the time working for us looking through the submissions, and he discovered Lawrence's in the pile we'd supposedly replied to, but he didn't think we *had* replied. He decided to look it over, out of courtesy, before sending the standard rejection letter (as the majority of the material we were sent was unusable), but after he had read it, he came to us and said that he couldn't reject it as it was very good – and that's how Lawrence started. The plot was mad, quite mad, and if anyone else had written it, I'd have rejected it, but Lawrence's talent just shone through.'

Miles also supplied three ideas for the book's cover. 'I thought doodling cover ideas was a normal thing for a writer to do,' he explains. 'It was not a success.' The second of Miles' ideas was actually taken forward and given to artist Jeff Cummins to realise, but unfortunately, due to various factors, including lack of time, the completed artwork was felt to be unsuitable.

'The first cover attempt for *Christmas on a Rational Planet* just didn't work,' admits Levene. 'A combination of a superb artist being given a duff brief by us and then not having enough time to do the art. And then our design department compounded the error by putting an awful yellow background on the book. Simply horrid.' Consequently, a replacement was commissioned.

LAWRENCE MILES

Lawrence Miles was born 15 March 1972 in Middlesex. His first professionally published fiction was a three-page comic strip drawn by Richard Elson and run under the generic title *Tharg's Time Twisters*; this appeared in Issue 722 of *2000 AD*, published in March 1991. His debut novel was *Christmas on a Rational Planet* for the New Adventures range. It was followed by *Down* and *Dead Romance*, two of the later titles with Bernice Summerfield as the central character, and then by *Alien Bodies*, *Interference* and *The Adventuress of Henrietta Street* for BBC Books' own *Doctor Who* range.

Miles' other original fiction includes the first title in the Faction Paradox range, *This Town Will Never Let Us Go*, and twelve titles in the Faction Paradox audio series produced by BBV and latterly Magic Bullet.

Non-fiction includes five titles in the *About Time* range, co-authored with Tat Wood, and *Dusted*, an unauthorised guide to *Buffy the Vampire Slayer*, co-authored with Lars Pearson and Christa Dickson.

Miles' writing can be found on two versions of his online blog, the Beasthouse, at http://beasthouse-lm.blogspot.com/ and http://beasthouse-lm2.blogspot.com/, in the latter of which can be found his *Doctor Who*-related musings.

THE WHO ADVENTURES

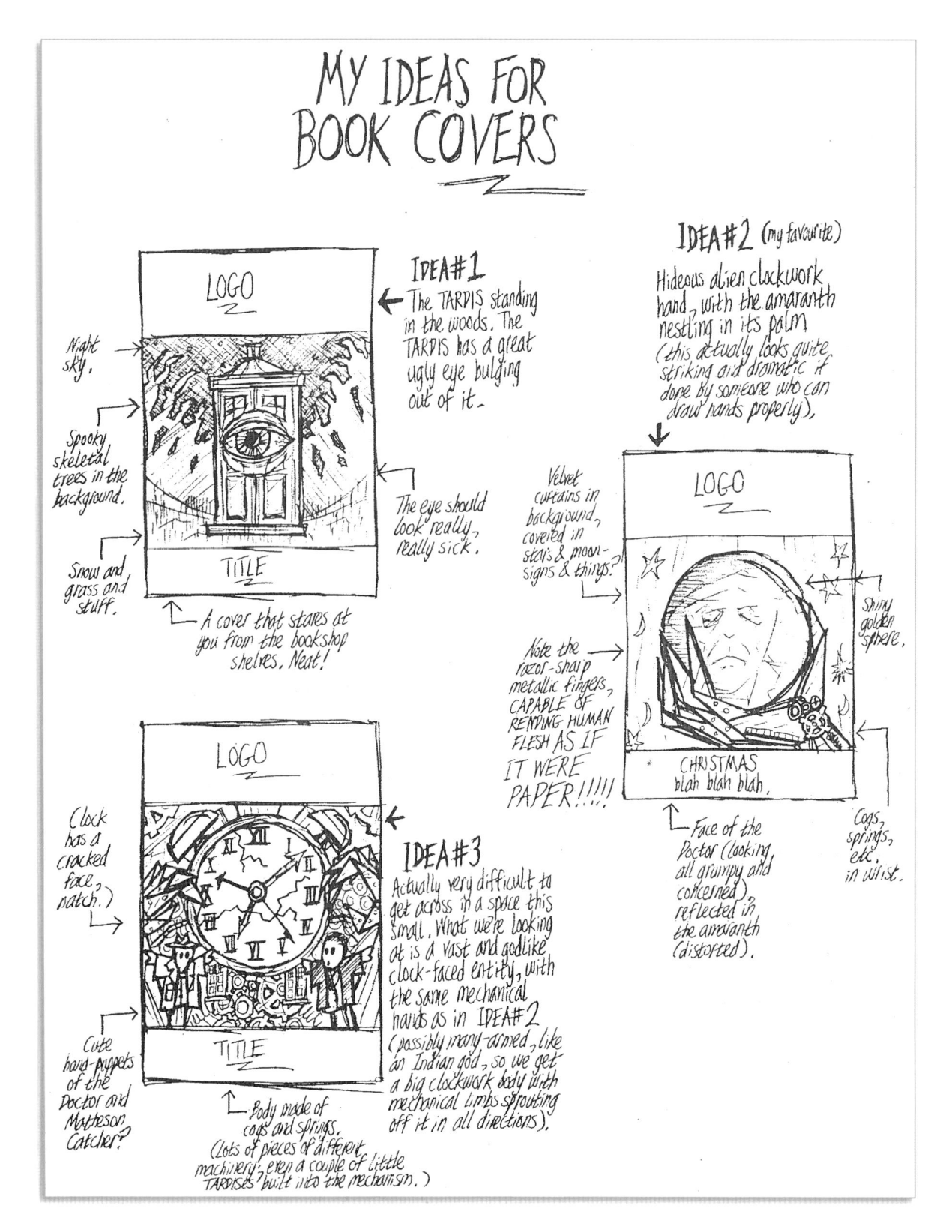

Lawrence Miles' sketched suggestions for the cover of his novel *Christmas on a Rational Planet*. The one marked Idea # 2 was selected for development by artist Jeff Cummins, but the finished artwork was ultimately dropped in favour of a different piece by Mick Posen.

VILE PROBLEMS

Above: Jeff Cummins' unused version of the cover art for *Christmas on a Rational Planet*. Below left: Cummins' rough for the piece. Below right: the cover proof prepared with this art, in the new format introduced in 1996.

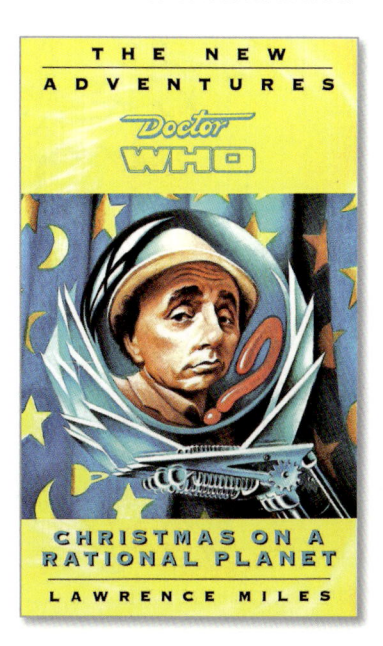

193

MICK POSEN

Mick Posen took a foundation course at Ravensbourne College of Art and Design in 1973, then studied illustration and graphic design at Brighton College of Art and Design. After pursuing an alternative career in music for a time, he moved back to the visual arts when his first daughter was born. He spent a couple of years putting together a portfolio – mostly caricature work – while at the same time picking up small advertising jobs. In 1986 he joined the Sarah Brown agency, specialising in fantasy and sci-fi artwork. They represented him for 12 years, during which time he painted numerous book covers. However, at the end of the '90s, this work sadly dried up. Posen then turned to the field of wildlife and nature illustration, at the same time making inroads into the new technique of 2D digital image creation; previously he had been using airbrush, paintbrush, gouache, acrylic and inks. Since then, he has taken on 3D digital modelling, and also animation. He now covers a variety of subject areas, such as historical reconstruction, earth sciences, natural history and medical illustration, for a variety of publishing and media outlets. He lives in Dorset with his wife Paulette.

Above: the as-published cover of *Christmas on a Rational Planet*, with Mick Posen's art replacing Jeff Cummins' first attempt. Opposite: Posen's rough for the piece, as faxed to Virgin on 12 February 1996.

Return of the Living Dad, with cover art by Mark Wilkinson.

VILE PROBLEMS

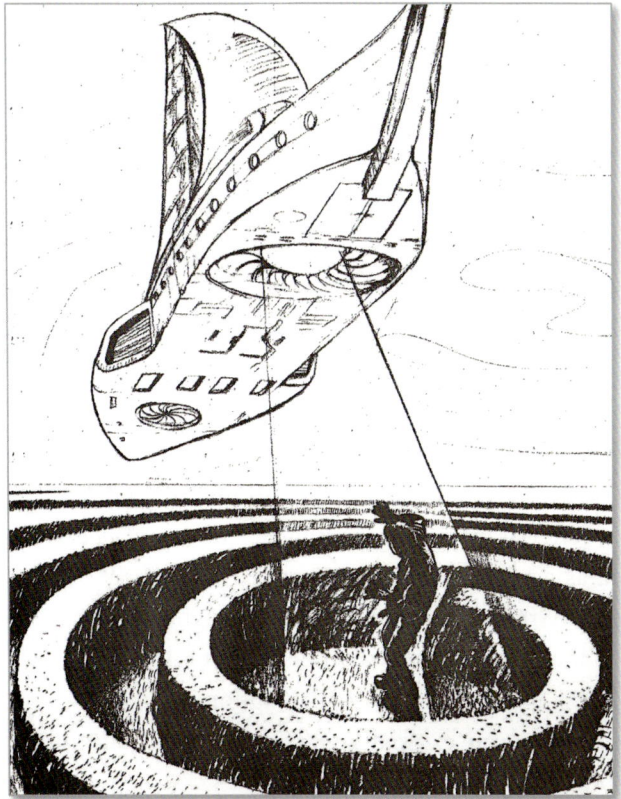

Mark Wilkinson's two roughs for *Return of the Living Dad*, as faxed to Virgin on 18 January 1996 (top) and 22 January 1996 (bottom).

MARK WILKINSON

Born in Windsor in 1952, Mark Wilkinson graduated from Watford College of Art in 1977 and joined a studio in Covent Garden with some friends under the direction of Graham Rogers, who had tutored him at art school. The agent David Lewis took him on shortly afterwards and managed to keep him busy for a number of years. He started out drawing in black-and-white in pen and ink for trade magazines including *Management Today*, but used airbrush for the occasional colour work that came his way, especially the more highly detailed and realistic type required for book publishing.

His two *Doctor Who* covers in the mid-'90s were among the last book covers he did. By that point, he had already been designing record sleeves for over ten years, and he then focused primarily on that type of work. He'd always been interested in fantasy art, so was fortunate to be asked to do covers in that style for the progressive rock band Marillion, and then for their lead singer Fish for his solo work. Some of the other bands for whom Wilkinson has designed covers and tour merchandise are Judas Priest, Iron Maiden, Europe and the Darkness. His pictures were chosen for the 2001 Best of British Illustration exhibition at the Royal College of Art, and he has exhibited in Denmark, Germany, Switzerland, Norway, Spain, Italy, Scotland and the USA. Two books of his work have been published: *Masque* in 2000 and *Shadowplay* in 2010.

SIMON BUCHER-JONES

Born in Liverpool in 1964, Simon Jones (Bucher-Jones since he married) was a civil servant working for the Home Office in London when his first book, *The Death of Art*, was published in 1996. This was just before Virgin lost the *Doctor Who* licence, and his second book, *Ghost Devices*, was a Bernice Summerfield New Adventure, with only a sneaky cameo by the Doctor. He has gone on to co-author two novels for BBC Books and pen a lot of short stories, and self-published poetry and a graphic novel adaption of his play *Thomas de Castigne's The King in Yellow*. For Obverse's Faction Paradox range he has written a novel, *The Brakespeare Voyage*, and edited an anthology, *The Book of the Enemy*. He has also contributed to the same company's Black Archive books about individual *Doctor Who* TV stories.

He retired from the civil service after 30 years and is now a freelance writer. As well as *Doctor Who* tie-ins, he's written Cthulhu mythos and Sherlock Holmes stories, and a series of mash-up novels with Charles Dickens and Wilkie Collins, set in an alternative spacefaring 1840s, that's also a prequel to *The War of the Worlds*.

He generally keeps his personal life out of these things, but has two children of whom he's really, really proud.

Artist Jon Sullivan's detailed rough for the cover of Simon Bucher-Jones' *The Death of Art*.

Russell T Davies, now a highly acclaimed TV scriptwriter, had already written extensively for the small screen by the time he contributed *Damaged Goods* to the New Adventures range; amongst his work were the popular BBC children's serials *Dark Season* (1991) and *Century Falls* (1993). He soon went on to write the Granada drama series *The Grand* (1997/98), starring Jean Marsh, and to create and write the groundbreaking Manchester-based Channel 4 series *Queer as Folk* (1999/2000), script-edited by fellow Virgin novelist Matthew Jones. There was interest at the time in *Damaged Goods* being adapted as a television property; on 2 February 1997 it was licensed to Granada for media and allied rights. The idea was to make the story as a television film, but excluding all BBC-owned *Doctor Who* characters. The option to do this was for one year only, and expired apparently without any further development being undertaken.

As things transpired, Ben Aaronovitch's *So Vile A Sin* gave Virgin the biggest headache they had to deal with during

VILE PROBLEMS

the whole run of the New Adventures. As the concluding Psi-Powers Series novel – during the course of which, in a dramatic development, Roz Forrester would be killed off – it formed a crucial part of the seven-title arc. However, it became subject to numerous delays, which eventually resulted in it being moved back from its scheduled slot and becoming the very last New Adventure published under the *Doctor Who* licence. 'It was a nightmare,' remembers Rebecca Levene. 'It was a really bad book for this delay to happen with. Ben was always a slow writer, but he always delivered. Late, most often, but he delivered, and you can't say that about most writers – in fact, the ones that delivered on time were the exception! Ben got us a synopsis in, not hugely detailed, but it was very

Jon Sullivan's original artwork for the cover of *The Death of Art*.

THE WHO ADVENTURES

Bill Donohoe's original artwork for the cover of *Damaged Goods*.

good. We had intended to kill Roz all along, ever since she first joined the Doctor in the TARDIS, and Ben always liked writing for her, so he got that honour. It was another thing to boost the books, and to remind readers that our characters can die, nothing is forever.

'We gave Ben lots of time, and he had sent in about 10,000 words by the time the deadline came, in April or May 1996. We then sent endless letters and made numerous phone calls. It got to the stage that he would not return our calls, and was not opening the letters I sent him, because he knew what they'd say. After it was all over, he sent me a very sweet letter apologising. The problem was simply that after his previous book, *The Also People*, was so well received, he just hit the block that he couldn't do better. It was a lot to live up to. We eventually realised that he was not going to deliver the book.'

'At one point,' adds Peter Darvill-Evans, 'in our desperation for news from Ben about how the book was progressing, I resorted to making an unannounced visit to his house one evening. This must have been in the late summer of 1996, I guess. Ben didn't reply to messages left on his answering machine and, as Bex says, we later found out that he wasn't even opening our letters. It wasn't until my personal call that we found out that Ben had written very little more finished text than the 10,000 words he'd submitted in the spring.'

'As the end of 1996 approached, we were talking to his agent,' continues Levene, 'and decided to pass the project on to Kate Orman, as we had to finish what we had started with the Psi-Powers Series. Ben was happy with this decision, and so that's what we did.'

'I volunteered to finish *So Vile A Sin*,' says Orman. 'The joke was that I was so desperate to read the new Aaronovitch book that I'd write it myself! SLEEPY and *Return of the Living Dad* had included only passing references to the arc, and suddenly, I was writing the climax to it.

'When I picked up the book, my writing partner (and now husband) Jon Blum and I were already working on *Vampire Science* [a novel later published as part of BBC Books' Eighth Doctor Adventures range], so he looked after that book while I raced to finish *So Vile A Sin*, based on Ben's synopsis for the first two-thirds and the chunk he'd already written. I hadn't paid much attention to the arc, so Jon also helped by reading all the arc books again and bringing me up to speed on how it all connected.

'Since everyone already knew about Roz's death [because it was heavily referenced in *Bad Therapy*, the book that was originally supposed

RUSSELL T DAVIES

Russell T Davies was born 27 April 1963 in Sketty, Swansea and studied at Worcester College, Oxford University where he gained a degree in English Literature. He initially worked in the theatre but soon turned to television. His early work was in children's television, including directing the BBC series *Why Don't You Just Switch Off Your Television Set and Go and Do Something Less Boring Instead?* (1973), writing the sci-fi adventure series *Dark Season* (1991) (starring a young Kate Winslet) and *Century Falls* (1993), and writing for Granada's *Children's Ward* (1994), for which he won a BAFTA in 1996.

Adult drama writing credits include: *The House of Windsor* (1994), *Touching Evil* (1997), *Coronation Street* (1997), *The Grand* (1997-1998), *Queer as Folk* (1999-2000) (which he also co-produced), *Bob & Rose* (2001), *The Second Coming* (2003), *Mine All Mine* (2004) and *Casanova* (2005).

In 2005 he regenerated *Doctor Who* after the show had been off the screen for 16 years, taking the role of lead writer and executive producer. He also created the *Doctor Who* spin-offs *Torchwood* (2006-2011) and *The Sarah Jane Adventures* (2007-2010).

In 2008 Davies was awarded an OBE for services to drama, and in May 2009 he collected the BAFTA Cymru award for best screenwriter for *Doctor Who*.

He has continued to work in television, co-creating the CBBC drama *Wizards vs Aliens* (2012-2013), and creating *Cucumber*, *Banana* and *Tofu* (all 2015), which looked at LGBT issues. His later work includes *A Midsummer Night's Dream* (2016), *A Very English Scandal* (2018), *Years and Years* (2019) and *It's a Sin* (2021).

to follow *So Vile A Sin* but ended up coming out in advance of it], it made sense to open with her funeral, and then tell the story that led up to it. A promised fax from Ben with the plot for the last third of the book failed to materialise, so I cobbled together the last part of the story on Boxing Day 1996, based on his rough notes. (Ben had created a huge guide to the 30th Century – history, family trees, even the names of all the ships in the Imperial fleet!)

'As an Australian expression goes, I was flat out like a lizard drinking, with barely two months to finish the book off – one night I fell asleep at the keyboard, and on another night, out of sheer desperation, I wrote up the events of a whole chapter as a telegram. (The next morning I realised this was nonsense and wrote it properly.)

'Even though I wrote four-fifths of the prose, all the best bits of the book, and the rich and often very funny ideas, are Ben's!'

Jon Blum adds: 'A lot of the material in the last third of *So Vile A Sin*, which connected *SLEEPY* into the arc, came from Kate filling in gaps in Ben's plot outline during her last high-speed burst of writing. So suddenly stuff that was never intended as arc material, like Chris's latent telepathy and the anti-telepath prejudices, became critical to the story. That wasn't a masterplan, that was Kate reaching back to what she could remember! And not only did she flesh out the climax of the story from a couple of phrases in the outline, and work out the fates of secondary characters like Ioamnet, Martinique and Walid, but she also came up with a *hell* of a

JON SULLIVAN

Jon Sullivan was born in 1973 in Plumstead, London. He started creating fantasy artwork and teaching himself how to paint with oils after leaving school in 1988 and built up an impressive portfolio, which he exhibited at the Glasgow Science Fiction WorldCon in 1995. His cover for the New Adventure *The Death of Art* in 1996 was his first commission, and he had two others that same year, for Philip G Williamson's *The Orb and the Sceptre*, published by Hodder and Stoughton, and David Gemmell's *Dark Moon*, from Bantam.

Since then, Sullivan has created a sizeable body of work, producing numerous covers each year, initially in oils, but later moving to add digital art to his repertoire. Authors whose covers he has worked on include Pierre Pevel, Neil Asher, Richard Morgan, Louise Cooper, Ed Greenwood, Mark Chadbourn, Richard A Knaak, Kate Jacoby, Simon R Green, Mercades Lackey, Stan Nicholls, Adrian Tchaikovsky, Terry Brooks, Mark Hodder and David Farlan. He has also contributed to the *Warhammer 40,000* series of books, and was one of seven artists providing internal art for the 2003 *Terry Pratchett Calendar*.

He was nominated for the Chesley Award in 2012 for his cover for Mark Holder's *The Curious Case of the Clockwork Man*, and again in 2015 for the cover for the same author's *The*

Jon Sullivan at work on the 1999 book cover for *Voice of the Demon* by Kate Jacoby.

Return of the Discounted Man, both published by Pyr. In addition, he was nominated for the 'Ravenheart' David Gemmell Legend Award in 2010 and 2011 for his covers for Pierre Pevel's *The Cardinal's Blades* and *Shadow King* and Graham McNeill's *Empire: The Legend of Sigmar*, all published by Black Library.

Sullivan's own website can be found at https://jonsullivancoverart.blogspot.com/.

Jon Sullivan's original rough for the cover of So Vile A Sin.

lot of good lines herself.'

The public explanation given for the delays at the time was that Ben Aaronovitch had suffered a disastrous computer hard-drive crash. What had really happened, however, was that he had run into a combination of daunting obstacles: a terrible case of writer's block, a change in family circumstances that made it hard for him to find time to write, and the intense pressure of having to live up to his critically-acclaimed previous novel *The Also People* while also providing the conclusion to an important and much-vaunted story arc. According to documentation held at Virgin, he eventually managed to deliver 16,000 words of the novel by 21 November 1996, and Kate Orman was formally engaged to complete the project on 21 January 1997, having previously been faxed all the available information from Aaronovitch. However, Orman had actually been working on the book since the end of the previous year.

The covers for the Psi-Powers Series novels

Jon Sullivan's original artwork for the cover of So Vile A Sin.

were supplied by Jeff Cummins (*Warchild*, with a photograph of his youngest daughter, Rhian, used as reference for the child); Mark Wilkinson (*SLEEPY*, *Return of the Living Dad*); Mike Posen (the second, published version of *Christmas on a Rational Planet*), Jon Sullivan (*The Death of Art*, his very first professional commission, and *So Vile A Sin*) and Bill Donohoe (*Damaged Goods*).

'The covers were a company-wide decision,' says Rebecca Levene. 'We'd have a weekly meeting where the finished covers were presented. The person with the most say at Virgin was the sales director, because the covers and information sheets are what you use to sell the books to the shops, so they have to work from that point of view.

'When commissioning a cover, I'd start by asking the writer for some suggestions, as we had to get that aspect well under way before the book was even written. I'd then send the brief off to the artists' agency with any associated material, and they'd come back with sketches and then the finished artwork. I can't remember when we decided to use one agency rather than individual artists, but I think it was around the time of these

VILE PROBLEMS

books. We did that as I had never been happy with the quality of the artwork, and hoped that using an agency might help improve matters.'

Jon Sullivan has fond memories of his debut commission. 'I had good times working on those New Adventures cover arts. I was 22 years old when I did the first. A few months previous to that I'd been exhibiting my art at the Glasgow Science Fiction WorldCon 1995, with a portfolio of art that I'd spent the past seven years since leaving school working on, just purely teaching myself how to paint with oils.

'I remember the deadlines as being quite relaxed, which was wonderful as it allowed me to enjoy and absorb the process of concept designing to finished art. My first professional cover art commission was *The Death of Art*. I remember receiving the book cover art proofs and being blown away by how it had printed up, with that darn cool *Doctor Who* font above the artwork. Of all the illustrations I've done over the years, that art is still one of my favourites. The fact it was my first helps.

'I was certainly more at home designing demons, aliens and the grotesque, so receiving that cover brief was right up my street.'

Reviewers were generally positive about this arc of books. Writing in *TV Zone* for the duration, Craig Hinton found that *Warchild* 'keeps you thinking well after you put it down' but that *The Death of Art* 'wasn't a book I particularly enjoyed reading', citing the lack of links into the arc, which was vague in itself, the overused setting of Paris, and the 'pointless' inclusion of Acc at the start. *Damaged* Goods, however, was better received: 'definitely not for children; it deals with some extremely adult themes, such as the late '80s drugs culture and homosexuality ... this is a brutal indictment of a society that has lost its way. Definitely one of the best New Adventures for a long time.'

Of Orman's offerings, Hinton felt that SLEEPY 'demonstrates her fascination with hurt/comfort, pain/angst, and pyramids, in a very

The cover of *So Vile A Sin* went through two different proofs, both with Ben Aaronovitch credited as sole author (below left and centre); the final, as-published cover (below right) had Kate Orman added as co-author and, owing to the imminent loss of Virgin's licence, was minus the *Doctor Who* logo.

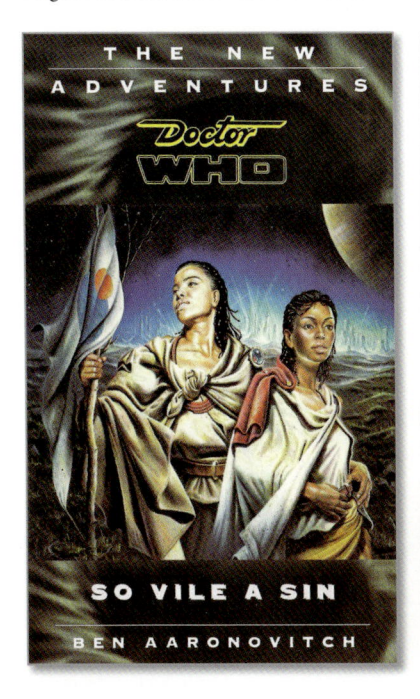

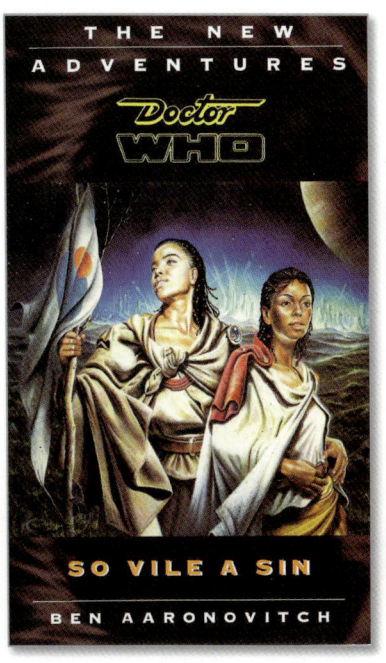

character-driven novel that you will either love or hate', while *Return of the Living Dad* was 'straightforward if implausible … Kate's penchant for being self-referential goes into overdrive in this one, with far too many references to her previous novels and the New Adventures in general, and her development of Cwej and Forrester is both illogical and vaguely distasteful. A good book for fans of the New Adventures but it might leave some people confused.'

On the subject of the arc's conclusion in *So Vile A Sin*, Hinton stated, 'Kate does her best to tie it all together, but the end result is sadly unsatisfying. In general [though, this is] … a tightly plotted and emotional read.'

Reviewing *Return of the Living Dad*, *Doctor Who Magazine*'s Dave Owen commented, 'It's a book for fans, by a fan, and often about fans,' while *Damaged Goods* elicited the following comment: 'Purists might argue that a book full of sex, drugs and squalor can't really be *Doctor Who*, but they would be forgetting that the essence of the series … is in portraying ordinary people's reactions to the unprecedented.'

BROADSWORD

The Virgin *Doctor Who* ranges even spawned a fanzine, *Broadsword*, created by Australians Richard Prekodravac and David Robinson. The first issue, in January 1995, ran to just six pages, but by the time of the fourteenth and final one, dated March-April 1997 but actually printed in August 1997, it had grown to 28 pages. Its contents included news and reviews, opinion pieces, author interviews and fan fiction. Inspired by the feature in *Doctor Who Magazine*, it also boasted author-written Preludes of two of the novels, Paul Cornell's *Happy Endings* and Craig Hinton's *GodEngine*, plus Kate Orman's complete draft of the one for *The Left-Handed Hummingbird*, which had been edited on its original publication. By the time the 'zine ended, its remit had expanded to cover also BBC Books' original *Doctor Who* novels ranges that started In June 1997.

Today, Prekodravac recalls, 'I started *Broadsword* with my co-editor David Robinson to be a positive celebratory voice for the New Adventures. We wanted to champion our support for the writers and the publisher. What I enjoyed the most about the New Adventures was that they were telling the Doctor's story in a novel context using new genres and concepts. We got to see *Doctor Who* from new perspectives and explore and discover new ideas and new truths. Also, Virgin was giving many new writers, most of them fans, an opportunity to publish their novels. It was a joy to see new writers at the early stages of their careers. I am very proud of the work we did. We got to celebrate and champion a chapter of *Doctor Who* history.'

Shown below are the covers of Issues 3, 8 and 12.

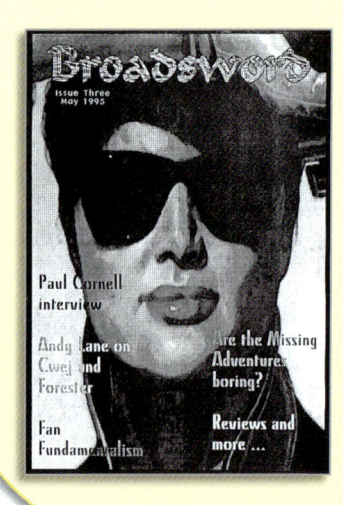

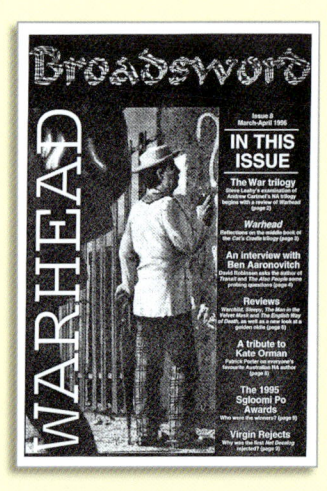

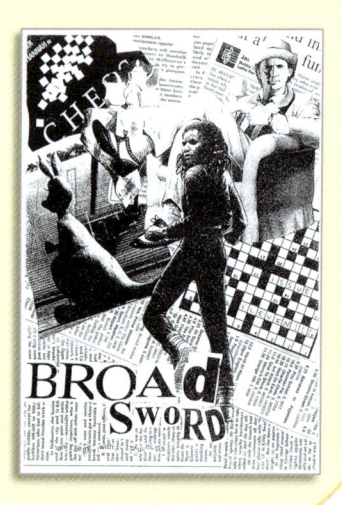

11: CELEBRATING FIFTY BOOKS

In the midst of the Psi-Powers Series, the New Adventures celebrated a milestone event: the publication of the fiftieth title in the range. Rather than have this be just another novel, a decision was taken to celebrate in style.

Rebecca Levene recalls that the idea for a special celebration book came up at one of Virgin's regular gatherings of authors. 'I remember we were talking about celebratory issues of comics with David Bishop, who had a lot of experience in that area, and the idea for a celebratory book came about. I think Paul Cornell might even have pitched his idea at that same meeting, and as he was one of our most popular writers, it made sense for him to do it. His idea of Benny getting married also seemed to fit.'

Cornell's initial outline for this book, which would feature the wedding of Bernice Summerfield, carried the lengthy title *The Wedding Book, or: Oops, It's the Bishop, or: Happy Endings (A silly, horny ramble about change and closure.)* The shortened title eventually chosen was *Happy Endings*.

In keeping with the party spirit, one of the chapters of the final manuscript was a joint effort by the majority of the authors to have contributed to the New Adventures up to that point. Each author wrote a couple of paragraphs featuring their originally-created characters, generally as guests at the wedding; Paul Cornell then took all these contributions and compiled them into a single piece of text. 'That was Paul's idea,' says Levene. 'I think we might have sent the letters out for him or something, but he put it all together.'

To add to the feel of the book recounting

You are cordially invited to the wedding of

Mr Jason Cane

and

Professor Bernice S Summerfield

to be held in the village of Cheldon Boniface

in the year 2010

Above: a promotional invitation mocked up by Virgin for *Happy Endings*' wedding of Bernice Summerfield to Jason Kane (whose surname is misspelt here).

REUNIONS

Happy Endings includes appearances by at least one character from almost every previous New Adventure, most of them as attendees at Benny's wedding – spanning from Gilgamesh, as featured in the range's first title, *Timewyrm: Genesys*, to the groom himself, Jason Kane, introduced in the immediately preceding book, *Death and Diplomacy*. One exception is that no character from *Cat's Cradle: Time's Crucible* shows up: although that novel's author, Marc Platt, did contribute, he chose to feature instead the artist Leonardo da Vinci.

HAPPY ENDINGS

The 50th New Adventure

By Paul Cornell

Virgin Publishing LTD
332 LADBROKE GROVE
LONDON W10 5AH
TEL 0181 968 7554
FAX 0181 968 0929

Virgin Publishing's *New Adventures* have been delighting Doctor Who fans and science fiction readers for five years, filling the void that was left when the BBC stopped making new Doctor Who stories in 1989. Now, in the year that Doctor Who returns to the screen with Paul McGann as the eight Doctor, Virgin is proud to publish the 50th *New Adventure* novel.

In **Happy Endings**, Paul Cornell's 5th **New Adventure**, one of the Doctor's companions gets married, and hosts a wedding with guests from every time and place in the universe. Everybody's coming: from Ice Warriors to Unit veterans, a flirtatious Ace to a suspicious Hamlet Mcbeth, and a very confused trio of Isley Brothers. The Doctor has to organise a buffet, Roz has a mystery to solve, and Chris has a girlfriend who used to be the Timewyrm.

However, between rows, fights and pre-emptive divorce proceedings, there may not be a wedding at all. Especially if there really is someone who wants to prevent it happening.

This celebratory book ties up plot threads from the previous novels, features guest appearances from well-loved characters, and includes a chapter written by many of the series' favourite authors. To add to the celebrations, we've given the *New Adventures* a new look: a modern cover design that will carry the series into the new millenium.

Happy Endings includes an off-the-page offer for an exclusive wedding poster.

Paul Cornell is a popular and prolific young talent in the world of Doctor Who writing. He has also written young adult horror, short stories and television drama.

PAUL CORNELL IS AVAILABLE FOR INTERVIEW

PRESS RELEASE

the events around a real wedding, it opened with a poem written by Vanessa Bishop and even included, in sheet music form, a song called 'Opposites Attract', with lyrics by Paul Cornell and music by Dave Owen, who was credited under the anagrammatical pseudonym Evan Dowe.

The cover artwork for *Happy Endings* posed some problems, as Rebecca Levene recalls. 'The cover for that one was a nightmare. We went through so many different ideas for it … It was meant to look like a comics special issue or something, but a lot of the early versions just looked appalling – our sales director nearly had a coronary when he saw our first attempt at it. What we ended up with was pretty good though.'

Because the art, commissioned from Paul Campbell, had a very complex brief – it was to take the form of a 'wedding photograph' of bride and groom surrounded by all their guests (including two seventh Doctors, Silurians, Ice Warriors and many others) – it took a lot longer than usual to complete, with the result that the finished artwork was not available at the point when proof covers needed to be produced for marketing purposes. To get around this, a cover was mocked up

Top left: Virgin's press release for the celebratory novel.

Bottom left: concept sketches for the depiction of the alien character Sgloomi Po in the book's cover artwork.

CELEBRATING FIFTY BOOKS

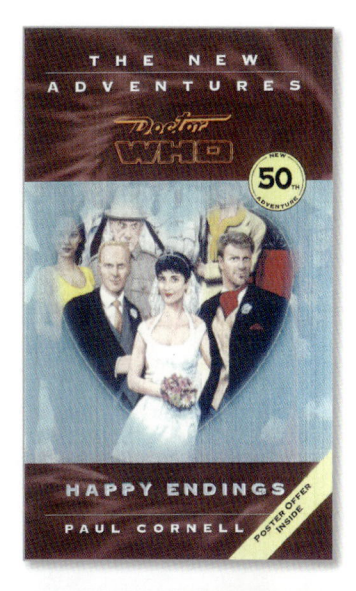

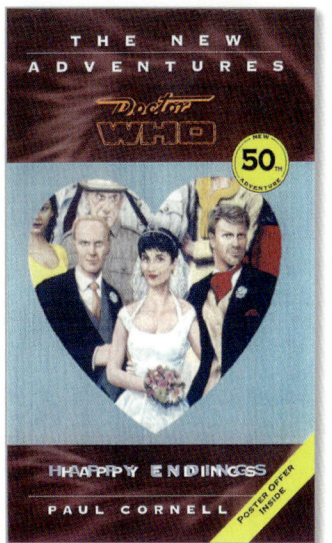

Above: the initial cover proof for *Happy Endings*. Created as a temporary measure purely for the purpose of marketing the novel to shops, this version used mocked-up artwork that took just selected elements from Paul Campbell's final composition and was never intended to appear on the book as published. Subsequently a proof of the final cover was also produced.

Also on this page: four more early, less-than-successful mock-ups of this celebratory novel's cover.

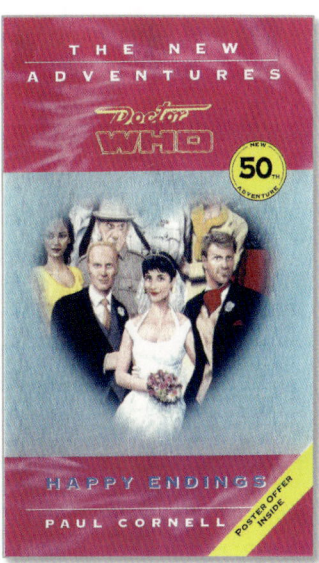

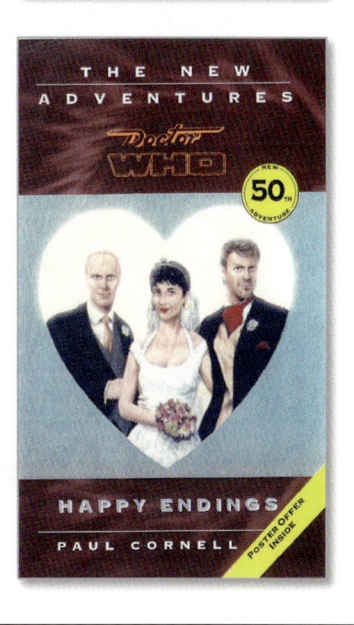

209

THE WHO ADVENTURES

The final cover for *Happy Endings*, with art by Paul Campbell. The 'Fiftieth New Adventure' flash was added to the cover as a silver foil stamp.

CELEBRATING FIFTY BOOKS

using just a few completed character likenesses from the final composition (see main image on page 209) – this was never intended to appear on the book when published, but Virgin had to have something to show to the shops. To make matters more complicated still, it had been decided that *Happy Endings* was to debut a new cover design for the range. 'We were never happy

Below: the poster made available of the *Happy Endings* cover artwork, and the key to the characters depicted.

THE WEDDING OF MR JASON KANE AND PROFESSOR BERNICE S. SUMMERFIELD

1. Bat 2. The Doctor 3. Muldwych 4. Kadiatu 5. William Blake 6. The Brigadier 7. Doris 8. Lord Savaar
9. Skog 10. Lisa Deranne 11. Braxiatel 12. Sskeet 13. The Doctor 14. Sanki 15. Danny Pain 16. Ruby Duvall
17. Hamlet Macbeth 18. The Master of the Land of Fiction 19. Sherlock Holmes 20. Dr Watson 21. Maire
22. Jacquilian 23. Keri 24. Chris Cwej 25. Bernice Summerfield 26. Jason Kane 27. Rev. Annie Trelaw
28. Roz Forrester 29. Dorothée McShane 30. Sgloomi Po

211

THE WHO ADVENTURES

Death and Diplomacy, with art by Bill Donohoe. The last New Adventure with the original cover design.

with the original cover design, and nor were our sales team,' explains Levene. 'The problem we always had was that the books looked like kids' books. They weren't kids' books, and yet the shops would always rack them there, even though we told them not to. That wasn't doing anyone any favours. The revised cover design looked more grown-up, and the landscape artwork design gave the artists more freedom over what to paint for us, without large parts of the image being obscured with logos and authors' names.'

Once Paul Campbell's final *Happy Endings* artwork was completed, Virgin decided to make it available as a poster, and an advert for this was included within the book, together with a checklist of everyone depicted in the painting (see page 211).

Commissioned and written before the Psi-Powers Series was developed, and published immediately before *Happy Endings*, was Dave Stone's latest contribution, *Death and Diplomacy*, which was originally titled *Summit* and then *Tact and Diplomacy*. Immediately after *Happy Endings* came another book with no connection to the arc, Craig Hinton's *GodEngine*. The year then ended with the publication of Matthew Jones' debut New Adventure, *Bad Therapy*, which explored the reactions of the Doctor and companion Chris Cwej to the death of their friend Roz. However, as previously mentioned, *So Vile A Sin*, the book in which Roz died, had yet to be finished at this time. This gave Jones a problem, in that he had to write his novel without knowing the full details of what happened in *So Vile A Sin*; and, when *Bad Therapy* was published, it gave readers a problem too, in that they didn't know that Roz *had* died in the first place.

The cover art for *Death and Diplomacy* was by Bill Donohoe; that for *GodEngine* was by Peter Elson; and that for *Bad Therapy* was by Mark Salwowski, another artist working for the Sarah

CRAIG HINTON

Craig Paul Alexander Hinton first became known for his fanzine articles about various science fiction TV shows, including *Doctor Who* and *Star Trek*. These brought him to the attention of *Doctor Who Magazine*, who offered him the role of regular book reviewer. His first published novels were the Missing Adventures *The Crystal Bucephalus* in 1994 and *Millennial Rites* in 1995; then came his only New Adventure, *GodEngine*, in 1996. Later, for BBC Books' *Doctor Who* ranges, he wrote *The Quantum Archangel* and *Synthespians™*, the latter of which was dedicated to his new husband, Ali, whom he'd 'waited a lifetime' to find. Under the pseudonym Paul C Alexander, he also wrote three books for Virgin's Idol erotica range: *Chains of Deceit*, *The Final Restraint* and *Code of Submission*. For audio, he scripted one *Doctor Who* adventure, *Excelis Decays* (2002), and one *Tomorrow People* one, *The Lords of Forever* (2005). In addition, he wrote short stories for a variety of collections. His last published pieces were reviews of the 2006 *Doctor Who* episodes for Shaun Lyon's Telos guide book *Second Flight*.

Hinton's *Doctor Who* novels often contained references to or explanations of elements of past continuity, and he coined the term 'fanwank' to cover this practice, happily applying it to his own work. Outside of science fiction, he was a noted IT journalist, editing magazines for VNU Business Publications in London in the mid-1990s and moving on to ITNetwork.com shortly afterwards.

Hinton died in December 2006 of a heart attack.

THE WHO ADVENTURES

COVER CONCEPTS

Craig Hinton wrote to Rebecca Levene at Virgin on 31 October 1995 outlining his ideas for the cover of *GodEngine*. At the start he asked: 'Will it be possible to bicapitalise this on the cover?' – i.e. he favoured the title being styled '*GodEngine*' rather than '*Godengine*'. He also expressed a desire for Peter Elson to do the artwork, and supplied a reference drawing by Mike Tucker of the Martian Grand Marshal Falaxyr. He suggested including a sword fight between an Ice Lord in the 'standard' green and other Ice Warriors, and 'if Peter is feeling adventurous – a female Ice Warrior as well. Females are slighter and a little more "curvaceous" than the males.'

This page: three drawings of the Ice Warriors as featured in *GodEngine*. These were created for Craig Hinton by fellow Virgin books author Mike Tucker, who had worked on the *Doctor Who* TV series while employed as a BBC visual effects assistant. The drawing to the right is captioned 'Nomad Ice Warrior adapted to desert conditions with built in air conditioning and heat exchanger.'

214

CELEBRATING FIFTY BOOKS

> ## MIKE TUCKER
>
> Mike Tucker began his career as a BBC visual effects assistant, *Doctor Who* being one of many shows he worked on as such in the late 1980s before being promoted to effects designer. By the mid-1990s, he was also branching out into writing. For Virgin, he worked with Sophie Aldred on her 1996 non-fiction book *Ace!* and co-wrote a *Decalog* short story. He has since gone on to gain many other writing credits on *Doctor Who* novels, short stories and audio dramas. In 2003, following the demise of the BBC Visual Effects Department, he set up the Model Unit, which has provided acclaimed and award-winning miniature effects for many productions, not least the post-2005 series of *Doctor Who*. Although he authored no New Adventures, he did have a late, peripheral input into the range by producing some concept sketches and designs, including for *GodEngine* (see opposite).

Brown Agency.

Once more, the titles received mostly praise from reviewers. 'ced *Death and Diplomacy* works on many levels,' wrote Paul Simpson in *Dreamwatch*, and *TV Zone*'s Craig Hinton agreed: 'One of the most fascinating and compelling New Adventures seen for ages … an amusing, moving and extremely entertaining read.'

'The single word which best describes *Happy Endings* is "indulgent",' opined *Doctor Who Magazine*'s Dave Owen. 'It reads like a series of jokes and sketches which Paul has been itching to use in his *Doctor Who* writing and has finally been given permission for.' Hinton felt the anniversary book was 'the most self-indulgent, continuity-bound piece of camp the series has seen. And I thoroughly enjoyed it.' However, Richard McGinlay, reviewing the book in *Dreamwatch*, identified a problem with it: 'Unless you have absorbed every single New Adventure you are liable to find this an occasionally dissatisfying read … it's unlike any other *Doctor Who* novel to date.'

Of the novels published during this period, only *GodEngine* received the sharp end of the reviewers' tongues. Owen had this to say: 'There are only two things wrong with *GodEngine*: the story is often dull, and the way it's told is often excruciating … This book is absolute proof that strong continuity and research do not alone guarantee a good Doctor Who novel. *GodEngine*? *Godawful* would have been more accurate.' David Bailey, writing in *TV Zone* (Hinton naturally being unable to review his own book), felt it was 'a novel filled to the brim with ideas. But it is not a *Doctor Who* novel. On the whole … while not truly bad, an unimpressive read.' *Dreamwatch*'s Paul Simpson, on the other hand, felt that it was 'a New Adventure that could have worked on screen … racy and occasionally repetitive.'

Simpson also liked *Bad Therapy*, specifically citing its emotional impact: 'It is rare for a New Adventure to pull at the heartstrings, but *Bad Therapy* does. Recommended.'

Bad Therapy was the final New Adventure to bear the *Doctor Who* logo on the cover and spine. This was an indirect consequence of the fact that, at the start of 1996, the BBC had announced, after months of speculation in the press, that a new *Doctor Who* television movie was in production, starring Paul McGann as the eighth Doctor. Although this was a cause for celebration amongst *Doctor Who* fans generally, Virgin Publishing had good reason to be concerned about the BBC's newfound interest in *Doctor Who* …

> ## BOOK DELAY
>
> Due to the delay in publication of *So Vile A Sin*, which it followed in story order, Virgin included an explanatory announcement at the front of *Bad Therapy*:
>
> 'The story in this volume, like that in most of the New Adventures, is a continuation of the events described in the preceding book, *So Vile A Sin* by Ben Aaronovitch.
>
> 'Unfortunately, it has proved impossible to publish *So Vile A Sin* on time. The publishers apologise for this; however the book will be published as quickly as possible.'

THE WHO ADVENTURES

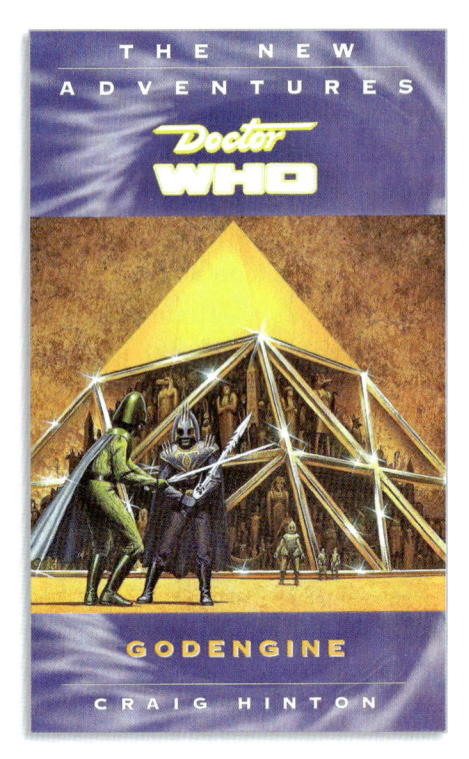

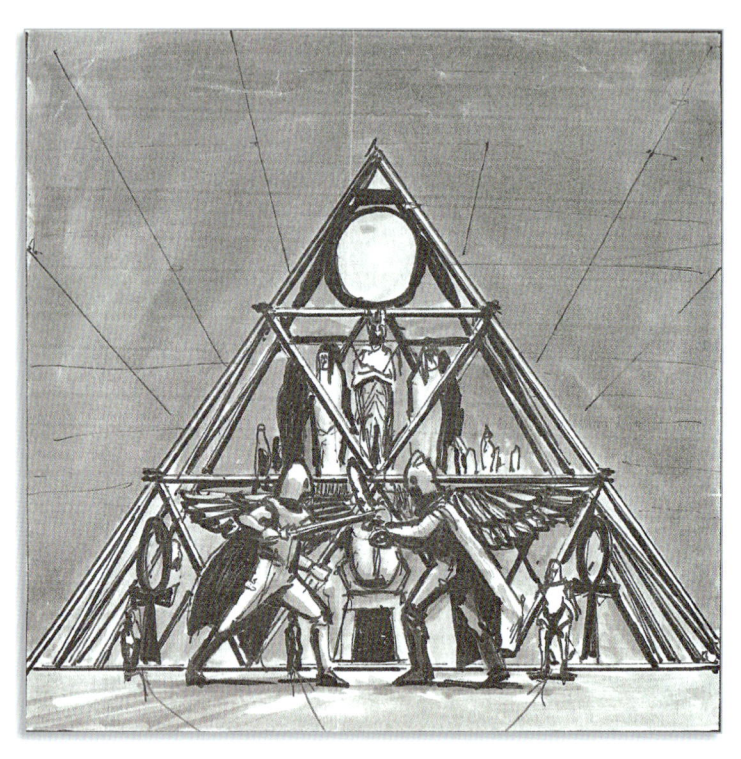

Above left: a proof version of the *GodEngine* cover, with an ultimately unused yellow-and-white take on the *Doctor Who* logo, also featured on the first proof of the *Happy Endings* cover (see page 209). Above right: Peter Elson's initial rough for the cover artwork. Below: Elson's revised rough, as faxed to Virgin on 29 November 1995, with his explanatory comments.

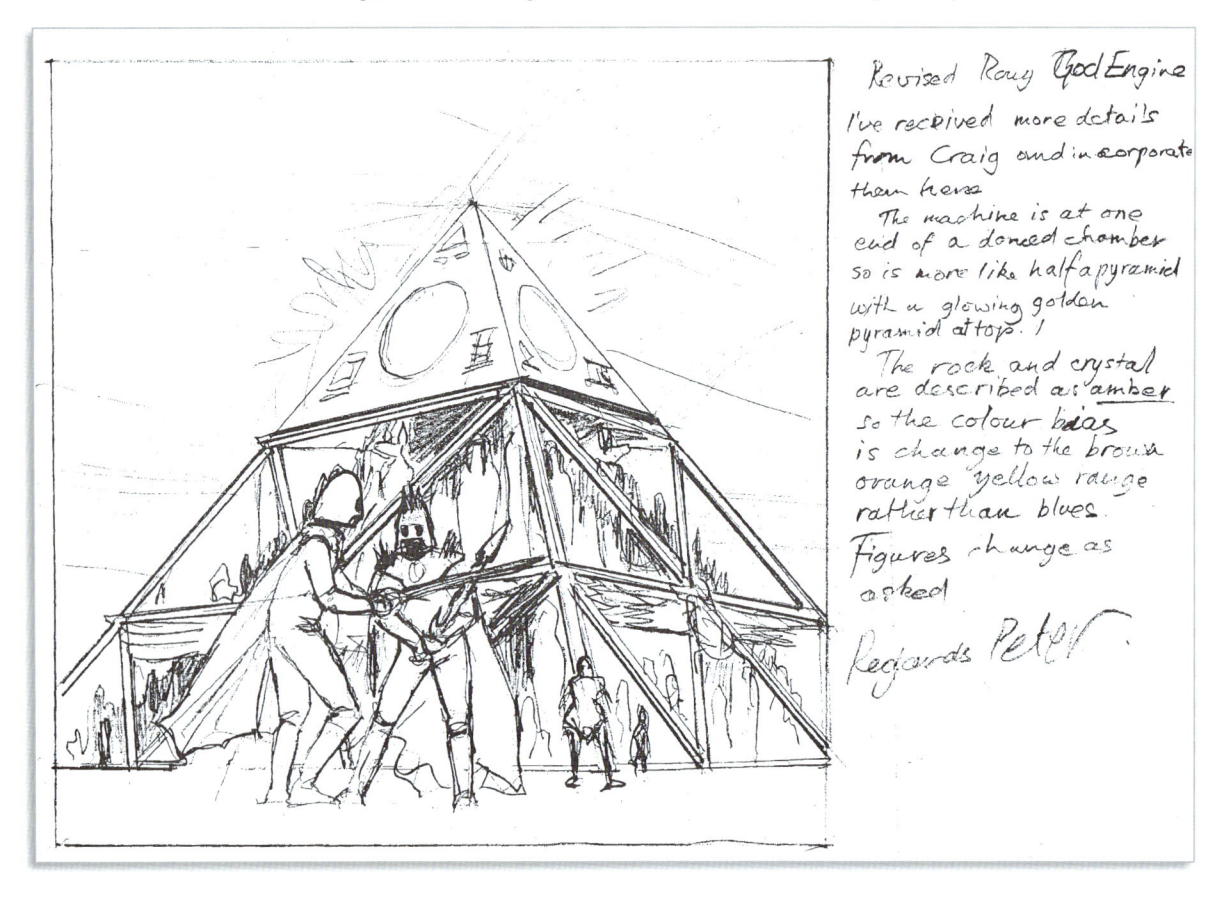

Revised Rough GodEngine

I've received more details from Craig and incorporated them here.

The machine is at one end of a domed chamber so is more like half a pyramid with a glowing golden pyramid at top.

The rock and crystal are described as amber so the colour bias is change to the brown orange yellow range rather than blues.

Figures change as asked.

Regards Peter

CELEBRATING FIFTY BOOKS

GodEngine as published, with cover art by Peter Elson.

MARK SALWOWSKI

Mark Salwowski was born in Enfield, north of London, in 1953 and lived there until migrating to Australia with his parents in 1964. The family arrived in Melbourne and lived and travelled around the east coast for a few years before settling in Sydney. After finishing high school, Salwowski started a Fine Art Diploma college course; but at the end of the second year his studies were cut short by a motorbike accident that led to months of hospitalisation and convalescence. In 1972, needing work, Salwowski took on several lowly positions before accepting a place at a large commercial printing establishment as an office junior in the games, greetings card and wrapping paper department. Although he rose to the position of senior product coordinator, gaining a thorough grounding in the printing industry and learning all about the operation of a modern commercial art studio, he still felt unfulfilled.

At that time, Salwowski was painting mainly abstracts in his spare time, exhibiting them occasionally, but through his association with the band Icehouse he started to move into sci-fi and fantasy art. After a particularly successful exhibition with a group of friends, in 1979 he and fellow artist Dennis Collins opened a gallery and studio specialising in the genre at Bondi Junction. The gallery side soon failed, but the studio, with plenty of work from the music industry and in advertising and magazine illustration for the likes of *Playboy*, *Penthouse*, *Cosmopolitan* and *Cleo*, went from strength to strength. But eventually the studio fizzled out as the artists began working for their own agents.

In 1984 Salwowski moved back to the UK and joined the Sarah Brown Agency, focusing on fantasy and sci-fi book covers. He worked for almost all the major publishers and dozens of different authors, and occasionally took on a bit of advertising work for the money. In 2000 he returned to Australia, where he still lives and works, though he is now semi-retired.

MATTHEW JONES

Matthew Jones has written episodes of the TV shows *The Split*, *Stan Lee's Lucky Man*, *Mr Selfridge*, *Doctor Who*, *Torchwood* and *Dirk Gently*. Working out of Los Angeles, he contributed a script and was supervising producer on the second season of the crime drama *Rogue*. As an executive producer, he has worked on twenty TV shows. He has produced or executive produced over eighty hours of drama, including Paul Abbott's BAFTA-winning *Shameless*, a show that he developed and went on to executive produce for its first four UK seasons. He also served as executive producer on the US remake of teen drama *Skins*, working between Toronto and New York. In 2019, he wrote the book for *Leave to Remain*, a musical at the Lyric Theatre Hammersmith. 'Theatre at its magnetic best,' wrote the *Evening Standard*. He lives in Clapham and writes full time.

Below: Mark Salwowski's original rough of the cover artwork for *Bad Therapy*.

CELEBRATING FIFTY BOOKS

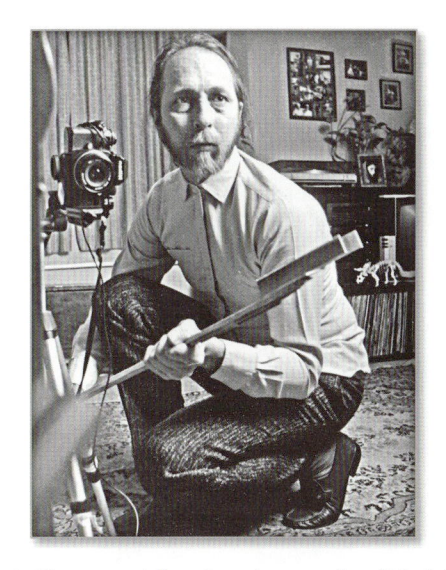

Above: specially-taken photographs of Mark Salwowski used as reference for his *Bad Therapy* cover. Below: Salwowski's completed original artwork for the cover.

BBC Books' Gary Russell-authored novelisation of the *Doctor Who* TV movie.

12: ALL CHANGE

The first clear indication of trouble ahead for Virgin Publishing's *Doctor Who* ranges came when BBC Books took the decision to publish themselves a novelisation of the new TV movie. Moreover, they commissioned one of Virgin's authors, Gary Russell, to write it. In addition to the novelisation, they published a script book and a postcard book of the movie, and news of *Doctor Who*'s impending small-screen return had also spurred other areas of merchandising into life, with the overall effect that BBC Worldwide – of which BBC Books was a part – was more aware than it had been previously of the show's enduring commercial potential.

At the end of 1995, just before the movie was announced, BBC Worldwide had reviewed all their then-current third party *Doctor Who* licences, and decided that BBC Books should in future publish any official tie-in titles. By coincidence – lucky for BBC Worldwide, unlucky for Virgin Publishing – Virgin's current licence period happened to expire in 1996, so BBC Worldwide simply declined to renew, signalling the end of Virgin's ranges of *Doctor Who* fiction.

'This wasn't an immediate decision,' reveals Peter Darvill-Evans. 'I actually spent some eighteen months prior to that trying to talk to BBC Worldwide about it.

'It was an intensely frustrating time. It was impossible to find out from BBC Worldwide what plans they had for *Doctor Who* licensing. At first, the only indication that they had any plans at all was the fact that I couldn't pin down Chris Weller, who at that time was in overall charge of the book ranges, Richard Hollis, the licensing manager, or anyone else to talk about renewing Virgin Publishing's licence. Then, once it became clear that BBC Worldwide wanted BBC Books to publish tie-ins to the new eighth Doctor TV movie, we still couldn't find out whether or not Virgin Publishing would be licensed to continue publishing all, some or none of the several sorts of *Doctor Who* books – New Adventures, Missing Adventures, non-fiction – that we and our predecessor companies had been producing for 25 years. It seemed hard to believe that such a long publishing history could be entirely swept away. I clung to the hope that BBC Worldwide would be interested mainly in the eighth Doctor, and that Virgin could be licensed to publish books – of all sorts – about the previous Doctors. Then, when it gradually became clear that BBC Books intended to create their own lines of *Doctor Who* fiction, we found ourselves negotiating over the rights to keep the existing Virgin titles in print and on sale. There

> **QUOTE, UNQUOTE**
>
> The Doctor: 'I've done so much. Saved entire races whose names I can't even remember. And why? Because of reasons. Because of principles. Truth, love, and harmony. Peace and goodwill. The best of intentions. Whatever I've done, I've done for these reasons. And there's been a price to pay. Sacrifices. People close to me have died. Four of my companions, hundreds of the universe's supporting cast. I could fill whole volumes with their names. Bystanders who helped me, perhaps for just a moment or two, and suffered for it. I've died myself, six times over. I have a responsibility. To every one of them, the living as well as the dead. If I let you succeed, if I let you make a world without reasons, then every sacrifice they've ever made in my name would be for nothing. They would have suffered, and died, and triumphed ... all for no purpose.'
>
> *Christmas on a Rational Planet*

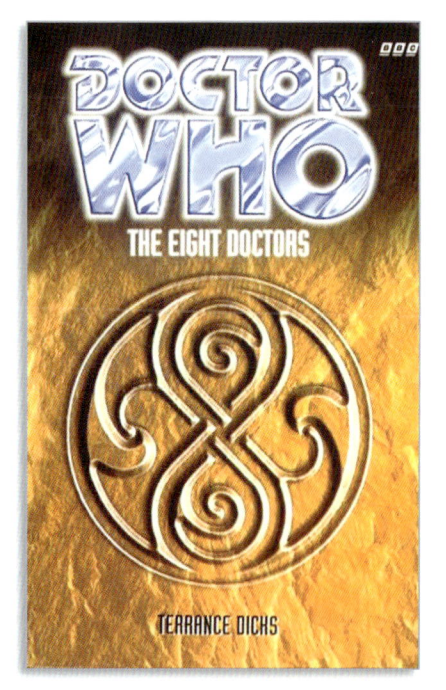

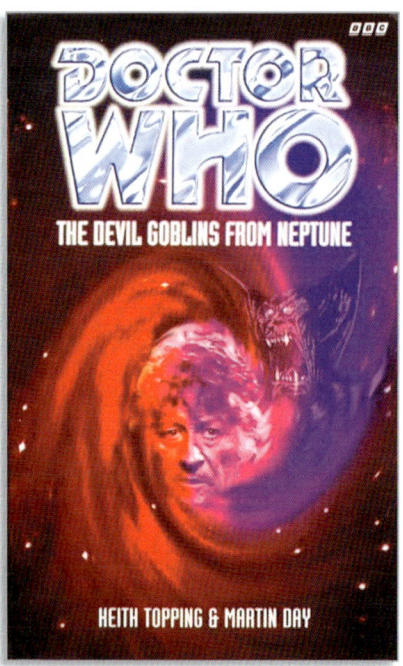

was talk of a continuing licence for the New Adventures, continuing to fill the continuity gap between the final story on television in 1989, "Survival", and the eighth Doctor.

'In the end, of course, it became apparent that BBC Worldwide wanted to be the sole publisher of *Doctor Who* material. I had to be grateful for a six month sell-off period in which to clear stocks of New Adventures and Missing Adventures, and for the concession that Virgin Publishing was allowed to sell most of its non-fiction books for a further period after the licence ended, including completing our range of non-fiction *Handbook* paperbacks on each Doctor's era. As we sought ways to clear stock of old books at knock-down prices and write off large amounts in the accounts, *Doctor Who* books came in 1996 to be seen by Virgin Publishing as a liability rather than an asset.

'Also, the delay and confusion meant that it was very difficult to make plans for the Fiction Department. A lot of energy that could have gone into creating new book series was expended in long, frustrating, fruitless meetings with BBC Worldwide people. I still don't know why they couldn't have just told us, back in 1995, that they intended to take back all *Doctor Who* publishing rights.'

The decision for BBC Worldwide to bring the publishing of the *Doctor Who* novels in-house was ultimately made by Chris Weller, then Managing Director of Consumer Publishing at BBC Worldwide. 'The decision to licence out the rights originally was taken at a time when BBC Worldwide was not the commercially aggressive publisher that it is today,' he explains. 'We were, by 1996, much more comfortable with specialist publishing and brand management and so felt equipped to take back the licence. We felt we could do a good job and make more money if we did it ourselves. The fact is that the BBC owns *Doctor Who* and it should be the BBC that fully benefits from the property.'

The possibility that the forthcoming TV movie might spawn a new ongoing *Doctor Who* series was also a factor in Weller's decision. 'We as a company made the movie happen, and it made sense that we should be in a position to experience any commercial upside as a result of it. We also published all the videos and managed all licensing activity, so we could co-ordinate our market approach.'

The day-to-day management of the BBC's new ranges of

The digital artwork covers created by the Black Sheep agency for *The Eight Doctors* by Terrance Dicks and *The Devil Goblins from Neptune* by Keith Topping and Martin Day – the debut titles in, respectively, the Eighth Doctor Adventures and Past Doctor Adventures ranges launched by BBC Books after the end of Virgin Publishing's *Doctor Who* licence. Both were issued on 2 June 1997.

ALL CHANGE

original *Doctor Who* novels fell to Rona Selby, Publishing Director of BBC Children's Books. 'It was an organisational thing,' says Weller. 'Rona identified the opportunity and pushed for us repatriating the rights. To the victor the spoils; plus she had a young editor, Nuala Buffini, who was keen to take on the publishing.

'As a publisher, I sympathise with Virgin. But a licence is not ownership. A commercial decision was made, but it was not a criticism of Virgin's stewardship of the brand, which had been energetic and exemplary. The reversion of rights was as a result of the expiry of the licence.'

With the knowledge that the licence was coming to an end, Rebecca Levene and her colleagues at Virgin decided that the best thing to do in the final four *Doctor Who* New Adventures was to start to wrap things up.

'We wanted to explain more what had been happening,' says Levene. 'Hence *Lungbarrow*. What was the point in keeping all these secrets that we would never be able to reveal, stuff that we'd been hinting at for ages? We wanted to wrap up the "Cartmel masterplan",' she adds, referring to the plans that script editor Andrew Cartmel had had for *Doctor Who* when it was cancelled as

Peter Elson's original artwork for the cover of *Eternity Weeps*.

223

THE WHO ADVENTURES

Above: Jon Sullivan's rough of the cover artwork for *The Room With No Doors*. Right: Sullivan at work on the final painting.

a BBC show back in 1989. These plans had been discussed with several writers at the time, among them Marc Platt and Ben Aaronovitch. 'It made sense for Marc to do this in *Lungbarrow*,' says Levene, 'as he had been talking about these things with Andrew. This felt right, and it was what had genuinely been talked about to end the seventh Doctor's era.

'We dropped the logo off these final books so that the bookshops would get used to getting the books without the *Doctor Who* branding – the company had already

ALL CHANGE

Jon Sullivan's completed original artwork for the cover of The Room With No Doors.

decided to continue the range but without the Doctor. It wasn't to try to trick people into buying them or anything like that, as we assumed that the readers were intelligent enough to work out what was going on.'

The final four *Doctor Who* books in the New Adventures range were Jim Mortimore's *Eternity Weeps*; Kate Orman's *The Room With No Doors*, originally titled *All That Glitters Is Not God*; Marc Platt's *Lungbarrow*; and Lance Parkin's *The Dying Days*.

The cover artwork for these four titles was commissioned from Peter Elson (*Eternity Weeps*), Jon Sullivan (*The Room With No Doors*) and newcomer Fred Gambino (*Lungbarrow* and *The Dying Days*). For *Lungbarrow*, it was suggested that visual effects designer Mike Tucker's talents be employed to create a model of the alien Badger – the Doctor's protector in the story – for the artist to use as reference for the character. Tucker – who had previously worked with Craig Hinton to develop new Ice Warrior designs for *GodEngine* (see page 214) and co-written with actress Sophie Aldred the non-fiction book *Ace!*, subtitled *The Inside Story of the End of an Era*, published by Virgin in March 1996 – duly created a small model of the character, and also a model of a lizard-like creature that ultimately was unused.

The Dying Days featured the eighth Doctor, as played by Paul McGann in the TV movie, in an adventure with the Ice Warriors. 'Unfortunately we only had time to do the one eighth Doctor book,' says Levene, 'or we would have done more. However, with needing to wrap up the seventh Doctor, and with the problems of having to commission so far in advance, we ended up with just the one.'

The Dying Days' author Lance Parkin put forward a cover idea intended to recall that of the very first New Adventure. As he explained in a letter to Virgin: 'The composition is a mirror image of the

Top left: the maquette – small model – that Mike Tucker created of Badger, for use as reference for the cover artwork of *Lungbarrow*.

Bottom left: Fred Gambino's rough of the artwork.

Below: the other maquette that Mike Tucker made, which in this case went unused.

Lungbarrow, with art by Fred Gambino.

THE WHO ADVENTURES

Lungbarrow artwork by Daryl Joyce, printed in Issue 305 of *Doctor Who Magazine* to tie in with a Marc Platt interview.

ALL CHANGE

> ### LUNGBARROW GENESIS
>
> Like his earlier New Adventure *Cat's Cradle: Time's Crucible*, *Lungbarrow* started life in the late 1980s as a proposal that writer Marc Platt submitted to script editor Andrew Cartmel for a potential *Doctor Who* TV story. Inspired in part by Mervyn Peake's *Gormenghast* novels, it involved the Doctor revisiting his family home, Lungbarrow, on the Time Lords' home planet Gallifrey. *Doctor Who*'s then producer John Nathan-Turner felt its ideas were too weird for it to be used in the show; however, its setting of a large, cobwebby, Victorian-style house was retained for Platt's televised story 'Ghost Light', which was commissioned in its stead and became the last 'classic era' *Doctor Who* to be recorded.

Timewyrm: Genesys cover, with a similar colour scheme for the lettering and "widescreen" bars. The background is the outside wall of the Tower of London. Gilgamesh's place is taken by Benny – wearing practical clothes that aren't too bright. She's looking defiant and not unlike Emma Thompson. Ishtar is replaced by the "new Ice Warrior". This is what Mark Jones and myself guess the Ice Warriors would look like with a big American budget. They don't look like the BBC version. McCoy is replaced by McGann. Again, his face is ghostly, although it is perhaps a little larger (and lower) than on the original. He's fairly angry/determined looking rather than smiling.'

In the end, this idea was not taken forward – although a drawing that Parkin had supplied of the proposed 'new Ice Warrior' (see page 231) was used as reference by Fred Gambino when he came to do the final cover art. Mark Jones, who had produced the drawing, was a friend of Parkin's with whom he would later co-author a book titled *Dark Matters* about the works of Philip Pullman, but he had no other involvement in the writing of this New Adventure.

Although *The Dying Days* was the final book commissioned, it was not the final one published. Following it in the shops a week later was the long-delayed *So Vile A Sin*, completing at last the Psi-Powers Series and allowing fans to discover exactly how Roz had come to die, and what had caused the Doctor and Chris such upset in *Bad Therapy*.

As usual, reviewers had mixed opinions on the books. *TV Zone*'s Craig Hinton described *Eternity Weeps* as 'Drivel. Distasteful rubbish,' but *Doctor Who Magazine*'s Dave Owen took a different view: 'arresting throughout … a return to form.' Hinton liked *The Room With No Doors*, extolling its virtues as 'an intriguing mystery, with enough lavish description and rich characterisation to keep both committed fans and casual readers hooked until the very end'. Marc Platt's *Lungbarrow*, though, was another book that split the vote. Hinton liked it: 'Marc weaves plot strands from all of the New Adventures to build *Lungbarrow* into a very complex yet extremely well written novel that answers every question that you ever had about the Doctor.' Owen, however, was unsure: 'rather more frustrating than rewarding. It's weird and wonderful – but, unfortunately, never simultaneously.'

Finally, comment on *The Dying Days* was largely positive. Hinton considered it to be 'a

> ### QUOTE, UNQUOTE
>
> The Doctor: 'I've dined at the tables of alien emperors and languished in their dungeons. I've seen whole galaxies born in the fires of the Aurora Temporalis. I've saved lives and taken them too. Which of you has even heard of the Frost-Fairs of Ice-Askar the Winter Star? Or dreamt of the torches burning on the canals of Venice?'
>
> *Lungbarrow*

SIMON WINSTONE

Working as editorial assistant for Virgin Publishing in the late 1990s was one of Simon Winstone's first jobs. He oversaw the Missing Adventures and was briefly in charge of the New Adventures after they had ceased to be a *Doctor Who* tie-in. His only novel, the post-*Doctor Who* New Adventure *Where Angels Fear*, was co-written with Rebecca Levene, his predecessor on the range.

In the late 1990s, Winstone moved into TV, initially on the popular ITV soap opera *Emmerdale*. He next worked on the BBC's *EastEnders*, starting in 2001 as a story editor and then from 2004 to 2005 as a producer. In 2005, he was announced as a script editor for the revived *Doctor Who* on TV, a post he held from 2006 to 2007. He also script-edited the first episode of the spin-off *The Sarah Jane Adventures* in 2007.

Winstone then moved to work for the independent production company Red Planet, and held posts such as head of drama for Wales, head of development and executive producer. His extensive credits include *Death in Paradise* (2013), *Dickensian* (2016), and *Hooten and the Lady* (2016).

In 2017, he was appointed BBC Studios' Head of Drama for Wales, overseeing drama series and serials and all productions out of the Cardiff scripted unit. In 2019, he served as an executive producer on the Amazon Prime and BBC Two show *Good Omens*.

---

splendid job … let down by its rather loose plot.' Owen felt it was 'a very atypical New Adventure to end the series, especially when compared to the gloomier style that has predominated over the past year. Yet it showcases perfectly the range's ability to actually expand *Doctor Who* and make its legend larger … Being creative within an existing framework is the difficult task facing all *Doctor Who* writers, and Lance Parkin here makes it look deceptively easy.'

Virgin's decision to continue the New Adventures without the Doctor once the licence expired meant that the focus would now shift to former companion Bernice Summerfield, a character created for the range itself and not owned by the BBC. 'This decision was, I suppose I must now admit, taken partly out of spite,' says Peter Darvill-Evans. 'I felt we'd been messed around. There was little chance that the New Adventures could succeed for long without the *Doctor Who* brand and the Doctor. I had always planned that they should be able to stand on their own feet and exist as a science fiction series without the Doctor; however, I had never anticipated that such a range would have to compete with a rival series that had both the Doctor and the full backing of the BBC.'

'I thought it was madness,' says Rebecca Levene. 'I just didn't think they'd sell at all. I knew the quality would be good, I just didn't think anyone would buy them. But Peter and other people at Virgin felt that they'd be okay, so I agreed to look after the books, and they did do much better than I'd expected. Not as well as the *Doctor Who* ones, though, and I was responsible for only the first four or so, and then our editorial assistant Simon Winstone took over, by which time I'd gone freelance.

'I stepped back from the Bernice New Adventure books to concentrate on setting up Virgin Worlds, a new original fiction line, for the company. I commissioned the first four Virgin Worlds titles before I left. Unfortunately, without me there pushing for it, there was no-one else with the enthusiasm, and Peter was being kept busy on other things. Fiction is very hard to do, and Virgin felt at the time that it wanted to concentrate on licensed music books, which always sold well.'

The termination of the *Doctor Who* ranges seemed to

mark the end of any real enthusiasm within Virgin Publishing to progress with original fiction.

'Bex and Simon read the writing on the wall far more clearly than I did,' recalls Darvill-Evans. 'They got out. First Bex and then Simon left Virgin Publishing, worked freelance for a while, and quickly found other work.

'I hung on. I inherited the last of the non-Doctor New Adventures. It was sort of fitting that I should have been the hands-on editor of the series at its birth and at its death. I also inherited the Virgin Worlds imprint, and I saw into print the four launch titles that Bex had commissioned.

'But by that time it was clear that my days at Virgin Publishing were numbered. I wasn't made redundant, it was far messier and more unpleasant than that. Since 1990 I had been a self-employed consultant, and Virgin could have simply told me that they didn't need me anymore. Instead, I was moved out of my office, I was no longer invited to management meetings about the Fiction Department, and I was subjected to increasingly harsh and personal criticism. I was getting on with commissioning more non-fiction books – the *Buffy the Vampire Slayer* guide and *The Complete Kubrick*, among many others – but I was given several additional projects – the website, supervising the editing of Richard Branson's own autobiography – that were complex and fraught with difficulties and stress.

'In the end, about a year after Bex and Simon left, after editing the Bernice books, the Virgin Worlds novels, and a

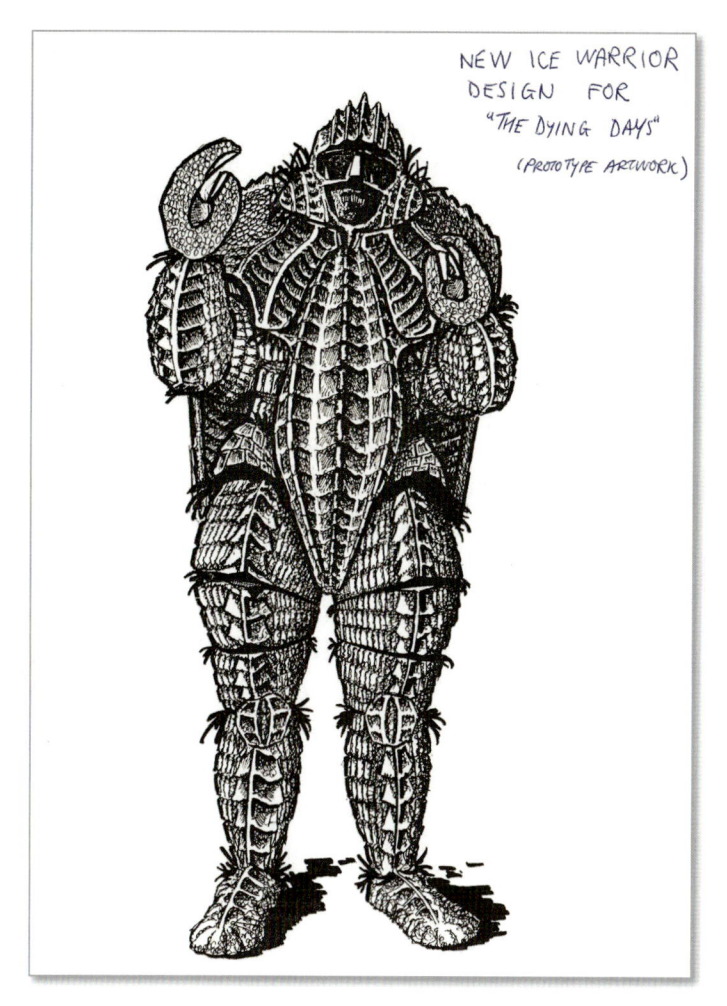

Above: Mark Jones' concept drawing of the new type of Ice Warrior featured in *The Dying Days*. This was used by Fred Gambino as reference for the cover art (see page 233) and Jones received a credit at the front of the book, where his design was described as 'Segalfied' – a reference to Philip Segal, producer of the 1996 *Doctor Who* TV movie.

THE VIRGIN DOCTOR …?

One aspect of *The Dying Days* much discussed amongst fans was the definite implication that the Doctor and Bernice at one point share a night of passion together – the first clear indication in any media of the Doctor having a friendship with one of his companions, or indeed anyone else, going beyond the purely platonic. One of Lance Parkin's working titles for the book was *Virginity Lost*, others being *Licence Revoked*, *Murder Eight* and *Morte D'Octor* – the first two of these referring obliquely to the loss of Virgin's *Doctor Who* licence. The book was commissioned in July 1996 on the basis of a three-page synopsis, in preference to a rival eighth Doctor novel proposal from a different author.

load of non-fiction titles, all the time under immense pressure for me to quit, I was told to go. It's a pity that my last year at Virgin Publishing was so bitterly unpleasant. And there can be little doubt that it was the ending of the *Doctor Who* licence that precipitated the end of my long and very happy reign as fiction bod-in-charge. The consolation is that, for the many years that the Fiction Department existed, it was a great place to work: the staff and the authors were wonderful, hugely talented people with whom it was great fun, and an honour, to work.

'The last New Adventure was published a few months before I finally left; the last of the Virgin Worlds books only a month or so before I went. Although the staff that remained from what had been my department – Kerri, James and Kathleen, editing the erotica imprints – were interested in publishing other fiction genres, once I had gone there was no-one at management level with any interest in fiction.

'And, in any case, some months later there began a series of redundancy programmes that shrank the workforce. In retrospect I can only assume that there were deeper and long-term problems at Virgin Publishing that I was unaware of. It may be significant that in my last year the practice of circulating management accounts to senior managers ceased. It's all too easy to take rejection personally, and to ascribe particular significance to those areas of an organisation about which one knows. The wider picture is often far more complex and impersonal.'

Despite the somewhat low-key ending to Virgin's *Doctor Who* ranges, Rebecca Levene is immensely proud of what they managed to achieve. 'I had a fantastic time working on those books. I met a lot of people who have become close friends. I worked with a load of very talented people. Had an absolute ball. I'm very proud of those books. I genuinely think we produced the best TV tie-in range going, and I think most of that was down to Peter. I learned a lot doing it. I don't think I'll ever be as happy as I was working on those books. It was a very nurturing environment both for us as staff and for the writers we worked with.

'I have two main memories of that time, that

Below: artist Fred Gambino's roughs for the cover of *The Dying Days*; the first was preferred by Virgin to the second.

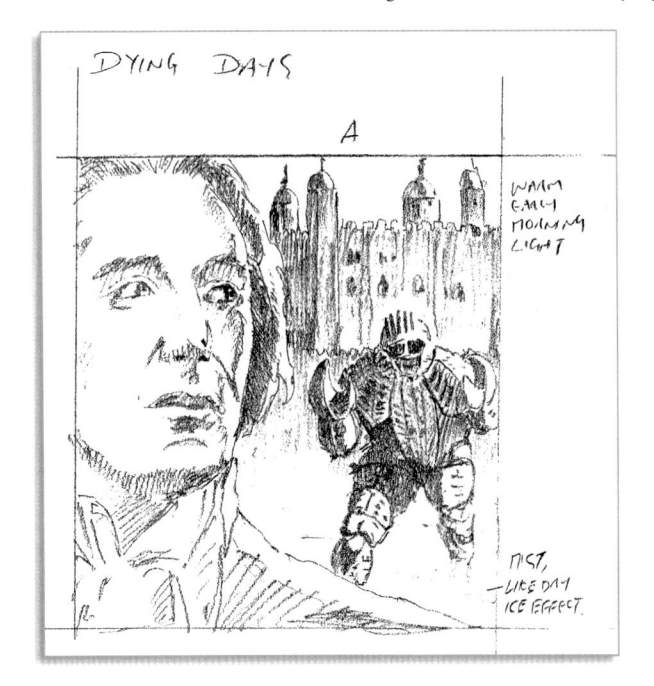

The Dying Days, with art by Fred Gambino.

FRED GAMBINO

Fred Gambino has been drawing for as long as he can remember, being inspired by iconic British sci-fi shows such as *Doctor Who* and the Gerry Anderson puppet series. After graduating from the Derby College of Art and Technology – now Derby University – he took a part-time job delivering groceries while painting in his spare time. Trips down to London with his portfolio eventually led to his first book cover commissions. He worked as an illustrator for clients on both sides of the Atlantic, including Penguin, Warner, Little Brown, Thames Television, National Geographic, *Scientific American*, Leo Burnet, *Der Speigel*, DNA Productions, Paramount, Agent 16, Whizzkids, Lego, Mattel, AVP and the US Postal service!

In 2001 Gambino was approached by DNA productions to work on the Oscar-nominated *Jimmy Neutron Boy Genius*, on which he was concept artist and matte painter. From 2002 to 2003 he worked on an ultimately unreleased Lego TV series – working title *Project X* – for Tinopolis TV. He was responsible for early visual development of all aspects of the show from environments to characters. This was followed by work on other ultimately unreleased projects: *C Horse*, *The Star Beast* and *Life in a Pickle*.

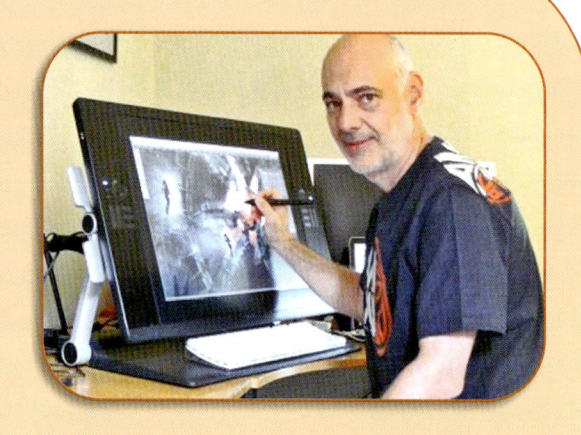

Further commissions that did see release include: *The Ant Bully* (2006), *Epic Mickey* (2015), *Escape from Planet Earth* (2012), *The Tale of Despereaux* (2008), *Firebreather* (2010), *Guardians of the Galaxy* (2014) and *Thor: Ragnarok* (2017).

A book of his work was published in 2000 by Paper Tiger entitled *Ground Zero*, and in 2014 Titan Books followed this up with *The Art of Fred Gambino: Dark Shepherd*.

---

sum up everything that it was about for me. I was on the phone to Lance Parkin, talking about his factual book *The History of the Universe*, and we were having a discussion about what year the Dalek invasion of Earth took place. I suddenly stepped back from myself and realised that I was being paid to have a conversation about when the Daleks invaded Earth. I said to myself then that this was never going to happen again. And indeed it never has.

'My second memory is of our editorial assistant Andy Bodle's demented letters to the authors – I believe a lot of the authors kept them. He used to write a sane version for the file, so we knew what he was doing, and then send these mad letters out. One I remember particularly was to Andy Lane, and read something like: "Dear Noddy Holder, I've always enjoyed your music. Oh, by the way, here are some books by Andy Lane. They're some old rubbish, but can you pass them on to him. Yours, Andy Bodle." And there were many more of that ilk.

'There's one final thing that I feel I now have to admit to. Not that I feel at all guilty, but inquiring minds might be interested to know … By the time we were doing the final books, Simon and I were so bored of writing cover copy that we used to play games, and one of them was to insert into the cover text as many of a particular type of thing as we could. If you look at the cover for … I think it's *Eternity Weeps* … we decided to insert as many books of the Bible as we could: there's *Revelation*, *Genesis*, *Numbers*, *Exodus* and so on. On the back cover of another book we decided to include titles of Virgin's erotic books – it might have been a Missing Adventure actually, probably

The Dark Path – and that was a lot harder to do, as many of the titles were full sentences. But we did our best.'

After six years and 61 books, the *Doctor Who* New Adventures finally came to an end. In that time, Virgin Publishing had managed to achieve what many critics had initially felt impossible: keeping a range of original novels alive and vibrant against a backdrop of no new *Doctor Who* on TV and decreasing publicity and interest in the show from the general public.

'What can I say …?' reflects Peter Darvill-Evans. 'The decade I spent at Virgin Publishing was the most rewarding and enjoyable of my life, so far, and I and the team around me achieved some remarkable successes, among the most significant being the wide range of long-lived *Doctor Who* publishing we created. It was a privilege to work with such a talented, enthusiastic and friendly network of editors, writers and artists. I don't know how much credit we can claim for keeping *Doctor Who* alive during the 1990s, but for at least the first half of the decade there was nothing being produced for *Doctor Who* fans except the books we were publishing and *Doctor Who Magazine*.'

In an afterword to *The Dying Days*, the final *Doctor Who* New Adventure, Peter Darvill-Evans, Rebecca Levene and Simon Winstone wrote a joint message to readers: 'We hope the books we've published have entertained more than they've irritated, and that we've contributed something worthwhile to the continuing universe that is *Doctor Who*. We're glad we were able to provide a forum for so many talented authors … Doctors may come and Doctors may go, but with your support the New Adventures can go on forever.'

Peter Darvill-Evans revisits the TARDIS.

The first Missing Adventure, *Goth Opera*, with cover art by Alister Pearson.

APPENDIX A:
THE MISSING ADVENTURES

The huge success of the New Adventures range, after its launch in 1991, soon led Peter Darvill-Evans and his colleague Rebecca Levene to start to think about how they might expand Virgin's *Doctor Who* fiction output. As noted in Chapter 2, Darvill-Evans was initially very resistant to the idea of producing novels with any but the most recent incarnation of the Doctor. Now, he found himself under increasing pressure to reconsider. There were, though, conflicting considerations.

'Bex and the authors were very much in favour,' recalls Darvill-Evans. 'They're creative people, and a new series of books would provide them with further challenges and opportunities. Some fans, as far as I could tell, were keen, but there were also murmurings from fandom that not everyone would be able to buy more than one book each month (the then publication rate of the New Adventures). Virgin, it was said, were becoming greedy, and not looking after the interests of fans. This latter point worried Virgin's management and salespeople – would the book trade, never mind the end readers, be prepared to stock a second series of *Doctor Who* novels? And would it harm Virgin's reputation – would people think Virgin was cashing in on *Doctor Who*? Was there a danger of killing the goose that laid the golden egg? I found myself in two minds: I had always thought of *Doctor Who* fiction as going forward, not looking back, and I didn't like the idea of publishing stories with old Doctors; on the other hand, I've always had a commercial attitude, and if new stories about old Doctors were likely to sell, I realised that I should publish them.

'As far as I can remember, I and Virgin came to support the idea in increments. Doubling the publication rate of the New Adventures hadn't harmed sales. John Peel's novelisations of the 1960s TV stories "The Power of the Daleks" and "The Evil of the Daleks" did well in 1993 – and were a powerful indicator that old Doctor stories

Below: the original proof cover of *Goth Opera*; the artwork was amended prior to publication to remove most of the blood from the blouse of the Doctor's companion Nyssa.

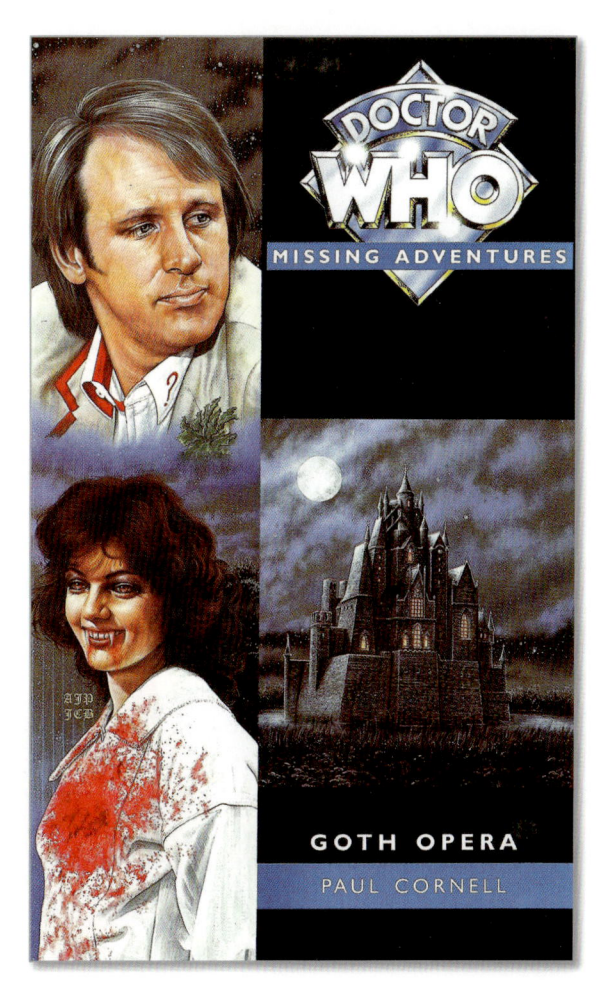

still sold well. The first *Decalog*, too, was a straw in the wind: short story collections were big publishing business in the '60s, but by the '90s they had become very difficult to sell. The fact that *Decalog* sold well into the book trade suggested to us that bookshops believed that anything with *Doctor Who* on the cover would sell okay.'

The success of the first *Decalog* collection was ultimately to make up Darvill-Evans' and Virgin Publishing's minds. This book had been proposed to them early in 1993 by Stephen James Walker and Mark Stammers, two of the authors who had been working on the company's non-fiction *Doctor Who* titles. It had been originally conceived but ultimately deemed unworkable as a potential fan fiction adjunct to *The Frame*, the popular *Doctor Who* fanzine that was edited and published at the time by Walker, Stammers and David J Howe. Eventually Stammers suggested that he and Walker try their luck with the project at Virgin (Howe being already tied up working on *Timeframe*, a celebratory book for *Doctor Who*'s thirtieth anniversary). 'It was I who came up with the title *Decalog* (originally *Decalogue*),' recalls Walker, 'and Peter suggested having a linking story running through the book – the idea being that people who read it cover-to-cover would get something extra out of it. Mark and I were quite happy with that suggestion, but realised it would make it a bit more difficult to pull the project together. For that reason, I decided to write the linking story myself, rather than ask one of the individual contributors to do it, which could have made the editing process a bit of a nightmare! The linking story's title, *Playback*, was borrowed from a Raymond Chandler crime novel, reflecting its 'private eye' theme.

'We invited a fair number of writers to submit ideas for stories – not only well-known names from the *Doctor Who* novels range but also people whom we had known for years and considered to be excellent writers, but who for one reason or another had never done any of the novels. David Auger and Tim Robins were two who fell into that category. We also received quite a lot of unsolicited ideas. In the end we had far more good ideas than we were able to use. We just had to pick what we thought were the best ones and reject the rest, which was actually a very difficult process.

'I was extremely pleased with how the book turned out. It received exceptionally positive feedback from individual readers (although some reviewers in certain specialist newsstand magazines, who, I understand, had themselves submitted short story anthology ideas that had been rejected by Virgin, were less kind), and I

The cover of the first *Decalog* volume, with artwork by Mark Salwowski.

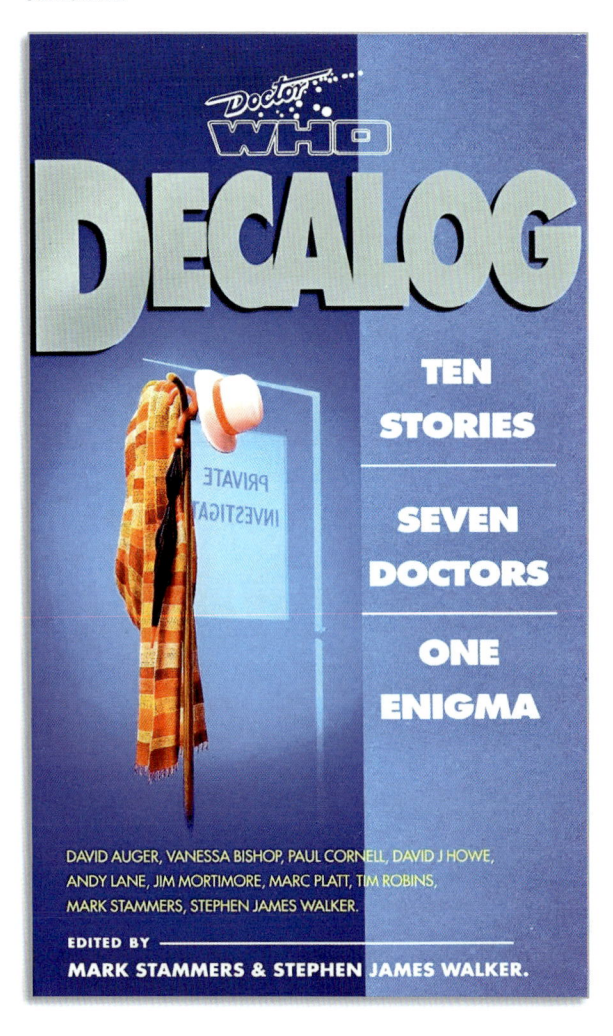

was subsequently told by Virgin that it had outsold all of the New Adventures novels.

'The second book, subtitled *Lost Property*, was put together in a similar way, and again I was very pleased with the end result, although I did feel that Virgin allowed us rather less editorial freedom on that one than they had on the first. For instance, they rejected our original idea for a linking story (which was somewhat akin to the idea that Terrance Dicks later used in his *The Eight Doctors* novel) and substituted another theme – the Doctor's homes – that we felt worked less well. I was also very disappointed when Peter vetoed our use of another David Auger story proposal, which we felt was one of the strongest that had been submitted, on the grounds that it was "too radical". It contained a number of ideas that were later echoed in Lawrence Miles' Faction Paradox concept in the BBC Books novels.

'Partly because of that perceived lessening of editorial freedom, and partly because we were aware that lots of other writers were vigorously lobbying Virgin to be given an opportunity to edit their own *Decalog* collections, Mark and I decided to call it a day after the second book.'

The third *Decalog*, subtitled *Consequences*, was edited by Andy Lane and Justin Richards, the linking theme this time being the consequences of the Doctor's actions running through a series of ten adventures. After Virgin lost the licence to publish *Doctor Who* fiction, two further *Decalog* titles followed. *Decalog 4: Re:Generations*, again edited by Lane and Richards, contained stories of Roz Forrester's family, while *Decalog 5: Wonders*, edited by Paul Leonard and Jim Mortimore, was an unthemed collection of science fiction tales, only one of which, with Bernice Summerfield, had any connection to *Doctor Who* (although characters from one of the others later gained a tangential connection when they were reused in a Faction Paradox story). The first *Decalog* was sold into shops some six months before its

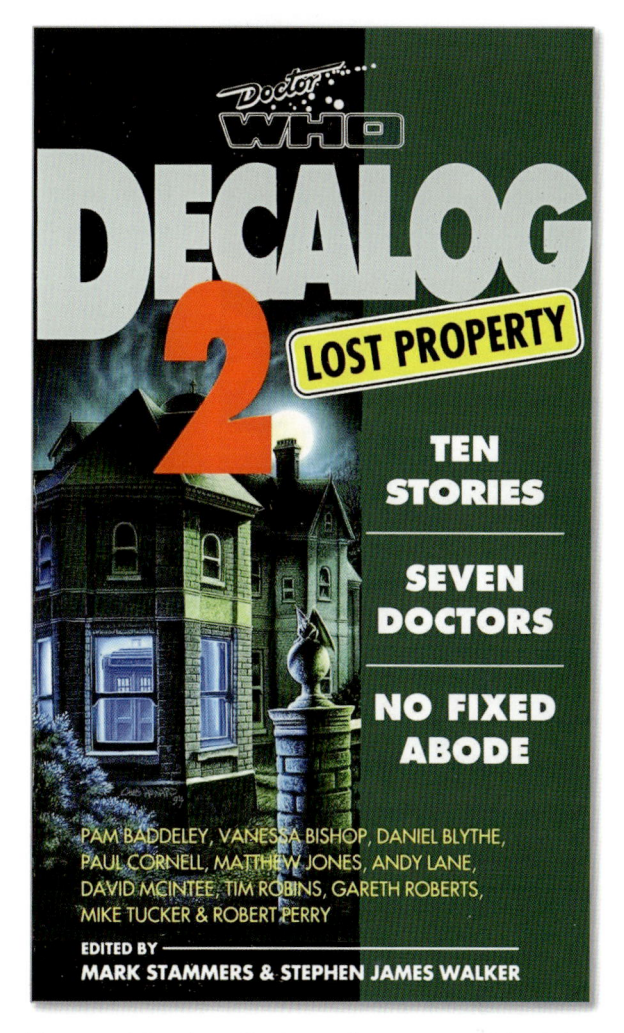

The second *Decalog* collection, with cover artwork by Colin Howard.

publication date of 17 March 1994, and Darvill-Evans quickly realised that he was onto a winner. There was clearly a market for books featuring earlier Doctors and so, around September 1993, he started to put together plans for the Missing Adventures range.

Like the New Adventures, these past Doctor titles were initially planned to be published once every two months, but such was the interest that, even before the first was in the shops, they were moved to a monthly schedule. 'The reason for this,' explains Darvill-Evans, 'was simply one of common sense. It was much easier for bookshops to take two books from us each month, every month, than for them to have to decide what to take on a changeable schedule. Also, our sales reps at Virgin could easily sell more books on the back of the success of the New Adventures – and so that's what they did.'

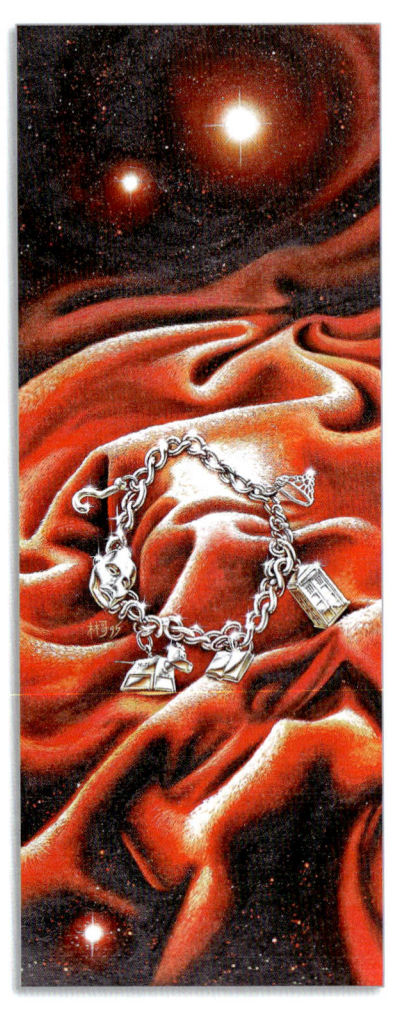

'They loved them!' confirms Rebecca Levene. 'They wanted them to be published one a month as quickly as possible, and this meant we had to commission twice as many books as we had been up to that point.'

On actual publication there was a two month gap between the first and second Missing Adventures, but from then on they became monthly.

'While I always retained a watching brief over the New Adventures – taking part in meetings and discussions about new characters, and story arcs, and so on – the Missing Adventures were very much Rebecca's fiefdom,' says Darvill-Evans. 'I approved cover artwork and cover copy, and I was always happy to read sample text and story submissions when Bex asked me to, but as far as the stories and the choice of authors went, I pretty much left her to get on with it – I knew she was more than capable of doing so without me sticking my nose in. And Bex, of course, delegated some of the work to Andy Bodle and even more so to Simon Winstone.'

The first of the Missing Adventures, Paul Cornell's *Goth Opera*, was published on 21 July 1994. As previously explained, its plot was linked to that of Terrance Dicks' New Adventures novel *Blood Harvest* as a further incentive for regular readers to check out the new range. However, Cornell recalls that its origins actually

Below: the third, fourth and fifth *Decalog* collections, all with Colin Howard cover art. Above left: Howard's original artwork for the third book.

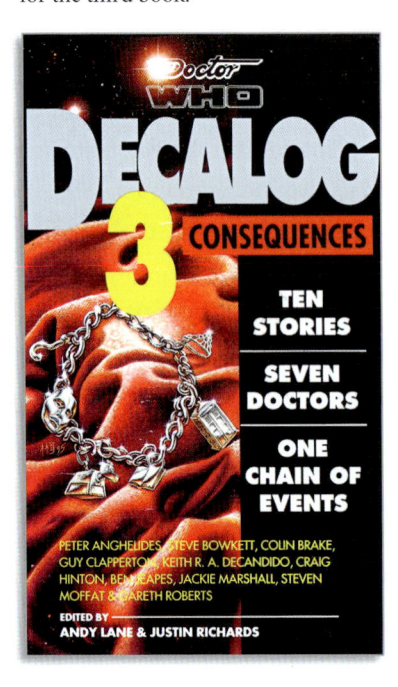

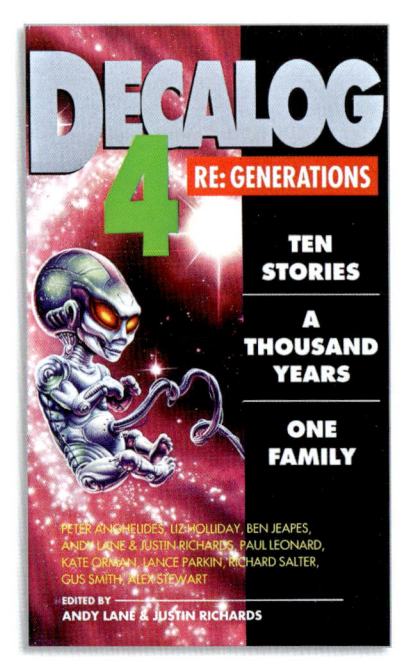

lay in an earlier comic strip proposal: 'I'd pitched a *Doctor Who Magazine* comic strip involving the fourth Doctor battling Dracula to the magazine's then editor, John Freeman. He turned it down, but when Peter Darvill-Evans told me that Virgin were starting a new line of Missing Adventures, I pitched it to him, changing the characters in my proposal from the fourth Doctor and Sarah to the fifth Doctor, Nyssa and Tegan.'

Cornell subsequently resubmitted the original proposal to new *Doctor Who Magazine* editor Gary Russell, who was unaware that his predecessor had previously turned it down. It eventually appeared as a fifth Doctor strip called 'Blood Invocation' in Marvel's 1995 *Doctor Who Yearbook*.

'While we were all waiting to see who'd get to write the first Missing Adventure,' says Cornell, 'I talked to Peter at one of Virgin's parties upstairs at the Café München in central London. He told me that Terrance also had a vampire book on the go and was wondering if they'd clash; so that got me talking to Terrance about how we could make them flow into each other.'

Darvill-Evans was very keen on his authors sharing ideas and so organised parties and other gatherings at which everyone could meet and swap suggestions. These sessions resulted in a great many developments in the book ranges: ideas such as the writing out of Ace, the introduction of new companions and the development of a hardback non-fiction book about the Doctor's companions were all brainstormed and eventually came to fruition as a result of the discussions. Some of the authors' feedback was also worked into Virgin's Writers' Guidelines; and it was in the February 1994 version of this document Darvill-Evans and Levene first added in a section on the Missing Adventures, planning for which was by then at an advanced stage. Several pieces of advice were offered to aspiring writers: 'Watch video recordings of TV stories that feature the Doctor and companions you want to use; read some of the New Adventures: the Missing Adventures will be similar in format and length; when it is published, read Barry Letts' novelisation of his script of "The Paradise of Death" –

BARRY LETTS

Barry Letts was born in Loughborough in 1925 and was originally an actor. He performed in repertory in York and worked for a local radio station in Leeds. He also appeared in a number of British films and TV series throughout the 1950s and 1960s.

In 1967 he took up directing, subsequently working on many BBC shows, including *Z-Cars*, *The Newcomers* and *Doctor Who* ('The Enemy of the World'). From 1970 to 1974 he took on the post of producer of *Doctor Who*, and was in charge of all but the first of Jon Pertwee's stories in the lead role. During that time he also directed and pseudonymously co-wrote several stories, including 'The Dæmons' (1971), which he later novelised for the Target range.

Letts then returned to directing, and also became producer on the BBC's Sunday classic serials; these included *Rebecca of Sunnybrook Farm* (1978), *The History of Mr Polly* (1980), *The Hound of the Baskervilles* (1982), *Beau Geste* (1983), *The Invisible Man* (1984), and *Sense and Sensibility* (1985).

Letts returned to *Doctor Who* in 1980 when he was appointed executive producer to oversee new producer John Nathan-Turner during the show's eighteenth season. In the 1990s he wrote two *Doctor Who* radio serials ('The Paradise of Death', 1994; 'The Ghosts of N-Space', 1995), and later novelised these for Virgin He collaborated with Terrance Dicks on the BBC Books *Doctor Who* novel *Deadly Reunion* (2003), published to coincide with the show's fortieth anniversary, and wrote *Island of Death* (2005) for the same range. In addition, he contributed a script to Big Finish's *Sarah Jane Smith* audio range (2003).

Letts died on 9 October 2009.

THE WHO ADVENTURES

The Paradise of Death, regarded by Virgin as a 'prototype Missing Adventure', with cover art by Alister Pearson.

it can be considered as a prototype Missing Adventure. It is a brand new story; it is more complex than a TV story; it contains scenes that would be too difficult and expensive to produce on TV; it fits into the continuity of the TV stories; it captures the flavour of the TV stories of its particular Doctor and companions; and it's a darn good read. All of these are attributes that we want to see in the Missing Adventures.'

The document went on to say: 'A Missing Adventure will be similar to a New Adventure in many respects. It will be about the same length, and it will be published in the same format – although the Missing Adventures will have their own distinctive cover design. Its plot will be more complex than that of a TV story. It will appeal to teenagers and adults, but unlike a TV story it will not have to appeal to young children. It will have an epic scale that most of the TV stories, restricted as they were by budgets and special effects technology, could not aspire to.

'But there will be differences, too, between a Missing Adventure and a New Adventure. Because a Missing Adventure should replicate the atmosphere of television *Doctor Who*, it should be written in a straightforward style and should eschew the stylistic experimentation of some of the New Adventures. The

STEPHEN MARLEY

Stephen Marley was brought up in Derby and later moved to London, Lyon in France, back to London, and then a few other cities before ending up back in Derby. In 1986, after departing Manchester, he left the academic life of a sociology lecturer gladly behind to take up writing full time. He has so far published nine novels and a number of short stories.

His first novels were three fantasy epics set in ancient China – the *Chia Black Dragon* series – and published by Harper Collins and Random House, but in 1995 his one and only *Doctor Who* novel was published by Virgin Publishing in the Missing Adventures series. The title was *Managra* (an anagram of 'anagram') and featured the fourth Doctor and his companion Sarah Jane Smith. The setting was Europa, a future version of Europe composed of numerous nations from the 16th Century to the 20th living cheek by jowl. Various historical characters in Europa include Byron (three of him), Torquemada, Mary Shelley and Casanova.

Marley has also written two *Judge Dredd* novels, *Dreddlocked* and *Dread Dominion*, again for Virgin in the early 1990s.

Marley has followed a parallel career in video games. In one PlayStation game he designed, *Martian Gothic*, he voice-directed, amongst others, Fenella Fielding and Julie Peasgood. In 2015 he brought out a religious/mystery thriller, *The Heresy*, that reached number eight in the mystery thrillers chart in America. At the time of writing, he is putting the finishing touches to a fantasy epic about the Virgin Mary.

readers of the New Adventures are mainly *Doctor Who* fans, but we publish them with an eye to reaching a wider readership; the Missing Adventures, on the other hand, will almost certainly appeal to no-one but *Doctor Who* fans. Some New Adventures are SF novels that happen to include a character called the Doctor; a Missing Adventure can't be like that, and must be Doctorcentric.'

The Guidelines went on to establish that Virgin was looking for 'original recipes, not reheated leftovers', and also gave some advice about where to place the original stories in the context of the TV adventures: 'Each Missing Adventure has to fit in a gap between two TV stories … the supply of gaps is finite, while the potential number of Missing Adventures is infinite. Therefore each gap must be able to accommodate several Missing Adventures, and therefore you must be careful not to link your novel to the TV stories on either side of your gap – while at the same time ensuring that the Doctor and his companions enter your novels in the clothing and frame of mind in which they ended the TV story before your gap, and leave your novel in the clothing and the frame of mind in which they first appear in the TV story that takes place after your gap – so that

> **BEHIND THE BOOK: *GOTH OPERA***
>
> Paul Cornell wanted to do a vampire novel, for which he had come up with a number of set-pieces, and since Terrance Dicks was already writing the New Adventure *Blood Harvest*, Virgin got the two writers together to link their books. Cornell says that *Goth Opera* was influenced by the story 'To Say I Love You' from the British TV drama series *Cracker*. The only thing that Cornell might have changed, in retrospect, is Chapter Six, which he calls 'the continuity chapter', featuring many elements taken from *Doctor Who* TV stories: Romana, Drashigs, Glitz, Miniscopes and more. Cornell explains that this was done as an example of how the Missing Adventures would link characters and concepts from the show's universe.
>
> (From *TSV* Issue 43 – courtesy Paul Scoones.)

> **CROSS-PROMOTION**
>
> In the spring of 1994, the earliest New Adventures, the *Timewyrm* series books, were reprinted, this time with newly-added Afterwords co-written by Peter Darvill-Evans and Rebecca Levene. The main aim of these was evidently to relay news of the forthcoming Missing Adventures range and encourage readers to buy those titles as well.

subsequent Missing Adventures authors can use the same gap.' On top of all this, continuity had to be adhered to; for example, there would be no third Doctor adventures in which he met Davros – a character first encountered by the Doctor on TV in his fourth incarnation. Also, mood had to be taken into account; there should not, for instance, be a story set immediately after 'Earthshock' – at the end of which the Doctor's companion Adric died – that started with the Time Lord and his other companions, Tegan and Nyssa, in a carefree party mood.

These detailed requirements constituted a daunting challenge for anyone not well versed in *Doctor Who* lore, so it is not really surprising that only one author unconnected with either the TV show or its active fanbase contributed to the range during its run. This was Stephen Marley, who had three fantasy novels under his belt and had also contributed two titles to Virgin's range of original *Judge Dredd* novels. 'Steve was a great writer,' says Levene, 'and he was a fan of the show, and wanted to do a *Doctor Who* novel – so we talked to him, and his book *Managra* was the result.'

The cover design devised for the Missing Adventures was an adaptation of that used in 1993 for the last of the TV story novelisations, John Peel's *The Power of the Daleks* and *The Evil of the Daleks*, and in early 1994 for Barry Letts' *The Paradise of Death* (see facing page), based on his 1993 *Doctor Who* radio drama. The main

THE WHO ADVENTURES

Annotations on cover mockup:

- All pix should have dark backgrounds
- Blue background on all books
- Logo will be computer-enhanced to have a metallic sheen.
- yellow / light strip/grey
- not required, of course. So this box will be smaller.
- Black stripe
- Dark blue of book spine
- this box could be smaller — depends on length of title. (GOTH OPERA / PAUL CORNELL — not long!)

Cover mockup text:

DOCTOR WHO
MISSING ADVENTURES

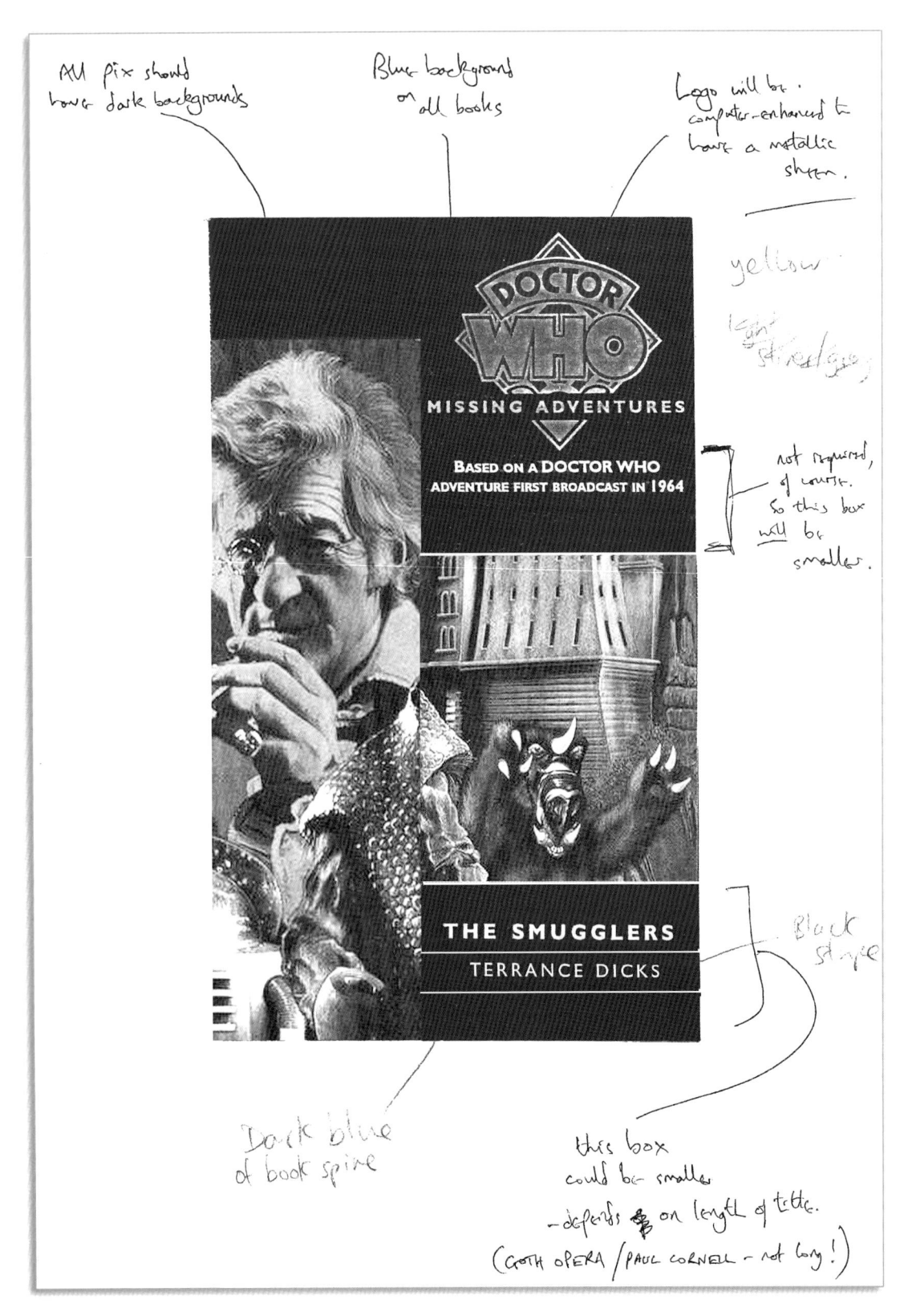

BASED ON A DOCTOR WHO ADVENTURE FIRST BROADCAST IN 1964

THE SMUGGLERS
TERRANCE DICKS

The original Missing Adventures cover design concept, assembled using elements from old Target novelisation covers. On the published books, the design was credited to the Slatter-Anderson agency. After the debut title, *Goth Opera*, an initial 'The' was added before 'Missing Adventures'.

change was that a Missing Adventures logo was developed, incorporating the old 1970s diamond *Doctor Who* logo rather than the final Sylvester McCoy-era one that the New Adventures had utilised. To provide the cover artwork, Darvill-Evans turned initially to Alister Pearson, who had painted all the covers for the final original Target novelisations and for the programme of reprints undertaken in the early '90s. Pearson's accurate likenesses were the prime reason for his being approached. He ended up painting 22 of the 33 Missing Adventures covers, and did no roughs for approval for any of them, Darvill-Evans being happy for him to work from written briefs supplied by himself, Levene, editorial assistant Simon Winstone, or sometimes the authors.

Virgin initially supplied Pearson with a rough layout created by sticking together a number of elements taken from various Target reprint covers, including sections of his own artwork for Brian Hayles' *The Curse of Peladon* (see facing page). The notes included on this

ALISTER PEARSON

Alister Pearson was born on the Isle of Wight. His first published *Doctor Who* artwork consisted of two pieces included in Peter Haining's *Doctor Who – The Key to Time* (1984).

He left art college after one term, and for three years often sent artwork in to Target editor Nigel Robinson and art director Mike Brett. Eventually he was given his first cover commission, for the novelisation of *The Underwater Menace*, and went on to contribute more covers to the Target range than any other artist, up until its demise in 1994. Following this, he painted 22 covers for Virgin Publishing's ranges of original *Doctor Who* fiction.

Before being commissioned for the Target range, Pearson sold paintings to *Doctor Who Magazine* under the editorship of Sheila Cranna, John Freeman and Gary Russell. His artwork adorned over a dozen of the magazine's covers, often being reproduced as free fold-out posters with the same issues. He also provided two covers for the short-lived sister publication *Doctor Who Classic Comics* (1992-93).

From 1990 to 1993, Pearson painted sixteen covers for the BBC Video releases of various *Doctor Who* stories. Much of this artwork was also used on concurrent reprints of the appropriate Target novelisations. He painted the covers for six of Titan Books' *Doctor Who – The Scripts* range (1992-94) and for twelve of the company's *Star Trek Adventures* reprints (1993-95). He also contributed to Titan's *Official Star Trek Fan Club Magazine* and their short-lived *Deep Space Nine* poster magazine. In addition, he has painted CD covers for Rod Stewart ('Changing Faces'), Nik Kershaw ('Then and Now') and Stock, Aitken and Waterman ('Gold').

In 2005, he emerged from a quiet period to provide the frontispiece for the newly relaunched *Doctor Who Annual* and the covers for all four of the subsequent *Doctor Who Storybook* titles issued by Panini. He has since provided further artwork for *Doctor Who* DVD and book releases, including *The Target Book*, telling the history of the Target range.

Most recently, he has supplied the cover artwork for a number of the BBC's *Doctor Who* audiobook releases.

Although he has always declined to produce prints of his work for sale, Pearson often provides very limited numbers of them for charity fundraising auctions and raffles and online competitions.

THE WHO ADVENTURES

rough indicated that the supplied paintings should all have dark backgrounds, and that the books would have blue borders and spines – although in the event black was used instead of blue. The design required that there be two artwork elements per cover: a side-bar depicting the Doctor/companion

Below: Alister Pearson's side-bar artwork for the second Missing Adventure, John Peel's *Evolution*, as later slightly modified by the artist.

> ### BEHIND THE BOOK: *VENUSIAN LULLABY*
>
> Paul Leonard was persuaded to write a *Doctor Who* novel by his friend Jim Mortimore. He had not watched the show for some years, so studied up on the subject by borrowing books and video tapes from Mortimore. His first Virgin submission, titled *Root of Evil*, did not get accepted, but led to him submitting a second, which eventually became his third novel, the New Adventure *Toy Solstice*. *Venusian Lullaby* was his third submission, and was put together in just two weeks (whereas the *Root of Evil* one had taken him five months). Leonard feels that the proposal for *Venusian Lullaby* was, as a result, 'more coherent and much tighter.' The title came about from his recollection of the third Doctor making comments about Venusians and their lullabies. The novel leads directly into Jim Mortimore's short story 'The Book of Shadows' in the first *Decalog*.
>
> (From *TSV* Issue 43 – courtesy Paul Scoones.)

Below: Jim Mortimore's concept sketches for the Globeroller vehicle (top) and one of the Venusian creatures (bottom) featured in Paul Leonard's *Venusian Lullaby*. The latter sketch was used by Alister Pearson as reference for his cover artwork (see opposite), and Mortimore received a credit for this at the front of the book.

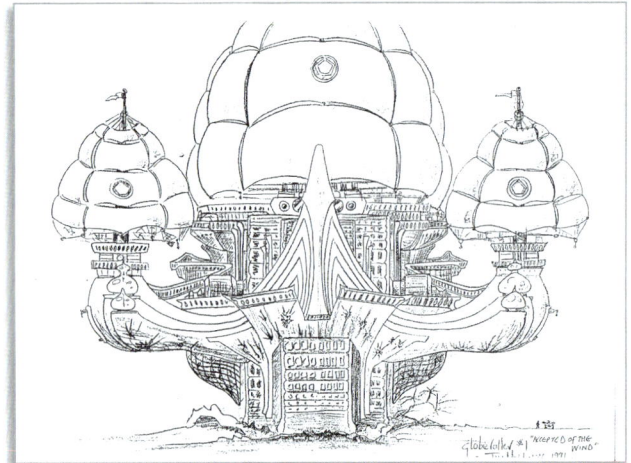

THE MISSING ADVENTURES

Venusian Lullaby, the third Missing Adventure to be published, with Alister Pearson cover art.

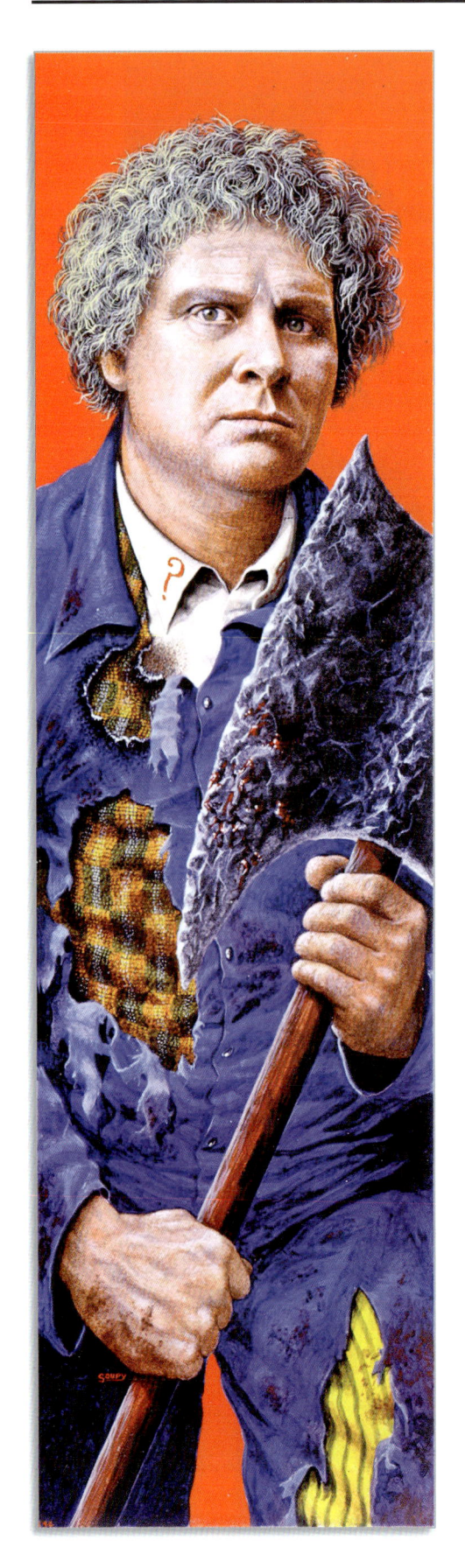

team featured in the novel, and the other showing a scene from the action. For *Goth Opera*, Pearson painted the fifth Doctor and a vampire Nyssa for the side-bar. However, once the cover was proofed and sent out to the bookshops, the major UK newsagents and booksellers W H Smith, who carry a lot of weight with regard to what should or should not appear on book jackets generally, stated that they would not stock the novel unless the artwork was made less gory. Pearson therefore had to retouch his painting to remove much of the blood he had included on Nyssa's blouse (see page 237), leaving just a few spots on her collar.

As the books were being published to a tight monthly schedule, to have had just one artist doing all the covers would have been risky. Therefore, to spread the load, a second regular artist, Paul Campbell, was brought in. Campbell, like Pearson, used a photo-realistic style, and his work for the range began with the cover for Steve Lyons' *Time of Your Life*, when Pearson's attempt – which, like Campbell's final version, featured a side-bar of the Doctor

Left and below: Paul Campbell's original cover artwork for *Time of Your Life*.

PAUL CAMPBELL

Paul Campbell was born in Derry, Northern Ireland, in 1964 and moved to the UK mainland in 1972. His first published work was in 1985, a commission for the *Proteus* role-playing magazine, and following this he supplied artwork for the magazine for two years.

From 1986 to 1989 Campbell attended Hull University to study Graphic Design, specialising in film and animation. After finishing University, he started supplying artwork for Games Workshop and *White Dwarf* magazine, on which he worked until 1992, eventually producing over 160 illustrations.

In 1991 he joined Meiklejohn Graphics, an art agency in London, and produced posters for Scandecor and Verkerke, who published them throughout Europe, including through the Athena UK brand.

From 1994 to 1996, Campbell produced numerous covers for Virgin's *Doctor Who* New Adventures and Missing Adventures ranges. He also provided for Panini the covers for Issues 22, 24 and 26 of the *Doctor Who Classic Comics* title in 1994, the cover for the *Doctor Who Magazine* Summer Special in 1995 and the cover and internal posters for the *Doctor Who Magazine* Spring Special in 1996. In 2011 he worked on covers for two of Penguin's *Doctor Who* range: the two-stories-in-one-book titles *The Good, the Bad and the Alien/System Wipe* and *Death Riders/Heart of Stone*.

He has also worked on many other projects: for advertising companies; for the interactive CD design company Binary Vision; for Boxtree books; and for *The Cawnpore Massacres*, a 1997 documentary in Channel 4's *Secret History* strand.

To supplement his income during the bulk of this period he has also worked in the building trade. He currently lives in Leyton, East London. His website can be found at https://porkamble.carbonmade.com.

---

in blue overalls clutching an axe, as this was a requirement of the brief – was abandoned as he could not manage the additional narrative image that was required. For the as-published cover, Campbell depicted a dinosaur rampaging through a city (see opposite).

Although Pearson and Campbell were the 'artists of choice' for the Missing Adventures, some of the authors would also occasionally be allowed a say in who they wanted to paint the covers for their novels. One such was Gary Russell who, as he explains, had particular reasons for opting for a certain artist when offered a choice of Alister Pearson, Colin Howard, Paul Campbell or Andrew Skilleter: 'Purely mercenary … I like to buy *Doctor Who* book cover artwork, but I already owned my all-time-favourite cover by Alister (for the Target novelisation *The Mutation of Time*), so I wanted to have the opportunity to buy something by a different artist. Hence I chose Colin for *Invasion of the Cat-People*, because I knew he'd do me some fab cats, and Andrew for *The Scales of Injustice*, as I didn't own any of his artwork.' For the latter novel, Russell also worked with artist Paul Vyse to come up with an image of a hybrid Silurian/Sea Devil creature, which was passed on to Skilleter as reference for the final cover art.

The cover for Justin Richards' *System Shock* was realised completely on computer by Martin Rawle, a graphic designer who at the time was

THE WHO ADVENTURES

Above: Colin Howard's original cover rough for *Invasion of the Cat-People*.

CAT PEOPLE COVER ART

Colin Howard's involvement in the cover of *Invasion of the Cat-People* came about at short notice, as he explains: 'I was happy to receive a phone call one day asking if I would be willing to step in at the last minute and supply the cover artwork for Gary Russell's novel. This was possibly one of the strangest commissions I had undertaken in the worlds of *Who*, as it required me to come up with giant domestic cats that walked upright, wearing skin-tight red catsuits and toting weaponry. Now I love cats – well, all animals, in fact – however, despite being gorgeous creatures, they look very strange when upright, so trying to think of how they might balance and walk was a challenge. I also had to think about the design of their weapons: as a race with no opposable thumbs, how would they hold their rifles and fire them? The cover features two of Gary's cats: Scratch, the tortoiseshell, and Tarot, the tabby, plus my own black and white cat, Albert. Another element I really enjoyed was to be able to design their warlike spacecraft. This had an extremely shiny metallic hull in the text, and I had fun with reflecting the colours of the Australian outback setting in its surface.'

INVASION OF THE CAT-PEOPLE: THE TV PRODUCTION!

Invasion of the Cat-People author Gary Russell amused himself by envisioning an imaginary television production of his novel. His casting choices for the guest roles included Jude Law, Carolyn Seymour, Jacqueline Pearce and Susan Engel, while his favoured director was Graeme Harper, who in the real world had handled several acclaimed *Doctor Who* stories, including the fifth Doctor's last, 'The Caves of Androzani'. Russell's choice to compose the music was the team of Mike Fillis and Adrian Pack, who had been responsible for the *Cybertech* and *Pharos* CDs (see page 162), and he had Michael Chapman earmarked as producer. It would have been a Virgin Films production.

SEQUELS, PREQUELS AND NOVELISATIONS

Four of the Missing Adventures were sequels to TV stories: *The Sands of Time* (a sequel to 'Pyramids of Mars'); *The Scales of Injustice* ('Doctor Who and the Silurians'); *The Shadow of Weng-Chiang* ('The Talons of Weng-Chiang'); and *Twilight of the Gods* ('The Web Planet'). In addition, two were novelisations: *The Ghosts of N-Space* (based on Barry Letts' BBC radio drama of that title); and *Downtime* (adapted from the Reeltime Pictures' video drama *Downtime*, a sequel to the TV stories 'The Abominable Snowmen' and 'The Web of Fear').

THE MISSING ADVENTURES

working for Richards' brother Toby (who in his spare time handled sound design for Big Finish's ranges of *Doctor Who* audio dramas). The original image created by Rawle featured the Doctor's companion Sarah Jane Smith in full tea-shop waitress garb, complete with lacy hat, apron and tight black skirt, and toting a machine pistol, but this was toned down for the finished cover as Richards felt 'she looked like she was out of an X-rated version of *'Allo 'Allo!*' – a reference to the BBC's long-running Second World War sitcom.

With the requirement to supply one Missing Adventure per month established, Darvill-Evans and Levene faced the additional problem of having to try to ensure that each of the six past Doctors was fairly represented in the range. This meant that sometimes when authors submitted ideas, they would be asked to change their Doctor/companion teams before their novels were commissioned. 'We did try to even things out,' says Levene. 'I didn't mind if there were more fourth Doctor stories, though – he had been the Doctor the

Left and below: Colin Howard's original cover artwork for *Invasion of the Cat-People*.

THE WHO ADVENTURES

COLIN HOWARD

Colin Howard was born 25 November 1965 in Harleston, Norfolk. His first involvement with *Doctor Who* was supplying artwork for several fanzines. He also had some black-and-white pieces included in the books *The Key to Time* and *25 Glorious Years*. In 1988 he was asked to paint the cover for the Target novelisation of 'Attack of the Cybermen'. In the early '90s he supplied art for the fanzine *The Frame* and the magazines *TV Zone* and *Space Junk*, and was also a regular contributor to *Doctor Who Magazine*, with numerous illustrations and cover paintings. For Virgin Publishing, he provided cover artworks for some of their range of *Doctor Who* tie-ins and in 1991 the cover and all of the internal illustrations for their role-playing book *Time Lord*.

In 1993, Howard was asked to paint the cover artwork for the BBC Video release of the *Doctor Who* story 'The Two Doctors', and this led to 33 VHS covers and then novel covers for BBC Books' *Doctor Who* ranges.

It was at this time that the BBC's science fiction sitcom *Red Dwarf* started to gain a lot of fans, and Howard supplied many covers for the tie-in *Smegazine* for Fleetway Publications, plus a cover for the EMI-released chart single 'Tongue Tied' performed by Danny John Jules, who played Cat in the show.

Photo-montage and digital art took precedence over traditional artists' work in the mid-'90s, so Howard taught himself how to paint digitally and began working for various art agencies. It was during this time that he helped out with digital detail on some DVD boxsets for Peacock design's Stuart Crouch.

In 2016 Howard was invited by producer Charles Norton to supply the black-and-white cover art for the BBC's upcoming animation of the 'lost' 1966 *Doctor Who* TV story 'The Power of the Daleks'. He agreed, and also ended up providing a 'digital artwork' TARDIS for episodes 1 and 6. He was then asked to return to work on backgrounds and 'prop elements' for the subsequent animations of 'Shada' and 'The Macra Terror'.

---

longest on screen and was the most popular. I found that certain TARDIS crews had the same or similar dynamics between them, and we could move them about. We were, of course, helped in this by the writers, who were occasionally faced with having either to wait to write their book, or to rework it using a different Doctor.'

Andy Lane remembers that this happened to him with his novel *The Empire of Glass*. 'The original intention was for me to write a third Doctor story

COVER STORY: *THE SCALES OF INJUSTICE*

In 1998, author Gary Russell wrote on his blog about how the cover design for *The Scales of Injustice* had come about:

'This is how I detailed the front cover and the blurb. I almost got what I wanted. Oh, and the hybrid Silurian I supplied was something Paul Vyse, *Doctor Who Magazine* design maestro extraordinaire, and I knocked up using Photoshop one night. The subsequent alterations came through discussions between Andrew [Skilleter] and myself.

'JON PERTWEE PIC from Season 7 – ideally the shot from the title sequence.

'CAROLINE JOHN PIC from 'The Ambassadors of Death' – long hair and wide-brimmed hat.

'Face to face: hybrid Silurian (based on enclosed photo) facing wire-frame almost isometric mirror-image head picked out in lime green. The real Silurian ought to be '[Doctor Who and the] Silurians' not 'Warriors of the Deep' colours. All on a black background to blend with cover black if allowed – this is an illo rather than a depiction of an actual scene.'

THE MISSING ADVENTURES

Above: Andrew Skilleter's original rough for the cover of Gary Russell's *The Scales of Injustice*. Left and below: the completed artwork.

253

System Shock, with digitally-created Martin Rawle cover art.

entitled *Broken Heroes*. Rebecca told me she needed first Doctor stories more than anything else, so I quickly wrote another proposal set in Venice. (I'd just come back from holiday there.) The proposal as originally conceived involved the first and seventh Doctors in separate but interlinked stories. The seventh Doctor strand was removed by Rebecca.'

Justin Richards has similar memories of a specific Doctor/companion request for his novel *The Sands of Time*. 'Bex asked me to think about the fifth Doctor. I've always been fascinated with Egyptology, and I'd just read a (non-fiction) book that mentioned that the Victorians had these mummy-unwrapping parties, where people went round for drinks and then they unwrapped a mummy and pretended it was all in the interests of research and not a cheap thrill at all. That got me thinking that it would be interesting if you turned up to one of these, and when the 4000-year old mummy was unwrapped it turned out to be Mr Smith from next door. Basically the whole plot with the time travel convolutions was then based round working out how on Earth this could have happened without "cheating".'

Martin Day also recalls Levene requesting that he use particular characters in his sole novel for the range: '*The Menagerie* was originally a New Adventure with Benny and Ace, which I submitted to Virgin around July 1993. I think it was Rebecca who suggested reworking it as a Missing Adventure with the second Doctor, feeling that his era better suited the plot I had, and I began to revise my outline accordingly around February 1994, retitling it *Freak Show* – which I always preferred to the final title. It was moved up the schedules to become the first second Doctor novel published in the range, when it became apparent to Virgin that Gary

MARTIN RAWLE

Martin Rawle was born on 31 March 1971 and is the son of a cartoonist and copywriter. He studied graphic design at Wallisdown Art College in Bournemouth from 1989 to 1991.

His first industry job was working for DSM Design as a trainee graphic designer and illustrator for four years. He then started his own company, TOMA, with his friend and fellow designer and artist Matt French.

Whilst Rawle was working for DSM design, another friend, Toby Richards, asked him if he would like to produce the cover art for the Missing Adventure *System Shock*, written by his brother, Justin Richards. A brief synopsis was supplied, and Rawle produced the art using an Epson painting tablet, Photoshop and Painter. This was his first endeavour in digital art, as up until that point he had used only traditional painting methods. It was a great learning experience, and set Rawle on the road to becoming a digital illustrator.

Rawle and French then became the heads of design for V4, a very successful marketing company based in Bournemouth, remaining there until 2001. Rawle then decided to start another company of his own, Martoons. Today, he still works for a few clients through Martoons, including Amuzo, an award-winning mobile computer games company, again based in Bournemouth. Rawle then decided to indulge his lifelong love of sculpting and model-making and formed BAF Studios along with Matt French. They are currently making film-related models.

MARTIN DAY

After gaining a degree in English Literature and Film Theory at the Polytechnic of North London in the late 1980s, Martin Day first worked on *The Guinness Book of Records* and wrote record reviews for the *NME*. His first books were co-authored reference guides to TV drama shows, including *The Avengers*, *Star Trek: The Next Generation*, *The Sweeney* and *The X-Files*. He also created *The Doctor Who Discontinuity Guide* with Paul Cornell and Keith Topping. Original *Doctor Who* fiction followed, including *The Menagerie* for Virgin and *Bunker Soldiers*, *The Sleep of Reason* and the tenth Doctor story *Wooden Heart* for BBC Books, plus a pair of novels co-written with Keith Topping. He's also written comic strip stories for *Doctor Who Adventures*, audio plays for Big Finish and audiobooks for the eleventh Doctor and for *The Sarah Jane Adventures*.

In his parallel career as a scriptwriter, Day has written for the Channel 5 show *Family Affairs* and for RTÉ's *Fair City*, and was lead writer on CBBC's *Crisis Control*. For nine years he was a regular contributor to BBC1's *Doctors*.

Day has an MA in Creative Writing from Bath Spa University and for three years he lectured undergraduates in the same subject. Currently a Royal Literary Fund Fellow at the University of Bristol, he is also the Wessex regional chair of the Writers' Guild of Great Britain. He is a member of the Royal Television Society and a voting member of BAFTA. He lives in Somerset and is married to a GP.

Russell, who at the time was writing his second Doctor novel *Invasion of the Cat-People*, was not going to be able to deliver it on time.'

Steve Lyons chose to use the sixth Doctor for his books, as he explains: 'I submitted the idea for *Time of Your Life*, under the title *Network*, sometime in February 1994. I hadn't submitted a Missing Adventure proposal when the line was first announced, because I had already had my second New Adventure, *Head Games*, provisionally accepted, and I was waiting to get started on that. However, *Head Games* got pushed back several months in the schedule – mainly due to the changeover of companions in the New Adventures – so I went for a Missing Adventure to fill in the gap. I was commissioned – verbally, at least – very quickly. I think my submission landed on Rebecca's

Concept design sketches drawn by Martin Day for the Mecrim monster featured in his novel *The Menagerie*. These were passed to Paul Campbell for him to use as reference when painting the cover artwork.

THE MISSING ADVENTURES

The Menagerie, with cover art by Paul Campbell.

THE WHO ADVENTURES

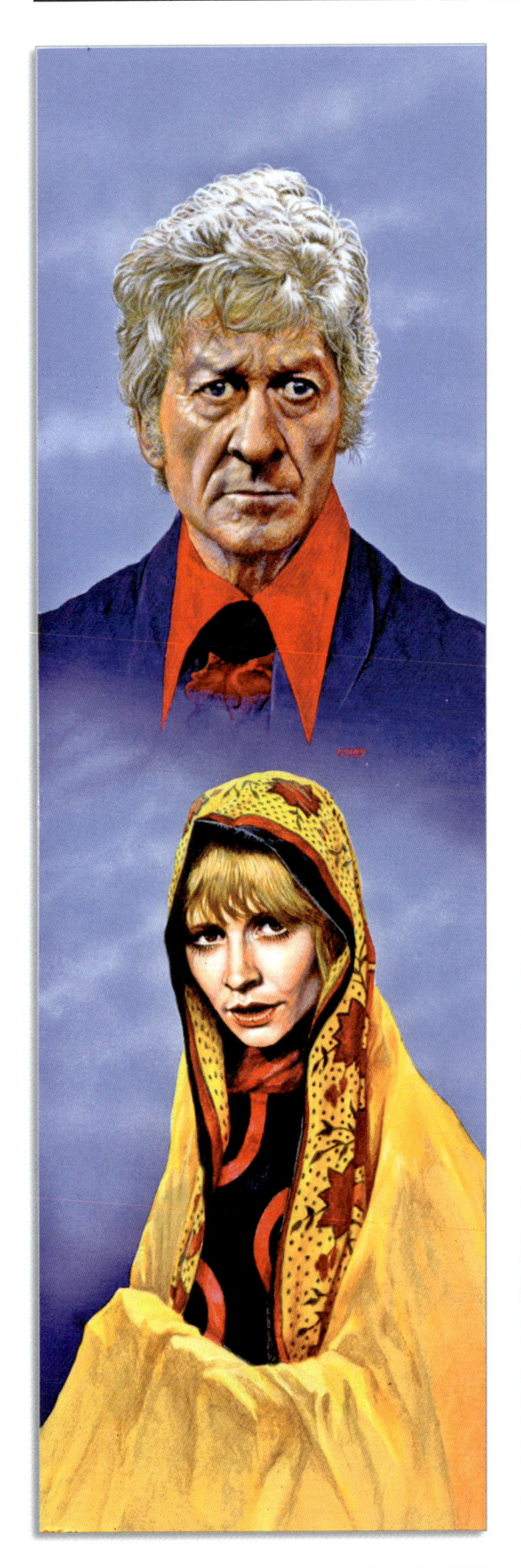

desk at exactly the right time: Virgin had just decided to go monthly with the Missing Adventures, so they were looking for some books fast.

'I really wanted to use the sixth Doctor, as I've always felt that his sometimes-violent, sometimes-amoral character was a very interesting one that was never really handled well on screen. I wanted to write a book in which he was forced to confront that side of his nature.'

The decision to use the sixth Doctor resulted in an interesting conundrum when it came to decide which companion to use. 'I originally submitted *Time of Your Life* as an introductory story for Mel,' explains Lyons. 'However, the book was set in the future, so an element of time travel was needed to get her involved. Rebecca asked me to take out that element, as she'd just commissioned *Set Piece* for the New Adventures range and *The Crystal Bucephalus* for the Missing Adventures, both of which dealt with human beings discovering time travel. Of course, this meant that Mel couldn't appear. It was Rebecca who solved the

Below and left: Paul Campbell's original artwork for the Paul Leonard-authored Missing Adventure *Dancing the Code*.

problem for me. Apparently, she'd been thinking about expanding the sixth Doctor's era anyway, so she suggested that I replace Mel in my book with a new companion. The story was already set in that strange gap between "The Trial of a Time Lord" part fourteen and … er, part nine, so it was an easy thing to do. I'd given Mel a lot of computer programming to do in the story, so the new character had to be a computer programmer too, in order to fill her shoes. That being the case, I thought I'd better make him as unlike her as I could in every other respect. Which is pretty much the only reason I made him a "him". I'd once played a computer programmer named Grant Markham in FASA's *Doctor Who* role-playing game – the only time I ever played it – so I expanded his character and used him.'

As well as being a challenge for Lyons to write, the advent of the new companion created an issue as to how he would be represented in the book cover artwork. For *Time of Your Life*, this was avoided by having the side-bar present just the sixth Doctor alone, however for *Killing Ground*, Lyons' second book with Grant, a decision was taken to include a depiction of him as well. 'As is perhaps widely known,' says artist Alister Pearson, 'Grant's face is based on my own likeness, with multiple alterations: I've never worn my – non-ginger – hair with a centre parting in my life; I don't wear glasses; I don't have freckles. Some of the details are actually based on the actor Mark Strickson [who played the fifth Doctor's companion Turlough in the TV show]! The only bit

Right and below: Phil Bevan's four internal illustrations for the Missing Adventure *The English Way of Death*.

> **QUOTE, UNQUOTE**
>
> The Doctor: 'Then what am I? A wanderer, my dear. A wanderer and a survivor. I am not of your race. I am not of this Earth. I am a wanderer in the fourth dimension of space and time, a refugee from an ancient civilisation, cut off from my own people by aeons of time and universes far beyond human understanding.'
>
> *The Empire of Glass*

THE WHO ADVENTURES

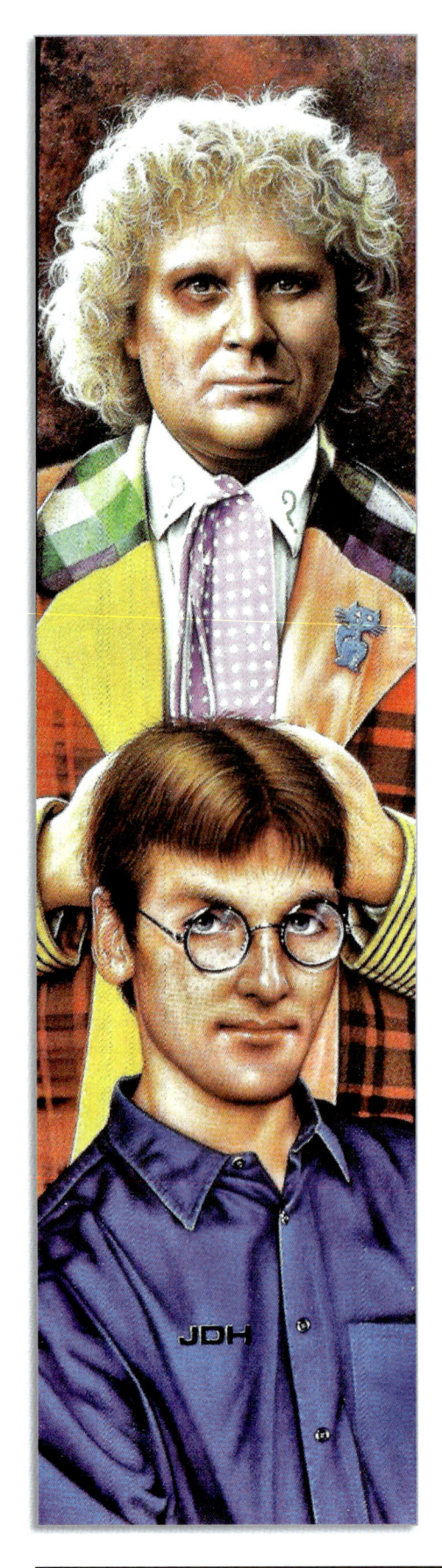

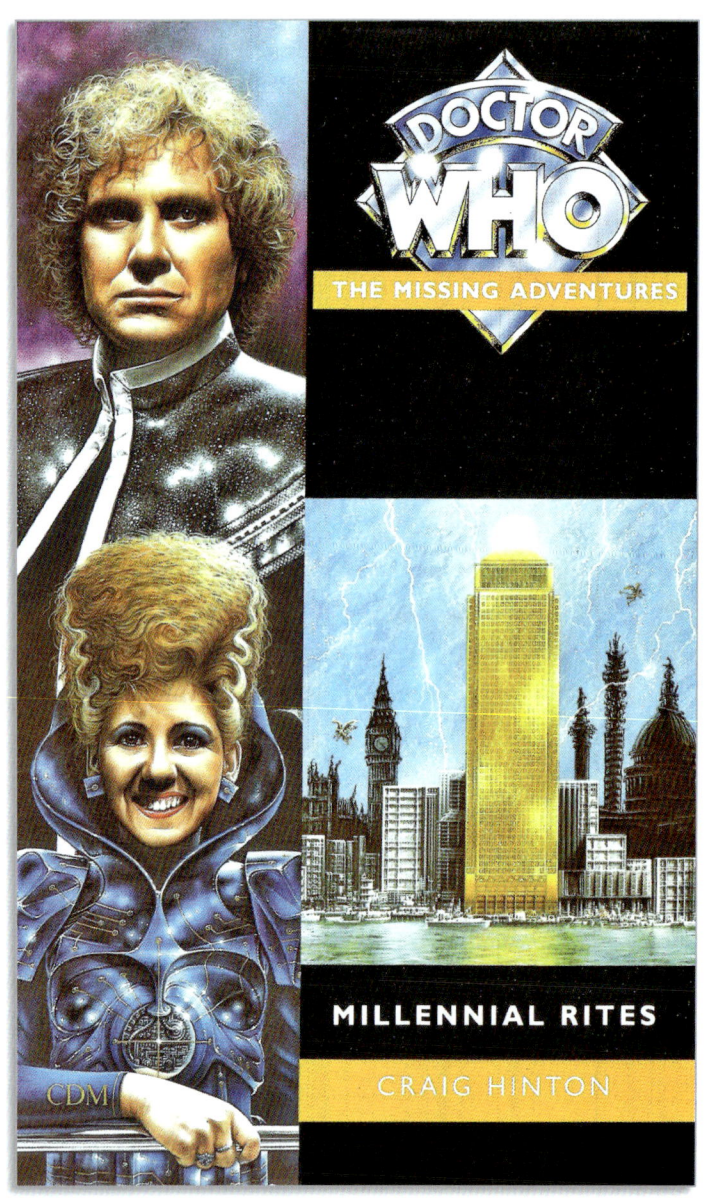

Left: Alister Pearson's side-bar artwork for *Killing Ground*, featuring new companion Grant Markham.

Above: *Millennial Rites*, also with Alister Pearson cover art.

I didn't alter at all was the ear – that's my ear!'

Daniel O'Mahony recalls that his contribution to the range, *The Man in the Velvet Mask*, was always intended to be for the first Doctor: 'Using William Hartnell's Doctor was a very deliberate decision on my part. Some people say that *The Man in the Velvet Mask* doesn't feel like a first Doctor story, but I imagined it very specifically as part of the very eclectic period when John Wiles and Donald Tosh were in charge of *Doctor Who*.

'I started with the idea of putting the Marquis de Sade

THE MISSING ADVENTURES

The Man in the Velvet Mask, with cover art by Alister Pearson.

THE WHO ADVENTURES

> ### BEHIND THE BOOK: *STATE OF CHANGE*
>
> Author Christopher Bulis started work on his early Missing Adventure *State of Change* with the intention of writing for a Doctor other than the sixth. However, as he explains, this was another case of Doctors being swapped during the course of the novel's development: 'I eventually latched on to the sixth Doctor and Peri. It was set in Ancient Egypt, with the obvious storyline of the Doctor meeting Cleopatra. Originally it was an epic: parallel universes, Gallifrey, time rifts, fleets of Egyptian starships … Peri and the Doctor would have been split in two by the rift, with one pair good and one evil. Although the bad Peri died, the evil Doctor survived and became the Valeyard.' After submitting this storyline to Virgin, Bulis discovered that the subject of parallel universes had already been extensively covered in the New Adventures' 'Alternate Universe Cycle'; that ancient Egypt had already featured in the *Decalog* story 'The Book of Shadows'; and that Virgin's policy was to avoid the subject of the Valeyard. He therefore heavily revised his proposal, instead setting the adventure mainly in Rome, in his favourite period of history. His story originally featured a group of immensely powerful energy beings responsible for changing the established course of events; it transpired that these beings were just children, and when the Doctor broke out of an energy barrier that surrounded Rome, this drew the attention of their elders, who told them off. Virgin, however, felt that the book needed a villain, so at editor Rebecca Levene's suggestion Bulis wrote in the Doctor's old enemy and fellow Time Lord the Rani.
>
> (From *TSV* Issue 43 – courtesy Paul Scoones.)

in a *Doctor Who* story, and I also knew I wanted to keep him in his historical context. I'd assumed while I was developing the ideas that it would be a New Adventure, but I felt it would be inauthentic to put the seventh Doctor – or, indeed, any of the later ones – into the sort of historical adventure I wanted to write. They weren't designed to interact with history on the same level as the first Doctor. I knew the Doctor and de Sade would be spending a lot of time together, and I couldn't see the story working if there wasn't an amount of respect between them. I imagined how de Sade would respond to each of the Doctors, and Hartnell won hands down.

'I knew it was going to be a sensitive choice, so I did suggest that, if there was any problem on Virgin's part, I could change the line-up to the third Doctor and Jo. That was for fairly prosaic reasons on my part, as I'd already written a sample chapter for them for another – rejected – novel called *The Drowned Towers*, and I didn't want to have to write more sample text for the first Doctor and Dodo! Fortunately, Rebecca liked my original choice. It would have been a horrible third Doctor story!'

As the Missing Adventures range progressed, so some of the authors contributed multiple titles. Christopher Bulis wrote five; Gareth Roberts four; David McIntee and Paul Leonard three apiece; while Craig Hinton, Gary Russell, Justin Richards and Steve Lyons completed two books each for the series. Solo offerings came from, amongst others, Andy Lane; Barry Letts, who novelised his third Doctor radio series *The Ghosts of N-Space*; Dave

Below: Christopher Bulis provided this frontispiece for his own Missing Adventure *Twilight of the Gods*.

THE MISSING ADVENTURES

Twilight of the Gods, with cover art by Alister Pearson.

263

THE WHO ADVENTURES

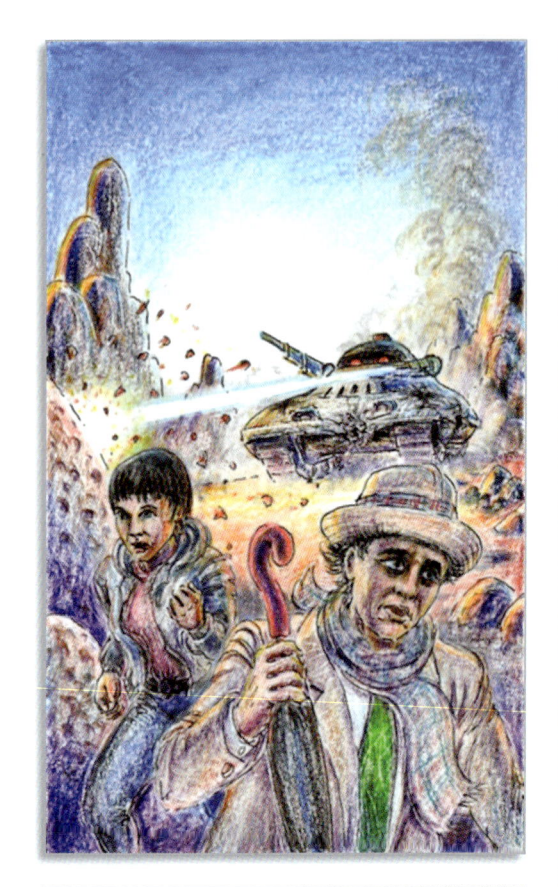

This page: four original roughs produced by Christopher Bulis for the cover artwork for his novel *A Device of Death*.

THE MISSING ADVENTURES

Stone; John Peel; and Lance Parkin.

Given how hard a challenge it must have been to ensure that the range gave equal coverage to all six of the past Doctors, Virgin succeeded remarkably well in this aim: all the Doctors ended up featuring in five books each, except for the second with four and the fourth with eight. There was, additionally, one book that hardly featured the Doctor at all. This was *Downtime*, Marc Platt's sole contribution to the range, adapted from his script for the independent video drama of the same title, which had been deliberately written to avoid using BBC copyright properties or properties for which permission had not been granted by the BBC. Thus both script and novelisation focused instead on the Doctor's old friend the Brigadier and one-time companion Sarah

Left: Christopher Bulis's rough showing his ultimately unused idea for the side-bar artwork for the cover of his novel *A Device of Death*.

COVER STORY: *A DEVICE OF DEATH*

Author Christopher Bulis had hoped to supply the cover artwork for his Missing Adventure *A Device of Death*, as he had previously for his New Adventure *Shadowmind*. 'I had hoped to get another cover for *A Device of Death*,' he confirms, 'but that did not work out. The story went through several stages, the first being a speculative screenplay I sent in to the BBC – badly timed, as it turned out, as production on *Doctor Who* had just shut down. Then I reworked it for a New Adventure with the seventh Doctor and Bernice. Then, with some more reworking, it became a Missing Adventure for the fourth Doctor, Sarah and Harry. Finally it got into print with a cover by Alister Pearson.'

The three portrait-shaped roughs on the opposite page were all produced by Bulis when the novel was still envisaged as a New Adventure. The square one on that page, and the one immediately to the left, show the compositions he had in mind for the main and side-bar artwork respectively for the revised, Missing Adventures version with the fourth Doctor and his companions. In the event, for the as-published artwork Alister Pearson came up with his own, completely different ideas.

THE WHO ADVENTURES

Jane Smith, battling the Great Intelligence – from the 1960s TV stories 'The Abominable Snowmen' and 'The Web of Fear' – who had taken over Professor Travers – a character from the same stories – and used him, its robot Yeti, and another of the Doctor's former companions, Victoria Waterfield, to engineer a bridgehead to take over the Earth via the internet. The Missing Adventures novelisation of this script also included a section of black-and-white photographs from the drama.

The Missing Adventures range came to an end at the same time as the New Adventures one. It concluded with a Gareth Roberts-authored fourth Doctor tale entitled *The Well-Mannered War* – which could have been an apt description of the war of words that had occurred between Virgin and the BBC with regard to the licence arrangements. Several authors were asked to pitch for the final book, among them Justin Richards, who recalls: 'I submitted a rather overwritten and under-developed proposal about alien steam-driven knights hunting for the Holy Grail. It was a third Doctor and UNIT story, and it was awful. Not surprisingly, Bex preferred Gareth's proposal.'

'I wasn't keen on the idea of the Missing Adventures at first,' says Roberts. 'One of the things that, for me, spoiled *Doctor Who* on TV was its obsession with its past. But as the years went by, that seemed to matter less and less.

'The Fourth Doctor, Romana and K-9 were my favourite TARDIS team. Three really intelligent minds: Romana is the most sane, the Doctor sort of bumbles through with his weird set of aesthetic priorities, and K-9 just can't make himself understood and doesn't even realise. I loved it on telly when the Doctor would wake up in a dungeon and say "I don't like those curtains" or whatever. That's my very favourite thing about the series, really. So I just did that again and again!

'When *The Well Mannered War* came out, everyone seemed to think that I was stomping round Cricklewood Broadway gnashing my teeth about Virgin losing the licence, but I wasn't. It was just done in a fairly cack-handed way; there was no direct communication to Virgin for ages. The ending of *The Well-Mannered War* was me saying, "These

Left: Alister Pearson's side-bar art for the penultimate Missing Adventure, *The Dark Path*, as slightly modified by the artist at a later date.

266

THE MISSING ADVENTURES

Speed of Flight, the final third Doctor Missing Adventure, with cover art by Alister Pearson.

THE WHO ADVENTURES

The Well-Mannered War, with cover art by Alister Pearson.

characters belong to the novel writers, we can do anything with them." Also, it was fun to make them characters in fiction in the fiction itself.'

Despite the commercial success of the Missing Adventure range, neither Darvill-Evans nor Levene holds much enthusiasm for it today. 'I guess my heart was never in the Missing Adventures as much it was in the New Adventures,' admits Darvill-Evans. 'With the latter I was creating something new – something personal, something that retained something of my personality, no matter how diluted, and transmitted at second and third hand by editors and authors. Whereas in publishing the Missing Adventures I felt I was obliged to recreate the style and atmosphere of the television Doctors – I was merely following the lead of others. And however much of an honour it was to be following in the footsteps of people such as Terrance Dicks and Barry Letts, I would always rather blaze my own trail.'

'It was a struggle,' comments Levene. 'It was hard to keep the books going, to find enough good writers and enough good ideas. The writers all did great work, and we delivered a range of books that people obviously wanted to read, which is always very pleasing. However, what people seemed to want was simply a good pastiche of the television show – stories that could have been episodes of the series on television – rather than something stretching and original.'

One of the problems that Levene had with the range stemmed from the original idea that every novel had to fit into a gap between two TV stories, which meant that no radical redevelopment could take place. 'I didn't like the rather clichéd *Star Trek* reset-button approach, where at the end of

> **QUOTE, UNQUOTE**
>
> The Doctor: 'Life's overrated anyway. The majority of places get along without it very well.'
>
> *The Well-Mannered War*

> **OLD FOES RETURN!**
>
> The Missing Adventures did a lot more than just bring back past Doctors and companions … many of the classic TV monsters and adversaries came back too! Amongst the many that featured were:
>
> - The Rani – *State of Change*
> - Ogrons – *The Romance of Crime*
> - The Valeyard, the Great Intelligence and Yeti – *Millennial Rites*
> - Sontarans and Rutans – *Lords of the Storm*
> - The Great Intelligence and Yeti – *Downtime*
> - Osirans and Servicer Robots (Mummies) – *The Sands of Time*
> - Cybermen – *Killing Ground*
> - Silurians, the Myrka – *The Scales of Injustice*
> - Mr Sin – *The Shadow of Weng-Chiang*
> - The Animus, Menoptra, Zarbi and Optera – *Twilight of the Gods*
> - The Master – *The Dark Path*
> - The Black Guardian – *The Well-Mannered War*

each book the status quo had to be restored,' she states. 'I didn't have a passion for the range or a vision for them, whereas with the New Adventures we could change, develop and build characters as we went, which is far more satisfying.'

Virgin had successfully steered the Doctor through 33 new adventures for his past selves. Old companions had been revitalised in ways that the original writers, actors and actresses could not have conceived, and new foes and enemies had been presented alongside some old favourites. In addition, Virgin had released several of their *Decalog* collections – although, it must be said, to diminishing returns.

Novels featuring past incarnations of the Doctor did not end there, however, as the month after publication of *The Well-Mannered War*, the BBC launched its own Past Doctor Adventures range, kicking off with *The Devil Goblins from Neptune*, a previously untold adventure for the third Doctor and Liz Shaw.

The adventures would continue.

THE WHO ADVENTURES

Jon Sullivan's original rough for the first post-*Doctor Who* New Adventure *Oh No It Isn't!* (bottom), and his original cover artwork for *Deadfall* (top left) and Mark Salwowski's for *Walking to Babylon* (top right).

APPENDIX B: AFTERLIFE

After the loss of Virgin's BBC licence, the New Adventures maintained an uninterrupted monthly publication schedule. *The Dying Days* and the much delayed *So Vile A Sin* both appeared in April 1997, and the next title, *Oh No It Isn't!*, followed straight on in May, making for a smooth transition between the novels with the Doctor and those without. *Oh No It Isn't!* wasn't the first Doctor-less entry in the range – Nigel Robinson's *Birthright* held that distinction – but the difference this time was that there was of course no *Doctor Who* branding, and whereas Robinson's novel had featured the TV companion character Ace alongside Bernice Summerfield, now Bernice was adventuring on her own. In all, 23 novels were published with Bernice as the central character before the range

Jon Sullivan's original cover artwork for *Oh No It Isn't!*.

#	Title	Author	Published
1	*Oh No It Isn't!*	Paul Cornell	May 1997
2	*Dragons' Wrath*	Justin Richards	June 1997
3	*Beyond the Sun*	Matthew Jones	July 1997
4	*Ship of Fools*	Dave Stone	August 1997
5	*Down*	Lawrence Miles	September 1997
6	*Deadfall*	Gary Russell	October 1997
7	*Ghost Devices*	Simon Bucher-Jones	November 1997
8	*Mean Streets*	Terrance Dicks	December 1997
9	*Tempest*	Christopher Bulis	January 1998
10	*Walking to Babylon*	Kate Orman	February 1998
11	*Oblivion*	Dave Stone	March 1998
12	*The Medusa Effect*	Justin Richards	April 1998
13	*Dry Pilgrimage*	Paul Leonard and Nick Walters	May 1998
14	*The Sword of Forever*	Jim Mortimore	June 1998
15	*Another Girl, Another Planet*	Martin Day and Len Beech*	August 1998
16	*Beige Planet Mars*	Lance Parkin and Mark Clapham	October 1998
17	*Where Angels Fear*	Rebecca Levene and Simon Winstone	December 1998
18	*The Mary-Sue Extrusion*	Dave Stone	February 1999
19	*Dead Romance*	Lawrence Miles	March 1999
20	*Tears of the Oracle*	Justin Richards	June 1999
21	*Return to the Fractured Planet*	Dave Stone	August 1999
22	*The Joy Device*	Justin Richards	October 1999
23	*Twilight of the Gods*	Mark Clapham and Jon de Burgh Miller	December 1999

* Len Beech was a pseudonym for Steve Bowkett

Jon Sullivan's revised rough for *Oh No It Isn't!*.

was finally cancelled by Virgin. These were as listed above.

One oddity published by Virgin while they still had the *Doctor Who* licence was a novel called *Who Killed Kennedy*. This was credited to James Stevens and David Bishop, although in fact the latter was the sole author – Stevens was a fictional character who served as the narrative's first-person protagonist. Bishop's novel was published on 18 April 1996 and detailed the supposed involvement of the Doctor and his UNIT associates in events surrounding the assassination of US President Kennedy in 1963. It was decided not to make this either a New Adventure or a Missing Adventure, as Bishop

Jon Sullivan's original cover artwork for *Ship of Fools*.

explained in the introduction to a 2016 e-book reissue: 'Bex and I both wanted the book to be published in the same style as the conspiracy tomes it was parodying, with big type on the cover and with a selection of blurry black and white photos in the centre pages. Ideally it would not even have the *Doctor Who* logo on the cover … In 1993 there had been a rash of books to coincide with the thirtieth anniversary of the assassination of US President John F Kennedy on 22 November, and then with the thirtieth anniversary of the first *Doctor Who* episode being broadcast on 23 November. Apparently it was running joke at Virgin that a book that hit both markets should be a bestseller. Why not use the JFK conspiracy to provide a hook on which to hang my *Doctor Who* proposal?'

In 2016, by arrangement with Bishop, the New Zealand *Doctor Who* Fan Club marked the novel's twentieth anniversary by putting out the aforementioned reissue, complete with revised opening and ending and extensive notes from the author. This version can be found online here: http://doctorwho.org.nz/archive/wkk/.

DAVID BISHOP

Born and raised in New Zealand, David Bishop worked as a daily newspaper journalist for five years before emigrating to London. He spent a decade editing *2000 AD* and other iconic British comics. During that time his first four novels were published, including his *Doctor Who* debut, *Who Killed Kennedy*. Since 2000 he has written award-winning screenplays, several episodes of the BBC's *Doctors* and numerous comics, radio plays, computer games, audio dramas and novels. His credits include the *Doctor Who* audio dramas *Full Fathom Five* (2003) and *Enemy of the Daleks* (2009), plus the BBC Books *Doctor Who* novels *Amorality Tale*, *The Domino Effect* and *Empire of Death*.

In 2009 Bishop helped create and launch a new Masters in Creative Writing course at Edinburgh Napier University, and he now leads that programme. He received a Robert Louis Stevenson Fellowship for his writing in 2017, and won a Sir Julius Vogel Award in 2020 for his *Doctor Who* audio original *The Elysian Blade*. In 2021 his first historical crime novel, *City of Vengeance*, written under the pseudonym D V Bishop, was published by Pan Macmillan.

Below: the cover of David Bishop's one-off Virgin novel *Who Killed Kennedy*.

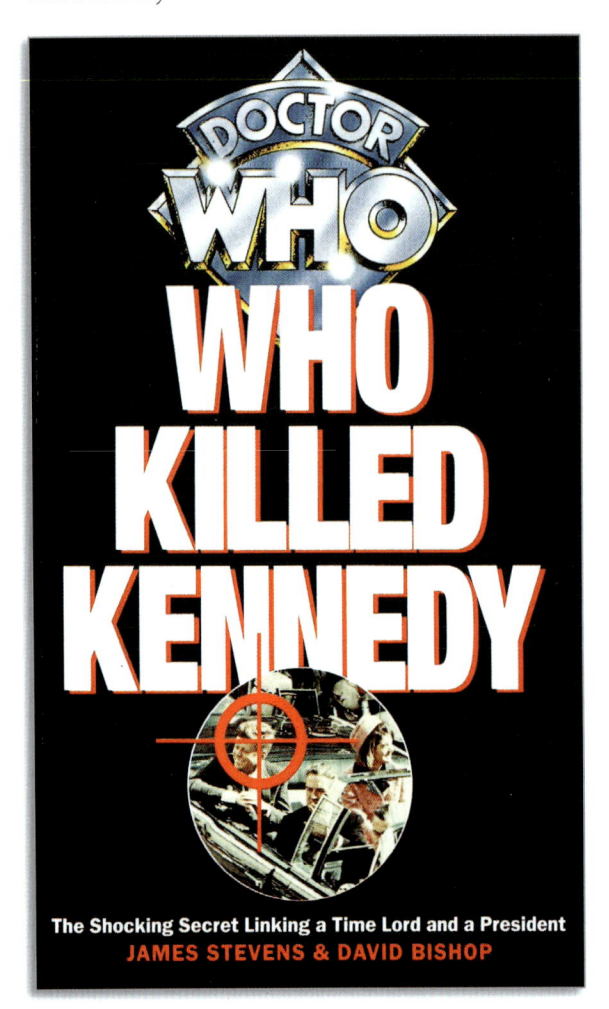

THE NEW NEW ADVENTURES

Writing in the fanzine *Broadsword*, author Lance Parkin explained the background to the new, Bernice Summerfield New Adventures: 'A summit conference at Virgin took place in mid-July 1996: the NA editorial team of Peter Darvill-Evans, Rebecca Levene and Simon Winstone were joined by Paul Cornell, Gareth Roberts, Andy Lane, Justin Richards and me. Our mission was to thrash out the basics of the Benny books. The idea of spinning Benny off into her own novels had come up a couple of times over the years – it was felt that she was a strong character able to sustain her own range of books, but with Virgin already publishing three *Doctor Who* books most months they might not be viable. Now Virgin felt there was much about the NAs that did not rely on *Doctor Who* – a "tone", the commitment to new authors, a strong cast of characters (note that in *Happy Endings* virtually all the guests are from the books, not the TV series). The decision was made that the NAs would continue until the end of 1997, and a new Writers' Guide was drawn up. The authors were very keen to sever the links with *Doctor Who* – the Benny NAs can retain a lot of the "Englishness" and "whimsy" of the TV series, but in no circumstances should they be *Doctor Who* stories without the Doctor. Immediately after the meeting was finished, *The Dying Days* was formally commissioned … the only stipulation was that now I somehow had to get Benny from 1997 to 2593 during the course of the book.'

Oblivion, with cover art by Jon Sullivan.

The Sword of Forever, with cover art by Mick Posen.

AFTERLIFE

Jon Sullivan's original cover artwork for Dry Pilgrimage.

Some of the books published by Virgin in the New Adventures and Missing Adventures ranges have gone on to enjoy further exposure since.

When the BBC started their own dedicated *Doctor Who* website in the early 2000s, they were looking for content to include, and the Virgin books gave them easy material. With new covers and internal illustrations, eight digital download titles were issued between 2002 and 2006 for fans to enjoy. They were eventually taken down in 2010.

The four New Adventures presented in this way were: *Nightshade* (art by Daryl Joyce); *Human Nature* (art by Daryl Joyce); *Lungbarrow* (art by Daryl Joyce); and *The Dying Days* (art by Allan Bednar). The four Missing Adventures were: *Empire of Glass* (art by Mike Nicholson); *The Scales of Injustice* (art by Daryl Joyce); *The Well-Mannered War* (art by Daryl Joyce); and *The Sands of Time* (art by Peter McKinstry).

These digital editions included a number of 'extras' in the form of authors' notes, and in some cases the text was slightly reworked by the authors.

Another Girl, Another Planet, with art by Fred Gambino, marking the debut of a new cover design.

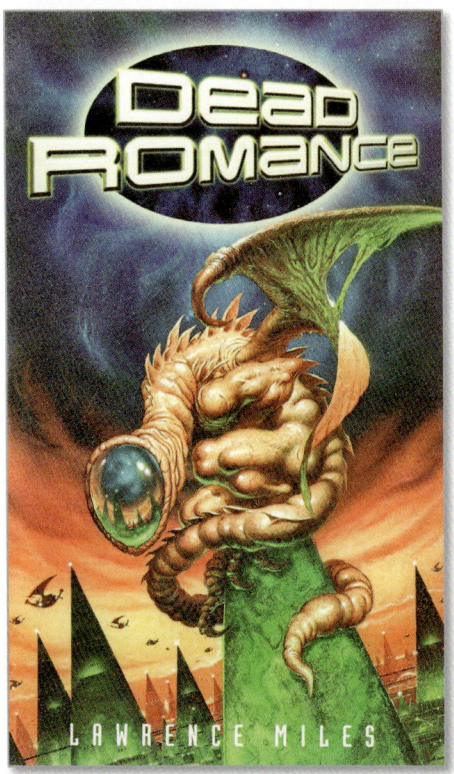

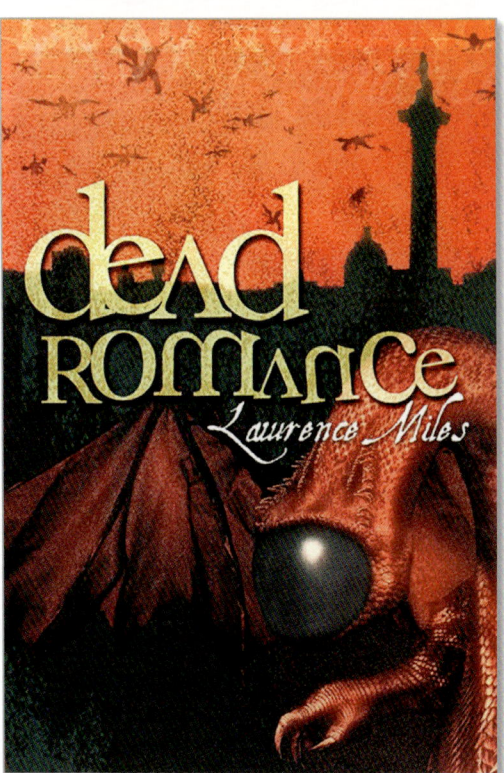

Top: Jon Sullivan's original rough (left) and final art (right) for *Where Angels Fear*. Bottom: *Dead Romance*, with David Wyatt art (left), and a 2004 reissue in Mad Norwegian's Faction Paradox range, with Steve Johnson art (right).

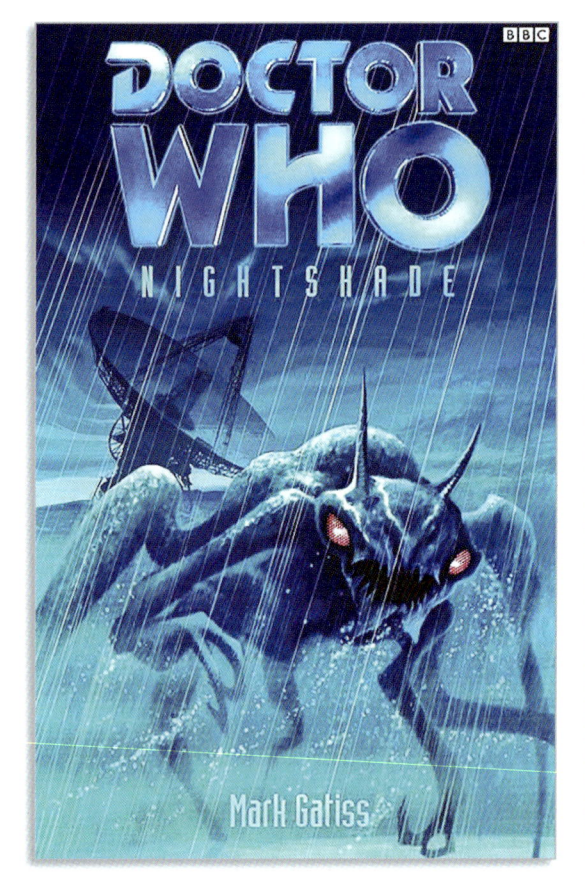

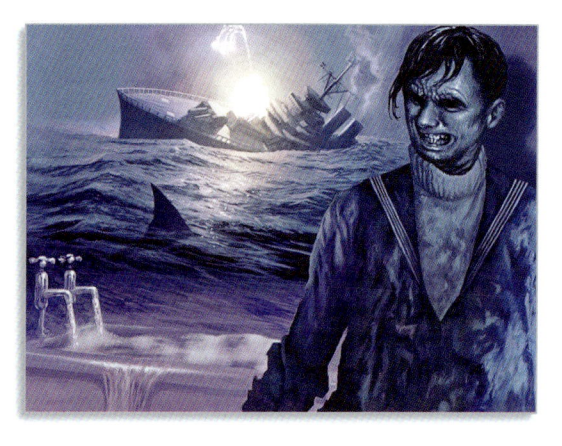

THE WHO ADVENTURES

This page and opposite: the cover of the BBC website e-book edition of Mark Gatiss's *Nightshade* (top left), plus Daryl Joyce's original cover artwork (top right) and eleven internal illustrations. The cover was styled to resemble that of one of BBC Books' Past Doctor Adventures novels. In his newly-written author's notes, Gatiss explained how the novel had been partly inspired by his love of the BBC's three Nigel Kneale-scripted *Quatermass* science-fiction serials of the 1950s. Of the main new character, he wrote: 'Edmund Trevithick is a composite character. He's a grumpy old actor (my favourite kind) who used to star in a TV series that isn't quite *Quatermass* and isn't quite *Doctor Who*.'

AFTERLIFE

THE WHO ADVENTURES

Daryl Joyce's cover art for the BBC website e-book edition of Paul Cornell's *Human Nature*.

AFTERLIFE

The first eight of Daryl Joyce's seventeen internal illustrations for the BBC website e-book edition of *Human Nature*.

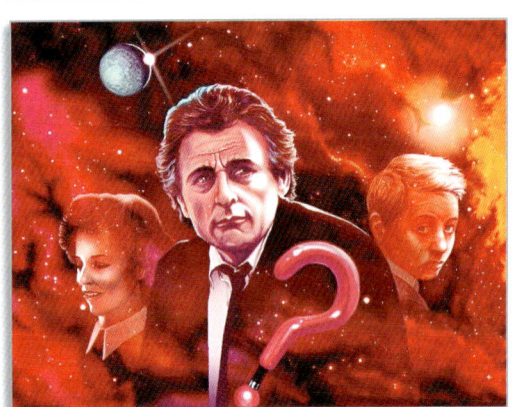

THE WHO ADVENTURES

A further eight of Daryl Joyce's seventeen internal illustrations for the BBC website e-book edition of *Human Nature*.

AFTERLIFE

The last of Daryl Joyce's internal illustrations for the BBC website e-book edition of *Human Nature*, depicting the Doctor and Bernice departing at the end of the story. In 2007, the BBC broadcast a two-part *Doctor Who* story, 'Human Nature'/'The Family of Blood', scripted by Paul Cornell and adapted from his novel. In this, the seventh Doctor was replaced by the tenth, played by David Tennant, and Bernice's part in the action was taken by his companion Martha Jones, played by Freema Agyeman.

DARYL JOYCE

Daryl Joyce is a freelance artist who has, over the years, had many *Doctor Who* commissions. Early examples included not only illustrations for the BBC's *Doctor Who* website but also numerous pieces for *Doctor Who Magazine* and for short stories in Panini's *Doctor Who Storybook* and *Doctor Who Annual* publications. In 2003 he painted a colour frontispiece for the deluxe edition of one of Telos Publishing's *Doctor Who* novellas, *Fallen Gods* by Jonathan Blum and Kate Orman.

From 2006, Joyce began providing background art for some of BBC Studios' animated recreations of 'lost' *Doctor Who* stories, such as 'The Power of the Daleks' and 'Shada', released on Blu-ray and DVD.

Many examples of Joyce's work can be seen at his website: https://www.daryljoyce-illustrator.com.

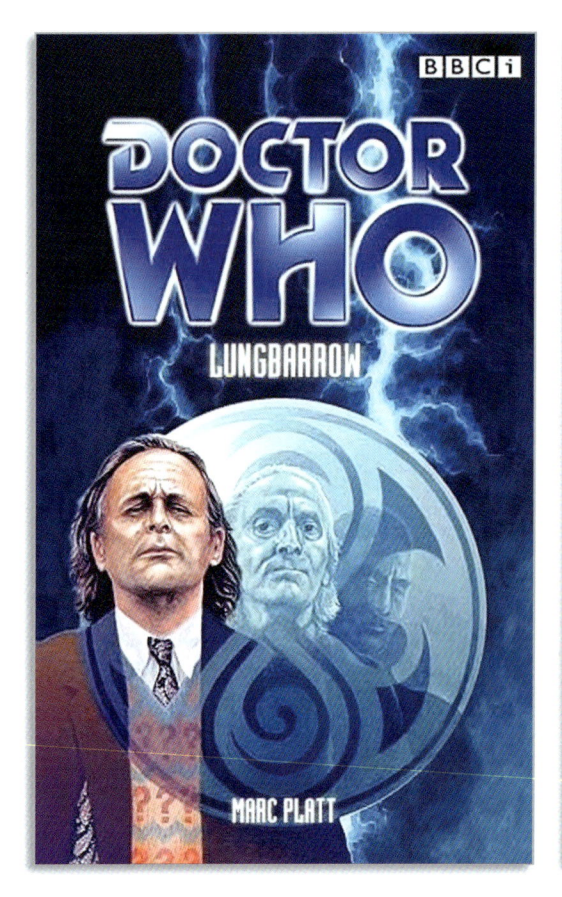

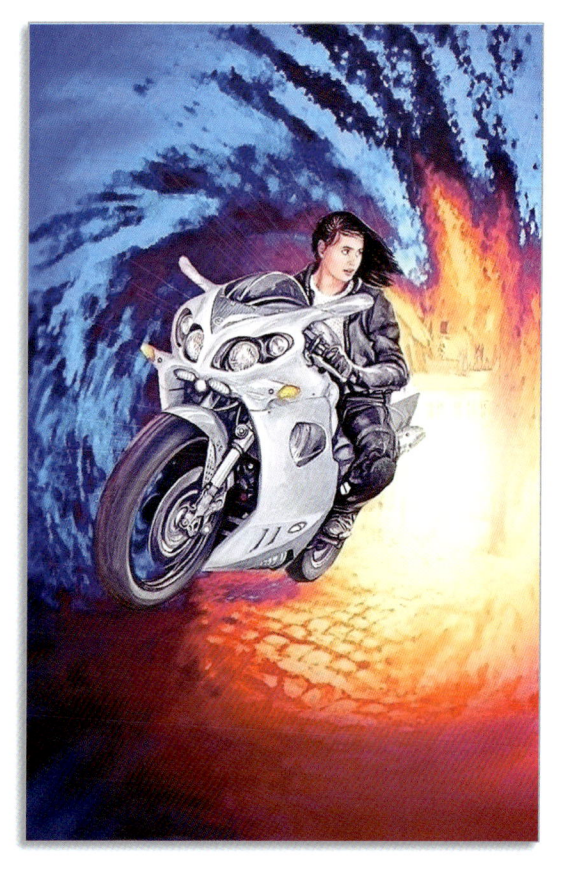

THE WHO ADVENTURES

Top left: the cover of the BBC website e-book of *Lungbarrow*.

Top right: Daryl Joyce's original cover artwork.

Immediately above: the first of seventeen internal illustrations that Joyce provided for this edition; it depicts the Doctor's companion Ace riding her newly-acquired time-travelling motorbike.

Right: in this instance, Joyce also created revised and reworked versions of a number of his illustrations, in some cases long after the e-book was first published; this is one example.

286

AFTERLIFE

A further eight of Daryl Joyce's seventeen internal illustrations for the BBC website e-book edition of *Lungbarrow*.

287

THE WHO ADVENTURES

The last eight of Daryl Joyce's seventeen internal illustrations for the BBC website e-book edition of *Lungbarrow*.

AFTERLIFE

Left: the introductory artwork for the BBC website e-book edition of *The Dying Days*; in this instance, rather than being presented in the style of a traditional book cover, with overlaid text, it took the form of a composite of some of the internal illustrations, which this time were commissioned from Allan Bednar, whose style was striking different from Daryl Joyce's.

Below: two of Bednar's internal illustrations for *The Dying Days*.

289

THE WHO ADVENTURES

Eight more of Allan Bednar's internal illustrations for the BBC website e-book edition of *The Dying Days*.

AFTERLIFE

The last of Allan Bednar's internal illustrations for the 2003 e-book edition of The Dying Days.

ALLAN BEDNAR

Allan Bednar is a Chicago-born artist who moved to the UK at age 16. After obtaining a degree in Graphic Design and Illustration, he got an early break in 1997 contributing under the name Neal Brand to the iconic *2000 AD* comic, under its then editor David Bishop. Since then he has continued to work in comics and also in computer games, including on *Broken Sword 3* for Revolution.

As well as supplying *The Dying Days* e-book illustrations for the BBC website in 2003, he worked on the independent Comeuppance Comics *Doctor Who* spin-off comic book *Miranda* (2003), contributed the colour frontispiece to the deluxe edition of one of Telos Publishing's *Doctor Who* novellas, *Companion Piece* (2003), provided various cards for *Fantasy Flight*, *AEG* and *Z-Man* games, and also the covers for a range of Powys Media novels based on the classic 1960s TV show *The Prisoner* (2005).

Bednar now works as a cognitive behavioural therapist in the NHS, but still draws and paints for fun and family.

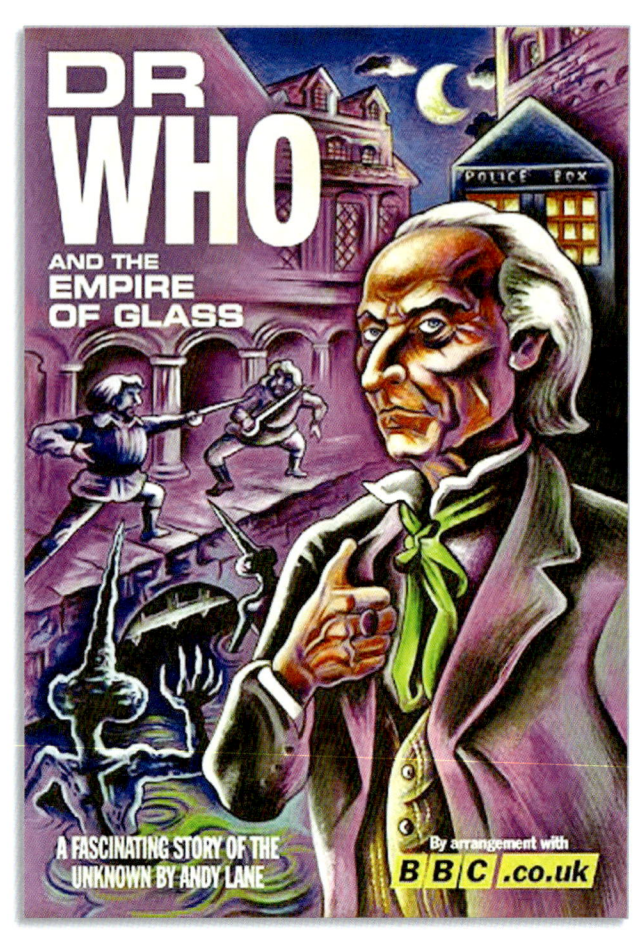

THE WHO ADVENTURES

Top left: the cover of the BBC website e-book edition of the *The Empire of Glass* by Andy Lane.

Bottom left: Mike Nicholson's original rough for the cover.

Bottom right: Mike Nicholson's original artwork; the colours were adjusted for the final version.

The Empire of Glass is a Missing Adventure with the first Doctor and his companions Steven and Vicki. Set in Venice in 1609, it features Shakespeare, Galileo and the Doctor's old enemies the Sontarans. Also involved in the action is Irving Braxiatel, a Time Lord character originally introduced by Andy Lane in his New Adventures novel *Theatre of War*, inspired by a throwaway mention of 'the Braxiatel Collection' in the 1979 TV story 'City of Death'. *The Empire of Glass* recounts his first chronological encounter with the Doctor.

Braxiatel has proved to be one of the most enduring new characters created for the Virgin ranges; he has since featured in several other novels – including the post-*Doctor Who* New Adventure *Tears of the Oracle*, in which it is suggested that he is actually the Doctor's brother – and also Big Finish audio dramas, in which he is portrayed by actor Miles Richardson.

AFTERLIFE

Nine of Mike Nicholson's eleven internal illustrations for the BBC website e-book edition of *The Empire of Glass*.

THE WHO ADVENTURES

Left-hand column: the pair of Mike Nicholson internal illustrations that appeared, respectively, immediate before the prologue and immediately after the epilogue of *The Empire of Glass*, both in its BBC website e-book edition and – in these two cases only – in the original Virgin paperback edition.

Below: some of Mike Nicholson's original roughs for his internal illustrations for this e-book.

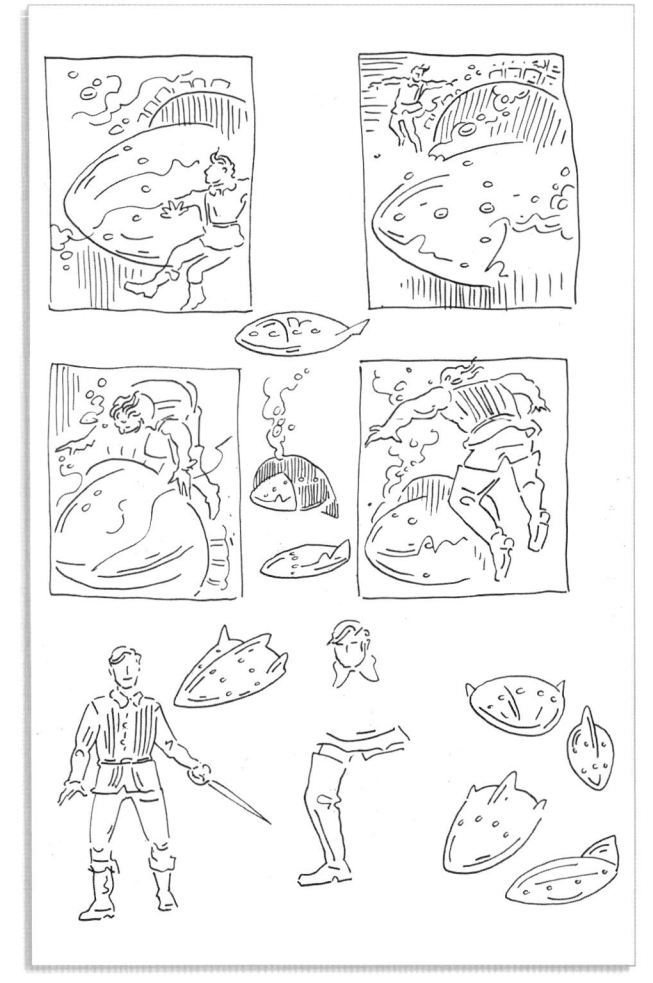

AFTERLIFE

Top right: a colour version of one of Mike Nicholson's *The Empire of Glass* illustrations. Entitled 'The Death of Shakespeare', this version was not included in the e-book itself but produced by the artist some time after its publication.

Other images: more of Mike Nicholson's original roughs for his *The Empire of Glass* illustrations.

THE WHO ADVENTURES

Daryl Joyce's cover artwork for the BBC website e-book edition of Gary Russell's *The Scales of Injustice*, executed in the style of a vintage 1970s Target novelisation cover, complete with added wear and tear.

On its initial publication, the BBC website e-book edition of *The Scales of Injustice* had six internal illustrations by Daryl Joyce. In keeping with his cover artwork (see opposite), these were done in the style of the internal illustrations that appeared in some of the early 1970s Target novelisations. Subsequently, a slightly revised version of the e-book was uploaded, with a different version of the first illustration substituted for the original, and a seventh added. Shown above are the first three illustrations, including both the original version (top left) and the revised version (top right) of the first.

THE WHO ADVENTURES

The other four internal illustrations for the BBC website e-book edition of *The Scales of Injustice*. At top left is the extra one added for the revised upload.

AFTERLIFE

This page: the cover and first four internal illustrations for the BBC's e-book edition of *The Well-Mannered War*. As for *The Scales of Injustice*, this Daryl Joyce artwork was intended to recall that of a vintage 1970s Target book of a fourth Doctor TV story, complete with creased cover and slightly yellowed pages. The internal illustrations – of which there were twelve in total – were presented over six double-page spreads, again in the manner of a paperback book.

THE WHO ADVENTURES

Daryl Joyce's original cover artwork for the BBC website e-book edition of *The Well-Mannered War*.

AFTERLIFE

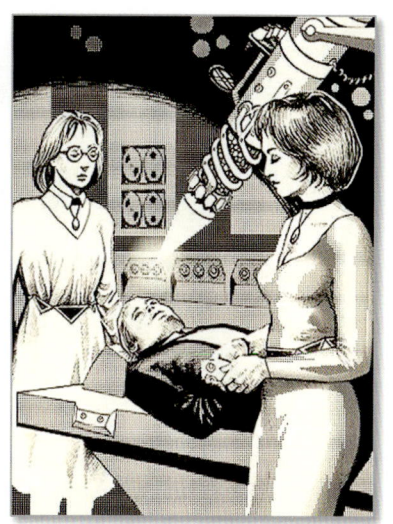

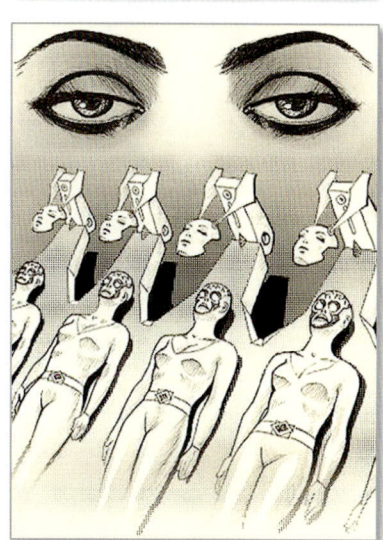

This page: the remaining eight Target book-type internal illustrations by Daryl Joyce for the BBC website e-book edition of *The Well-Mannered War*. The last Missing Adventure to be issued in the original run, this story, pairing the fourth Doctor with the turtle-like Chelonians, was felt by many commentators to recall well the style of late-1970s *Doctor Who* TV stories script-edited by Douglas Adams, of *The Hitch-Hiker's Guide to the Galaxy* fame.

301

The striking cover for the BBC website e-book edition of *The Sands of Time*, with art by Peter McKinstry.

This page: five of Peter McKinstry's eleven black-and-white internal illustrations for the BBC website e-book edition of Justin Richards' Missing Adventures novel *The Sands of Time*. Featuring the fifth Doctor, as played on screen by Peter Davison, with his companions Tegan and Nyssa, this serves as a sequel to the 1975 TV story 'Pyramids of Mars', involving the powerful alien race the Osirans, and is likewise heavily influenced by classic 'Egyptian mummy' horror movies.

THE WHO ADVENTURES

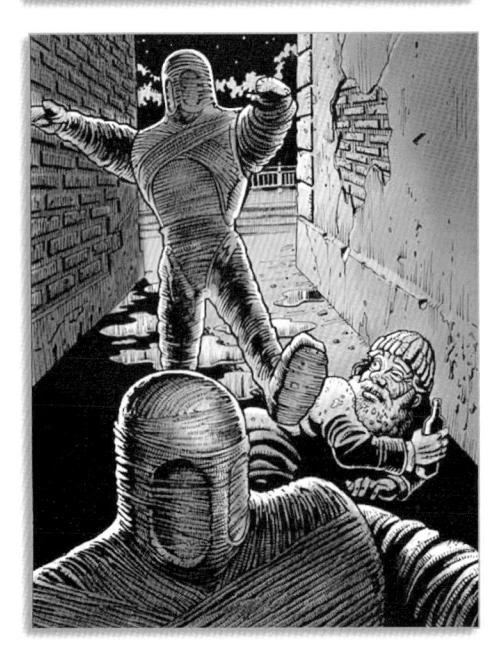

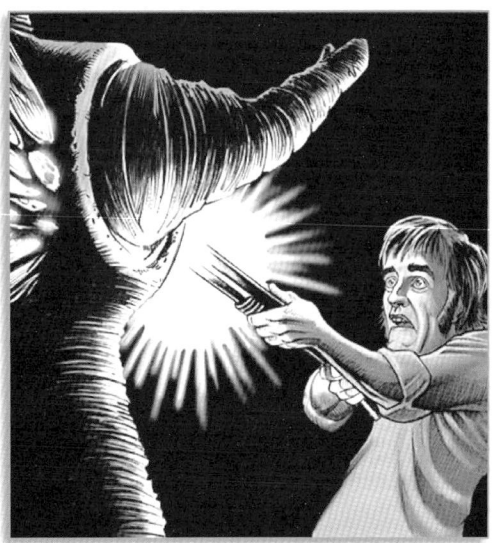

The other six Peter McKinstry internal illustrations for the BBC website e-book edition of *The Sands of Time*.

PETER McKINSTRY

Peter Mckinstry is a freelance concept artist working in film, television and video game art departments. His most recent feature film projects include *Star Wars: Andor*, *Eternals*, *Wonder Woman 1984*, *Morbius* and *Pacific Rim: Uprising*. He provides a broad range of concepts including environments, props, weapons, vehicles and creature design. Other projects have included *Game of Thrones*, *Pan*, *Snow White and the Huntsman* and *Jack the Giant Slayer*. Prior to these he provided concepts for three of the *Harry Potter* films, and before that, from the late 2000s, he spent five years as concept artist on *Doctor Who*. Other illustration work includes comic book covers for IDW's *Star Trek* title, and commissions for BBC Books, Dorling Kindersley, Topps and Carlton Books.

The BBC's *Doctor Who* website is not the only place where certain New Adventures and Missing Adventures novels have enjoyed an afterlife since Virgin lost their licence in 1996. BBC Books have also reissued five of them (along with some of their own *Doctor Who* titles) in a pair of themed collections, as B-format paperbacks with new cover designs credited to Two Associates. Details of these are as follows. (Where a book's title included an initial 'The', this was dropped from the cover but retained in the text inside.)

THE MONSTER COLLECTION

Published 6 March 2014:

- *Shakedown* (ISBN: 978-1-84990-766-8)
- *The Sands of Time* (ISBN: 978-1-84990-767-5)
- *The Scales of Injustice* (ISBN: 978-1-84990-780-4)

THE HISTORY COLLECTION

Published 12 February 2015:

- *The English Way of Death* (ISBN: 978-1-84990-908-2)
- *Human Nature* (ISBN: 978-1-84990-909-9)

Three of these BBC-reissued editions of Virgin titles have also been translated into German by publishers Cross Cult:

- *Doctor Who* Monster-Edition 3: *Rückkehr der Sontaraner* (5 October 2020) (*Shakedown*)
- *Doctor Who* Monster-Edition 4: *Waage der Ungerechtigkeit* (11 January 2021) (*The Scales of Injustice*)
- *Doctor Who* Monster-Edition 7: *Sand der Zeit* (6 September 2021) (*The Sands of Time*)

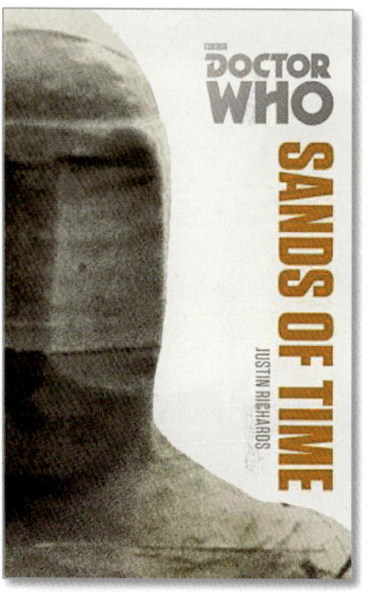

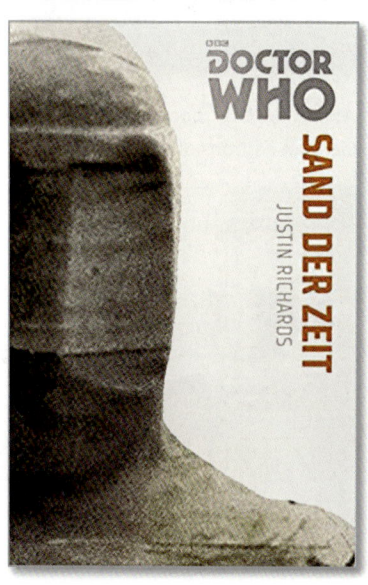

THE WHO ADVENTURES

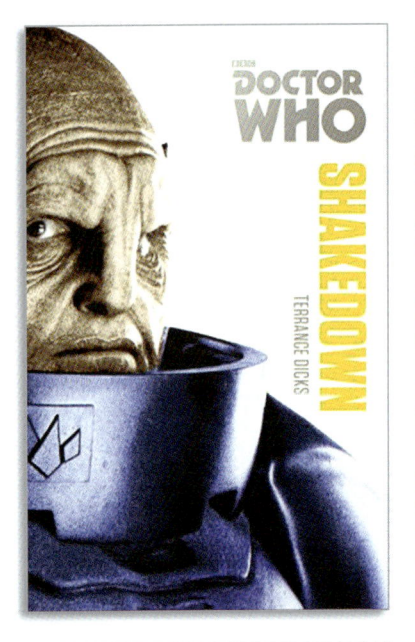

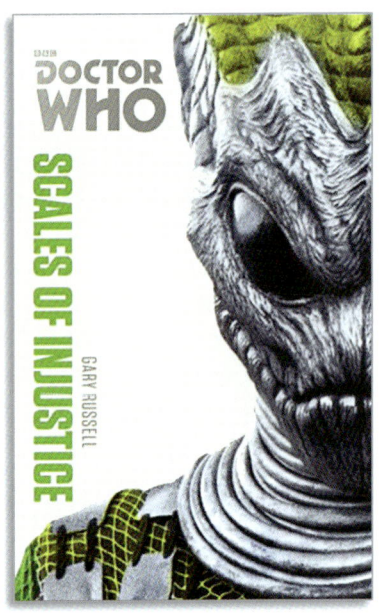

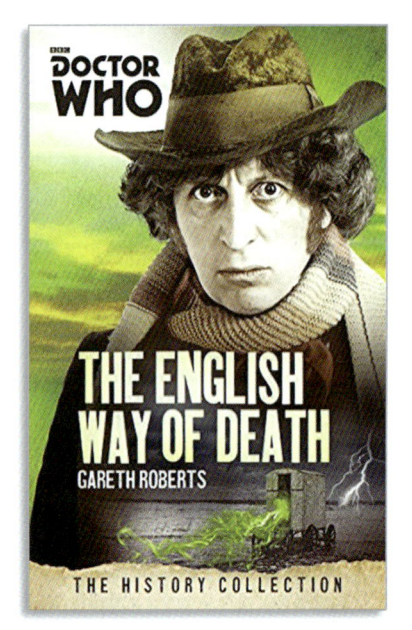

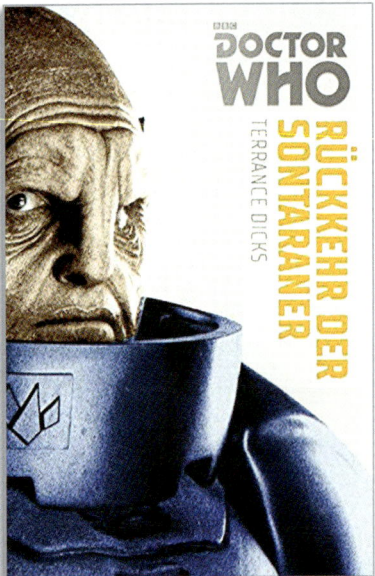

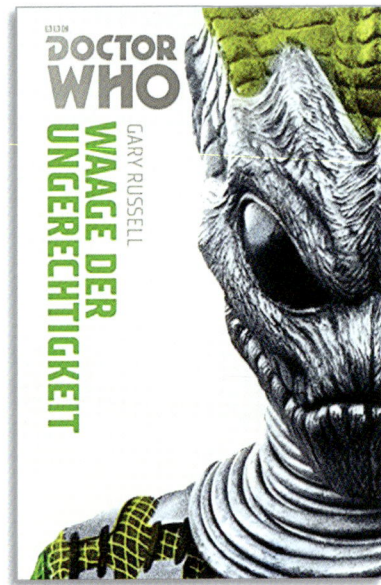

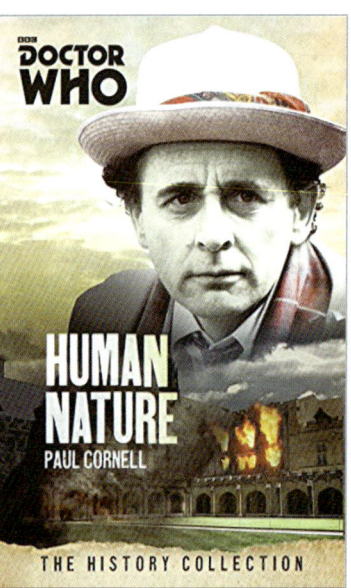

Above: the BBC Books reissue editions of *Shakedown*, *The Scales of Injustice* and *Human Nature*, together with the equivalent German editions of the first two. Below: the BBC audiobook editions of three of the titles.

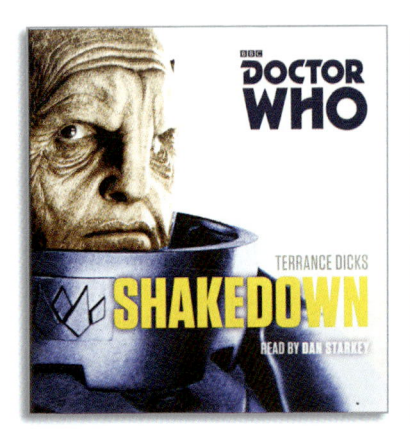

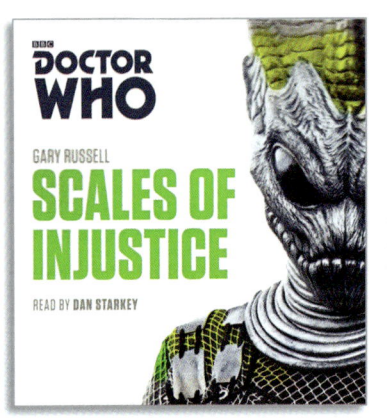

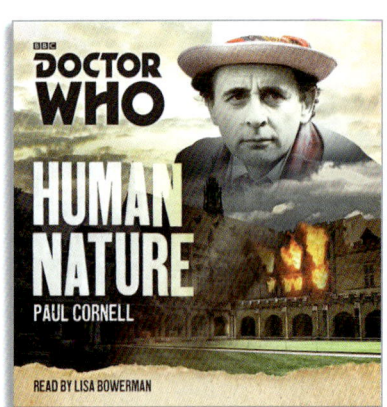

Four of the Virgin titles have also, over the years, been made available in audiobook form:

- *Iceberg* (Royal National Institute for the Blind, released on 1 March 2004). A 9-hour cassette version produced for distribution via the charity and the public library system. Unabridged reading by author David Banks.
- *Human Nature* (BBC Worldwide, released on 20 August 2015, ISBN: 978-1-78529-140-1). Eight CDs. Read by Bernice Summerfield actress Lisa Bowerman.
- *Shakedown* (BBC Worldwide, released on 5 May 2016, ISBN: 978-1-78529-302-3). Seven CDs. Read by regular Sontaran actor Dan Starkey.
- *The Scales of Injustice* (BBC Worldwide, released on 1 December 2016, ISBN: 978-1-78529-325-2). Seven CDs. Read by Dan Starkey.

Around November 2015, an expanded hardback edition of Jim Mortimore's New Adventure *Blood Heat* was self-published by the author. Described by Mortimore as a 'Director's Cut', this version was nearly twice as long as the original, including both previously-deleted sequences and around 40,000 words of newly-written material; a new prologue; and an updated version of the Prelude originally published in *Doctor Who Magazine*.

At Mortimore's request, artist Tim Keable produced three colour illustrations, akin to the black-and-white ones he had supplied for the original Virgin paperback, for reproduction as colour plates in a mooted deluxe edition of this 'Director's Cut', which ultimately failed to come to fruition.

Below: the cover of Jim Mortimore's self-published version of *Blood Heat*.

Bottom row: Tim Keable's colour illustrations for the mooted deluxe edition.

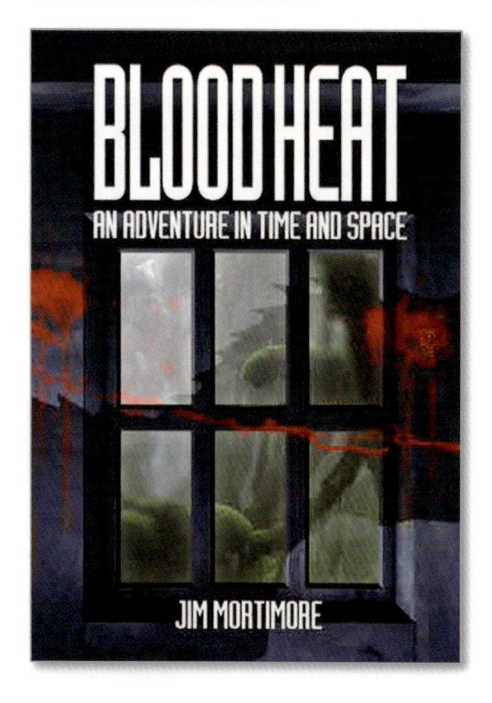

THE WHO ADVENTURES

Seventeen New and Missing Adventures have been adapted by Big Finish as full-cast audio dramas. Two of these, *Birthright* and *Just War*, were reworked as Bernice Summerfield solo stories, as they were released before the company secured a BBC licence, and four were Bernice Summerfield New Adventures to start with. See Appendix E for full details of the thirteen *Doctor Who* adaptations.

Right-hand column: the CD covers of the Bernice Summerfield solo adaptations, with main artwork by Mark Salwowski (*Oh No It Isn't!* and *Beyond the Sun*) and Fred Gambino (*Dragon's Wrath*) and inset illustration of Bernice by Lee Sullivan.

Below: the initial cassette releases of *Oh No It Isn't!* and *Beyond the Sun*.

Bottom: the CD booklet cover of Big Finish's reworked adaptation of *Birthright*.

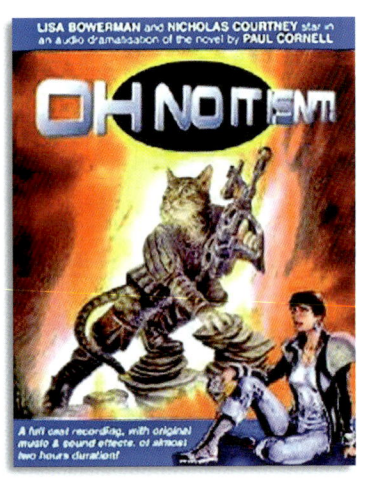

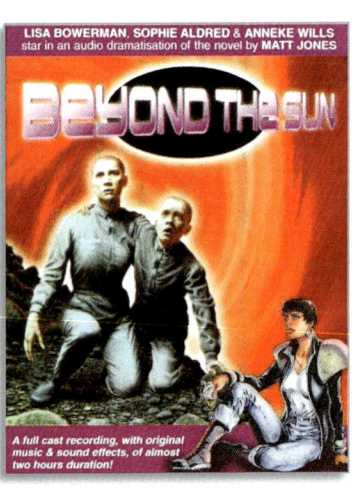

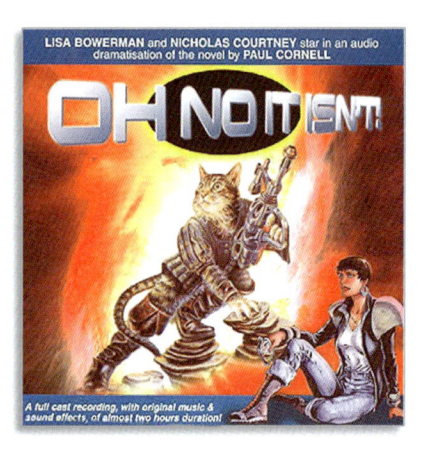

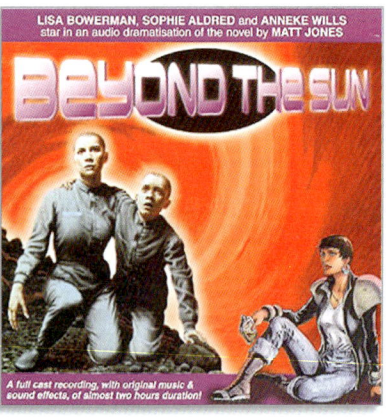

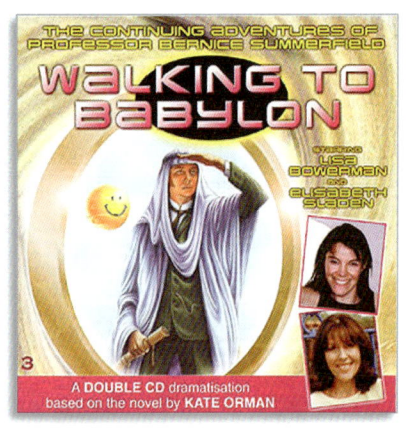

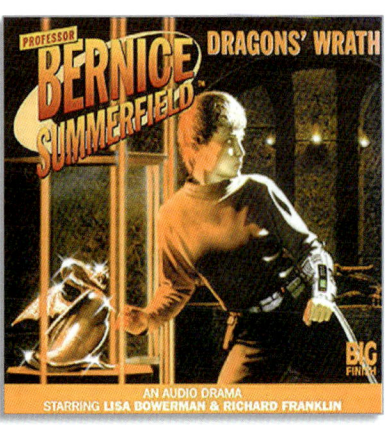

308

AFTERLIFE

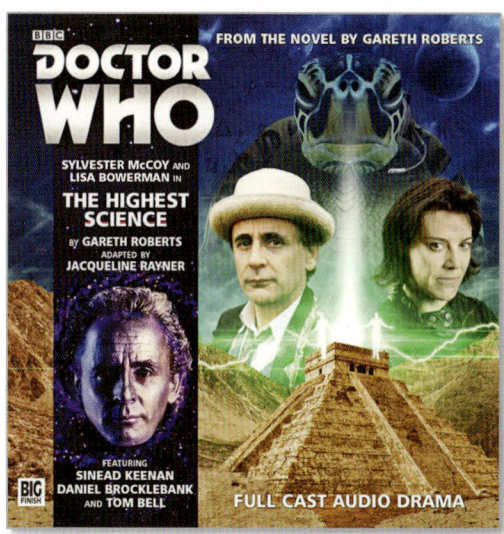

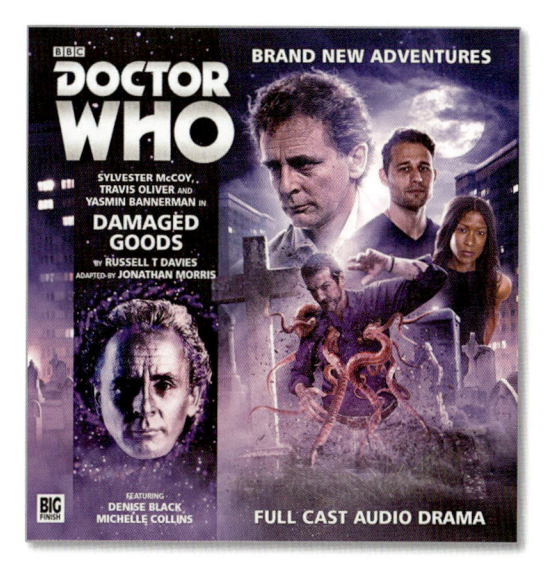

The CD booklet covers of six more of Big Finish's New Adventures and Missing Adventures adaptations.

309

THE WHO ADVENTURES

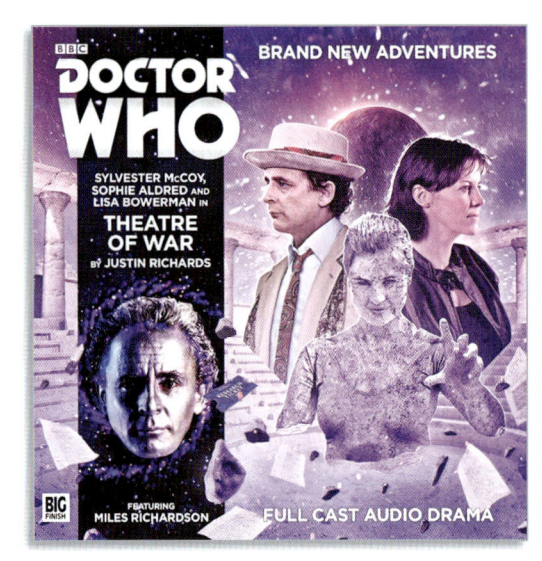

The CD booklet covers of, to date, the last six New and Missing Adventures adaptations from Big Finish.

310

APPENDIX C: CHECKLIST: THE NEW ADVENTURES

1	*Timewyrm: Genesys* (John Peel)	20/06/91	ISBN 0-426-20355-0	£3.50 p/b	Cover by Andrew Skilleter. Preface by Peter Darvill-Evans. Foreword by Sophie Aldred.
2	*Timewyrm: Exodus* (Terrance Dicks)	22/08/91	ISBN 0-426-20357-7	£3.50 p/b	Cover by Andrew Skilleter.
3	*Timewyrm: Apocalypse* (Nigel Robinson)	17/10/91	ISBN 0-426-20359-3	£3.50 p/b	Cover by Andrew Skilleter.
4	*Timewyrm: Revelation* (Paul Cornell)	12/12/91	ISBN 0-426-20360-7	£3.50 p/b	Cover by Andrew Skilleter.
5	*Cat's Cradle: Time's Crucible* (Marc Platt)	12/12/91	ISBN 0-426-20365-8	£3.50 p/b	Cover by Peter Elson.
6	*Cat's Cradle: Warhead* (Andrew Cartmel)	16/04/92	ISBN 0-426-20367-4	£3.50 p/b	Cover by Peter Elson.
7	*Cat's Cradle: Witch Mark* (Andrew Hunt)	18/07/92	ISBN 0-426-20368-2	£3.99 p/b	Cover by Peter Elson.
8	*Nightshade* (Mark Gatiss)	20/08/92	ISBN 0-426-20376-3	£3.99 p/b	Cover by Peter Elson.
9	*Love and War* (Paul Cornell)	15/10/92	ISBN 0-426-20385-2	£3.99 p/b	Cover by Lee Sullivan. **Bernice joins/Ace leaves**
10	*Transit* (Ben Aaronovitch)	03/12/92	ISBN 0-426-20384-4	£3.99 p/b	Cover by Peter Elson.
11	*The Highest Science* (Gareth Roberts)	18/02/93	ISBN 0-426-20377-1	£3.99 p/b	Cover by Peter Elson.
12	*The Pit* (Neil Penswick)	18/03/93	ISBN 0-426-20378-X	£3.99 p/b	Cover by Peter Elson.
13	*Deceit* (Peter Darvill-Evans)	15/04/93	ISBN 0-426-20387-9	£3.99 p/b	Cover by Luis Rey. **Ace rejoins**
14	*Lucifer Rising* (Andy Lane and Jim Mortimore)	20/05/93	ISBN 0-426-20388-7	£4.50 p/b	Cover by Jim Mortimore. Illustrated by Lee Brimmicombe-Wood.
15	*White Darkness* (David A McIntee)	17/06/93	ISBN 0-426-20395-X	£4.50 p/b	Cover by Peter Elson.
16	*Shadowmind* (Christopher Bulis)	15/07/93	ISBN 0-426-20394-1	£4.50 p/b	Cover by Christopher Bulis.
17	*Birthright* (Nigel Robinson)	19/08/93	ISBN 0-426-20393-3	£4.50 p/b	Cover by Peter Elson.
18	*Iceberg* (David Banks)	16/09/93	ISBN 0-426-20392-5	£4.50 p/b	Cover by Andrew Skilleter.
19	*Blood Heat* (Jim Mortimore)	21/10/93	ISBN 0-426-20399-2	£4.50 p/b	Cover by Jeff Cummins. Illustrated by Tim Keable.
20	*The Dimension Riders* (Daniel Blythe)	18/11/93	ISBN 0-426-20397-6	£4.50 p/b	Cover by Jeff Cummins.
21	*The Left-Handed Hummingbird* (Kate Orman)	02/12/93	ISBN 0-426-20404-2	£4.50 p/b	Cover by Pete Wallbank.
22	*Conundrum* (Steve Lyons)	20/01/94	ISBN 0-426-20408-5	£4.99 p/b	Cover by Jeff Cummins.

23	*No Future* (Paul Cornell)	17/02/94	ISBN 0-426-20409-3	£4.99 p/b	Cover by Pete Wallbank.
24	*Tragedy Day* (Gareth Roberts)	17/03/94	ISBN 0-426-20410-7	£4.99 p/b	Cover by Jeff Cummins. **Rebecca Levene takes over as editor**
25	*Legacy* (Gary Russell)	21/04/94	ISBN 0-426-20412-3	£4.99 p/b	Cover by Peter Elson.
26	*Theatre of War* (Justin Richards)	19/05/94	ISBN 0-426-20414-X	£4.99 p/b	Cover by Jeff Cummins. Illustrated by Martin Rawle.
27	*All-Consuming Fire* (Andy Lane)	16/06/94	ISBN 0-426-20415-8	£4.99 p/b	Cover by Jeff Cummins. Illustrated by Mike Nicholson.
28	*Blood Harvest* (Terrance Dicks)	21/07/94	ISBN 0-426-20417-4	£4.99 p/b	Cover by Bill Donohoe.
29	*Strange England* (Simon Messingham)	18/08/94	ISBN 0-426-20419-0	£4.99 p/b	Cover by Paul Campbell.
30	*First Frontier* (David A McIntee)	15/09/94	ISBN 0-426-20421-2	£4.99 p/b	Cover by Tony Masero.
31	*St Anthony's Fire* (Mark Gatiss)	20/10/94	ISBN 0-426-20423-9	£4.99 p/b	Cover by Paul Campbell.
32	*Falls The Shadow* (Daniel O'Mahony)	17/11/94	ISBN 0-426-20427-1	£4.99 p/b	Cover by Kevin Jenkins.
33	*Parasite* (Jim Mortimore)	01/12/94	ISBN 0-426-20425-5	£4.99 p/b	Cover by Paul Campbell.
34	*Warlock* (Andrew Cartmel)	19/01/95	ISBN 0-426-20433-6	£4.99 p/b	Cover by Tony Masero.
35	*Set Piece* (Kate Orman)	16/02/95	ISBN 0-426-20436-0	£4.99 p/b	Cover by Tony Masero. Afterword by Sophie Aldred. **Ace leaves**
36	*Infinite Requiem* (Daniel Blythe)	16/03/95	ISBN 0-426-20437-9	£4.99 p/b	Cover by Barry Jones.
37	*Sanctuary* (David A McIntee)	20/04/95	ISBN 0-426-20439-5	£4.99 p/b	Cover by Peter Elson.
38	*Human Nature* (Paul Cornell)	18/05/95	ISBN 0-426-20443-3	£4.99 p/b	Cover by Bill Donohoe. From a plot by Paul Cornell and Kate Orman. **Wolsey the cat joins**
39	*Original Sin* (Andy Lane)	15/06/95	ISBN 0-426-20444-1	£4.99 p/b	Cover by Tony Masero. Illustrated by Tony Masero. **Roz and Chris join**
40	*Sky Pirates!* (Dave Stone)	20/07/95	ISBN 0-426-20446-8	£4.99 p/b	Cover by Jeff Cummins. Illustrated by Roger Langridge.
41	*Zamper* (Gareth Roberts)	17/08/95	ISBN 0-426-20450-6	£4.99 p/b	Cover by Tony Masero.
42	*Toy Soldiers* (Paul Leonard)	21/09/95	ISBN 0-426-20452-2	£4.99 p/b	Cover by Peter Elson.
43	*Head Games* (Steve Lyons)	19/10/95	ISBN 0-426-20454-9	£4.99 p/b	Cover by Bill Donohoe.
44	*The Also People* (Ben Aaronovitch)	16/11/95	ISBN 0-426-20456-5	£4.99 p/b	Cover by Tony Masero.
45	*Shakedown* (Terrance Dicks)	07/12/95	ISBN 0-426-20459-X	£4.99 p/b	Cover by Peter Elson. Foreword by Jason Haigh-Ellery and Gary Leigh. Video tie-in, with 8pp section of black-and-white photos by Robin Pritchard.

CHECKLIST: THE NEW ADVENTURES

46	*Just War* (Lance Parkin)	18/01/96	ISBN 0-426-20463-8	£4.99 p/b	Cover by Nik Spender.
47	*Warchild* (Andrew Cartmel)	15/02/96	ISBN 0-426-20464-6	£4.99 p/b	Cover by Jeff Cummins.
48	*SLEEPY* (Kate Orman)	21/03/96	ISBN 0-426-20465-4	£4.99 p/b	Cover by Mark Wilkinson. Illustrated by Jason Towers.
49	*Death and Diplomacy* (Dave Stone)	18/04/96	ISBN 0-426-20468-9	£4.99 p/b	Cover by Bill Donohoe.
50	*Happy Endings* (Paul Cornell)	16/05/96	ISBN 0-426-20470-0	£4.99 p/b	Cover by Paul Campbell. Poster offer of the cover artwork to mark the fiftieth New Adventure. Includes a poem by Vanessa Bishop. ****Bernice leaves/Cover design changes****
51	*GodEngine* (Craig Hinton)	20/06/96	ISBN 0-426-20473-5	£4.99 p/b	Cover by Peter Elson.
52	*Christmas on a Rational Planet* (Lawrence Miles)	18/07/96	ISBN 0-426-20476-X	£4.99 p/b	Cover by Mick Posen.
53	*Return of the Living Dad* (Kate Orman)	15/08/96	ISBN 0-426-20482-4	£4.99 p/b	Cover by Mark Wilkinson. ****Features Bernice and Jason****
54	*The Death of Art* (Simon Bucher-Jones)	19/09/96	ISBN 0-426-20481-6	£4.99 p/b	Cover by Jon Sullivan.
55	*Damaged Goods* (Russell T Davies)	17/10/96	ISBN 0-426-20483-2	£4.99 p/b	Cover by Bill Donohoe.
56	*So Vile A Sin* (Ben Aaronovitch and Kate Orman)	17/04/97	ISBN 0-426-20484-0	£4.99 p/b	Cover by Jon Sullivan. Publication originally scheduled for 21/11/96. ****Roz dies/Features Bernice and Jason****
57	*Bad Therapy* (Matthew Jones)	05/12/96	ISBN 0-426-20490-5	£4.99 p/b	Cover by Mark Salwowski.
58	*Eternity Weeps* (Jim Mortimore)	16/01/97	ISBN 0-426-20497-2	£4.99 p/b	Cover by Peter Elson. ****Features Bernice and Jason/*Doctor Who* logo dropped from books ****
59	*The Room With No Doors* (Kate Orman)	20/02/97	ISBN 0-426-20500-6	£4.99 p/b	Cover by Jon Sullivan.
60	*Lungbarrow* (Marc Platt)	20/03/97	ISBN 0-426-20502-2	£4.99 p/b	Cover by Fred Gambino. ****Chris leaves****
61	*The Dying Days* (Lance Parkin)	17/04/97	ISBN 0-426-20504-9	£4.99 p/b	Cover by Fred Gambino. Eighth Doctor novel. Final *Doctor Who* New Adventure. Afterword by Peter Darvill-Evans/ Rebecca Levene/Simon Winstone. ****Reintroduces Bernice as a regular****

THE WHO ADVENTURES

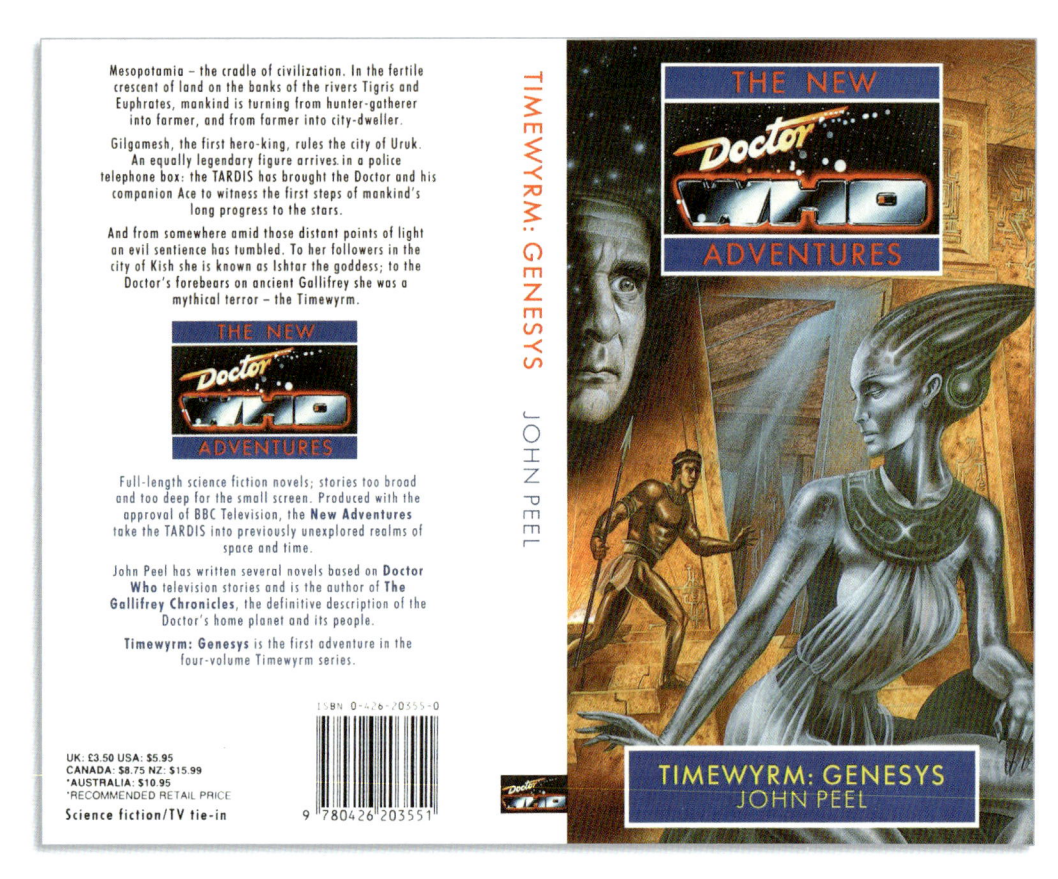

The two Virgin ranges' respective first titles, showing their standard spine and back cover designs.

APPENDIX D: CHECKLIST: THE MISSING ADVENTURES

1	*Goth Opera* (Paul Cornell)	21/07/94	ISBN 0-426-20418-2	£4.99 p/b	Cover by Alister Pearson. Doctor 5, Tegan, Nyssa. Cover has no 'The' on it. Preface by Peter Darvill-Evans. Sequel to the NA *Blood Harvest*.
2	*Evolution* (John Peel)	15/09/94	ISBN 0-426-20422-0	£4.99 p/b	Cover by Alister Pearson. Doctor 4, Sarah.
3	*Venusian Lullaby* (Paul Leonard)	20/10/94	ISBN 0-426-20424-7	£4.99 p/b	Cover by Alister Pearson. Doctor 1, Ian, Barbara. Venusian based on a Jim Mortimore sketch.
4	*The Crystal Bucephalus* (Craig Hinton)	17/11/94	ISBN 0-426-20429-8	£4.99 p/b	Cover by Alister Pearson. Doctor 5, Tegan, Turlough, Kamelion.
5	*State of Change* (Christopher Bulis)	01/12/94	ISBN 0-426-20431-X	£4.99 p/b	Cover by Alister Pearson. Doctor 6, Peri.
6	*The Romance of Crime* (Gareth Roberts)	19/01/95	ISBN 0-426-20435-2	£4.99 p/b	Cover by Alister Pearson. Doctor 4, Romana 2, K-9.
7	*The Ghosts of N-Space* (Barry Letts)	16/02/95	ISBN 0-426-20434-4	£4.99 p/b	Cover by Alister Pearson. Doctor 3, Sarah, Brigadier.
8	*Time of Your Life* (Steve Lyons)	16/03/95	ISBN 0-426-20438-7	£4.99 p/b	Cover by Paul Campbell. Doctor 6, Grant.
9	*Dancing the Code* (Paul Leonard)	20/04/95	ISBN 0-426-20441-7	£4.99 p/b	Cover by Paul Campbell. Doctor 3, Jo, Brigadier, Yates, Benton. Xarax helicopter based on a Jim Mortimore sketch.
10	*The Menagerie* (Martin Day)	18/05/95	ISBN 0-426-20449-2	£4.99 p/b	Cover by Paul Campbell. Doctor 2, Jamie, Zoe.
11	*System Shock* (Justin Richards)	15/06/95	ISBN 0-426-20445-X	£4.99 p/b	Cover by Martin Rawle. Doctor 4, Sarah, Harry. Internal map by Martin Rawle.
12	*The Sorcerer's Apprentice* (Christopher Bulis)	20/07/95	ISBN 0-426-20447-6	£4.99 p/b	Cover by Paul Campbell. Doctor 1, Susan, Ian, Barbara.
13	*Invasion of the Cat-People* (Gary Russell)	17/08/95	ISBN 0-426-20440-9	£4.99 p/b	Cover by Colin Howard. Doctor 2, Ben, Polly. Foreword by Anneke Wills.
14	*Managra* (Stephen Marley)	21/09/95	ISBN 0-426-20453-0	£4.99 p/b	Cover by Paul Campbell. Doctor 4, Sarah.
15	*Millennial Rites* (Craig Hinton)	19/10/95	ISBN 0-426-20455-7	£4.99 p/b	Cover by Alister Pearson. Doctor 6, Mel.
16	*The Empire of Glass* (Andy Lane)	16/11/95	ISBN 0-426-20457-3	£4.99 p/b	Cover by Paul Campbell. Doctor 1, Vicki, Steven. Internal illustrations by Mike Nicholson.

17	*Lords of the Storm* (David A McIntee)	07/12/95	ISBN 0-426-20460-3	£4.99 p/b	Cover by Alister Pearson. Doctor 5, Turlough.
18	*Downtime* (Marc Platt)	18/01/96	ISBN 0-426-20462-X	£4.99 p/b	Cover by Paul Campbell. Doctor 2 briefly at the start, Doctor 3 briefly at the end, Victoria, Sarah, K-9, Brigadier. Video tie-in, with 8pp section of black-and-white photos by Robin Pritchard. Foreword by Keith Barnfather.
19	*The Man in the Velvet Mask* (Daniel O'Mahony)	15/02/96	ISBN 0-426-20461-1	£4.99 p/b	Cover by Alister Pearson. Doctor 1, Dodo.
20	*The English Way of Death* (Gareth Roberts)	21/03/96	ISBN 0-426-20466-2	£4.99 p/b	Cover by Alister Pearson. Doctor 4, Romana 2, K-9. Internal illustrations by Phil Bevan.
21	*The Eye of the Giant* (Christopher Bulis)	18/04/96	ISBN 0-426-20469-7	£4.99 p/b	Cover by Paul Campbell. Doctor 3, Liz, Brigadier, Yates, Benton.
22	*The Sands of Time* (Justin Richards)	16/05/96	ISBN 0-426-20472-7	£4.99 p/b	Cover by Alister Pearson. Doctor 5, Tegan, Nyssa.
23	*Killing Ground* (Steve Lyons)	20/06/96	ISBN 0-426-20474-3	£4.99 p/b	Cover by Alister Pearson. Doctor 6, Grant.
24	*The Scales of Injustice* (Gary Russell)	18/07/96	ISBN 0-426-20477-8	£4.99 p/b	Cover by Andrew Skilleter. Doctor 3, Liz, Brigadier, Yates, Benton. Sea Devil/Silurian hybrid by Paul Vyse.
25	*The Shadow of Weng-Chiang* (David A McIntee)	15/08/96	ISBN 0-426-20479-4	£4.99 p/b	Cover by Alister Pearson. Doctor 4, Romana 1, K-9.
26	*Twilight of the Gods* (Christopher Bulis)	19/09/96	ISBN 0-426-20480-8	£4.99 p/b	Cover by Alister Pearson. Doctor 2, Jamie, Victoria. Frontispiece by Christopher Bulis.
27	*Speed of Flight* (Paul Leonard)	17/10/96	ISBN 0-426-20487-5	£4.99 p/b	Cover by Alister Pearson. Doctor 3, Jo, Yates.
28	*The Plotters* (Gareth Roberts)	21/11/96	ISBN 0-426-20488-3	£4.99 p/b	Cover by Alister Pearson. Doctor 1, Ian, Barbara, Vicki. Internal illustrations by Paul Vyse.
29	*Cold Fusion* (Lance Parkin)	05/12/96	ISBN 0-426-20489-1	£4.99 p/b	Cover by Alister Pearson. Doctors 5 and 7, Adric, Tegan, Nyssa, Chris, Roz.
30	*Burning Heart* (Dave Stone)	16/01/97	ISBN 0-426-20498-0	£4.99 p/b	Cover by Alister Pearson. Doctor 6, Peri.
31	*A Device of Death* (Christopher Bulis)	20/02/97	ISBN 0-426-20501-4	£4.99 p/b	Cover by Alister Pearson. Doctor 4, Sarah, Harry.
32	*The Dark Path* (David A McIntee)	30/03/97	ISBN 0-426-20503-0	£4.99 p/b	Cover by Alister Pearson. Doctor 2, Jamie, Victoria.
33	*The Well-Mannered War* (Gareth Roberts)	17/04/97	ISBN 0-426-20506-5	£4.99 p/b	Cover by Alister Pearson. Doctor 4, Romana 2, K-9. Afterword by Peter Darvill-Evans, Rebecca Levene and Simon Winstone.

APPENDIX E: CHECKLIST: THE BIG FINISH AUDIOS

Title	Date	ISBN/Code	Price	Notes
Bernice Summerfield: Birthright (Nigel Robinson, adapted by Jacqueline Rayner)	02/1999	Physical ISBN: 1-903654-36-X Digital ISBN: 978-1-83868-477-8 Production Code: BFPCD4	£12.99	Recorded 05/11/98 and 06/11/98. Cover by Peter Elson. Director Nicholas Briggs. Bernice, Jason.
Bernice Summerfield: Just War (Lance Parkin, adapted by Jacqueline Rayner)	08/1999	Physical ISBN: 1-903654-35-1 Digital ISBN: 978-1-83868-478-5 Production Code: BFPCD5	£12.99	Cover by Nik Spender. Director Gary Russell. Bernice, Jason.
Doctor Who: Love and War (Paul Cornell, adapted by Jacqueline Rayner)	10/2012	Physical ISBN: 978-1-78178-024-4 Digital ISBN: 978-1-78703-977-3 Production Code: BFPDWLWCD01	£14.99	Twentieth anniversary of Bernice Summerfield. Recorded 28/01/12 and 29/01/12. Cover by Andy Lambert. Director Gary Russell. Doctor 7, Ace, Bernice.
Doctor Who: The Highest Science (Gareth Roberts, adapted by Jacqueline Rayner)	12/2014	Physical ISBN: 978-1-78178-366-5 Production Code: BFPDWLWCD03	£14.99	Recorded 06/01/14 and 07/01/14. Cover by Mark Plastow. Director Scott Handcock. Doctor 7, Bernice.
Doctor Who: The Romance of Crime (Gareth Roberts, adapted by John Dorney)	01/2015	Physical ISBN: 978-1-78178-342-9 Digital ISBN: 978-1-78575-321-3 Production Code: BFP4DGRCD01	£14.99	Also available in a deluxe edition with *The English Way of Death*. Recorded 31/10/13 and 01/11/13. Cover by Tom Webster. Director Nicholas Briggs. Doctor 4, Romana 2, K-9.
Doctor Who: The English Way of Death (Gareth Roberts, adapted by John Dorney)	01/2015	Physical ISBN: 978-1-78178-343-6 Digital ISBN: 978-1-78575-407-4 Production Code: BFP4DGRCD02	£14.99	Also available in a deluxe edition with *The Romance of Crime*. Recorded 10/09/13, 11/09/13 and 13/09/13. Cover by Tom Webster. Director Nicholas Briggs. Doctor 4, Romana 2, K-9.
Doctor Who: Damaged Goods (Russell T Davies, adapted by Jonathan Morris)	04/2015	Physical ISBN: 978-1-78178-439-6 Production Code: BFPDWLWCD02	£14.99	Also available in a deluxe edition with *The Well-Mannered War*. Recorded 28/07/14 and 29/07/14. Cover by Tom Webster. Director Ken Bentley. Dr 7, Chris, Roz.
Doctor Who: The Well-Mannered War (Gareth Roberts, adapted by John Dorney)	04/2015	Physical ISBN: 978-1-78178-443-3 Production Code: BFP4DGRCD03	£14.99	Also available in a deluxe edition with *Damaged Goods*. Recorded 19/08/14, 20/08/14 and 01/09/14. Cover by Tom Webster. Director Ken Bentley. Doctor 4, Romana 2, K-9.

THE WHO ADVENTURES

Title	Date	ISBN/Code	Price	Notes
Doctor Who: Theatre of War (Justin Richards, adapted by Justin Richards)	12/2015	Physical ISBN: 978-1-78178-699-4 Production Code: BFPDWLWCD04	£14.99	Recorded 04/06/15 and 07/06/15. Cover by Will Brooks. Director Scott Handcock. Doctor 7, Ace, Bernice.
Doctor Who: All Consuming Fire (Andy Lane, adapted by Guy Adams)	12/2015	Physical ISBN: 978-1-78178-701-4 Production Code: BFPDWLWCD05	£14.99	Recorded 05/06/15, 15/06/15 and 16/06/15. Cover by Joseph Bell. Director Scott Handcock. Doctor 7, Ace, Bernice.
Doctor Who: Nightshade (Mark Gatiss, adapted by Kyle C Szikora)	04/2016	Physical ISBN: 978-1-78178-703-8 Production Code: BFPDWLWCD06	£14.99	Recorded 13/04/15, 16/10/15 and 17/10/15. Cover by Lee Binding. Director Scott Handcock. Doctor 7, Ace, Susan.
Doctor Who: Original Sin (Andy Lane, adapted by John Dorney)	12/2016	Physical ISBN: 978-1-78178-705-2 Digital ISBN: 978-1-78178-706-9 Production Code: BFPDWLWCD07	£14.99	Recorded 01/09/15 and 17/09/15. Cover by Tom Newsom. Director Ken Bentley. Doctor 7, Bernice, Chris, Roz.
Doctor Who: Cold Fusion (Lance Parkin, adapted by Lance Parkin)	12/2016	Physical ISBN: 978-1-78178-707-6 Production Code: BFPDWLWCD08	£14.99	Recorded 24/05/16 to 26/05/16. Cover by Tom Newsom. Director Jamie Anderson. Doctors 5 and 7, Adric, Nyssa, Tegan, Chris, Roz.

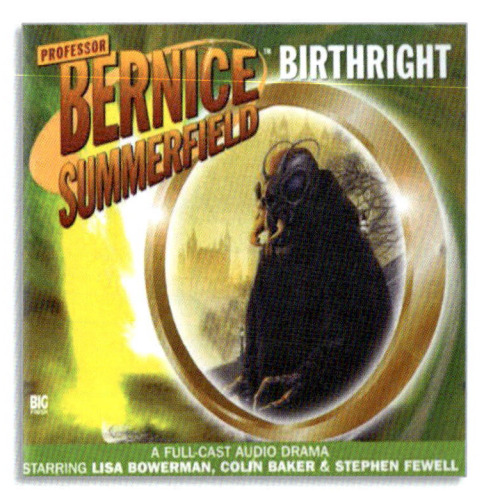

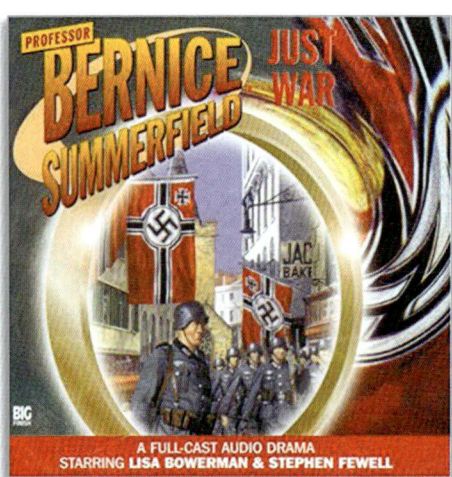

Above left: reissues of the *Birthright* and *Just War* CDs, with revised artwork now incorporating the *Bernice Summerfield* range logo, designed by Paul Vyse. Above right: the deluxe edition of *Damaged Goods* and *The Well-Mannered War*.

COVERS GALLERY

APPENDIX F: COVERS GALLERY

This Appendix presents a complete gallery of the as-published covers of Virgin Publishing's original *Doctor* Who-related fiction titles, in three sections: the New Adventures; the one-off *Who Killed Kennedy* book and the *Decalog* collections; and the Missing Adventures. In each case the books are in intended publication order, and the artist is identified by initials.

ARTIST KEY:

AP - Alister Pearson
AS - Andrew Skilleter
BD - Bill Donohoe
BJ - Barry Jones
CB - Christopher Bulis
CH - Colin Howard
DW – David Wyatt
FG - Fred Gambino
JC - Jeff Cummins
JM - Jim Mortimore
JS - Jon Sullivan

KJ - Kevin Jenkins
LR - Luis Rey
LS - Lee Sullivan
MP - Mick Posen
MR - Martin Rawle
MS - Mark Salwowski
MW - Mark Wilkinson
NS - Nik Spender
PC - Paul Campbell
PE - Peter Elson
PW - Pete Wallbank
TM - Tony Masero

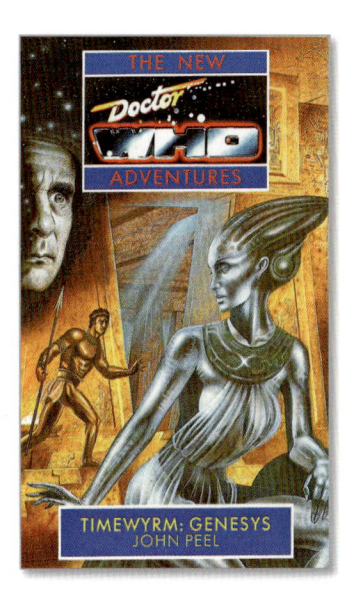

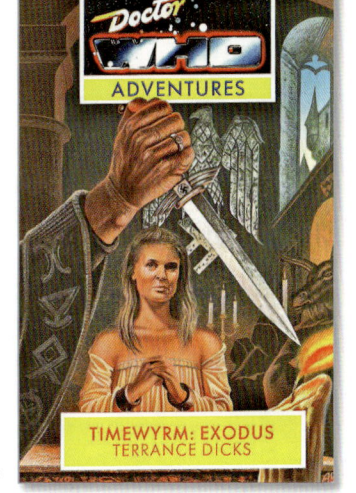

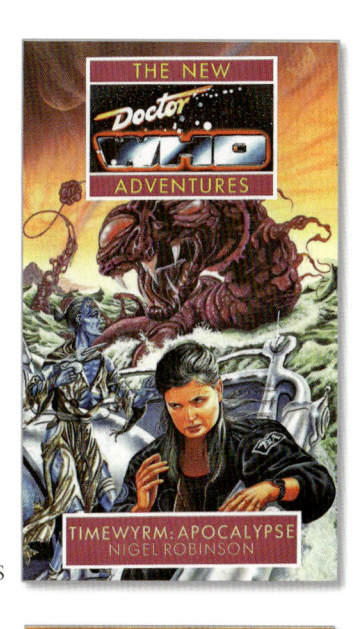

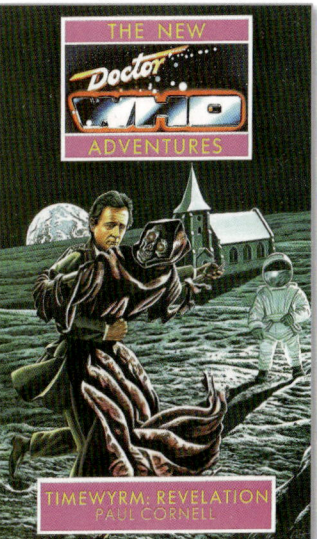

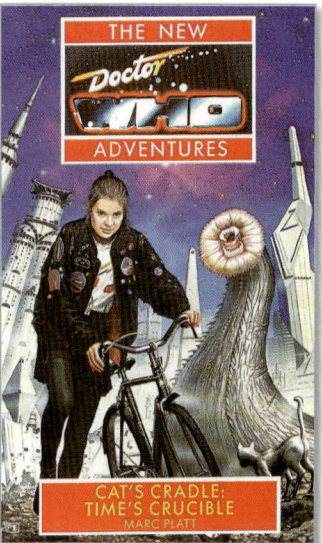

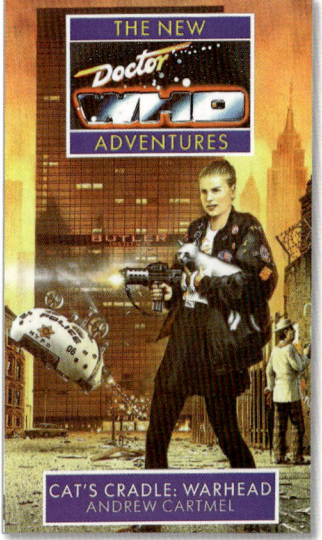

319

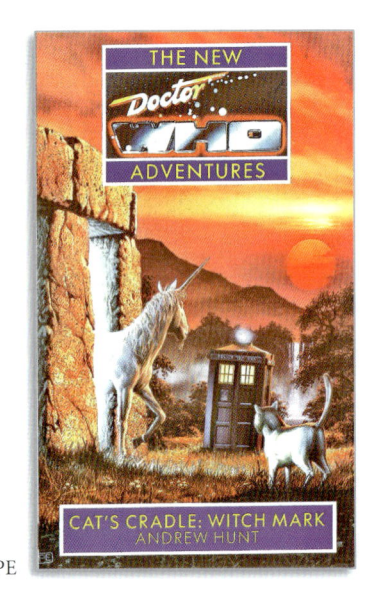

THE WHO ADVENTURES

CAT'S CRADLE: WITCH MARK
ANDREW HUNT
PE

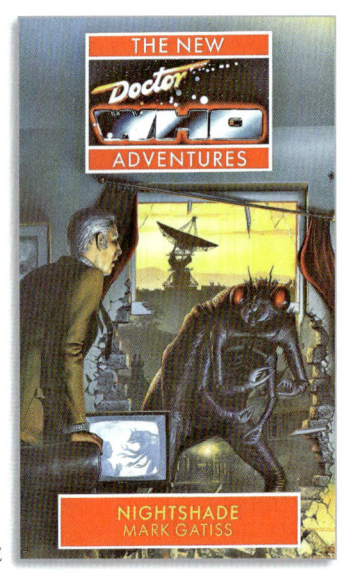

NIGHTSHADE
MARK GATISS
PE

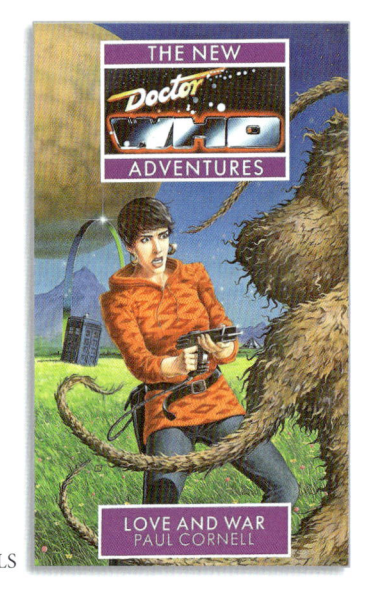

LOVE AND WAR
PAUL CORNELL
LS

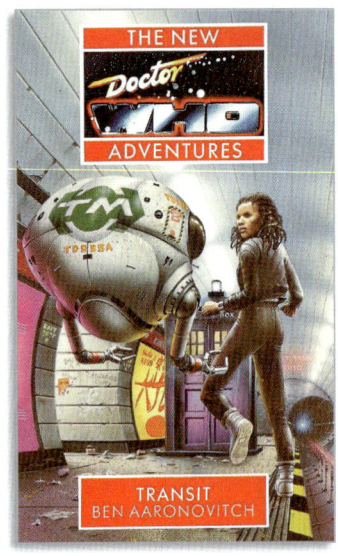

TRANSIT
BEN AARONOVITCH
PE

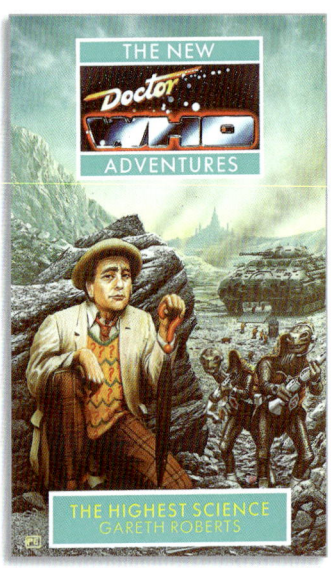

THE HIGHEST SCIENCE
GARETH ROBERTS
PE

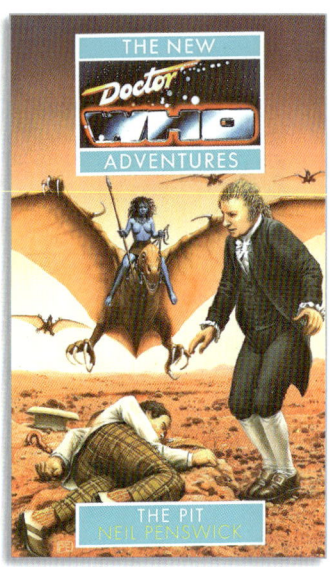

THE PIT
NEIL PENSWICK
PE

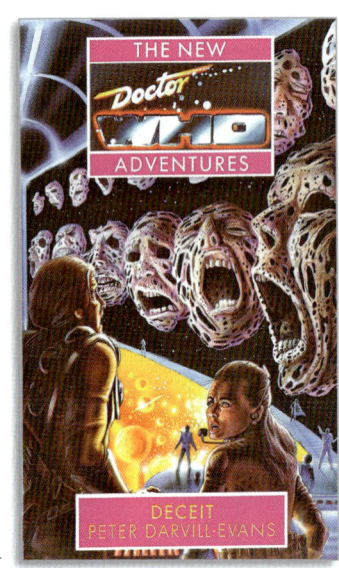

DECEIT
PETER DARVILL-EVANS
LR

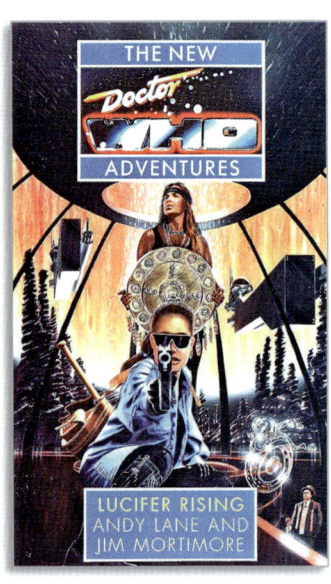

LUCIFER RISING
ANDY LANE AND JIM MORTIMORE
JM

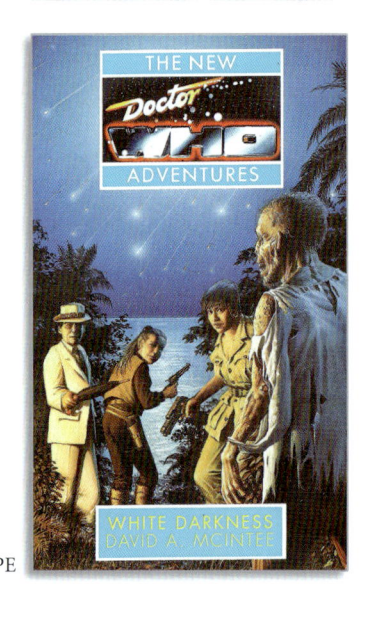

WHITE DARKNESS
DAVID A. MCINTEE
PE

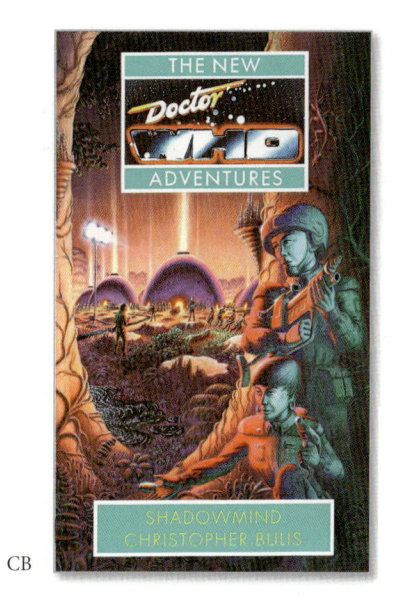

COVERS GALLERY

SHADOWMIND
CHRISTOPHER BULIS
CB

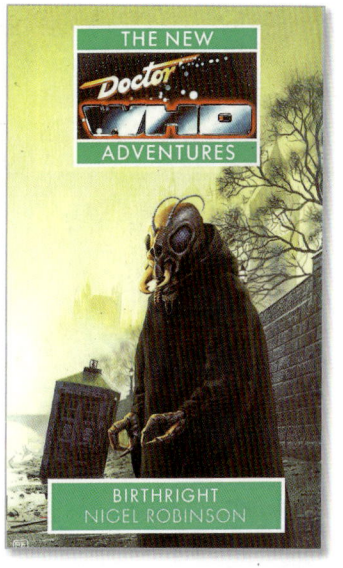

BIRTHRIGHT
NIGEL ROBINSON
PE

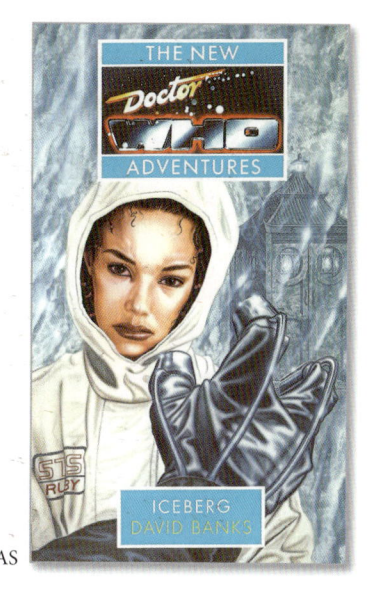

ICEBERG
DAVID BANKS
AS

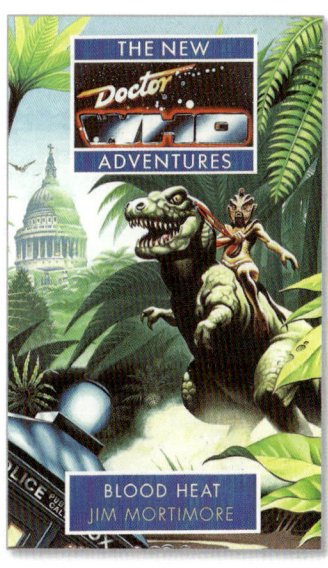

BLOOD HEAT
JIM MORTIMORE
JC

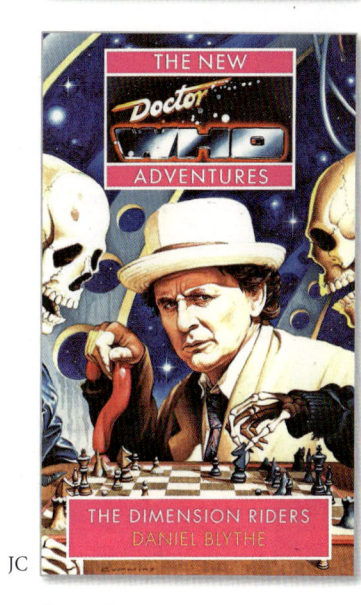

THE DIMENSION RIDERS
DANIEL BLYTHE
JC

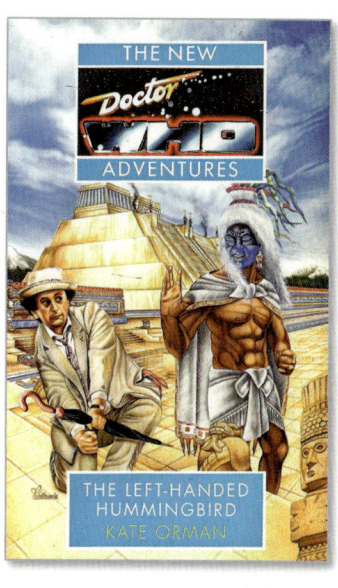

THE LEFT-HANDED HUMMINGBIRD
KATE ORMAN
PW

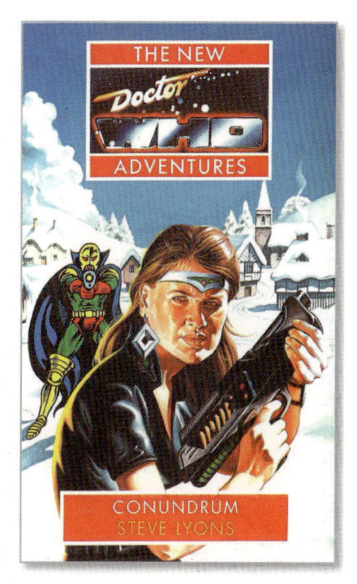

CONUNDRUM
STEVE LYONS
JC

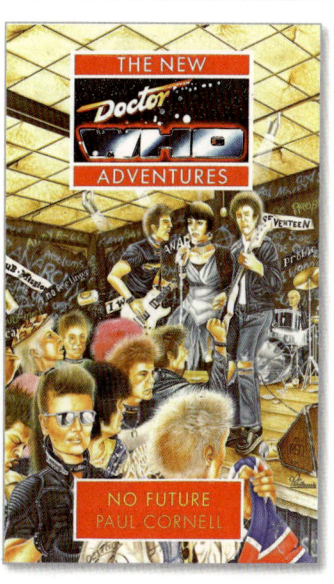

NO FUTURE
PAUL CORNELL
PW

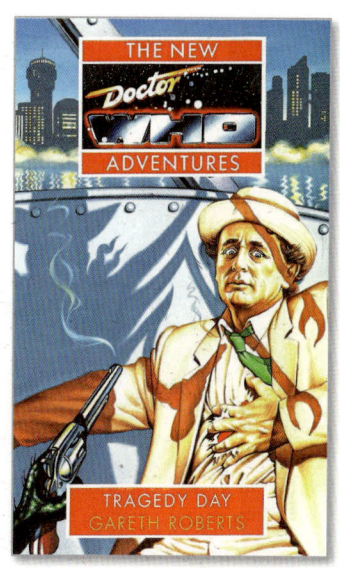

TRAGEDY DAY
GARETH ROBERTS
JC

321

THE WHO ADVENTURES

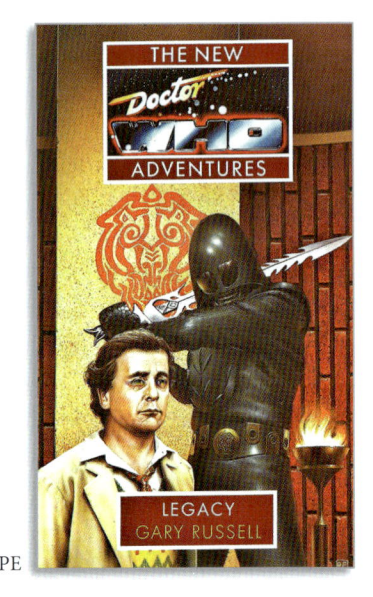

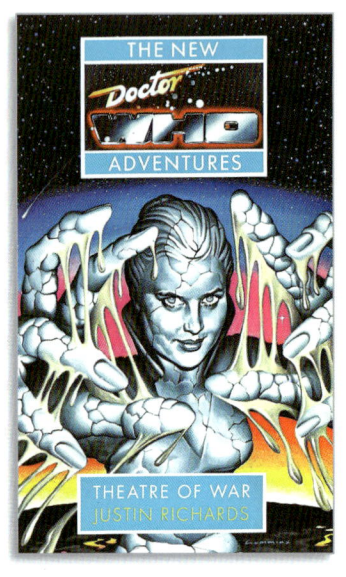

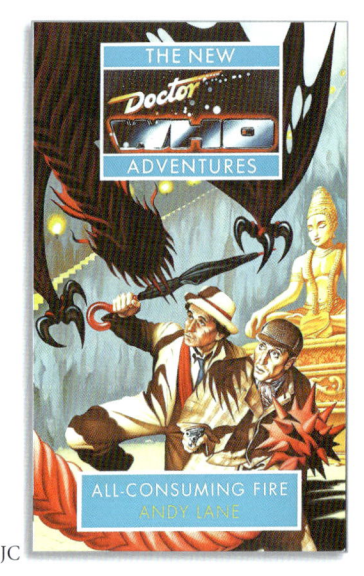

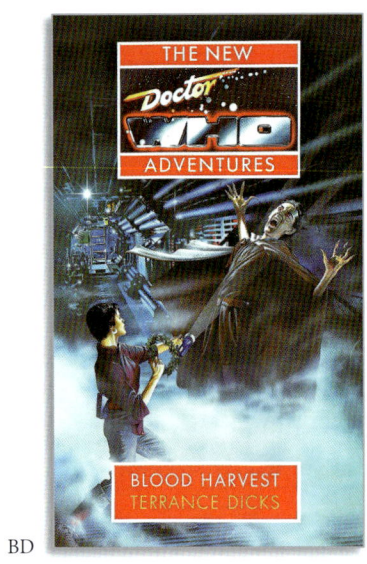

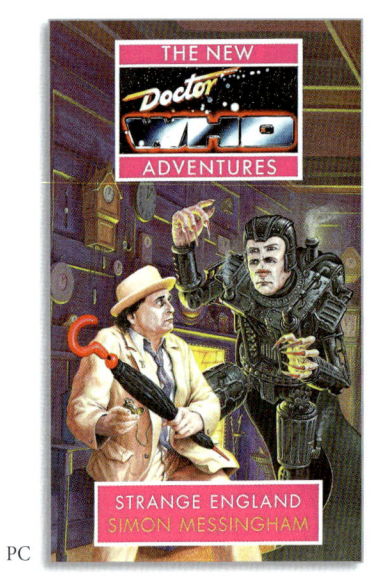

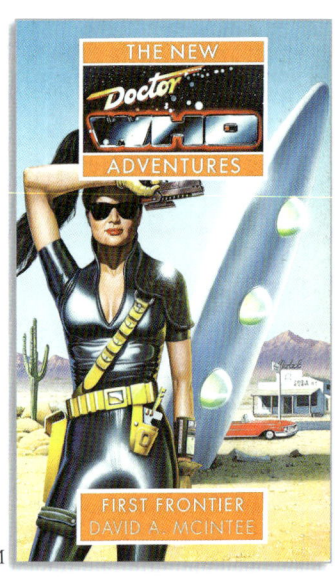

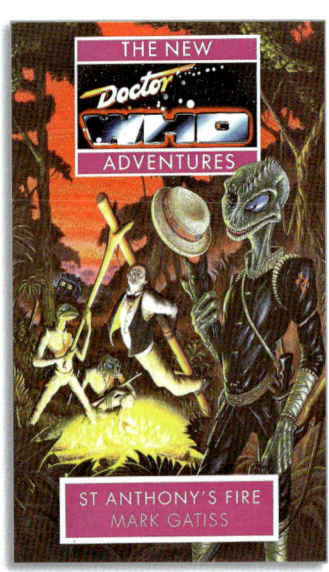

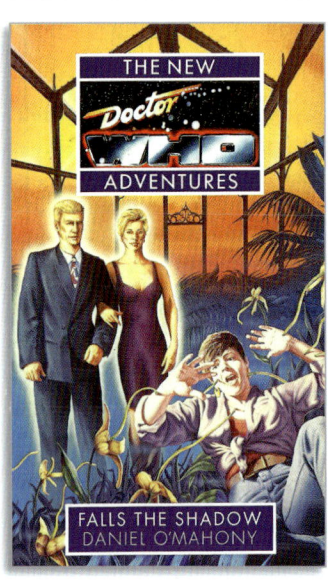

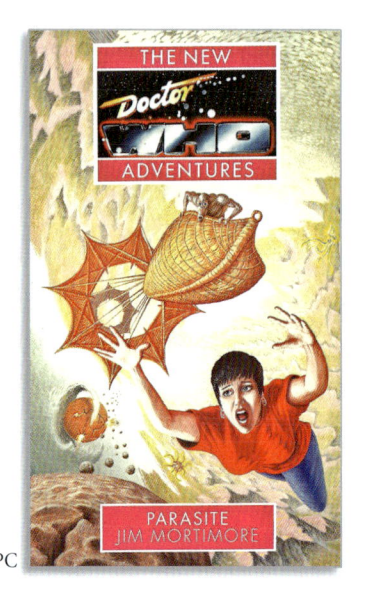

LEGACY — Gary Russell (PE)	**THEATRE OF WAR** — Justin Richards (JC)	**ALL-CONSUMING FIRE** — Andy Lane (JC)
BLOOD HARVEST — Terrance Dicks (BD)	**STRANGE ENGLAND** — Simon Messingham (PC)	**FIRST FRONTIER** — David A. McIntee (TM)
ST ANTHONY'S FIRE — Mark Gatiss (PC)	**FALLS THE SHADOW** — Daniel O'Mahony (KJ)	**PARASITE** — Jim Mortimore (PC)

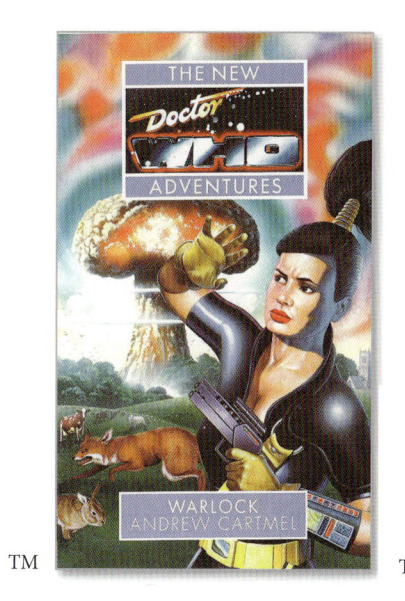

COVERS GALLERY

WARLOCK — ANDREW CARTMEL — TM
SET PIECE — KATE ORMAN — TM
INFINITE REQUIEM — DANIEL BLYTHE — BJ
SANCTUARY — DAVID A. McINTEE — PE
HUMAN NATURE — PAUL CORNELL — BD
ORIGINAL SIN — ANDY LANE — TM
SKY PIRATES! — DAVE STONE — JC
ZAMPER — GARETH ROBERTS — TM
TOY SOLDIERS — PAUL LEONARD — PE

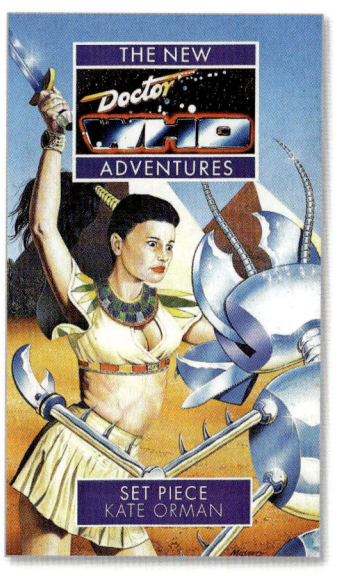

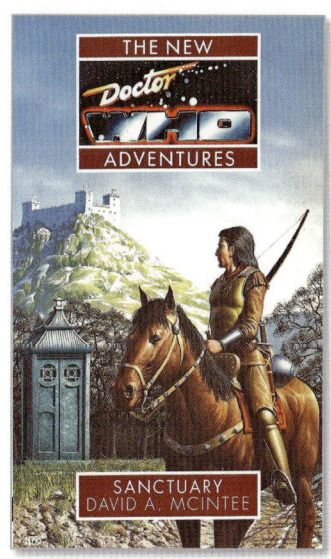

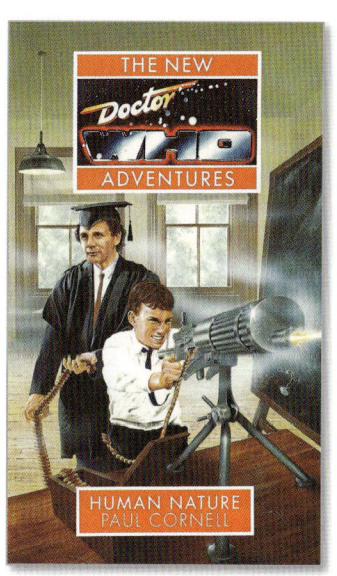

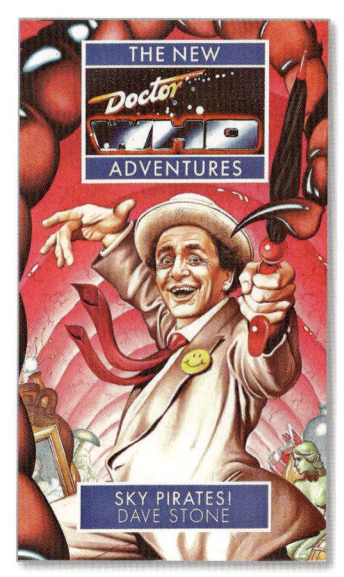

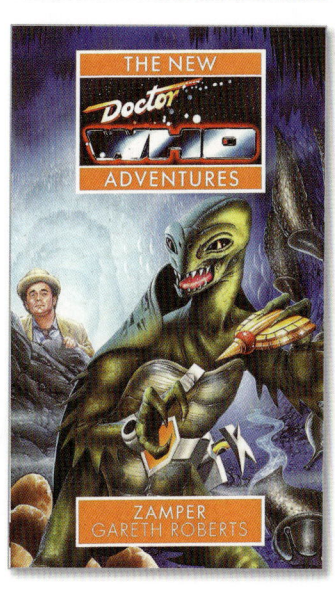

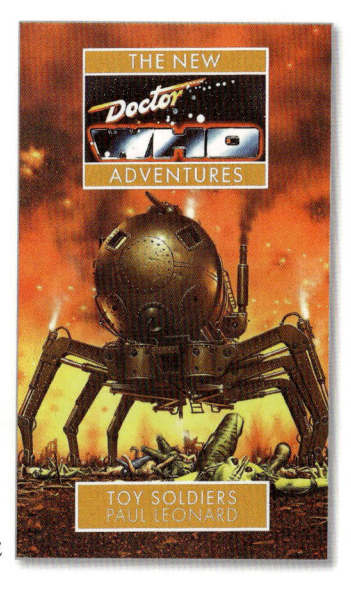

323

THE WHO ADVENTURES

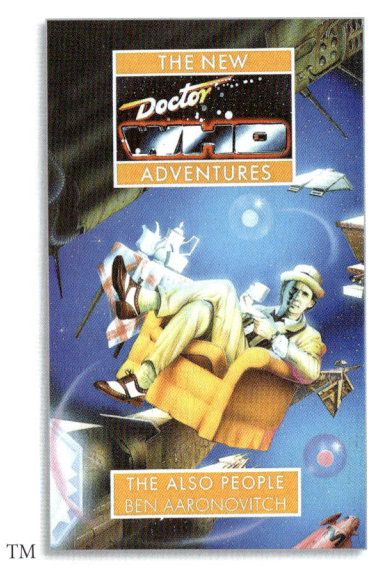

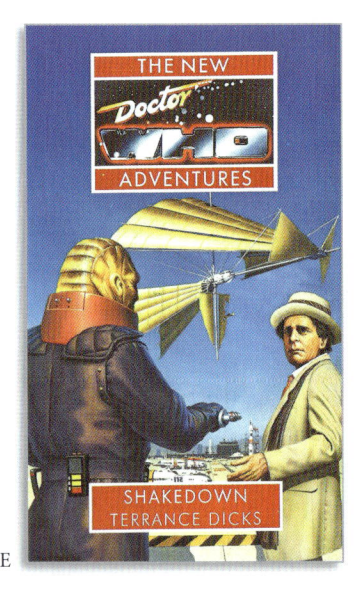

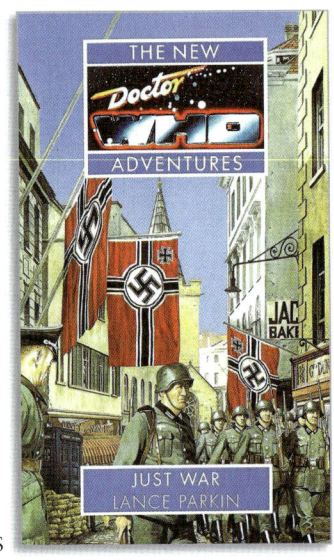

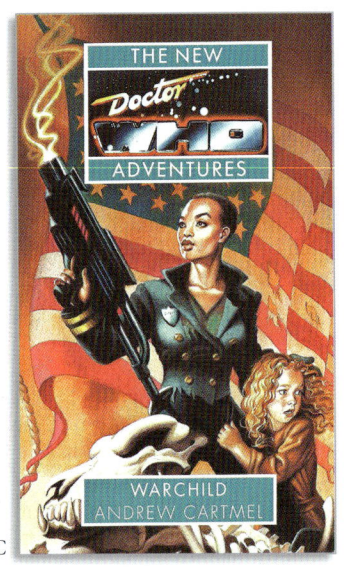

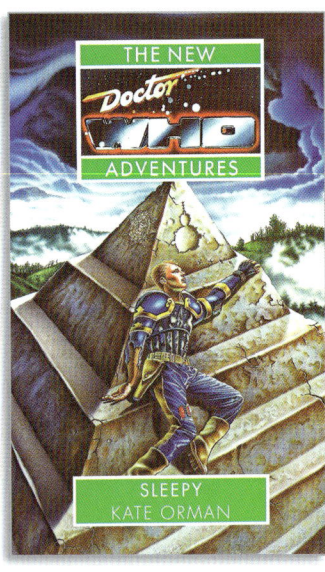

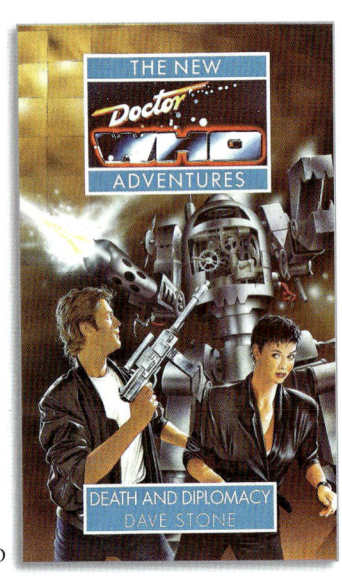

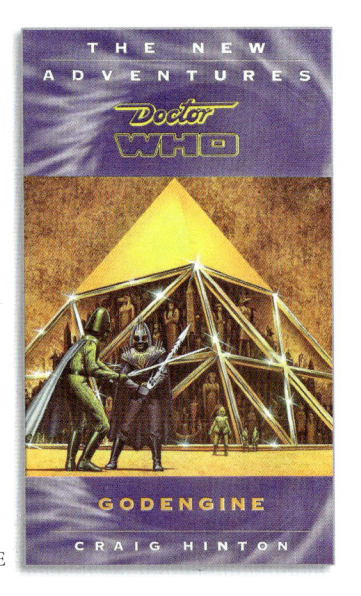

HEAD GAMES — STEVE LYONS (BD)	THE ALSO PEOPLE — BEN AARONOVITCH (TM)	SHAKEDOWN — TERRANCE DICKS (PE)
JUST WAR — LANCE PARKIN (NS)	WARCHILD — ANDREW CARTMEL (JC)	SLEEPY — KATE ORMAN (MW)
DEATH AND DIPLOMACY — DAVE STONE (BD)	HAPPY ENDINGS — PAUL CORNELL (PC)	GODENGINE — CRAIG HINTON (PE)

324

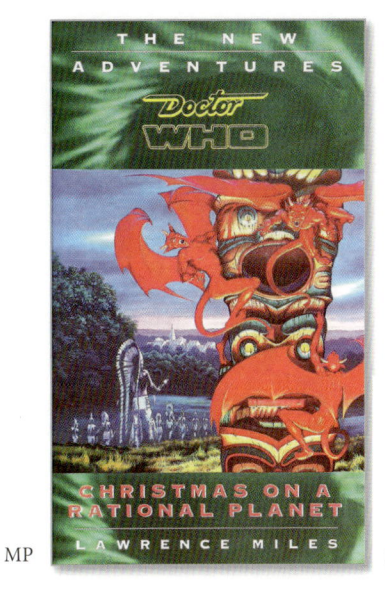

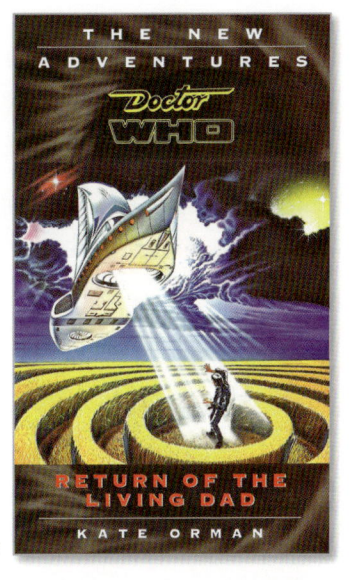

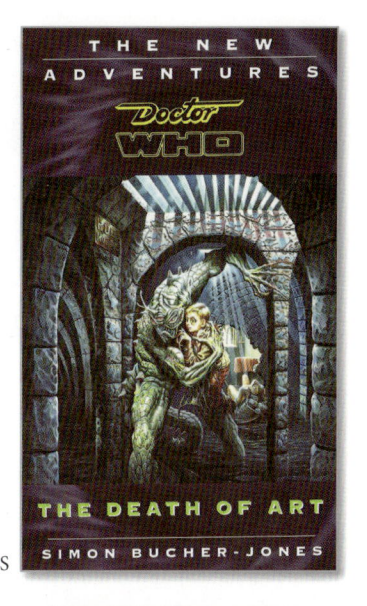

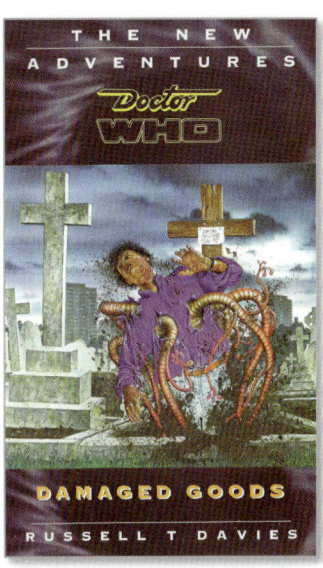

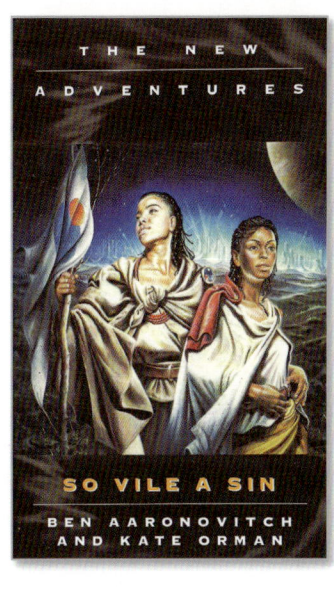

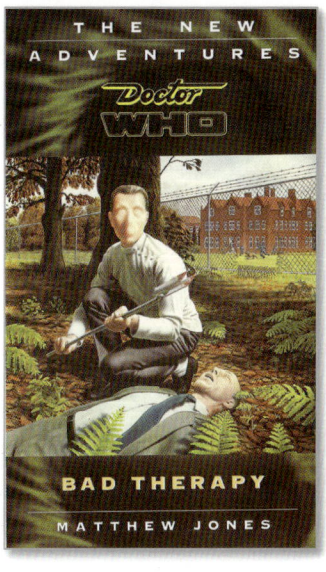

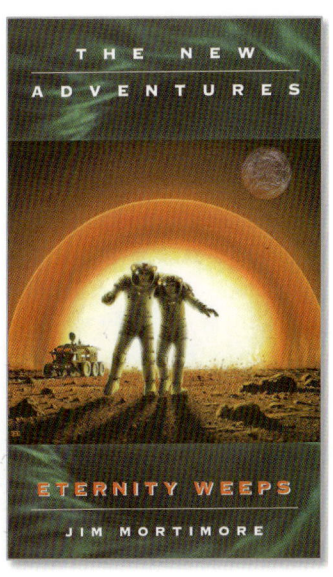

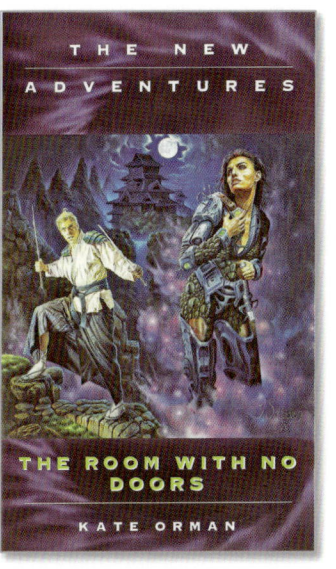

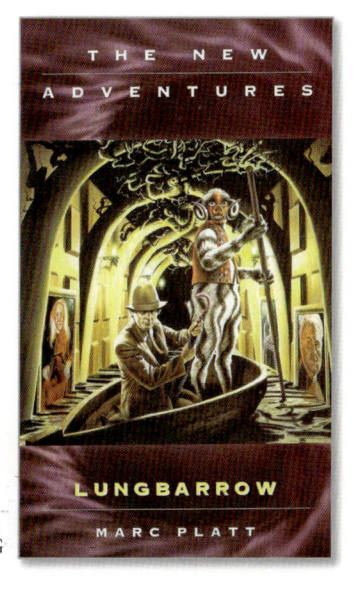

COVERS GALLERY

CHRISTMAS ON A RATIONAL PLANET — LAWRENCE MILES (MP)	**RETURN OF THE LIVING DAD** — KATE ORMAN (MW)	**THE DEATH OF ART** — SIMON BUCHER-JONES (JS)
DAMAGED GOODS — RUSSELL T DAVIES (BD)	**SO VILE A SIN** — BEN AARONOVITCH AND KATE ORMAN (JS)	**BAD THERAPY** — MATTHEW JONES (MS)
ETERNITY WEEPS — JIM MORTIMORE (PE)	**THE ROOM WITH NO DOORS** — KATE ORMAN (JS)	**LUNGBARROW** — MARC PLATT (FG)

THE WHO ADVENTURES

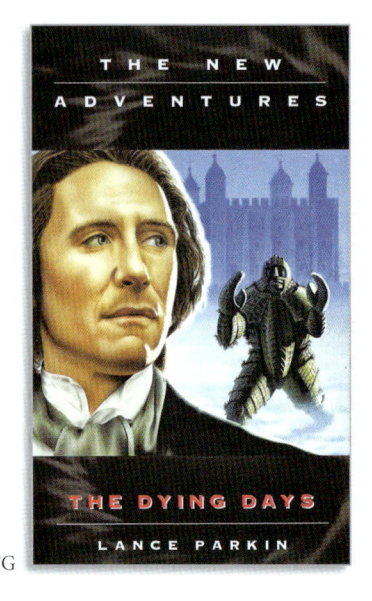

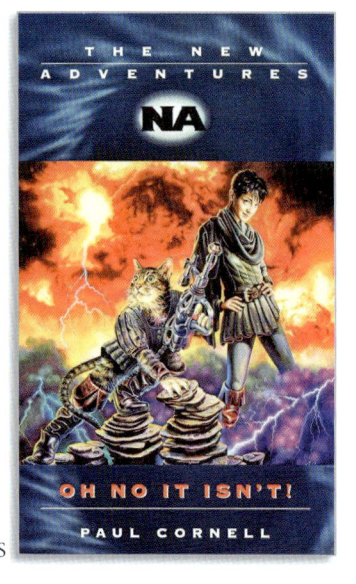

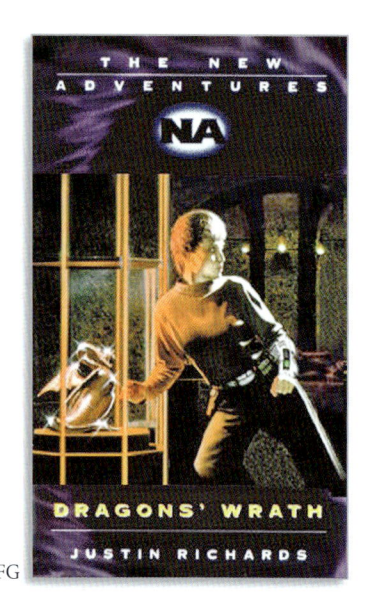

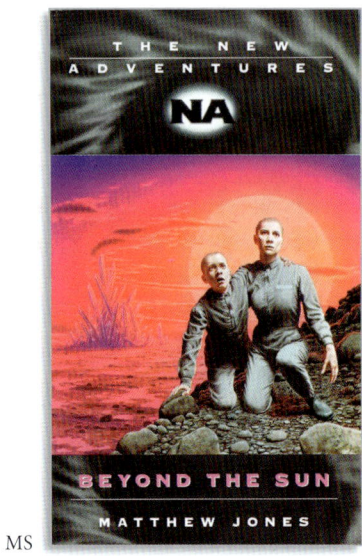

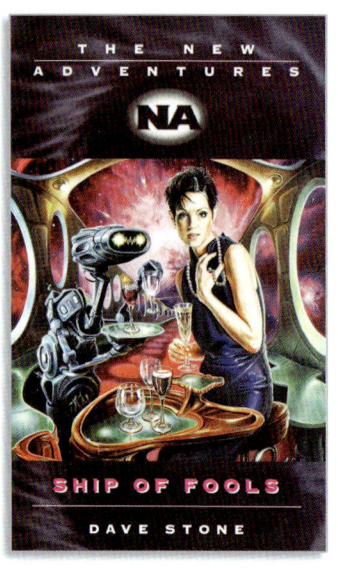

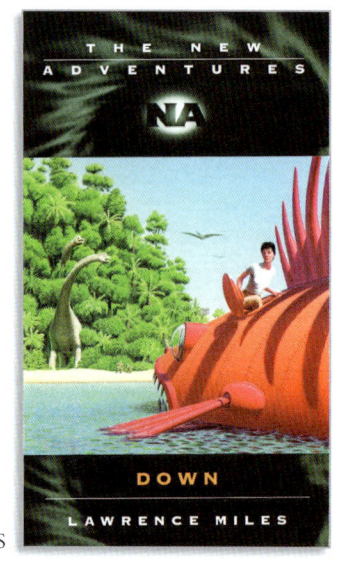

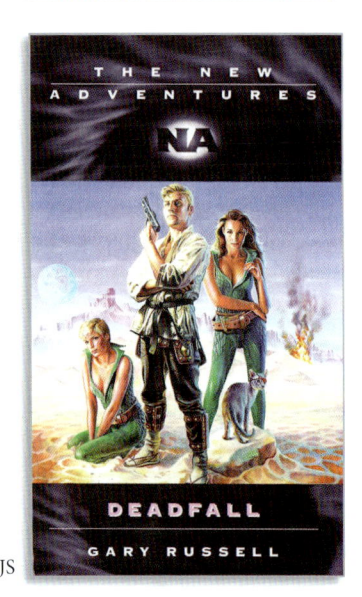

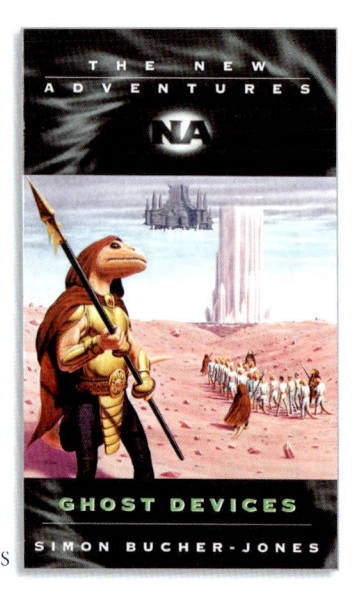

THE DYING DAYS — LANCE PARKIN (FG)	**OH NO IT ISN'T!** — PAUL CORNELL (JS)	**DRAGONS' WRATH** — JUSTIN RICHARDS (FG)
BEYOND THE SUN — MATTHEW JONES (MS)	**SHIP OF FOOLS** — DAVE STONE (JS)	**DOWN** — LAWRENCE MILES (MS)
DEADFALL — GARY RUSSELL (JS)	**GHOST DEVICES** — SIMON BUCHER-JONES (MS)	**MEAN STREETS** — TERRANCE DICKS (FG)

326

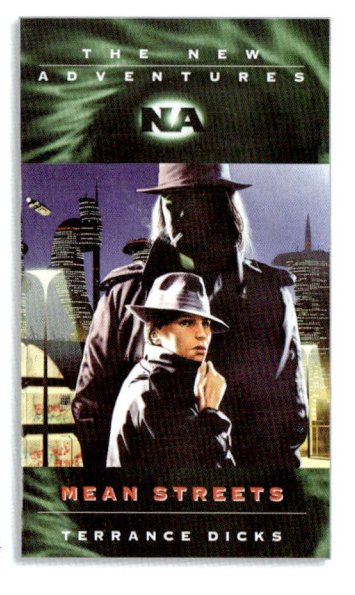

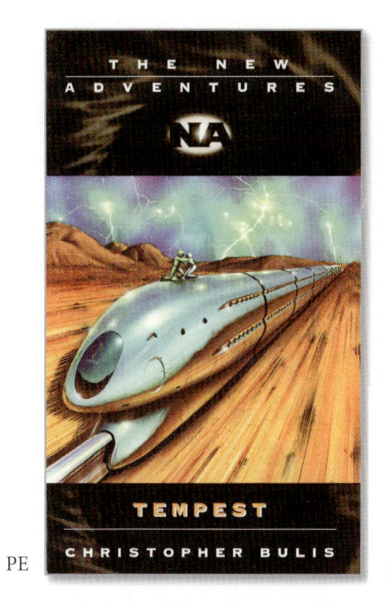

COVERS GALLERY

THE NEW ADVENTURES — TEMPEST — CHRISTOPHER BULIS	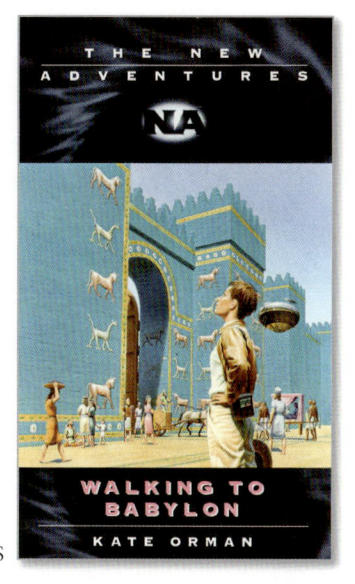 THE NEW ADVENTURES — WALKING TO BABYLON — KATE ORMAN	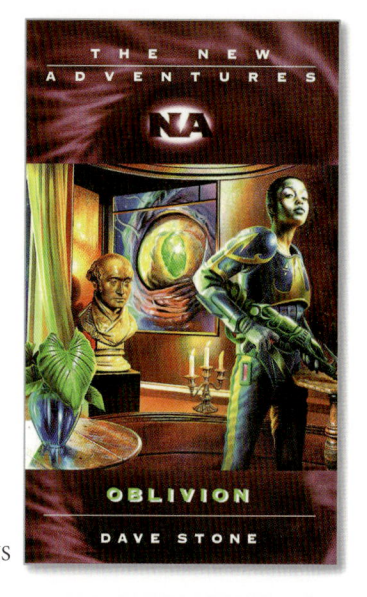 THE NEW ADVENTURES — OBLIVION — DAVE STONE
PE	MS	JS
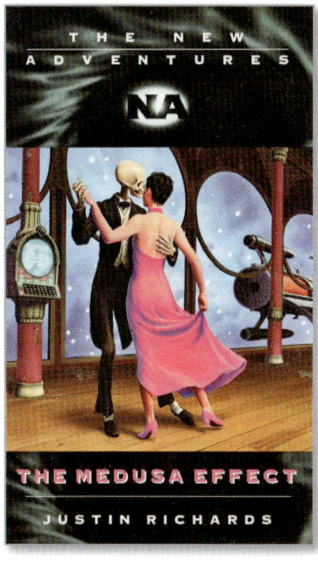 THE NEW ADVENTURES — THE MEDUSA EFFECT — JUSTIN RICHARDS	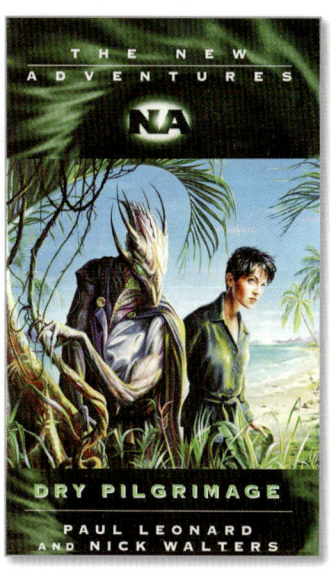 THE NEW ADVENTURES — DRY PILGRIMAGE — PAUL LEONARD AND NICK WALTERS	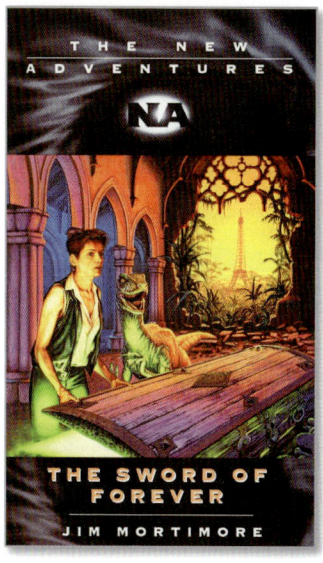 THE NEW ADVENTURES — THE SWORD OF FOREVER — JIM MORTIMORE
MS	JS	MP
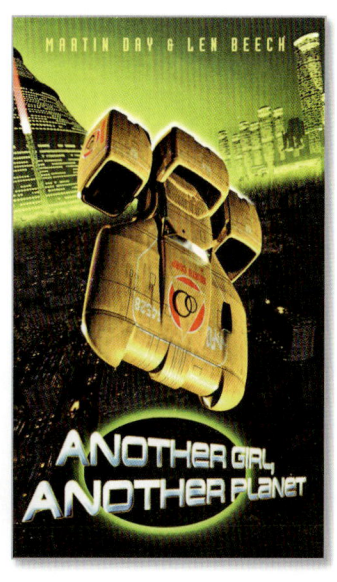 MARTIN DAY & LEN BEECH — ANOTHER GIRL, ANOTHER PLANET	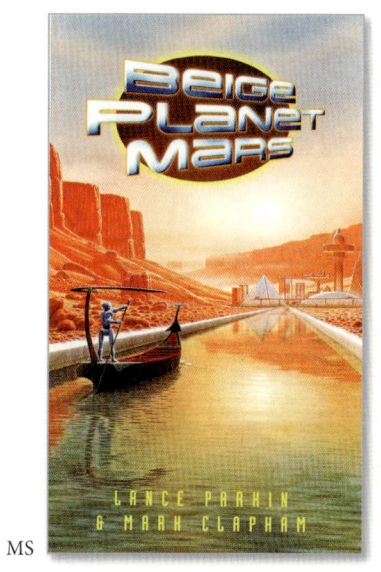 BEIGE PLANET MARS — LANCE PARKIN & MARK CLAPHAM	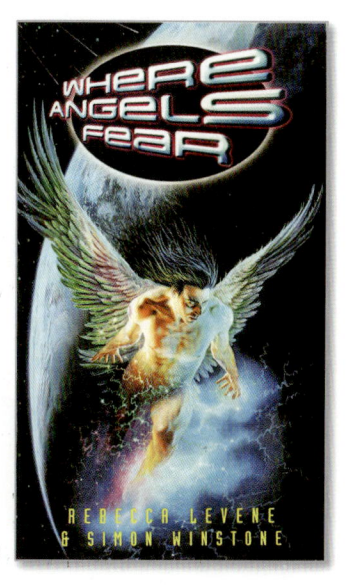 WHERE ANGELS FEAR — REBECCA LEVENE & SIMON WINSTONE
FG	MS	JS

327

THE WHO ADVENTURES

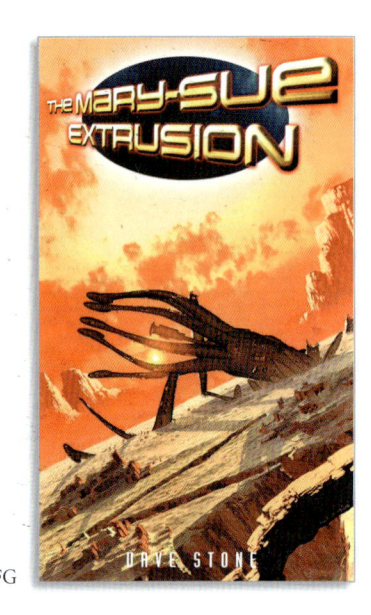

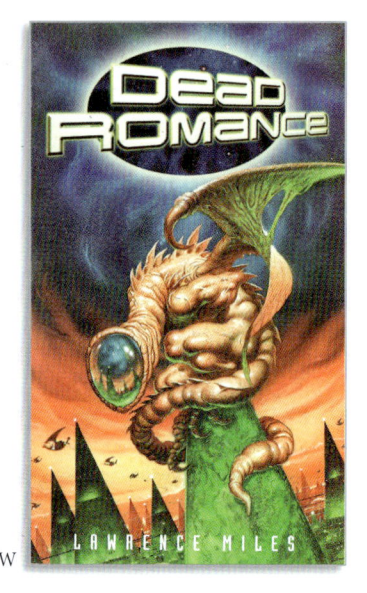

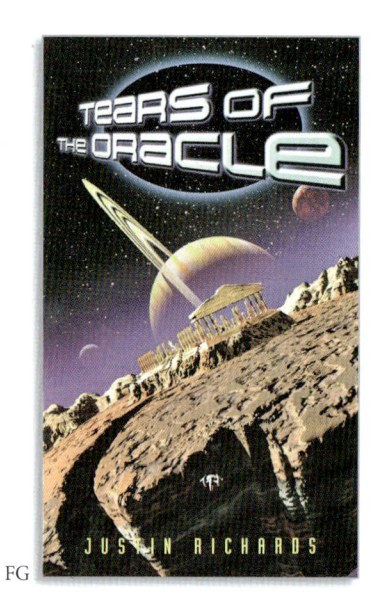

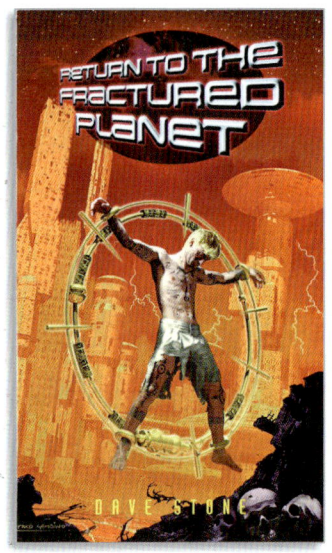

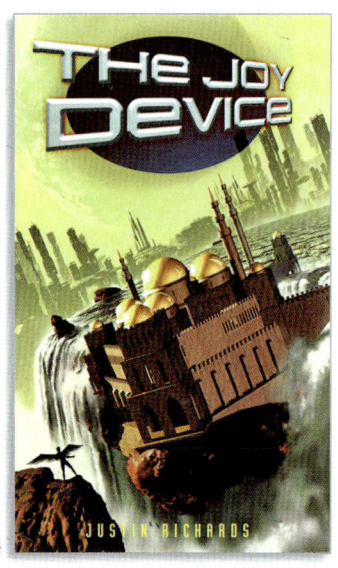

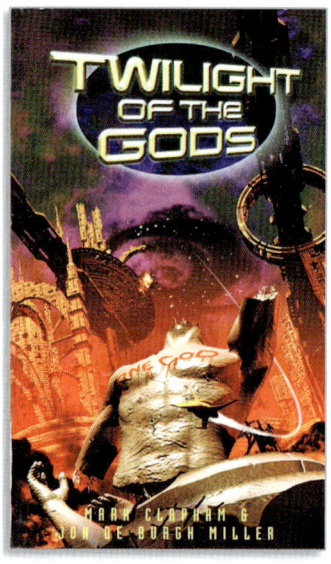

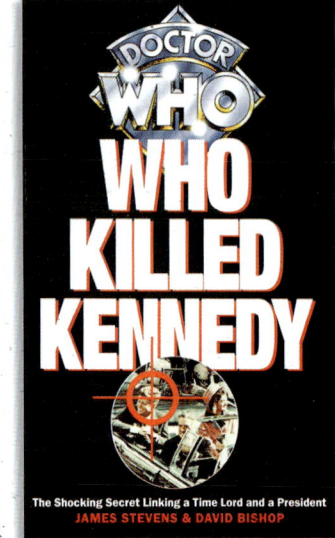

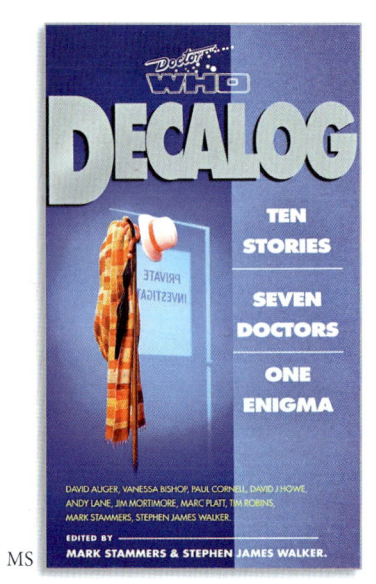

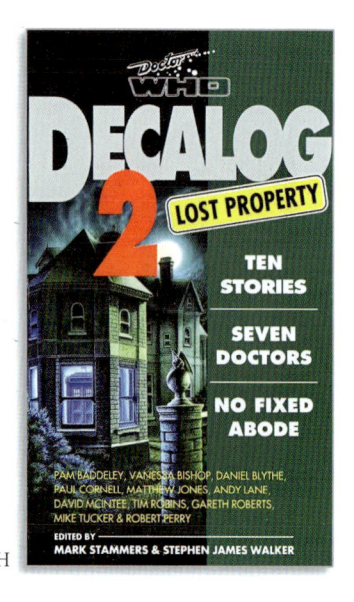

FG — The Mary-Sue Extrusion (Dave Stone)
DW — Dead Romance (Lawrence Miles)
FG — Tears of the Oracle (Justin Richards)
FG — Return to the Fractured Planet (Dave Stone)
FG — The Joy Device (Justin Richards)
FG — Twilight of the Gods (Mark Clapham & Jon de Burgh Miller)
LR — Who Killed Kennedy (James Stevens & David Bishop)
MS — Decalog (edited by Mark Stammers & Stephen James Walker)
CH — Decalog 2: Lost Property (edited by Mark Stammers & Stephen James Walker)

328

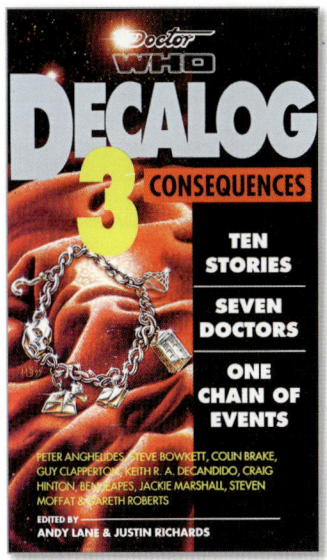

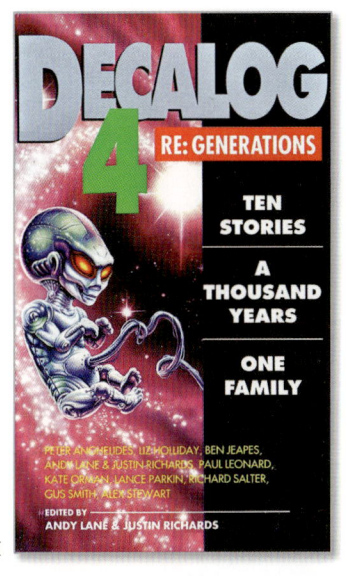

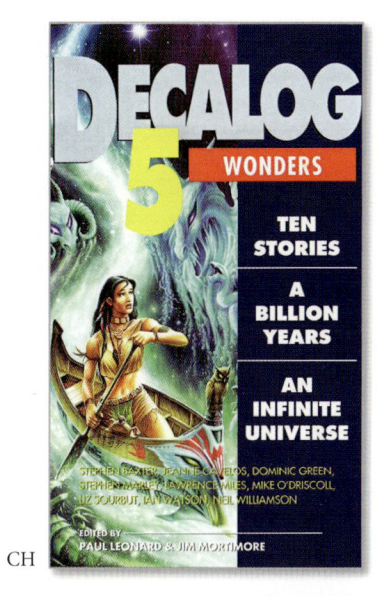

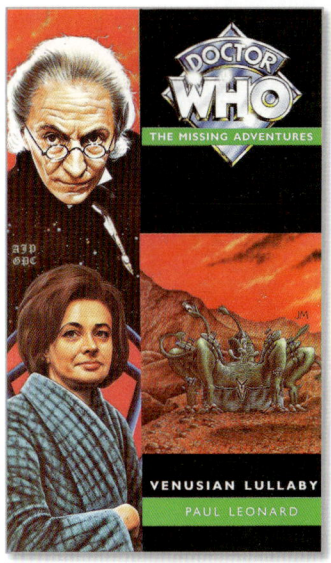

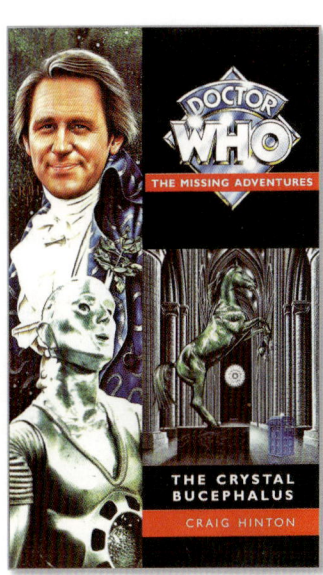

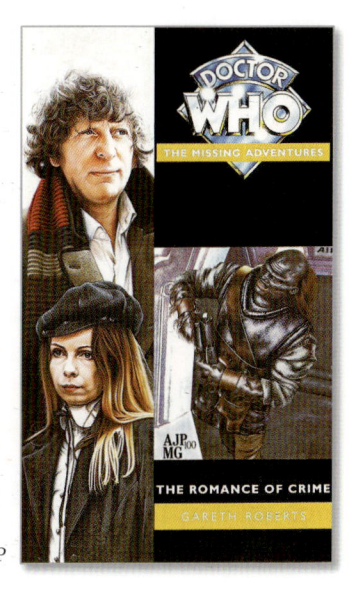

COVERS GALLERY

329

THE WHO ADVENTURES

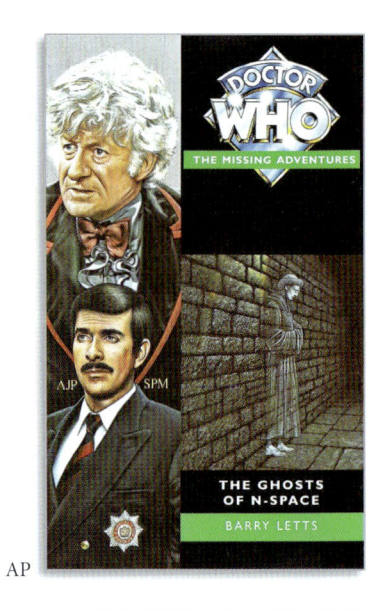

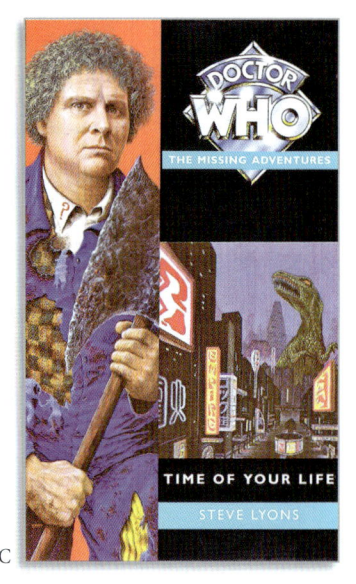

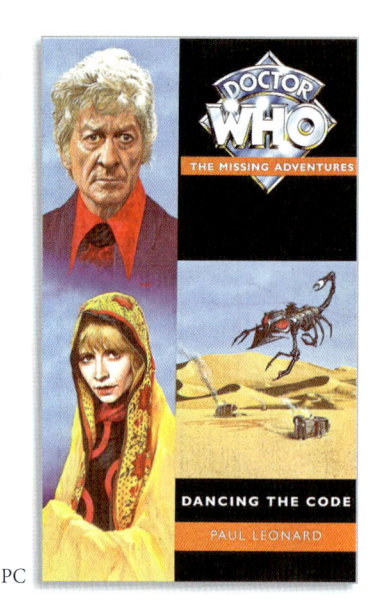

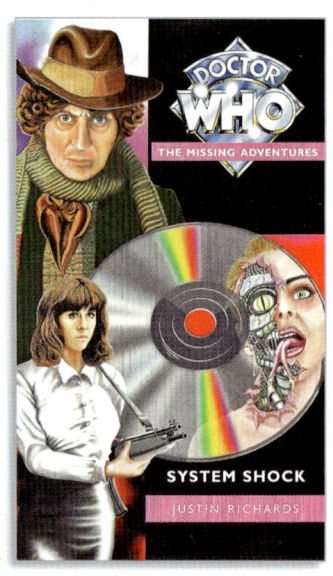

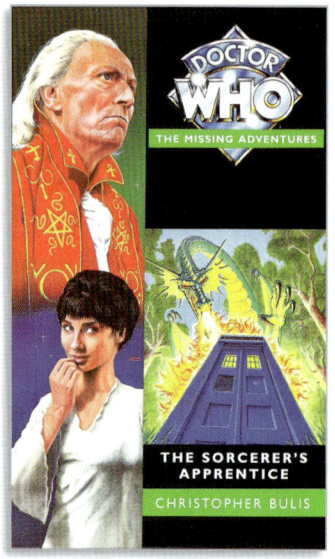

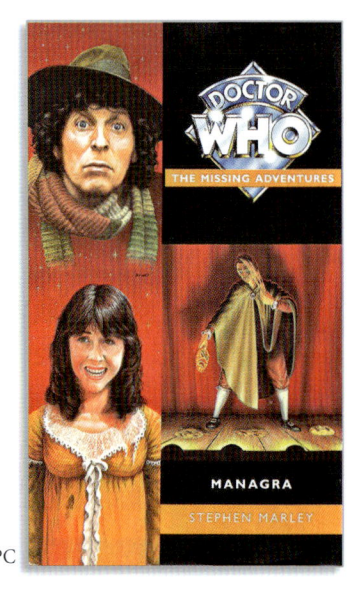

THE GHOSTS OF N-SPACE — BARRY LETTS	TIME OF YOUR LIFE — STEVE LYONS	DANCING THE CODE — PAUL LEONARD
AP	PC	PC
THE MENAGERIE	SYSTEM SHOCK — JUSTIN RICHARDS	THE SORCERER'S APPRENTICE — CHRISTOPHER BULIS
PC	MR	PC
INVASION OF THE CAT-PEOPLE — GARY RUSSELL	MANAGRA — STEPHEN MARLEY	MILLENNIAL RITES — CRAIG HINTON
CH	PC	AP

330

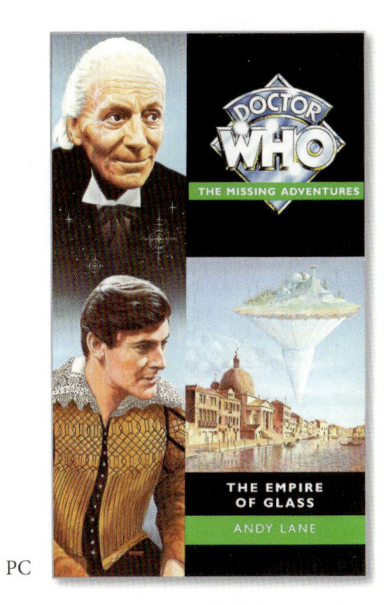

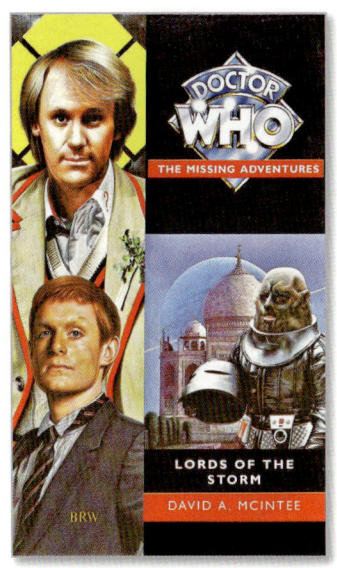

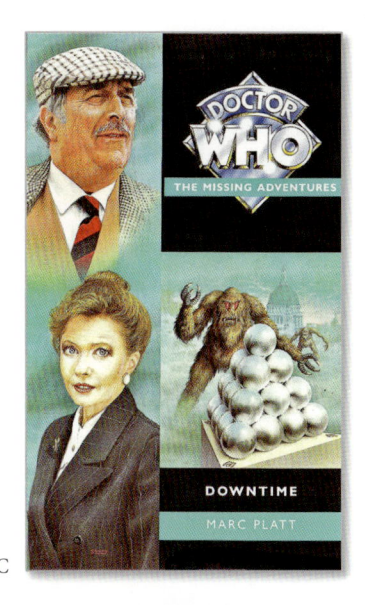

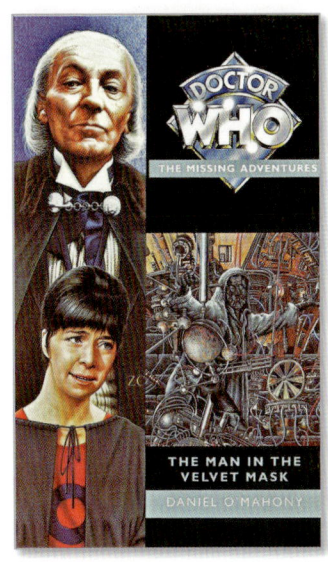

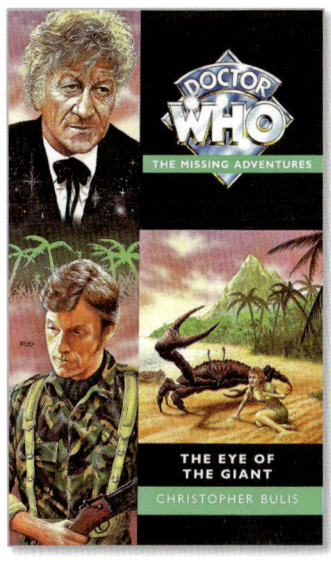

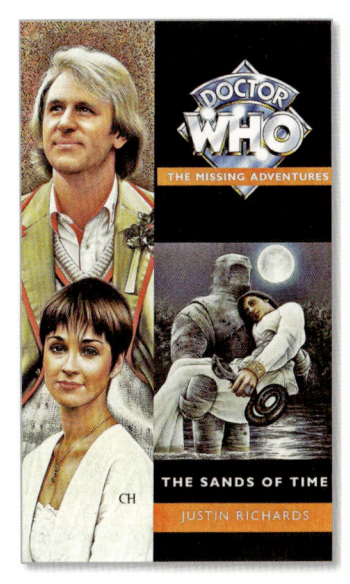

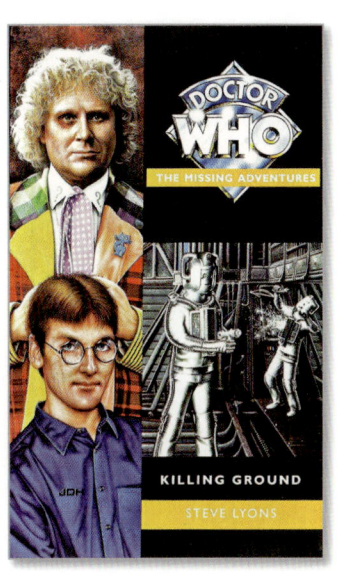

COVERS GALLERY

331

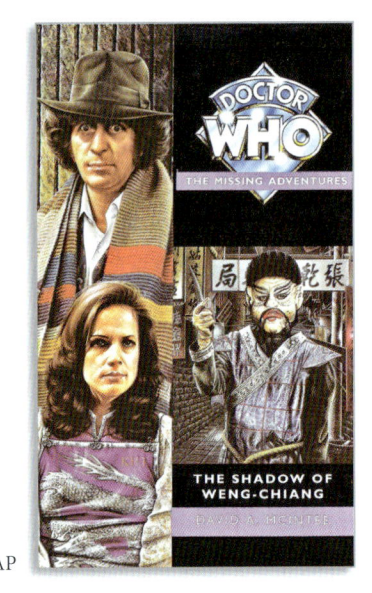

THE WHO ADVENTURES

THE SHADOW OF WENG-CHIANG
DAVID A. McINTEE
AP

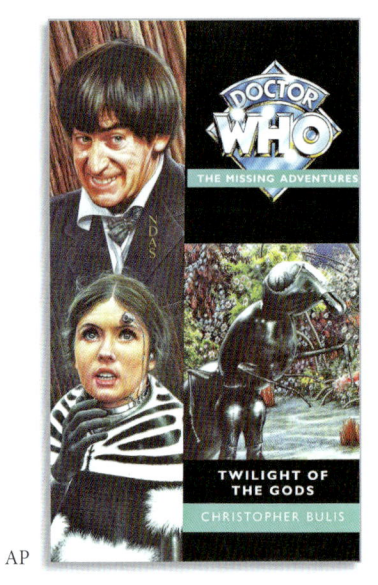

TWILIGHT OF THE GODS
CHRISTOPHER BULIS
AP

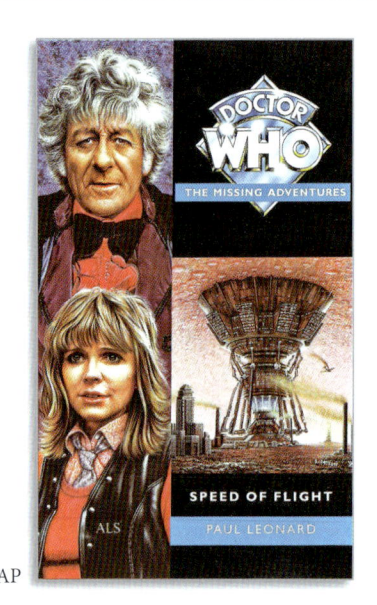

SPEED OF FLIGHT
PAUL LEONARD
AP

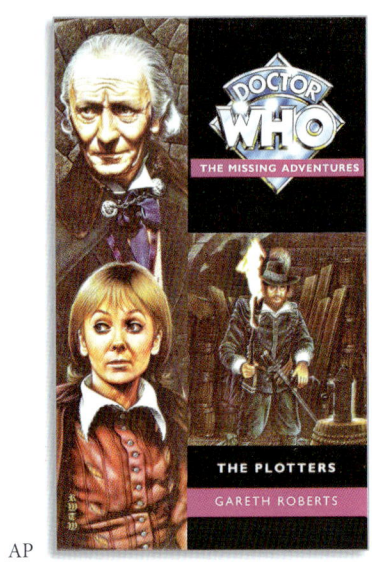

THE PLOTTERS
GARETH ROBERTS
AP

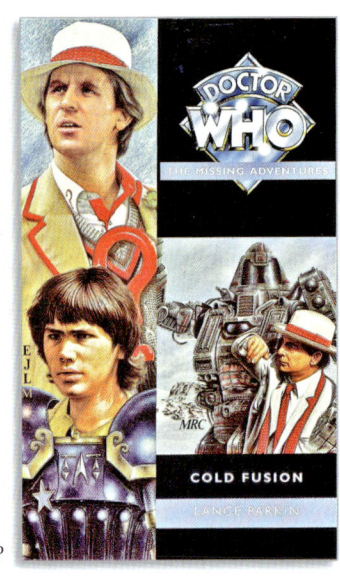

COLD FUSION
LANCE PARKIN
AP

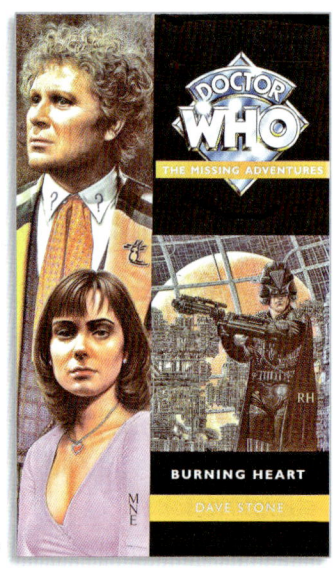

BURNING HEART
DAVE STONE
AP

A DEVICE OF DEATH
CHRISTOPHER BULIS
AP

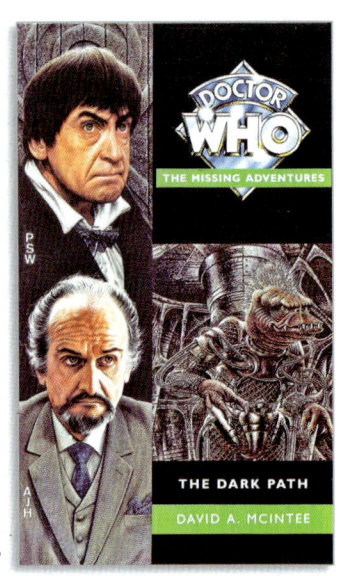

THE DARK PATH
DAVID A. McINTEE
AP

THE WELL-MANNERED WAR
GARETH ROBERTS
AP

AFTERWORD: THE LEGACY

The New Adventures may have come to an end in the late 1990s, along with their sister range the Missing Adventures, but the incredible impact they made on *Doctor Who* has continued to be felt ever since.

Bernice Summerfield has proved to be a far more popular and enduring character than could ever have been imagined when Paul Cornell created her for *Love and War* back in 1992. Her adventures have continued, courtesy of producers Big Finish, in extensive ranges of novels, short story collections and audio dramas – with Lisa Bowerman in the lead role – that are still ongoing today and have sometimes included other New Adventures characters such as Jason Kane and Kadiatu Lethbridge-Stewart. In 2015, Bernice also guest-starred in one of BBC Books' original twelfth Doctor novels, *Big Bang Generation* by Gary Russell. Even Chris Cwej, a companion introduced relatively late in the New Adventures' run, has enjoyed further outings, most notably in the Faction Paradox novel *The Book of the War* (Mad Norwegian, 2002) and the short story anthology *Cwej: Down the Middle* (Arcbeatle Press, 2020), the latter including contributions from the character's creator Andy Lane and fellow Virgin author Simon Bucher-Jones, amongst others. Although these New Adventures spin-offs fall outside the scope of this book, anyone interested in learning more would be well advised to seek out a copy of *Bernice Summerfield: The Inside Story*, written by Simon Guerrier and published by Big Finish, which details all of Bernice's exploits up to its June 2009 publication date.

More significant still, though, is the huge influence that the New Adventures have had on the *Doctor Who* TV show itself since it returned to the screen in 2005. It is sometimes said that there is a clear stylistic through-line from the last classic-era story, 'Survival' (1989), to the first new-era one, 'Rose' (2005), but it is really the New Adventures that form the main plank in the bridge that connects the two. *Doctor Who*'s first 21st Century showrunner and head writer, Russell T Davies, who was instrumental in its revival, was a contributor to the Virgin

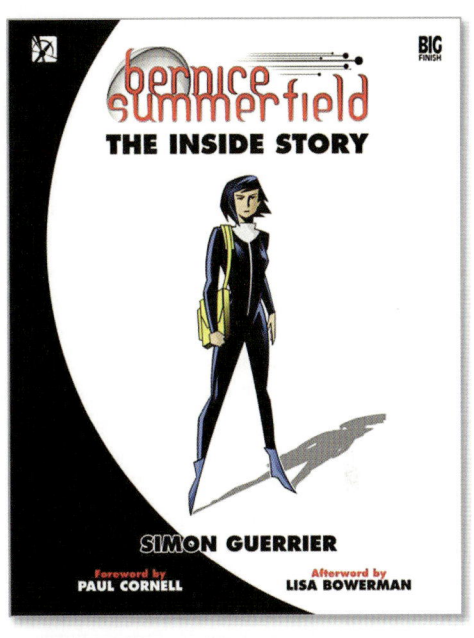

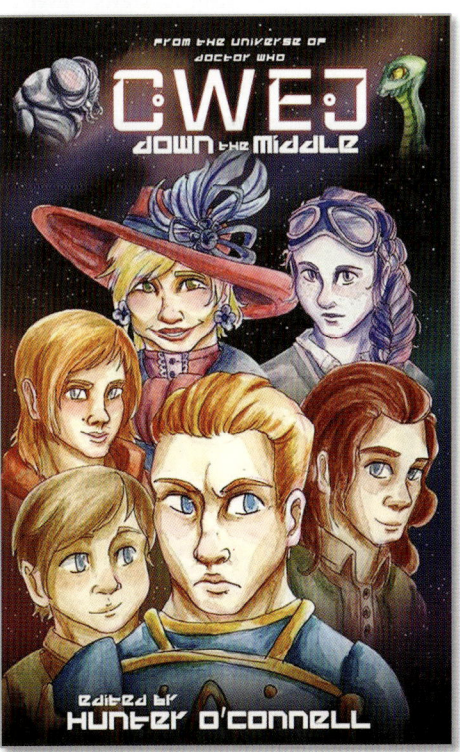

Big Finish's *Bernice Summerfield: The Inside Story* and Arcbeatle Press's *Cwej: Down the Middle*, with cover artwork by Adrian Salmon and Bri Crozier respectively.

THE WHO ADVENTURES

> **CASTING THE ADVENTURES**
>
> When Big Finish produced their New and Missing Adventures audios (see Appendix E), the characters carried over from *Doctor Who* on TV were all played by their original actors: Tom Baker, Peter Davison and Sylvester McCoy all returned as the fourth, fifth and seventh Doctors respectively, while Ace actress Sophie Aldred reprised her role, and in *Cold Fusion* – a unique cross-over between the Missing and New Adventures, featuring both fifth and seventh Doctors – the former's companions Adric, Nyssa and Tegan were played as usual by Matthew Waterhouse, Sarah Sutton and Janet Fielding. For the characters newly created for the novels ranges, however, Big Finish had to make their own casting choices. The key role of Bernice Summerfield went to Lisa Bowerman, who had a previous *Doctor Who* connection, having played the Cheetah Person Karra in the final classic-era TV story 'Survival'. Her sometime husband Jason Kane was played by Stephen Fewell, while the parts of Chris Cwej and Roz Forrester went to Travis Oliver and Yasmin Bannerman respectively.

ranges, as were his successor Steven Moffat (who wrote a *Decalog* short story) and scriptwriters Mark Gatiss, Paul Cornell, Gareth Roberts and Matthew Jones, while one-time New Adventures editor Simon Winstone worked as a script editor on some of the tenth Doctor episodes, and they and their colleagues all brought a distinct New Adventures ethos to the show. This went far beyond the fact that one of the novels, Paul Cornell's *Human Nature*, was actually adapted as a highly-acclaimed two-part tenth Doctor story, 'Human Nature'/'The Family of Blood' (2007); or the fact that various New Adventures plot elements found their way into other TV episodes, such as when *Human Nature*'s inclusion of an alien family directly inspired Russell T Davies to make his Slitheen from 'Aliens of London'/'World War Three' (2005) an alien family, or when *The Highest Science*'s idea of a bus being transported to another planet was repeated in 'Planet of the Dead' (2009); or even the fact that

The CD covers for six of Big Finish's numerous Bernice Summerfield audios; Adrian Salmon was the regular artist before photographic covers were introduced. As seen here, classic *Doctor Who* monsters such as Ice Warriors, Cybermen and Daleks have sometimes featured.

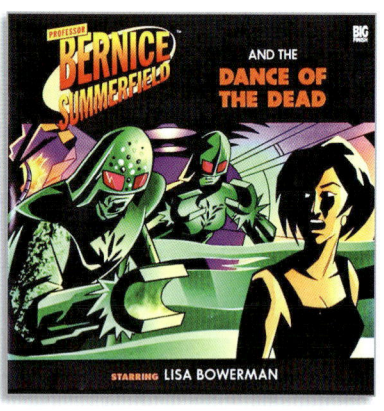

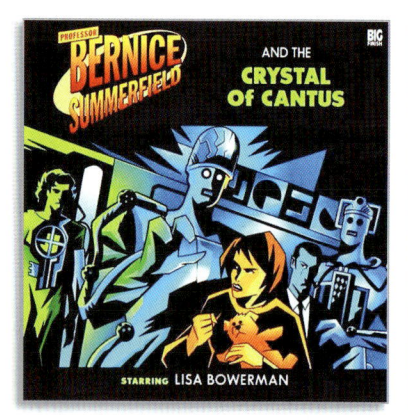

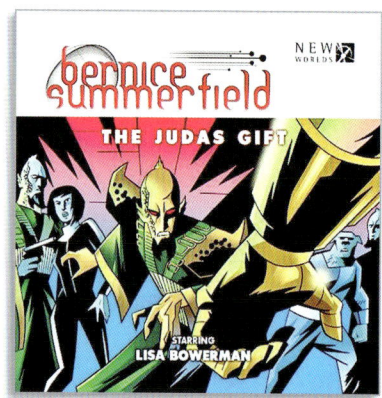

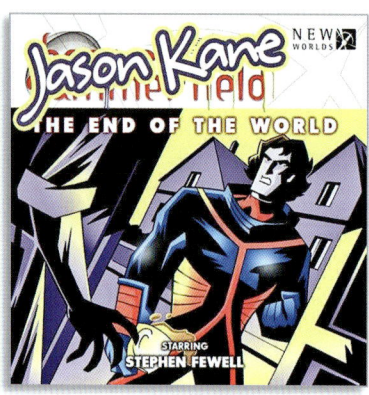

AFTERWORD: THE LEGACY

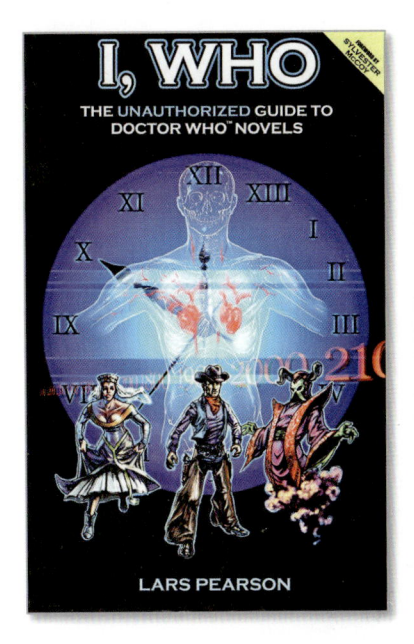

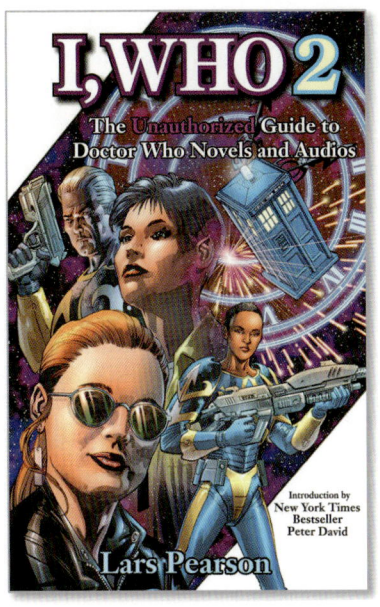

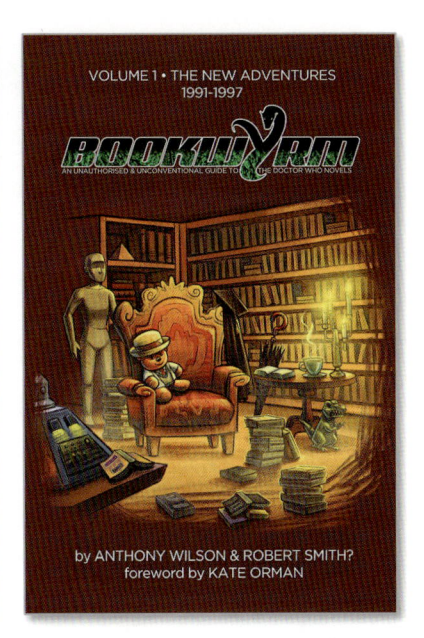

Over the years, the Virgin novels have been detailed and analysed in a number of guide books, including the initial two volumes of Lars Pearson's *I, Who* series (above left and centre), the first published by the author's own Mad Norwegian Press in 1999 with cover art by Alan Evans, and the second in 2001 with cover art by Bryan Hitch; and Volume 1 of Anthony Wilson and Robert Smith?'s *Bookwyrm* (above right), published in 2019 by Dr Arnold T Blumberg's ATB Publishing with cover art by Dani Jones.

Below: the first of Big Finish's many original Bernice Summerfield novels, published in 2000, with cover art by Carolyn Edwards.

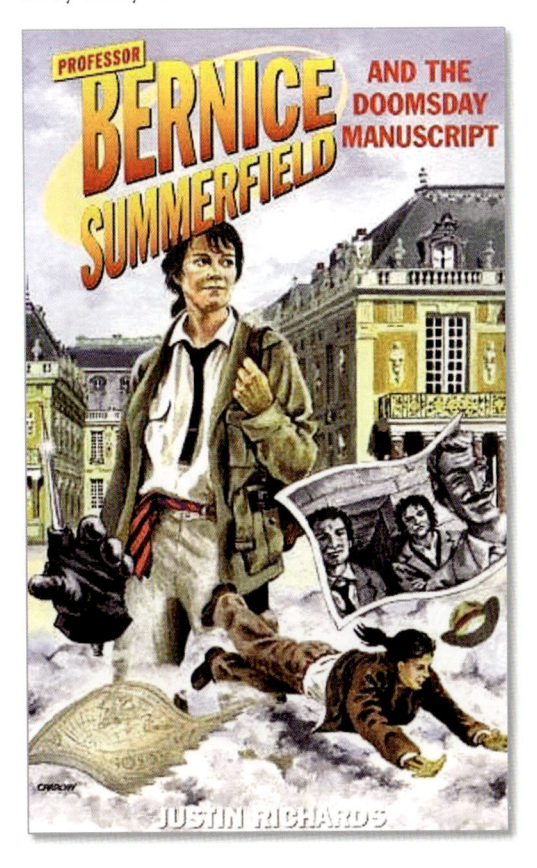

Bernice Summerfield, an archaeology professor from Earth's far future, who has a sassy attitude and becomes romantically involved with the Doctor, was an obvious inspiration for Steven Moffat's popular River Song character. Following the New Adventures' lead, the new-era episodes have boasted much greater emotional content and ongoing character development than the classic-era ones, and have dealt in many cases with subject matter and themes – sexual, familial, political, psychological and moral – that, back in the time of the classic-era episodes, really would have been considered 'too broad and too deep for the small screen', to quote a line often used in the novels' publicity.

Arguably, *Doctor Who* would never have been revived at all, and certainly not in the form it was, had it not been for the Virgin books helping to keep the flame of interest in the show still burning during the long years when it was off the air. At any rate, the incredible wealth of New Adventures to which Peter Darvill-Evans, Rebecca Levene, their Virgin colleagues and their team of gifted authors and artists gave birth will live long in the memories of all those who've read them, and stand as one of *Doctor Who*'s greatest ever eras.

THE WHO ADVENTURES

An evocative Lee Sullivan portrait of Bernice Summerfield with the seventh Doctor, created to accompany a Paul Cornell interview about the New Adventures in Issue 267 of *Doctor Who Magazine*, dated 29 July 1998.

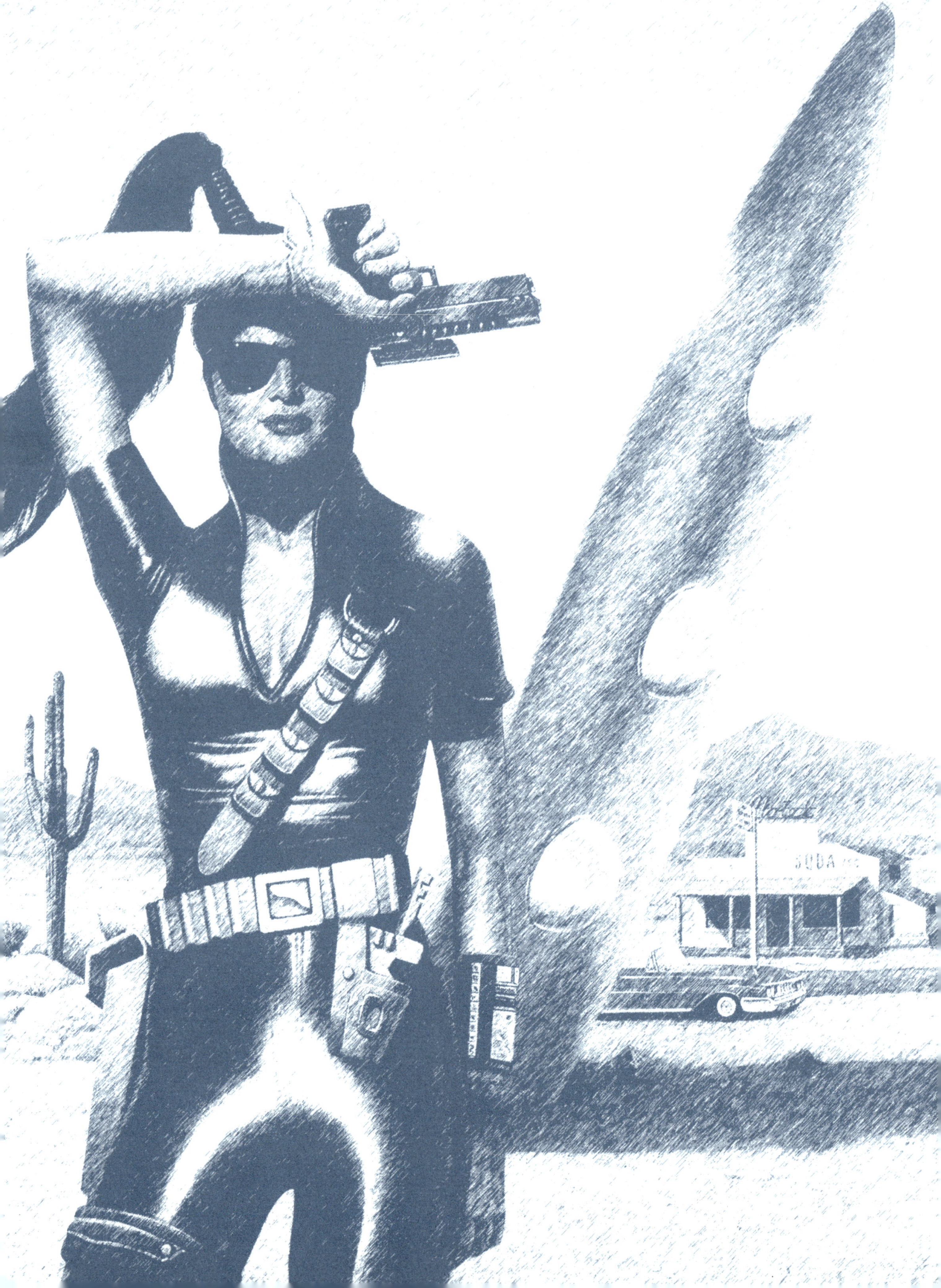